Strategic Survey 2021
The Annual Assessment of Geopolitics

published by

 Routledge
Taylor & Francis Group

for

The International Institute for Strategic Studies

The International Institute for Strategic Studies

Arundel House | 6 Temple Place | London | WC2R 2PG | UK

Strategic Survey 2021
The Annual Assessment of Geopolitics

First published October 2021 by **Routledge**
4 Park Square, Milton Park, Abingdon, Oxon, OX14 4RN

for **The International Institute for Strategic Studies**
Arundel House, 6 Temple Place, London, WC2R 2PG, UK

Simultaneously published in the USA and Canada by **Routledge**
52 Vanderbilt Avenue, New York, NY 10017

Routledge is an imprint of Taylor & Francis, an Informa business

© 2021 The International Institute for Strategic Studies

DIRECTOR-GENERAL AND CHIEF EXECUTIVE Dr John Chipman

EDITOR Dr Nigel Gould-Davies

ASSOCIATE EDITOR Alice Aveson
ASSISTANT EDITOR Gregory Brooks
EDITORIAL Flora Bell, Jill Lally, Michael Marsden
KEY EVENTS RESEARCH Catherine O'Connor, Ben Kibblewhite
DRIVERS OF STRATEGIC CHANGE RESEARCH Graham Ivory, Kevin Jewell
COVER/PRODUCTION/CARTOGRAPHY John Buck, Carolina Vargas, Kelly Verity
COVER IMAGES Getty

British Library Cataloguing in Publication Data
A catalogue record for this book is available from the British Library

Library of Congress Cataloguing in Publication Data

ISBN 978-1-032-21227-2
ISSN 0459-7230

Contents

Chapter 1

Introduction

Editor's Introduction

2021 is the second year of pandemic and the first of recovery. While some countries emerge from lockdown, others face further devastation. But everywhere, COVID-19 remains a commanding issue shaping every aspect of life. For geopolitics, it is a global natural experiment testing state effectiveness, social cohesion and international relations. It has forced massive, urgent and complex decisions, especially in striking difficult balances between state power and citizens' rights; between openness and security in flows of people across states; and between short-term national interest and the collective global good in vaccine production and distribution.

But the politics of pandemic are constantly and rapidly changing. Few countries have performed uniformly well or poorly – and some that fared worst in 2020 now fare best. What we at the IISS call 'strategic sports commentary' – the pundit stream of today's 'hot takes' that become tomorrow's myths dispelled – is soon forgotten. It is thus too early to draw reliable conclusions about the geopolitical consequences of COVID-19. And a great deal of geopolitics in an exceptionally eventful year has had little or nothing to do with the pandemic but remains rooted in the enduring features of international life: war, power and rules. All this vindicates the view we took in 2020 that *Strategic Survey* should remain geopolitics-centric, not become COVID-centric. The pandemic has not displaced geopolitics, merely refracted it.

New wars erupted in 2020–21 even as old ones in the Middle East and the Sahel ground on. China and India fought their most deadly clash since 1967. Azerbaijan's defeat of Armenia in the second Nagorno-Karabakh war produced the biggest geopolitical shift in Eurasia since 2014 and prompted military planners elsewhere to study drone warfare more intently. Africa's second-most-populous country, Ethiopia, began a major assault on its province of Tigray. America's allies and adversaries alike are absorbing and interpreting both the fact and the manner of its withdrawal from Afghanistan.

War expresses irreconcilable interests; rules embody shared ones. Here, too, there were significant developments. With the end of the Brexit transition period in December 2020, that most ambitious rule-maker, the European Union, decoupled from the United Kingdom – whose readiness to consider a 'specific and limited' breach of international law sat ill with its commitment to a rules-based order. With one week to spare, the two sides agreed a Trade and Cooperation Agreement (TCA) to define their new relationship. But this remained unsettled and discordant, notably over the status of Northern Ireland – an issue that might yet erode the stability, and even integrity, of the UK. On the same day that the EU signed the TCA it also announced an ambitious Comprehensive Agreement on Investment with China. But the future of these rules, too, remained uncertain: in May 2021, the European Parliament suspended ratification of the agreement against the background of a deteriorating Sino-EU relationship.

There were breakthroughs too. The Abraham Accords that Israel signed with Bahrain, Morocco, Sudan and the United Arab Emirates marked an important shift in norms and relationships underpinning Middle Eastern politics, setting precedents that others may follow. Several countries, including China, bolstered the 2015 Paris Agreement on climate change – itself a landmark of global governance – with national commitments to achieve carbon neutrality. United States

President Joe Biden rejoined the Agreement on his first day in office, signalling America's return as an active multilateralist. His agreement with Russian President Vladimir Putin soon afterwards to renew the New START treaty saved strategic arms control from collapse. With remarkable speed, the new administration demonstrated the United States' unique ability to concert ambitious cooperation by securing G7 adoption of a global minimum corporate tax rate on multinationals. No other country can still make rules like America.

In short, the unprecedented 'cooperation gap' between the demand for and supply of global governance identified by *Strategic Survey 2020* did not widen and in some ways narrowed. But this hopeful development may not last. For the possibilities of cooperation, as of war, depend on power. And some of the most powerful states have been honing weapons short of war as their relations deteriorate. Russia's hack of SolarWinds illustrated the wider escalation of cyber espionage and attack. Its biggest military build-up on Ukraine's border since 2014 was a slow-motion exercise in coercive diplomacy. And regardless of any final judgement about the origins of COVID-19, the pandemic prompted a larger debate about the growing threat of biological weapons.

War, power and rules drive geopolitics. Leaders matters too: their choices turn these forces into effects. This was also a year of major leadership change. Japan's and Israel's long-serving prime ministers, Abe Shinzo and Benjamin Netanyahu, left office, as did the EU's longest-serving leader, German chancellor Angela Merkel. Chad's Idriss Déby, one of Africa's veteran presidents, died in battle. Belarusian leader Alexander Lukashenko faced the most serious challenge to his 26-year rule as the country erupted in protest.

But most consequential of all was Donald Trump's defeat in the November 2020 US elections. The events that followed drove America into uncharted territory. Genuine uncertainty over whether the military would support or remove Trump if he refused to leave; the unfounded yet widespread belief that the election was 'stolen'; and the insurrection on Capitol Hill on 6 January 2021: all this amounted to the most serious challenge to American democracy and cohesion since the Civil War.

This reminds us that, within states as well as between them, power may become zero-sum, rules may wear thin, and even large-scale conflict is imaginable. When this happens in the world's most powerful country and oldest democracy, the global implications must be great. At a minimum, it means America may be better at securing international cooperation than domestic consensus – its internal divisions could yet derail the historic G7 tax plan. Further polarisation would be more fateful – and there is no sign that the forces driving this have eased. No less than the wars, agreements and rivalries, America's political turmoil may prove one of the most important geopolitical events of the past year.

September 2021

Drivers of Strategic Change

Geopolitics is driven by changes in the ability of states to use and resist power. The first depends on power resources, and the second on domestic resilience. Our Drivers of Strategic Change measure and compare key trends in both areas. They illuminate recent shifts in geopolitics and sources of potential future change.

Geopolitics is a craft, not a science: judgement, skill, chance and other immeasurable factors also shape international relations. But they do so within a range of possibilities set by the underlying domestic and external capacities of states. We encourage you to explore the rich data in our Drivers and the insights they yield.

The Drivers begin each geographical chapter. Unless otherwise stated, they chart change over 20 years by plotting data from 2000, 2010 and 2020.

Regional Share of Global Population, GDP and Defence Budget
(Sources: United Nations Department of Economic and Social Affairs; IMF; IISS, *Military Balance*; IISS, Military Balance+)

The first Driver depicts the region's share of global population, GDP and defence budget. These are key power resources: the more of each that a country or region possesses, the greater its potential power, especially in combination. This Driver thus shows how the relative power of each region has changed over the past two decades.

The next six Drivers depict data for key selected countries in each region.

Population
(Source: United Nations Department of Economic and Social Affairs)

The second Driver shows population, age structure and median age. These are important for several reasons. Population is a power resource. A high proportion of young people – a 'youth bulge' – is a strong predictor of civil violence. It also presages a 'demographic dividend' of higher economic growth through future workforce growth, especially if fertility rates subsequently fall. Conversely, an ageing population means a high dependency ratio of economically inactive to active citizens, creating fiscal and productivity challenges that can limit resources needed to sustain power.

GDP

(Source: IMF)

The third Driver shows GDP and global ranking. The larger a country's economy, the more of other forms of strength, including military hardware, it can procure.

GDP per Capita

(Source: IMF)

The fourth Driver shows GDP per capita, which has been shown to have a significant impact on the development of social values. Rising affluence leads to robust and predictable changes in political orientation – in particular, a decline in deference towards authority and a rise in demands for inclusion and participation.

Defence Budget and Active Military Personnel

(Sources: IISS, *Military Balance*; IISS, Military Balance+)

The fifth Driver shows defence budget and active military personnel, which are indicators of hard power.

Human Development Index (HDI)

(Source: UN Development Programme)

The sixth Driver shows Human Development Index scores, a composite measure of human well-being. This indicates a country's ability to provide well-being and life chances for its population, with positive implications for governmental legitimacy and stability.

Political System

(Source: Freedom House, 'Freedom in the World')

The seventh Driver shows how democratic a political system is. Democratic legitimacy tends to produce stable and responsive government that is more resilient in a crisis. Conversely, the recent decline of democracy in some high-income countries, where the underlying demand for accountability remains high, may presage declining stability.

Regional Trends

The final Driver for each chapter uses a range of data to illuminate region-specific trends.

For Asia, Europe, Latin America and North America:

Trust in Government

(Source: Edelman Trust Barometer)

This Driver shows the general public's average percentage of trust in government. Falling trust in governmental institutions – a recent feature of many countries – implies a decline in stability and cohesion. Questions that afforded respondents the opportunity to criticise their government were not asked in China, Russia and Thailand.

For Russia and Eurasia:

Approval Rating for President Vladimir Putin, and Assessment of the Current State of Affairs in Russia

(Source: Levada Center)

This Driver shows approval ratings for Russian President Vladimir Putin and popular views about the state of affairs in Russia. It highlights declining confidence that Russia is going 'in the right direction'.

For the Middle East and North Africa:

Breakeven Oil Prices

(Sources: BP Statistical Review of World Energy 2021; IMF)

This Driver shows the oil price per barrel needed to ensure that planned government spending will not incur a budget deficit for 2016–21, together with the average annual oil price. This highlights the impact of post-2014 oil-price decline on the fiscal sustainability of oil-export-dependent states.

For sub-Saharan Africa:

Percentage of Children in Education
(Source: World Bank)

This Driver shows the gross percentage of children in education. The strong recent growth of education is a major investment in human capital that should lead to significant development and growing prosperity.

Chapter 2

Key Events
July 2020–June 2021

July 2020

01 The United States–Mexico–Canada Agreement (USMCA) comes into effect, replacing the North American Free Trade Agreement (NAFTA).

14 In response to China's adoption of an Internal Security Act for Hong Kong on 30 June, US president Donald Trump signs an executive order revoking Hong Kong's special status with the US in the areas of national security, foreign relations and economics.

29 The US secretary of defense, Mark Esper, announces plans to withdraw almost 12,000 troops from Germany. President Joe Biden freezes this decision in February 2021 pending a deployment-of-forces review.

August 2020

4 A massive explosion destroys the port of Beirut and damages many areas of the city, leading to the resignation of the government and a worsening of Lebanon's economic and political crisis.

10 Belarusian President Alexander Lukashenko claims a sixth term in office. Official results give him 80.1% of the vote. Mass protests begin.

20 Russian opposition leader Alexei Navalny is poisoned by military-grade nerve agent Novichok.

28 Abe Shinzo, Japan's longest-serving prime minister, steps down due to poor health and is succeeded by Suga Yoshihide.

31 In Sudan, government and rebel groups sign a peace deal promising to end a 17-year civil war based predominantly in the Darfur region.

September 2020

15 Israel, Bahrain and the United Arab Emirates (UAE) sign the Abraham Accords at the White House following intense US diplomacy. These normalisation agreements are the first between Israel and Arab states.

27 War breaks out between Armenia and Azerbaijan over the disputed Nagorno-Karabakh region.

October 2020

15 Mexico's former secretary of defence, General Salvador Cienfuegos, is arrested in the US on drug-trafficking and money-laundering charges.

15 Sooronbai Jeenbekov resigns as president of Kyrgyzstan following post-election protests. He is succeeded by Sadyr Japarov.

18 Trump hosts delegations from Israel, Bahrain and the UAE to sign the Abraham Accords to normalise relations between Israel and the two Gulf states.

23 The UN brokers a permanent ceasefire agreement among Libya's warring parties, paving the way for elections in December 2021.

November 2020

3 Joe Biden wins the US presidential election.

4 Civil war in Tigray begins as clashes between the Tigray People's Liberation Front (TPLF) and the Ethiopian National Defense Force (ENDF) escalate.

10 Armenia, Azerbaijan and Russia sign an agreement to end fighting over the Nagorno-Karabakh region.

10 The European Council announces an agreement with European Union member states on a €1.8 trillion spending package for the next seven years, including a €750 billion COVID-19 recovery fund.

18 Pressured by the Mexican government, the US drops charges against Cienfuegos ahead of his return to Mexico to face investigation. Cienfuegos is then cleared of all charges in December.

24 Foreign donors pledge a projected US$12bn in civilian aid to the Afghan government over the next four years and promise to support the country's peace process.

27 Mohsen Fakhrizadeh, Iran's top nuclear scientist, is assassinated. In April 2021, the Natanz enrichment facility is hit by a sabotage act that knocks several thousand centrifuges out of commission. Iran accuses Israel.

December 2020

6 President Nicolás Maduro's Socialist Party and its allies win Venezuela's legislative elections, which were boycotted by the main opposition parties. All political institutions of the country are now under Maduro's control.

22 Morocco and Israel normalise relations. The US recognises Morocco's claim to the disputed territory of Western Sahara.

24 The EU and UK reach agreement on a new Trade and Cooperation Agreement (TCA), which enters into force on 1 January 2021.

24 Maia Sandu is sworn in as Moldova's first woman president following her election victory in November on a pro-EU platform.

January 2021

01 China's free-trade agreement with Mauritius, its first with an African state, comes into force.

05 Saudi Arabia, the UAE and Bahrain agree to restore diplomatic relations with Qatar, after imposing an embargo against the country since 2017.

06 Following incitement from Donald Trump, a mob of his supporters storm the US Capitol in a bid to overturn the presidential election.

06 Sudan signs the US-brokered Abraham Accords.

11 The Trump administration puts Cuba back onto the US State Department's list of state sponsors of terrorism. The measure will further restrict business between the two countries.

13 After the storming of the Capitol by Trump supporters, the US House of Representatives votes to impeach Donald Trump, making him the first US president to be impeached twice. The Senate acquits him on 13 February.

17 Alexei Navalny is arrested on his return to Moscow after being treated in Berlin.

22 A row develops over whether the EU is receiving its fair share of vaccine supplies from AstraZeneca, leading the EU to suggest it could trigger Article 16 of the Northern Ireland Protocol to prevent vaccines entering the UK.

25 Mexican President Andrés Manuel López Obrador announces that Russia will supply Mexico with 24 million doses of its Sputnik V vaccine, and that he has invited Russian President Vladimir Putin to visit Mexico.

26 US President Biden and Russian President Putin agree to extend the New START nuclear treaty for five years.

February 2021

01 New Chinese legislation apparently giving the China Coast Guard enforcement powers in all waters claimed by Beijing takes effect.

01 The armed forces in Myanmar seize power following an election victory by the National League for Democracy led by State Counsellor Aung San Suu Kyi in November 2020.

02 US President Biden issues Executive Order 14010 directing executive agencies to address the root causes of, and collaboratively manage, migration in Central America.

07 The Houthi movement renews its campaign to seize Marib, the last major city held by forces loyal to the internationally recognised government of Yemen.

09 Colombia grants almost 1m undocumented Venezuelans the right to remain for ten years.

19 The US rejoins the Paris Agreement on climate change.

March 2021

09 A Supreme Court judge in Brazil annuls former president Luiz Inácio 'Lula' da Silva's corruption convictions, opening up the possibility of his running for Brazil's presidency in 2022.

09 The outgoing head of US Indo-Pacific Command, Admiral Phil Davidson, tells the US Senate Armed Services Committee that China might attempt to use force to take control of Taiwan 'in the next six years'.

16 The UK publishes the Integrated Review setting out the country's role in the world over the next decade. It includes a decision to increase the UK nuclear stockpile.

18 Senior US and Chinese officials publicly clash at a summit meeting in Anchorage, Alaska.

25 Russia begins its biggest military build-up on Ukraine's border since 2014.

April 2021

04 The Jordanian government places former crown prince Hamzah bin Al-Hussein under house arrest and arrests several senior figures, accusing them of plotting to destabilise the country.

05 Mozambique's military reclaims full control of the town of Palma, just over one week after it was raided by jihadists.

13 Biden announces that all US forces will leave Afghanistan before 11 September 2021.

16 The US announces sanctions on Russia over cyber attacks and other hostile activities.

19 Miguel Díaz-Canel becomes first secretary of the Cuban Communist Party, marking the first time in 60 years that Cuba is not ruled by a Castro.

28 Biden announces the second part of an investment plan for infrastructure (US$2.3trn, announced in March) and jobs, education and social care (US$1.8trn).

28 Border clashes between Kyrgyzstan and Tajikistan lead to the deaths of over 50 people.

28 Reports emerge that Sudan has suspended plans to allow Russia to open a naval logistics base in Port Sudan.

May 2021

04 The EU suspends ratification of a Comprehensive Agreement on Investment (CAI) with China, following China's imposition of sanctions on several senior EU politicians and European academics.

07 Clashes between Palestinians and Israeli police erupt in East Jerusalem. Heavy fighting spreads to Gaza and ends two weeks later thanks to Egyptian mediation between Israel and Hamas.

20 The Biden administration suspends sanctions on companies building the controversial Nord Stream 2 pipeline between Russia and Germany.

22 The UK's Carrier Strike Group, led by the aircraft carrier HMS *Queen Elizabeth*, departs on a seven-month deployment, much of which will be spent in Asian waters.

23 Belarusian opposition journalist Roman Protasevich is detained after his flight from Greece to Lithuania was forced to land in Minsk.

24 In the second Malian coup in nine months, president Bah Ndaw and prime minister Moctar Ouane are ousted by Colonel Assimi Goïta.

26 Switzerland abandons several years' worth of efforts aimed at establishing a single framework agreement with the EU.

26 The corruption trial of South Africa's former president Jacob Zuma begins. He faces 18 charges relating to his US$2bn arms deal in 1999.

28 US Senate Republicans block a bill to establish a bipartisan commission to investigate the insurrection at the Capitol in January.

June 2021

06 Political novice Pedro Castillo from the far-left Free Peru party wins the second round of Peru's presidential elections, reinforcing perceptions of a new 'Pink Tide' sweeping Latin America.

09 A Russian court bans organisations founded by Alexei Navalny, classifying them as 'extremist'.

10 China's National People's Congress passes a law to counter foreign economic sanctions, as part of an effort to reduce pressure from the US and EU over technology, trade, Xinjiang and Hong Kong.

10 French President Emmanuel Macron announces that *Operation Barkhane* in the Sahel will end in its present form.

11 Leaders of the G7 countries meet in Cornwall, UK, for their first summit in two years, and the first for Joe Biden as US president.

12 US President Biden and the G7 leaders agree to establish a new global infrastructure project, 'Build Back Better World' (B3W), explicitly intended to counter China's Belt and Road Initiative (BRI).

13 Naftali Bennett is sworn in as Israeli prime minister, ousting Benjamin Netanyahu after 12 years in office.

14 President Rodrigo Duterte of the Philippines extends the suspension of the abrogation of the country's Visiting Forces Agreement with the US for a further six months.

16 US President Biden and Russian President Putin hold a summit meeting in Geneva.

19 Ebrahim Raisi, the head of Iran's judiciary, wins an Iranian presidential election marred by low turnout.

21 The European Council imposes a fourth package of restrictive measures against Belarusian individuals and entities in response to escalating human-rights abuses and the forced landing of a Ryanair flight in Minsk.

23 Southern African nations agree to deploy forces to Mozambique to help combat terrorism and extremism in Cabo Delgado province.

28 Following the rebels' capture of the Tigrayan capital, Mekelle, Ethiopia's government announces a unilateral ceasefire.

28 Moscow and Beijing agree to extend their 2001 friendship and cooperation treaty for a further five years, from 2022 until 2027.

Chapter 3

Strategic Prospects

The present strategic situation does not lend itself to easy typology or summary. Phrases like the 'post-Cold War order', 'the return of great-power conflict', 'the Asian century', a 'G2 world', 'multipolarity' or its clever obverse 'G Zero' fail to capture any vital essence. Commentators frustrate themselves in attempting to capture the nature of the current world order in a single phrase.

As for drawing together the threads of disparate events to form a purposeful assessment – that too is vulnerable to intellectual fashion or individual experience. How best to weigh the relative importance of COVID-19, China's emergence as a superpower, the new technology rivalry and the prospects of decoupling, the growing appeal of economic statecraft, the frequent deployment of state-sponsored 'influence networks', the proliferation of cyber threats, the withdrawal of America from current battlefields, the rise of authoritarians on both the right and the left, the dissipation of the 'rules-based order' or the urgency of climate change? The variety of issues that have strategic impact daunts even the most confident of analysts. Nevertheless, good strategic thinking requires separating the trend from the trendy to judge which subjects should, or will, seize the attention of policymakers who must address international tensions. This is what the IISS *Strategic Survey* attempts each year.

As 2022 approaches, several regional conflicts will become more local-ised. International intervention fatigue has set in. It has gripped the United States most particularly in Afghanistan. The announcement by the Biden administration that all US forces would withdraw from Afghanistan by the anniversary of the 9/11 attacks predictably led to the reinvigoration of the Taliban offensive. That in turn led many forces fighting for the government, with which they had lost faith, to change sides.

The burden of containing Taliban-ruled Afghanistan will fall on those in the immediate region. Pakistan's attitude will be crucially important. India will see Afghanistan as potentially breeding an intensified terrorist threat. Russia and the Central Asian states will revive their direct interest in the country. Iran will share an interest with the Taliban to defeat the Islamic State–Khorasan Province (ISIS–KP), though sectarian differences could still stall the creation of a strategic partnership. China will need to discern how close a relationship it is prudent to form with the Taliban, whose support for the East Turkestan Islamic Movement (ETIM) it would like to end. Gulf states will be wary of any resurgence of al-Qaeda or other extremist terrorist groups, but will consider the new realities in their regional diplomacy. Afghanistan's neighbours will struggle to contain flows of refugees, drugs or terrorism. Security in South Asia will decline from a low bar.

The US decision to withdraw led all other NATO countries to do so. The manner of leaving a military engagement is consequential. People who speak of an exit strategy tend to think more of 'exit' than of 'strategy'. Afghanistan has been left to its own sadly dysfunctional devices – indeed challenged to do so – by the US, which feels it has done its bit.

Intervention fatigue also affected, to a degree, the French in Mali, who decided to draw down their military engagement to a force of hundreds rather than thousands. Here too, there will be an uncertain and inevitably fragile reliance on local forces to contain terrorist threats. Security in the Sahel will be further fractured. The implications for European security are uncertain, but not negligible. North Africa is a strategically significant part of southern Europe's near abroad. While a Europe with a new German chancellor and a French president entering electoral season tries to develop a common approach towards Russia, insecurity on the southern shores of the Mediterranean will still tug on both the strategic and humanitarian consciences. Europeans will need to deal with security challenges on all flanks, but with only intermittent US attention.

In the Gulf, Saudi Arabia and the United Arab Emirates (UAE) judged that their military intervention in Yemen was not yielding the desired results and scaled down their military operations too, aiming instead for a political solution. That is proving elusive as divisions in the Houthi opposition emerge and elements of its leadership consider that progress on the ground justifies seeking a military solution rather than a diplomatic compromise. The risks to commercial maritime traffic in the Gulf – as evidenced by the uninhabited aerial vehicle (UAV) attack on the *Mercer Street* tanker in July 2021 – may well persist. Iran will see this traffic as offering easy pickings and has an array of superficially deniable ways of threatening it. Strategies will have to be developed to better protect commercial shipping in the area and to contain the proliferation of weaponry that is used to disrupt it.

These developments in South Asia, North Africa and the Gulf make it likely that, next year, counter-terrorism will again appear as a priority on the international agenda. It is a maxim of counter-terrorism professionals that when little is being heard, sometimes that is a sign that one should worry more. Silence invites its own suspicions. As Afghanistan, Mali and Yemen face a reduction in external military engagement with no commensurate increase in the quality of national governance, the risk of renewed or intensified terrorist activity potentially increases locally, regionally and internationally. Intervention fatigue and strategic impatience are two sides of the same coin. Neither attitude can prevent threats from developing, and their coexistence may inspire malign transnational actors to try their luck. Leaders in North America and Europe, perhaps to their strategic irritation, will need to find ways to cooperate on counter-terrorism instruments in these new conditions. The lethal disruption of emerging threats may become more necessary in these circumstances, though more difficult given the loss of intelligence that results from serial disengagement from key theatres.

In the Middle East, there is less sign of intervention fatigue from Iran, whose well-maintained international influence networks remain capable of affecting political outcomes in several countries in which they operate. The manipulated election to office of President Ebrahim Raisi will strengthen the role of the Islamic Revolutionary Guard Corps (IRGC) at the centre of Iran's governing apparatus. This will in turn ensure that the IRGC is in complete charge of regional relationships, raising the prospect of intensified efforts to weigh the regional balances of power towards Iran's interests. As the IRGC values its international influence network and the state's ballistic-missile programme even more than the nuclear project, the odds of reaching a satisfactory follow-on agreement to the nuclear agreement known as the Joint Comprehensive Plan of Action (JCPOA) are limited. The new government needs sanctions to be lifted but is unlikely to agree to a reduction of its regional influence operations – even if this could be defined in a negotiated text – to achieve it.

Tensions with Israel are bound to rise. The Gulf countries worry equally about an Iran that develops nuclear weapons, and a war to prevent this from happening. The Abraham Accords, which led to the establishment of official diplomatic relations between the UAE, Bahrain and Israel, were in large part founded on shared strategic antipathy towards Iran and its policies. The arrival of the IRGC at the centre of Iranian regional policymaking will cause very substantial disquiet on the other side of the Gulf. The simultaneous acceleration of Iran's nuclear programme and the likely redoubling of its influence operations in the Gulf, Iraq, Syria, Lebanon and Yemen will pose a dizzying challenge to the US and its regional partners. The likelihood of a labour-intensive strategy being developed to counter Iran's regional policies is low. The window to slow Iran's nuclear programme is closing. Security in the Gulf will be tenuous.

These unhappy trends collide with the reality that dealing with China is at the top of almost every state's foreign-policy consideration. China has for some time been the swing player geo-economically. The economies of so many countries go up or down in rhythm with Beijing's purchasing power and tastes. It is now a swing player geostrategically as well, given the role it wishes to play not just in Asia but globally as it asserts its recently acquired status. The US Department of Defense has declared the Indo-Pacific as its primary strategic theatre of interest. Several European countries have Indo-Pacific policies, and the European Union and NATO have announced the need to have China strategies. 'What is your China policy?' is a question to which most governments, and all international businesses, now need an answer. Providing that answer and adapting it to ever-changing conditions is a huge task.

China's strategic extroversion now extends beyond defending core Chinese interests. The ambitions of the Belt and Road Initiative (BRI) have a global character. China has expressed national interests in every corner of the world. It complains about the internationalisation of issues that it thinks are purely domestic, while it keenly domesticates issues that others rightly consider international. President Xi Jinping's goals are also tethered to a diplomatic mindset extremely sensitive to any perceived attack on national pride. The resulting so-called 'wolf warrior' diplomatic posture has officials on 'high alert' to any affront to, or criticism of, China. Australia, among others, has been heavily sanctioned for public statements and domestic legislation that appear insufficiently respectful of China's status and intentions.

The US, for its part, has developed a bipartisan consensus that China presents a competitive challenge on multiple fronts. The Pentagon is concentrating its military strategy in the Indo-Pacific and welcomes the 'purposeful presence' of European navies in theatre. The intelligence agencies are focused on China's cyber activity and on developing a better understanding of Chinese decision-taking and aims. The State Department and White House are strengthening relations among the so-called Quad countries: Australia, India, Japan and the US. Yet these military, intelligence and diplomatic efforts have not yet been married to an economic strategy that can woo friends and compete with a China that is the leading commercial partner for every country in the region.

This strand of US policy will likely mature in the next year, given the growing place of economic statecraft in US and allied policies. Trade, arrangements, sanctions policies, standard-setting, investment regimes and supply-chain management are all strands of US policy that are bound to be more tightly drawn together in addressing China. Certainly, in the technology and digital realm, this will be a priority. The US continues to sanction China's technology firms and seeks to control the supply chain of semiconductors to slow China's pre-eminence in this area. It recognises that China's Digital Silk Road, little blocked by the Trump administration's effort to slow the growth of Chinese 5G, will be a major source of Chinese influence across large swathes of the developing world. The US will seek to develop new digital rules of the road and gain greater Asian collaboration in that effort. It will have a very willing partner in Japan, which is keen to create digital technologies that can compete with China. And in today's Japan, the US has an Asian ally that is also actively concerned about the growth of Chinese military power and its use to encroach on neighbouring seas. Australia has weathered sanctions from China well, and opinion there is hardening on the need to restrain China strategically. India's own frontier struggles with China have equally bolstered the sense in New Delhi that strategic engagement in the Indo-Pacific must be more than a regular appearance at all key meetings.

The question for the future is whether the Biden administration's declared preference for multilateralism translates to an effective policy for coalition creation and alliance building. Strengthening the Quad, engaging effectively with the Association of Southeast Asian Nations (ASEAN) and building on formal bilateral alliances require persistent attention. The region will feel the more immediate influence of the large neighbour. The allure of the Chinese economy exerts a strong magnetic pull. The absence of a clear economic and trade strategy in Asia may hinder America's case in the region. And however specific the circumstances that led to the US withdrawal from Afghanistan, the question of strategic reliability will hang over American promises of support. Trust in China is low in the region, strategic self-confidence is weak and belief in the US is not yet fully revived.

Europeans are now collectively more wary of China. The largely commercial approach of the past has ceded ground to a more clear-eyed geostrategic attitude. China's ability to peel off EU states through economic and technological inducements persists, but it is now sufficiently observed to be a matter for critical debate. The ratification of the EU's Comprehensive Agreement on Investment (CAI) with China was suspended after China placed sanctions on some EU parliamentarians. Such agreements will be subject to more scrutiny in future as Europeans also adopt the techniques of economic statecraft to protect interests and advance international goals. Standard-setting in the technology realm will become one of the more important features of economic diplomacy. It will be a key element in relations with China and a theme that will invite both cooperation with other countries in Asia, particularly Japan, and constructive engagement with the US.

Alliance and partnership structures are changing to accommodate greater strategic self-determination in a shifting environment. Traditional US allies are aware that arguments over burden-sharing will become more vigorous. Withdrawal from Afghanistan, wounding as it may be to South Asian security, is consistent with America's shift of attention further into the Indo-Pacific. The White House multilateralist catchphrase 'America is back' struck a dissonant chord at the time of the Afghan withdrawal. The intrusions of the outside world on the US will not cease because of a well-publicised desire to focus on the home front. Allies and partners of the US will nevertheless need to be more extrovert in designing an agenda for cooperation with the US that chimes with the times and can win wider engagement. So-called 'great-power competition' is inescapable. In Europe, Russia; in the Middle East, Iran; and in Asia, China – all will absorb plenty of attention. As a consequence, at least five thematic national-security challenges will require concerted effort in 2022.

Firstly, developing standards for technology that incorporate security considerations and invite effective digital cooperation is a natural priority that emerges out of the tense debate over 5G. Secondly, advancing norms and laws that support 'responsible cyber' policies internationally is required given the growing role of cyber power in national-security strategies, and the rise of cyber criminality. Thirdly, maintaining a capacity for counter-terrorism operations is bound to remain important in Europe, the Middle East and Asia. Fourthly, the climate-change crisis must now be framed as a first-order security issue, as well as an environmental and social one, to galvanise more international cooperation. That said, a combination of nationalism and geopolitical distrust between the major state contributors to global warming is bound to disappoint the proponents of this.

This leaves the fifth issue, which is the recasting of the multilateral order, putatively the prime foreign-policy objective of the Biden administration. The president will host a summit of democracies in December 2021. This will no doubt celebrate the great virtues of democratic systems. Yet it would be unwise to turn this into a rallying cry for the spread of democracy, however worthy a goal that might be. As this publication has argued in the past, good governance without democracy is safer strategically than is democracy without good governance. That is an important maxim to bear in mind as governments come to office eager to shape international relations along lines with which they are domestically familiar.

Agreement is easier to reach with those with whom you already agree on almost everything else. But those who argue passionately about inclusion in domestic politics should take care to avoid being too exclusive in their international relations. The view that others should adopt one's own domestic model of governance displays a missionary zeal that is unbecoming in modern times. Throughout the world there are unhappy examples of states wishing to export their government, economic and other models to others without regard for the specific conditions that obtain elsewhere. Principles of good governance, both domestic and international, can arise from a variety of legitimate sources.

As the world swings perilously between an old rules-based order that seems poorly maintained for contemporary purposes, and a new order yet to be well designed and strategically engineered, it is important to place emphasis on new rules and norms that are required to govern the world more effectively in the third decade of the twenty-first century. There is no requirement for fundamental changes in international law. But as the IISS has regularly argued, the need for active diplomacy to modernise the legal underpinnings of the international order is urgent.

The international principles that can support healthy inter-state relations in the digital age, shaped by transnational threats, as great-power competition returns, need to be elaborated. Allies and partners must develop shared strategic visions, but they then require legal inter-operability to work together 'at the speed of relevance'. Politicians committed to 'build back better' should apply that rallying cry to their efforts within the international community. Otherwise, their domestic tasks will be rendered futile by a further deterioration of the international situation. The COVID-19 pandemic should have reminded leaders of the ease of transmission of global threats. Rediscovering extroversion in the service of a revived multilateralism following a period of hibernation will require huge diplomatic energy, but *'stratégie oblige'*.

Chapter 4
Strategic Policy

How Have Global Power and Influence Shifted?

Acceleration

At first blush, the shock of the COVID-19 pandemic has not reordered the hierarchy of global power. The United States remains the most broadly based of the major powers and the only one that has global heft across the spectrum of power: it continues to occupy the commanding heights of the world's financial and monetary system and retains unparalleled global power-projection capability, both hard and soft. Indeed, as a result of Donald Trump's defeat in the November 2020 presidential elections, the US was better placed to retain its pivotal role at the heart of the European and Asia-Pacific security systems than before the pandemic – or so it seemed before the chaotic withdrawal from Afghanistan in August 2021.

China's rise has continued unimpeded under the control of the Chinese Communist Party (CCP), confirming its standing as the United States' peer competitor established after the great financial crisis of 2007–09. Indeed, that crisis arguably had a deeper effect on the hierarchy of states than the pandemic: America's strategic prudence and pivot to Asia under Barack Obama; China's rise to become the second-largest world economy; the return of Russia as a global strategic player; and the beginning of the European Union's decade-long lurching from one existential crisis to another all pre-date COVID-19.

The same set of remarks apply in varying degrees to the other major actors: India is no closer to catching up with China than it was before the pandemic; Brazil remains no less dependent on raw-materials markets; and Turkey's slide into neo-Ottoman governance and foreign policy has been reinforced rather than attenuated.

Indeed, the pandemic has accelerated most of these trends. US President Joe Biden may have dropped Trump's 'Make America Great Again!' slogan, but the United States' focus is first and foremost on rebuilding America's strength: 'Trumpism with a human face', as it were. Abroad, continuity was deliberate vis-à-vis the winding up of America's force presence in Afghanistan. The self-declared 'wolf-warrior' rhetoric accompanying China's rise has taken on a stridency reminiscent of Germany's Wilhelmine era. The CCP has tightened its grip, with 'Xi Jinping Thought on Socialism with Chinese Characteristics for a New Era' now enjoying close-to-equal status with that of Mao Zedong: Lenin has been put back into 'market-Leninism'. Vladimir Putin's Russia is accelerating its slide into authoritarian rule in the service of its overt quest for a liquidation of the post-Cold War order in Europe. During the pandemic, the EU has demonstrated the strength of its survival instincts, even if these continue to be in inverse proportion to its ability to shape its future.

Meanwhile, the nature and content of power relationships are changing substantially under the pressure of the pandemic.

Kindleberger's trap

It has become an intellectual fashion to point out the risk of China and the US falling into a Thucydides Trap of inevitable war. Another analogy may be more apposite. In 1973, in *The World in Depression 1929– 1939*, Massachusetts Institute of Technology (MIT) Professor Charles Kindleberger argued that it was the breakdown in global hegemonic stability that turned the Wall Street Crash into an epoch-changing disruption, eventually leading to the Second World War: the British Empire no longer had the will or the ability to keep the global system working whereas the US was unwilling or unable to do so. This trap was avoided during the 2007–09 global financial crisis. Unlike the precedent of the Great Depression, Washington and Beijing worked together as 'responsible stakeholders' with the shared objective of heading off a global depression.

Conversely, this is what decidedly did not happen during the pandemic, in any of its dimensions – sanitary, economic, political or ideological: the US under Trump and China under Xi displayed no interest in assuming separately or jointly the mantle of global leadership.

The United Nations served only the narrowest of national interests, as was evident at the suddenly pivotal World Health Organization (WHO). The difficulties the WHO faced in determining the origin of and reacting promptly to CoV-SARS-2 (the virus that causes the disease COVID-19) contrast starkly with what is required to fully understand the ongoing pandemic and to prepare against future outbreaks. As ever, the multilateral system is only as good as its member states allow it to be. Trump's decision to withdraw the US from the WHO rather than to leverage the West's majority contribution to the organisation's budget did not help. However, this proved to be reversible. China's power has grown immeasurably during the intervening years and its views of what the WHO is allowed or not allowed to do are proving less amenable to revision.

This 'pandemic nationalism' has prevailed at the expense of the poorer and less powerful parts of humanity. The US policy before March 2021 was to withhold all vaccines from export customers, rich or poor. China energetically practised 'vaccine bilateralism' with its refusal to distribute its vaccines through the multilateral COVAX programme. Such policies have sent a powerful message, notably in Africa, that 'the poor do not count'. This is likely to have long-term consequences for the global order, as the global north's vaccine egotism will rekindle resentment vis-à-vis the former colonial powers. It remains to be seen whether China or Russia will be the beneficiaries of this development, given the limitations of their own policies, notably their 'vaccine diplomacy', which was stronger in words than in deeds.

The economic responses to the pandemic were no less fractured. The democracies universally decided to sustain domestic demand with state spending unprecedented in peacetime, while China emphasised supply-based export-oriented policies. China was the first country to experience the pandemic and the first to return to a form of economic normality. It could therefore fuel its economic recovery through consumer exports paid for by Western 'helicopter money', while much of the West's economy was still in lockdown. This Chinese approach contrasted starkly with the fiscal expansion that underpinned its response to the 2007–09 crisis. As for the cash-strapped countries of the global south, the IMF proved to be rather slow in expanding its Special Drawing Rights. Lack of international support for the poor compounded the sense that they did not matter.

At the strategic level, the divide between the US-centric alliance system in Europe and the Asia-Pacific and a rising China has deepened, but in a manner that is for the time being closer to Kindleberger than to Thucydides. The Biden administration asserts the need for a return to a degree of multilateralism and a consolidation of the alliance system. However, this runs against powerful headwinds, of which the priority given to domestic affairs is only one. 'Leading from behind' (Libya, 2011), 'red lines' (Syria, 2013), 'Normandy format' (handing prime responsibility of the Ukrainian nexus to Europe, 2014) and, most recently, the debacle in Kabul tell a story of ten years of American retreat. This backdrop fuels the scepticism of allies and rivals alike as to America's willingness and ability to back its global vision with the sort of determination that prevailed during the Cold War contest with the Soviet bloc. Nor is the foreground generating confidence in America's political staying power, with looming midterm elections that are rarely favourable to the incumbent.

China, for its part, is clear about what it does not want, but gives little sense of its vision of the future international order. This makes it different from the USSR, which harboured a coherent alternative vision of this order. Hence, the US–China power contest is not set to look like the comparatively stable bipolar confrontation of the Cold War, even if the latter was never as predictable as flawed hindsight has painted it. This rejectionist tendency is reinforced by China's strategic relationship with Russia, which is based in part on a common rejection of Western political values and systems. This stands in contrast to the period that followed the fall of Saigon, when a weaker but regionally influential China was a strategic partner of the West.

In this context, the occasional agreement to perpetuate the strategic status quo becomes the outlier, such as the US–Russian decision to extend the provisions of the New START treaty until 2026 and to prepare for the aftermath by opening nuclear strategic-stability talks. More typical is the unravelling of the grand compromise struck between China and the US during the 1970s that has enabled regional stability in East Asia for more than four decades. By extension, it fuelled the blistering economic growth of East Asia in general, and China's emergence as the main beneficiary of globalisation in particular. With Beijing dismantling the 'One Country, Two Systems' compromise that has underpinned Hong Kong's status since 1997, and escalating its shows of force against Taiwan, the constructive strategic ambiguity is set to become a thing of the past. This is possibly the single most destabilising development currently under way in the global strategic arena.

Deglobalisation or decoupling

In the lexicon of instant comments about post-pandemic power shifts, deglobalisation stands out. Global merchandise trade fell by 5.3% in 2020 while air travel in passenger miles dropped by a colossal two-thirds. However, this does not signal a turning point, for the basic reason that the crisis of globalisation, like so many other trends, began not with the pandemic but as an outcome of the great recession of 2007–08. During that episode, trade fell harder than during the pandemic, with a 12% drop, and recovered less than the global economy as a whole: during 2010–19, foreign trade grew by one-sixth whereas the world's economic output increased by nearly one-third. For more than a decade, globalisation may have continued to enable economic growth, but it was no longer driving it.

Flows of data, not goods, will be the main driver of future globalisation. This in turn means not only some institutional reordering – a greater role for the International Telecommunication Union (currently headed by a Chinese secretary-general), for example, and a lesser one for the World Trade Organization (run by a Nigerian director-general). More fundamentally, digital asymmetries, such as China's unfettered access to the global cyber domain on the one hand and its restrictions to foreign entry into its national cyber realm on the other, will take on ever greater salience, fuelling disaffection and confrontation. Conversely, the pandemic also demonstrated that the global economy and society could carry on despite the raising of high barriers to the circulation of people. In 2020, the number of passengers travelling by air between China and the outside world stood at some 13% of the pre-pandemic number (9.6 million versus 74.2m in 2019), extending its collapse into 2021 (0.14m passengers in January). This did not appear to impair China's economic recovery. Globalisation is changing, not disappearing.

Economic decoupling of the West from China, rather than a more general deglobalisation, is likely to be the main source of declining connectivity. It responds to powerful strategic rationales rather than to purely economic considerations, and is also strongly mutual, since China and the global West share this goal to varying degrees. China's 'Made in China 2025' plan was launched before the pandemic, and has since been superseded in semantic terms by the call for a 'dual-circulation' economic strategy, with 'internal circulation' – domestic production, distribution and consumption – destined to be protected from unwelcome outside dependency but supported by 'external circulation'. For instance, China imports some US$350 billion of semiconductors a year, many of which are designed and produced using proprietary US technology. By comparison, it spends less than US$200bn a year on oil, despite being the world's biggest importer. In important respects, China has never 'coupled' with the global economy, most notably in its early building of the Great Firewall to keep out many Western online platforms.

The push for decoupling from China, which began in the US before the pandemic, has been ramped up, including from substantial restrictions on technology transfers – notably against Huawei – and a toughening of Committee on Foreign Investment in the US (CFIUS) regulation. In Europe, the debate was relatively low-key until China pressured governments to give Huawei pride of place in its fifth generation (5G) of online networks in late 2019. This backfired when the sudden shortage of protective medical equipment at the beginning of the pandemic, and China's vigorous 'mask diplomacy', stunned public opinion. For their part, Australia, India and Japan have launched discussions on supply-chain resilience in the Indo-Pacific region.

The key to the West's future decoupling from China will be the implementation of the US and EU recovery plans, with their strong focus on technology and innovation. If successful, these plans will enable both domestically based innovation and the repatriation (or 'reshoring') of key capabilities. At more than US$2.2 trillion and €750bn respectively, these ventures could lead to substantial 'Made in the West' effects, as well as the transfer of Chinese-based Western value chains to less strategically sensitive countries. Economic decoupling and strategic bipolarisation are thus mutually reinforcing forces.

Rule-breakers versus rule-makers

The Westphalian conception of state sovereignty and the temptation to use power independently of legal strictures confines the reach of international law to limited areas and specific circumstances. The novelty of the current era is that states do not simply ignore international law when convenient, as the US did when it invaded Iraq; as Beijing does when it ignores the UN Convention on the Law of the Sea in the South China Sea; and as Russia does in carrying out assassinations and sabotage abroad – sometimes abusing diplomatic privilege to do so. Rather, there is a concerted movement, exacerbated by the pandemic, to reject the very idea of universal values and thus the desirability of a rules-based order.

Indeed, the readiness to use force outside the framework of international law has drawn together powers that are otherwise divided by deep differences of national interest. This, along with the shared aim of removing Western players from contention, helps explain the permutations of the conflictual partnership between Putin's Russia and Recep Tayyip Erdogan's Turkey. Moscow and Ankara support opposing factions in Libya, Syria and the Black Sea, yet they belong together by virtue of their shared modes of operation.

The extraterritorial extension of national law, notably in the monetary and financial arenas, is a major feature of US international practice, whether in the form of primary or secondary sanctions. It reached a high point during the Trump administration with twice as many yearly additions to the Department of the Treasury's Office of Foreign Assets Control (OFAC) sanctions list as during the presidencies of Obama and George W. Bush. This approach is now being adopted by China and Russia, and its grasp is broadening. Over time, the United States' abuse of its financial and monetary preponderance may speed up the demise of the very system that it has shaped and dominated since the Second World War. Rapidly developing Chinese fintech and blockchain technology or the ongoing dedollarisation of Russia's international economic relations are portents for a future that will be not only multipolar but bereft of common legal and regulatory norms.

If the world is being divided between those states that assert their support for an international rules-based order and those that aim to subvert it, it is less certain that this division based on differing principles will translate into a directly political 'democracies versus autocracies' bipolarity. China, for which democracy is the handmaiden of decline, and the US, with its vision of a global grouping of democracies, may both be comfortable with such a bipolar political narrative. In practice, however, the historical record suggests that keeping the democracies safe in the face of totalitarian powers may entail bringing 'on side' countries that are not democracies by any stretch of the imagination. During the Cold War, the Portugal of Antonio de Oliveira Salazar and coup-ridden Turkey were members of NATO, and South America's military dictatorships were part of the 'Free World'. The defeat of Nazi Germany during the Second World War was brought about by an extraordinary alliance between the democracies and the Soviet Union. A narrative pitting an alliance of the democracies against a Sino-Russian partnership of the autocracies may run into similar limits.

Among the rule-makers, the Europeans have been particularly prominent, both in the legal arena and in terms of technical norm-setting: the latter field is unspectacular and hence does not capture much public attention, but it enables the smooth functioning of globalisation, not least in its digital incarnation. One of the more visible instances of norm-setting has been the EU's General Data Protection Regulation (GDPR), rolled out in 2018, which online operators with global ambitions cannot afford to ignore. The collective ability of the EU to play this role of a global 'normative empire' is threatened in the longer term by the relative weakening of the EU's single market as its share of the global economy shrinks: US and Chinese reactions to ongoing EU attempts to regulate artificial intelligence will be a test of that proposition. The alternative to the 'Brussels effect' will presumably be neither US nor Chinese preponderance or cooperation, but the setting up of competing spheres of geo-economic, and by extension geostrategic, influence.

The return of the state

Before COVID-19 struck, the rise of non-state actors – non-governmental organisations (NGOs) without borders, consumer-driven multinationals, online behemoths and terror franchises – had begun, with border-bound nation-states hard-pressed to catch up. This trend has been reversed. The state has led the response to the public-health and economic challenges of COVID-19. There would have been no timely roll-out of vaccines in Trump's US without the 1950 Defense Production Act and *Operation Warp Speed*, and no UK vaccines without successful British industrial strategy in support of Oxford University.

The Biden administration's plan for the renewal of US infrastructure and research and the 'Next Generation EU' plan are hardly libertarian in their approach. Chinese online giants and unicorns (privately held start-up companies valued at more than US$1bn) may have hoped for a time when the CCP would let them operate with minimal interference. When Alibaba's CEO Jack Ma 'disappeared' for two months during the pandemic, any residual illusions were dissipated. The general trend is towards the reassertion of state power, including in democracies: digital taxation; the stifling of offshore tax optimisation; tougher controls on the funding and activities of NGOs; and maybe even trust-busting à la Theodore Roosevelt are the prospective new normal.

For better or for worse, the state is back, whether democratic or autocratic, ideocratic or kleptocratic, competent or dysfunctional.

The unglobal commons

One of the pillars of a rules-based international order has been the understanding that only global responses, and thus common rules, could possibly deal with global challenges.

This did not happen during the pandemic. Although scientific co-operation remained relatively unfettered (minus much of the crucial data relating to the origins of COVID-19 in Wuhan), in every other dimension, nationalism was the default option. This was not an encouraging portent of the world's ability to handle the immense challenge of climate change, despite the United States' return to the Paris Agreement on climate change under the Biden administration. China became the world's largest emitter of greenhouse gases in 2006. From 1990 to the eve of the pandemic, its emissions increased by 370%, while EU emissions decreased by 24%. The Chinese government has indicated that it will continue to increase its emissions until 2030, while giving itself until 2060 to achieve carbon-neutrality. At the global level, such policies are incompatible with meeting even the most permissive interpretation of the Paris Agreement. In the meantime, the EU has pledged a 55% reduction from 1990 emissions by 2030, and the US has set a goal of a 52% reduction on 2005 levels by 2035. Tensions between China and the main Western countries will heighten as the consequences of climate change worsen and as the economic costs of measures to fight them increase.

The largely 'orderless order' that is emerging from the pandemic's shadows is not the best backdrop for dealing with the existential challenge posed by climate change. Nor does it provide a robust framework for the peaceful resolution of the strategic competition between the world's two biggest powers.

Vaccine Diplomacy
How is global politics shaping the fight against COVID-19?

In 2020, COVID-19, the greatest public-health crisis in a century, shook the world's economic, social and political foundations. The crisis came at a moment when global politics were becoming increasingly contentious. US–China relations had lost the trust that had underpinned cooperation after the global financial crisis in 2008. China's lack of transparency and communication in the early phase of the crisis, and its failure to allow a full international investigation of the origins of the novel coronavirus (SARS-CoV-2) that caused the COVID-19 disease, further damaged this relationship. From the very beginning, the pandemic had a major geopolitical dimension.

While a substantial part of the world moves into a more optimistic phase of the pandemic in 2021, it remains highly geopolitical. If the great negative shock of 2020 was the speed and scale of COVID-19's spread around the globe, the positive shock of 2021 was the speed at which successful vaccine development took place. This in turn has given rise to 'vaccine diplomacy', as China, Russia, the United States, India and the European Union compete for credit – and thus influence – in providing vaccines to other countries that lack the capacity to develop and produce them. But, at least in the first half of 2021, the impetus of vaccine diplomacy came into conflict with leaders' imperatives to administer vaccines to their own citizens. For the developed democratic countries, vaccine nationalism prevailed over vaccine diplomacy. The result was that the wealthy and powerful secured early access to vaccines while less wealthy and powerful countries were generally forced to wait. It also meant that Russia and China were able to dominate the early phase of vaccine diplomacy.

Vaccine diplomacy dates back to the Cold War era and does not inherently have a competitive connotation. In the 1950s, US and Soviet scientists collaborated in the successful quest to contain polio. A decade later it was a Soviet innovation that enabled the freeze-drying of the smallpox vaccine, allowing the World Health Organization (WHO) to deliver

Countries of the world by vaccines used, July 2021

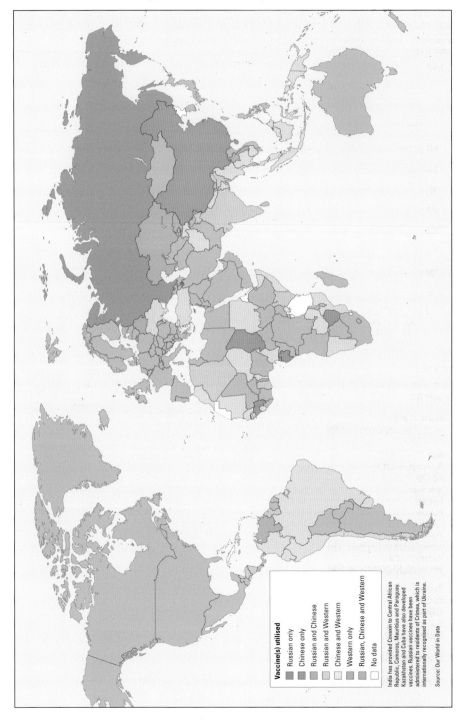

Vaccine(s) utilised

- Russian only
- Chinese only
- Russian and Chinese
- Russian and Western
- Chinese and Western
- Western only
- Russian, Chinese and Western
- No data

India has provided Covaxin to Central African Republic, Comoros, Mauritius and Paraguay. Kazakhstan and Cuba have also developed vaccines. Russian vaccines have been administered to residents of Crimea, which is internationally recognised as part of Ukraine.

Source: Our World in Data

Vaccination rates for selected countries

Total vaccinations administered in selected major countries

For vaccines that require multiple doses, each individual dose is counted. As the same person may receive more than one dose, the number of doses can be higher than the number of people in the population.

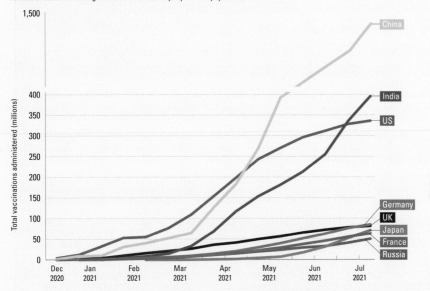

Selected low vaccination-rate countries

Share of people fully vaccinated against COVID-19 (31 July 2021)

World: 11.60%

Asia
Afghanistan: 0.60%

Indonesia: 7.40%

Pakistan: 2.30%

Thailand: 5.60%

Vietnam: 0.60%

Russia and Eurasia
Kyrgyzstan: 1.80%

Tajikistan: 0.60%

Ukraine: 4.70%

Uzbekistan: 3.6%

Middle East and North Africa
Egypt: 1.70%

Iraq: 1.20%

Syria: 0.05%

Yemen: 0.04%

Sub-Saharan Africa
Chad: 0.04%

Democratic Republic of the Congo: 0%

Mali: 0.30%

Nigeria: 0.70%

Latin America and the Caribbean
Guatemala: 1.80%

Haiti: 0%

Nicaragua: 2.40%

Venezuela: 3.80%

Source: Our World in Data

it to tropical areas and eradicate the disease. But, even then, there was awareness that manufacturing and distributing live-saving medicines could enhance the prestige and influence (and commercial advantages) of states. This notion has been prevalent in discussions of 'soft power' since Harvard University's Joseph Nye coined the concept in the late 1980s. Generally, the world's major vaccine producers – China, the EU, India, Russia and the US – reject the charge that they engage in competitive vaccine diplomacy. For China, this is part of a larger insistence that their external policies are not motivated by any geopolitical aims. But for all involved, the starting point of vaccine diplomacy is claiming to be acting as a responsible major power.

In the case of COVID-19 vaccines, in 2020 both Russia and China ignited concern when they developed their vaccines with limited co-operation with WHO guidelines. This concern was reinforced when Russia launched a disinformation campaign in Africa and the Middle East to disparage vaccines made in the US and Europe. This campaign had shades of the last big Soviet disinformation campaign in Africa, which promoted the myth that the US introduced the HIV virus to Africa in order to prevent the continent from developing. The aggressive nature of Russia's vaccine programme in Africa alarmed Western governments, with French President Emmanuel Macron warning in February 2021 of a 'war of influence over vaccines' and urging Europe to supply COVID-19 doses to Africa in order to counter Russian and Chinese vaccine diplomacy.

The race to develop vaccines

In the early months of COVID-19, there was pessimism in the scientific community about the prospects for developing a vaccine fast enough to stem the pandemic. Even in the best-case scenarios, vaccines typically take years to develop and test. In June 2020, Dr Anthony Fauci, director of the US National Institute of Allergy and Infectious Diseases, sought to dampen expectations about the effectiveness of a vaccine, stating that he would view anything above a 50% effectiveness rate as a 'success'. But president Donald Trump, anticipating a challenging re-election campaign and aware of public disapproval of his handling of the pandemic, threw the White House's weight behind vaccine-development efforts as a central element of his re-election bid. In May 2020, he initiated *Operation Warp Speed*, a public–private partnership propelled by a US$14 billion investment from the federal government to hasten development of vaccines, in part by covering the cost of manufacturing millions of doses before they were known to be effective. Even so, few expected rapid or decisive results.

The US government, and American and other Western companies, were not the only actors in the race to develop, manufacture, test and distribute COVID-19 vaccines. By late summer 2020, nearly 200 vaccine-development efforts were under way around the world. In the West, the effort to develop and distribute effective vaccines was led by private pharmaceutical companies with support from governments, philanthropic foundations and international organisations. Four Western vaccines dominated this element of the market until the first half of 2021: Moderna, Oxford-AstraZeneca, Pfizer-BioNTech, and Johnson and Johnson. There will almost certainly be further entrants into this group.

In China, the government both promoted and oversaw efforts, with state-owned firm Sinopharm being the national champion along with private company Sinovac. In August 2020, Russian President Vladimir Putin surprised the world by approving the country's first domestically developed COVID-19 vaccine, before phase III clinical trials had even begun. The Sputnik V vaccine was developed and produced entirely domestically, and its name invoked Soviet success in the space race of the 1950s. Even before the WHO had declared COVID-19 a pandemic in early March 2020, the Gamaleya National Center of Epidemiology and Microbiology in Moscow was working on a vaccine prototype, funded by the country's sovereign wealth fund.

Another, more multilateral, initiative was launched by the Coalition for Epidemic Preparedness Innovations (CEPI), a global alliance founded in 2017 by Norway, India, the Bill & Melinda Gates Foundation, the UK-based Wellcome Trust and the World Economic Forum. In June 2020, CEPI, the WHO and others launched COVAX, a global initiative aiming to distribute 2bn vaccine doses by the end of 2021. While the COVAX platform aspired to become the clearing house for global vaccine development and distribution – some 75 countries signed onto it by summer 2020 – it has largely fallen victim to vaccine nationalism and unilateralism in vaccine diplomacy.

Early vaccine diplomacy: Russia and China

By late 2020, it was clear that both the US and the most developed European countries were going to prioritise vaccinating their own citizenry, creating an opportunity for China and Russia to dominate the export arena, especially in poorer countries. But while most of the vaccines that were advancing most rapidly in the West drew on an entirely new technology that utilised nucleic acids containing genetic material that triggered an attack on the virus itself, the Chinese vaccines were of the more traditional type, based on inactivated viruses. The Russian Sputnik V was of a third variety, utilising the recombinant-viruses technique that also underlies the now widely used Oxford-AstraZeneca vaccine.

But the real concern was the lack of transparency around both information about and testing results of the Russian and Chinese vaccines. Russia had compounded this challenge by approving vaccines for 'emergency' use before phase III trials – by far the most important – had begun. For China, transparency concerns were multiplied by the growing frustration over its lack of cooperation in investigating the origins of COVID-19. While China allowed a WHO investigation team to travel to Wuhan in January 2021, it sharply restricted access to sources and sites the team was allowed to examine. This trip, which coincided with the inauguration of President Joe Biden in the US, marked a tipping point after which many more scientists were willing to take a second look at the possibility that the original outbreak was linked to research at the Wuhan Institute of Virology, rather than being the outcome of zoonotic transmission.

Meanwhile, both Russia and China were enjoying only partial success in their vaccine-export programmes. On 9 December 2020, the United Arab Emirates (UAE) became the first country to approve the

Sinopharm vaccine. Bahrain followed shortly thereafter. Both countries had participated in the clinical trials for the vaccine and made rapid progress in vaccinating the majority of their populations. But while the UAE and Bahrain were successful in securing and administering vaccines, the number of new COVID-19 cases in both countries increased dramatically during and immediately following the vaccination period. While cases began to abate in June 2021, at mid-2021 both countries continued to suffer among the highest per capita rates of infections in the world. No doubt this was partly due to much wider testing that is capturing a larger volume of cases than in most countries and partly due to the time lag involved in vaccine effectiveness. But the limited efficacy of the Sinopharm vaccine was almost certainly part of the problem. Both governments have begun to provide booster shots of non-Chinese vaccines to their populations, an implicit admission of scepticism about the effectiveness of the Sinopharm vaccine.

Serbia had a much better experience with non-Western vaccines. President Aleksandar Vučić has been a vocal critic of the EU response to the pandemic, and has sought support from both Russia and China, both of which responded eagerly. As a result, Serbia has rolled out vaccines more rapidly than almost all the EU member states. Vučić even delivered thousands of vaccines to North Macedonia and to Bosnia-Herzegovina. In March 2021, he reached an agreement with China and the UAE for the construction of a Sinopharm factory in Serbia, and in June, Belgrade's Torlak Institute for Virology, Vaccines and Serums officially launched the production of Sputnik V, making Serbia the first European state to produce the Russian vaccine. Serbia also procured both Pfizer and Oxford-AstraZeneca doses, enabling Vučić to proclaim an 'all-of-the-above' approach to vaccine acquisition. Unlike the UAE and Bahrain, Serbia has not faced a COVID-19 spike in the aftermath of its vaccine efforts. Indeed, its successful balancing act has made the country the envy of its neighbours frustrated with the slow roll-out of Western vaccines. Hungary became the first EU country to administer both Sputnik and Sinopharm after Prime Minister Viktor Orbán said that he had studied Serbia's approach.

Western responses

These early successes by China and Russia evoked consternation in the West. Macron, speaking at a US Atlantic Council event in February 2021, called Chinese and Russian efforts a 'clear diplomatic success' and admitted that Europe found this to be 'a little bit humiliating'. Both he and German Chancellor Angela Merkel declared their readiness to consider purchasing Russian vaccines, but by the end of June 2021, the European Medicines Agency indicated that it had not yet received sufficient testing data for Sputnik V to make a decision on authorisation.

The first moves by the West to counter China's and Russia's vaccine efforts took place at the virtual summit of the Quad group (comprising Australia, India, Japan and the US), hosted by Biden in March 2021. The centrepiece of the summit was the announcement of a plan to provide 1bn doses of Johnson and Johnson's COVID-19 vaccine to Southeast Asian countries by the end of 2022 – implicitly an effort to counter the influence of Chinese vaccine diplomacy. The Quad plan envisaged the two richest partner countries, the US and Japan, financing production at the Serum Institute of India (SII) – the world's largest manufacturer of vaccines – while Australia would play the leading role in distributing them across Southeast Asia.

The plan would enable the US to the enter the vaccine-diplomacy arena while avoiding any trade-off with its domestic vaccination programme – Biden's most important commitment upon entering office. When the plan was announced, the COVID-19 new-case count in India was less than 20,000 per day, and Prime Minister Narendra Modi was balancing a modest pace of domestic vaccination with substantial exports. But almost immediately after the Quad summit, India's second COVID-19 wave hit, and case numbers skyrocketed. By early May, India was recording nearly 400,000 new cases per day.

In this context, Modi's strategy of combining domestic vaccination with exporting substantial quantities of vaccines was no longer viable. This was exacerbated by the inability of the SII to expand its vaccine-production capacity to 100m doses per month as had been planned, following a major fire at its facility in Maharashtra in January 2021. As a result, the timing of the Quad vaccine campaign, which envisaged front-loading the bulk of its exports during 2021, had to be shifted to later in 2021 and throughout 2022. Given the US commitment to focus on domestic vaccinations and Japan's need to ramp up vaccine administration in order to prepare for the holding of the postponed 2020 Olympics in July 2021, there was no plan B for the Quad to fall back on when Indian-produced vaccines failed to become available.

The first round of COVID-19 vaccine diplomacy ended in May 2021 with no clear winner, but an edge to China. But Beijing was stung by the strong resurgence of COVID-19 in the UAE and Bahrain despite their comprehensive Sinopharm vaccination programmes and faced broader diplomatic and public scepticism over the origins of COVID-19 and resentment at aggressive 'wolf-warrior' diplomacy. Russia had some success with Sputnik V outside its borders but suffered from 'guilt by association' with Chinese vaccines because they had all been developed without a transparent testing process. The other main producers – India, the US and European states – remained focused on domestic vaccination programmes.

A turning point?

At this point, international organisations like the United Nations and CEPI, along with non-governmental organisations and foundations, began an effort to focus attention on the limited access of poorer countries to vaccines. The focal point of these pressures was the G7 summit hosted by UK Prime Minister Boris Johnson in Cornwall on 11–13 June 2021. In the run-up to the summit there were numerous calls, perhaps made most cogently by former UK prime minister Gordon Brown, for the G7 to massively expand its efforts to provide vaccines for developing countries, and to take on responsibility for organising and managing efforts that would involve increased manufacturing capacity, pooled purchasing efforts and supply-chain expansion. In the US, there were calls for the Biden administration to follow the example of president George W. Bush, who in 2003 dramatically expanded US efforts to combat the scourge of AIDS across the globe by creating the President's

Emergency Plan for AIDS Relief (PEPFAR). This led to enormous gains in the fight against HIV/AIDS, especially in sub-Saharan Africa, which faced a health disaster at the time. PEPFAR is estimated to have saved 15–20m lives in Africa.

The timing of the 2021 G7 meeting had parallels to that of the launch of PEPFAR in the US. In both cases, the domestic threat from a deadly disease had dramatically lessened in rich countries, but much less so across the developing world. While the US was substantially ahead of most European states in terms of vaccinations in the early months of 2021, by the end of June, this gap had narrowed considerably. By contrast, in sub-Saharan Africa, for example, at mid-2021, only about 1% of the population was fully vaccinated. In both situations, rich-country governments had begun to broaden their scope of action to focus more on the international side. In late 2000, the UN Security Council had declared HIV/AIDS to be a threat to international peace and security. Around the G7 summit, UN Secretary-General António Guterres took an active role in pushing for stronger action, arguing that:

> … vaccines are our only way out of this crisis. They must be considered as a global public good, available and affordable to all. Vaccine equity is not only the greatest moral test of our times. It is also a matter of effectiveness.

Before the G7 meeting, Biden responded to the pressure for stronger action by waiving the patent protection that pharmaceutical companies have for COVID-19 vaccines in May. He stated that 'we know America will never be fully safe until the pandemic that is raging globally is under control'. European governments refused to go along with the US decision, but most public-health experts believe that the US move did little to address the underlying financial challenges involved in providing vaccines to the developing world.

The G7 meeting did not achieve the breakthrough on vaccines that Brown and Guterres had sought, though progress was made. In their communiqué following the summit, G7 leaders committed to strengthening global action against COVID-19 and prioritised the need for an acceleration of the vaccine roll-out, stating: 'We are committed to share at least 870 million doses directly over the next year and ... aim to deliver at least half by the end of 2021.' The communiqué further stated that the G7 'will support manufacturing in low income countries ... and continue to work with partners, regional organizations and recipient countries, including through COVAX'. According to a White House statement, the G7 announcement meant that since 2020, the G7 has committed to financing and providing approximately 2.3bn vaccines for the world, including support for expanding local production capacity to add more than 1bn doses to the global vaccine supply by the end of 2022.

In terms of vaccine burden-sharing, about half of the G7 commitments were to be undertaken by the US, with the other G7 countries together covering the other half. The size of the US contribution, and America's unique convening and coordinating power, means that its policy thinking is exceptionally important. While the G7 commitment was a belated start, a more dramatic approach will be needed if Biden's aspiration to get COVID-19 under control globally is to be realised. The United States' capacity to export vaccines is increasing due both to declining domestic demand as its own vaccination rates rise, and to the growing production capacity of major US companies (for instance, Moderna is increasing its supply capacities by 50% over the final months of 2021 and early 2022). Biden appointed his top administrative talent, Jeffrey Zients, to coordinate his administration's COVID-19 vaccine efforts. The US is shifting its focus from vaccine nationalism to vaccine diplomacy. But the aspiration has not yet been matched by the commitment to act, and so remains less ambitious than the Bush administration's efforts against global AIDS.

What might change this? The US is unlikely to face increased vaccine competition from China, whose initial aspirations focused on providing a vaccine that would be safe and effective at preventing severe cases of COVID-19. Less certain was how successful Chinese vaccines would be at curbing transmission. Evidence so far suggests they are not very effective at preventing the spread of the virus, particularly of the new variants. As a result, the politics of accepting Chinese vaccines is becoming complicated for recipient governments, and the pressure to expand the availability of Western vaccines is growing. The damage to the credibility of Chinese vaccines has in turn undermined China's vaccine diplomacy. A more compelling driver of US and Western efforts to provide vaccines globally is the challenge posed by new and more contagious COVID-19 strains. The spread of the Delta variant to the world's poorest countries not only creates a humanitarian catastrophe but poses a direct risk to the success of vaccination efforts in the US and other wealthy countries.

Mid-2021 appears to be a turning point in COVID-19 vaccine diplomacy, with Western vaccines replacing the Chinese and Russian versions as the focal point of global efforts. Several factors are driving this: declining demand for vaccines in rich countries as those states reach their vaccination goals; growing scepticism about Chinese vaccines (which appears to have bled over to the Russian Sputnik V vaccine despite its much better track record); a sharp downturn in new cases in India, which should allow production and export under the March 2021 Quad agreement; and the increasing pressure on Western governments to take decisive action on the vaccine-production and export front to ensure domestic protection against future waves of infection.

This new phase will not necessarily be the final one for vaccine diplomacy. It will take around 11bn doses to vaccinate 70% of the world's population to achieve herd immunity. But this estimate assumes that no additional boosters will be needed for those already vaccinated, which most scientists believe will be necessary. As of mid-2021, about 4–5bn vaccine doses have been produced. Existing large producers are expanding their production capacities, and potential new producers are planning large production runs. China's first domestically developed vaccine using the same advanced techniques as those developed by Pfizer-BioNTech and Moderna has recently started large-scale phase III trials and could be in production in late 2021. UNICEF estimates that global production capacity could rise to well over 10bn doses per year in 2022.

These numbers suggest that vaccine supply per se is likely to be a diminishing constraint on vaccination levels. But financing, distribution capacity and implementation of jabs will remain significant challenges.

This implies that a combination of competitive and cooperative vaccine diplomacy will remain into late 2021 and 2022. The main players – China, Europe, Russia and the US – will be joined by India. The US and Europe will face growing pressure to expand the G7 commitments made in Cornwall. The low uptake of vaccinations in Russia means that Moscow will likely focus greater attention on the domestic market. China will face the challenge of restoring the credibility of its vaccine diplomacy, especially given growing global scepticism about its broader behaviour. Beijing is also likely to face a new vaccine competitor in India, which sees its vaccine-diplomacy collaboration with Australia, Japan and the US as giving it an opening to increase its influence, especially in Southeast Asia.

Digital Conflicts
Higher intensity, inadequate responses?

A spate of high-profile incidents in 2020–21 escalated concerns about the intensity of cyber competition among major powers, but their governments seemed unable to match their responses to the growing threats.

In December 2020, the United States announced that a Russian state actor had carried out the hack of US IT company SolarWinds – a major cyber-espionage campaign conducted over several months against government and other institutions. In March 2021, at the first high-level Sino-US meeting under the Biden administration in Anchorage, Alaska, China publicly called the US the 'champion' of cyber attacks. In May 2021, US President Joe Biden issued an Executive Order on Improving the Nation's Cyber Security, one week after a ransomware attack caused serious disruption to the Colonial Pipeline on the East Coast. The following month, at the US–Russia summit in Geneva, Biden pushed Russian President Vladimir Putin to rein in the cyber attacks originating from Russia. The US explicitly mentioned attacks on US elections and government, and on private business, including operators of critical infrastructure. Biden threatened further retaliation if the cyber attacks on US sovereignty did not stop.

Restraint and strategic stability in cyberspace are not currently central organising concepts for the great powers, even though most states less capable in cyber power clamour for them. Many governments also worry about the underlying shifts in strategic power that might be occurring as digital competition expands its reach into almost every sector of economic and social life and almost all aspects of military affairs. Combating influence-seeking and interference in national elections though cyber operations has become an urgent new priority alongside more familiar technically oriented security concerns.

Digital power potential
Cyber power is based on the willingness and capability of states to conduct both offensive and defensive cyber operations. It depends on

three factors: how well organised a country is (strategy and doctrine, command and control); how well it can defend itself (through its own cyber security and resilience or through international partnerships); and how effectively its digital economy can support its cyber needs and ambitions. As a result of the intensifying conflict in cyberspace, many states are trying to ramp up their cyber capabilities in both the military and civil sectors. Three trends have emerged over the past year that suggest responses to the growing intensity of cyber competition have so far been incomplete or inadequate: the slow pace of transition to cyber-enabled military capability; increasing realisation of the centrality of formal cyber-education systems; and the deepening cross-border entanglement of the underlying technologies.

Transition to cyber-enabled military capability

By 1998, states had begun to discuss at the United Nations the ways that cyber capabilities would shape international security. At the time, a few countries recognised that they would need to reform and reshape their military strategies and armed forces in order to exploit new opportunities and respond to new threats in cyberspace. While scores of countries are now moving in that direction, none of them – except perhaps the US – has succeeded in aligning national-security strategies and ambitions for digital power with appropriately reformed and restructured military forces.

While some countries, especially the US, can point to significant cyber-related reforms in their armed forces, these remain largely organisational in others, including in China. Where there has been capability building, this has been concentrated in specialist units that are very small compared with the scale and scope of military cyberspace. In terms of operational potential, reforms in other countries do not match either the US ambition declared in 2015 for cyber options in all phases of operations or China's declaration the same year that 'outer space and cyberspace have become new commanding heights in strategic competition among all parties'.

The main universal reason for the lack of progress is that force-structure reform to accommodate new capabilities is an inherently slow and complex process in any country's armed forces. For example, in 2006, the US Air Force announced its intention to set up a Cyber Command and changed its declared mission accordingly to one of fighting in the air, space and cyberspace. The Air Force Cyber Command was set up in 2008, but implementation was suspended to allow the Pentagon to begin setting up the new joint-service Cyber Command (USCYBERCOM) in 2009. It took until 2018 for all the cyber-mission forces in Cyber Command to reach full operational readiness. This did not prevent the Command's engagement in offensive cyber operations against the Islamic State, also known as ISIS or ISIL, in 2016 and other adversaries during those ten years. It is understood that in 2021, Cyber Command retaliated against criminal gangs in Russia responsible for some of the ransomware attacks, including the attack on the Colonial Pipeline, but critics still found fault with the United States' organisational arrangements, including Cyber Command, for not being able to prevent the attacks in the first place.

Progress in military cyber transformation has also been slow for organisational reasons. The US and United Kingdom have concluded that 'military' cyber capabilities are best organised jointly between the military and intelligence agencies. But it has taken some time to develop structures that manage the complexity of the civil–military relationship in this domain. The UK solution culminated in the new National Cyber Force announced in 2021, which built on close collaboration between the Ministry of Defence and GCHQ, the UK's lead cyber-intelligence agency, while in the US a similarly close organisational relationship has existed between Cyber Command and the National Security Agency, which are both commanded by the same individual. It remains to be seen whether these arrangements prove optimal or are subject to further organisational innovation as they are tested by practice.

The time frame by which governments can expect to achieve substantial and widely distributed military cyber reform is shaped in large part by the diversity and uniqueness of the technical skills required – most of which have to be learned or taught on the job – and by the relatively small numbers of adequately trained personnel at the start of the reform process. This development pathway of cyber military skills at very high technical standards explains the long delay that USCYBERCOM faced in reaching full operational readiness in 2018. Not all governments would be as demanding as the US has been in this regard, so time frames could potentially be shortened.

The retarding effect of the pipeline of qualified personnel applies not only to front-line military operators but also to the leadership levels of the armed forces and supporting civilian agencies, as well as the administrators and planners in between. Apart from learning about the technical aspects of complex cyber military operations, the leaders need to develop confidence in the reliability of both offensive and defensive operations and their political utility in armed conflict. This can only be done through a relatively long period of experimentation and experience.

Centrality of national cyber-education systems

The second key trend that emerged with more force in the past year is the realisation of the centrality of formal national cyber-education systems, both for research and as a source of operational personnel. This will determine the extent of a country's indigenous research and development (R&D) potential in relevant disciplines (including cyber security, wireless computer communications, artificial intelligence (AI), super-computing and quantum information sciences). Like military reform, education reform is a complex and protracted process, unique to each country's education system. Education reform is also shaped in large part by a country's private-sector demand in industries associated with information and communications technologies.

This topic was one of the more strident elements in a speech given in private by Chinese President Xi Jinping in 2018 but released in 2021, in which he said: 'Hard power or soft power, when it comes down to it, it all depends on the power of talent.' The release of the speech corroborated other evidence of Chinese leadership concerns about the slow pace of development of China's information and communications technology (ICT) education systems. China's highly centralised system should lend itself to direction from the top leadership to expand its output of graduates in cyber-related fields, both in civilian universities and in military education facilities. Expansion of R&D capabilities depends in particular on growth in the number and quality of PhD graduates, and increased funding to their university departments for additional staff (PhD supervisors). Yet China's education reforms in cyber-related fields and civilian and military universities have made only gradual progress. In 2020, Chinese researchers concluded that 9% of the senior research personnel working globally on AI were based in China, compared with 46% in the US. They also concluded that China was not among the top-three most-attractive destinations for AI researchers thinking about moving to another country for work. While this result came only three years after the Chinese government's launch of an ambitious AI development strategy, it came a decade after the Chinese Academy of Sciences issued a national road map for information technology, of which AI was to be a key component. Chinese universities have found it difficult to adjust to the demands for radical increases in AI researchers who want to work in China on completion of their research. Baidu, the leading Chinese search-engine company, is stepping up its programmes with leading Chinese universities to recruit and train more AI teachers.

The military education system in China can move a little more quickly than its civilian counterpart, though the two are not completely independent of each other. In 2019, the People's Liberation Army (PLA) Information Engineering University introduced a new undergraduate major in AI and planned to enrol 30 students.

A country's national cyber-education system is part of its larger national cyber ecosystem, especially private-sector businesses. In the most cyber-capable countries, there is also a third leg to this partnership: the role of government and military-related agencies in funding R&D. This three-way relationship has been referred to as the 'triple helix' (by analogy to DNA) of national innovation. If China's goal is to match the levels of cyber power of the US, where there is a well-functioning and long-entrenched cyber–industrial complex organised on this triple-helix principle, then it will probably also need to match that system as well as the decades of experience that it takes to maximise its effective functioning.

Migration practices for education abroad also play a fundamental part in the national accumulation of cyber power, especially to redress gaps in capability that cannot be met by the national education system or the wider innovation system. Some countries have increasingly acknowledged this in their national cyber strategies, with an expansion of highly skilled visa arrangements directly targeting cyber skills (as in Australia), but other countries with less open approaches to inward migration – such as China, Iran or Russia – seem more reluctant to exploit this avenue to compensate for weaknesses in national education systems. China continues its long-standing policy of temporary outward migration for its citizens to acquire advanced technology skills and has introduced incentive schemes to attract its scientists working abroad to return home. But the rate of return of researchers in key fields does not, and could not, fill the very large gaps that will need to be filled if China is to meet its ambitions.

Technology entanglement

The third trend of note is the intensification of 'digital entanglement'. This comprises two elements: the physical infrastructure through which data is moved, stored and processed; and the data flows themselves that pass over digital networks.

As national-security concerns around cyberspace have increased, countries have become more interested in exercising sovereign control over it. But there are major challenges to doing so. On the infrastructure side, complex global supply chains source ICT products and services from around the world. Many less-capable countries rely on cyber-security services delivered remotely from foreign countries. Governments now seek to regulate their sourcing more tightly – the United States' 'trusted vendor' policy being an example of this. On the data side, the internet is designed to ignore national borders in favour of maximising speed. These global data flows include financial-services transactions worth trillions of dollars every day as well as personal data on hundreds of millions of individuals. Here, too, some governments, notably in the European Union, have sought to tighten regulation, especially through data localisation to prevent the export of data on national firms and citizens held by foreign corporations.

In its final year, the Trump administration stepped up its campaign to reduce the integration of China and its companies in the ICT systems of the US and its allies. This was supported by Australia and Japan, which were opposed to Huawei 5G systems before the American efforts began to gather pace. The US campaign was quite successful, with the UK, other European allies and several countries in Asia eventually agreeing to go along with US demands. As the US administration progressively broadened the exclusion efforts to cover, potentially at least, all ICT goods and services provided by or administratively connected with Chinese entities, private-sector interests that were adversely affected mobilised to dilute the exclusion regimes, largely by seeking exemptions. The Biden administration has decided to extend this pattern of exclusions but is arguably more sensitive to the tension between concerns about the risks to national security from Chinese equipment, its firms and even its personnel on the one hand, and the immutable reality that the ICT sector has long been a multinational phenomenon, with global supply chains and knowledge-production processes in which firms from the US and its close allies are entangled, on the other.

Concerns about security risks from Chinese ICT were amplified by larger ones about China's international behaviour, its domestic repression in Xinjiang and Hong Kong, and its prospects for overtaking the US as leader in the great-power technological competition. The antagonistic view has been fuelled by exaggerated assessments of China's ICT power and by inflated estimates of the economic gains to China from cyber theft of intellectual property (IP). The IISS has assessed that China is not in the same class of cyber power as the US even on a bilateral basis, and that China's relative inferiority is magnified when the cyber power of US allies such as Australia, Canada, France, Israel, Japan and the UK is taken into account. On the question of the contribution of cyber-enabled IP theft to China's civil-sector economic power, the confirmed cases that trace IP theft to competing Chinese products in the marketplace are few, especially in the ICT sector. There have probably been more disputes among Western ICT corporations than between Chinese and Western corporations about IP theft leading to a drop in commercial viability of products. Furthermore, too little attention has been paid to the much larger contribution of lawful technology transfer directly encouraged by foreign governments.

In this increasingly heated environment, techno-nationalist arguments remain dominant: anything that supports gains by the home country in ICT capability is *ipso facto* good, regardless of the cost to international relationships. Revelations that Chinese universities had been sending military personnel to the US and allied countries under false identities to collect information, and that they were also channelling funds to several leading Western scholars through less-than-transparent processes, added fuel to the fire.

In this atmosphere, most nuances about the relationship between national cyber power and open-source scientific research by a global community of scholars have been abandoned. During the Cold War, when the Allies imposed severe restrictions on technology transfer and exchanges with the USSR, there was a sharp distinction between basic science and applied R&D. During the years of detente (1972–79), and again in the Reagan–Gorbachev era (1985–88), the two countries signed agreements for cooperation in basic science, even though the CIA assessed that the Soviets were exploiting these agreements for military and national-security advances. A return by the US under Biden to the risk appetite shown towards the USSR in technology transfer seems unlikely, but America will still have to come to terms with the entanglement of its ICT ecosystems with those of its allies and China. This entanglement has not been studied as closely as it needs to be.

While global supply chains of goods (such as the iPhone and its components) can be documented quite easily, it is difficult to document supply chains of ICT services. Governments have tried to mitigate this through new regulations on data localisation. But documentation for the purposes of regulation of knowledge production – the basic scientific research that underpins a globalised digital economy – is almost impossible. This is one reason why some governments have resorted to the blunt instrument of blocking scientific exchange with citizens of certain countries, most visibly China. However, such globalised knowledge production, represented by, for example, the 700–800 foreign laboratories in China or the tens of thousands of Chinese nationals working abroad in universities and corporations on technical research, cannot be easily restricted without major negative impacts on the economies and freedom of scientific research of the countries seeking to exert such controls.

Implications for the coming year

The digital conflicts of the past year will likely accelerate since they are a manifestation of growing insecurities in all regions of the world and there are few effective mechanisms available for reducing tensions. In several important cases, one or both sides confront a security dilemma because one believes the other is so much stronger in many aspects of conventional or cyber-enabled military power. This exacerbates other tensions arising from political interests, such as conflicting systems of government, human-rights issues, inappropriate use of force or perceived existential threat.

Another reason for the likely aggravation of existing cyberspace tensions is that many countries are intent on maximising their own cyber potential as quickly as they can. They are acutely aware that existing deficits in underlying cyber power cannot be overcome quickly, but will take a decade, if not two, to redress. Most governments, even the most powerful, do not believe they are adequately defended in cyberspace and that it is probably unwise to consider measures of restraint until their cyber defences are in a better state.

European Geo-economic Strategies Towards the Indo-Pacific
Diversifying engagement to enhance resilience?

In 2020, leading Western European economies began to change their geo-economic approaches to the Indo-Pacific region. For the previous half-decade, the promise of access to Chinese markets and opportunities for enhanced trade with China had dominated the European agenda. In 2015, the United Kingdom government's announcement of a 'golden era' in Sino-British trade relations during President Xi Jinping's state visit epitomised wider efforts across Europe to prioritise engagement with China. The pursuit of a profitable relationship with Beijing was prioritised due to the potential of the country's considerable domestic market.

By 2020, the exclusion of Chinese telecommunications companies like Huawei, considered to be 'high-risk vendors', from digital networks in France, the UK and other European countries highlighted the nature of the policy shift that had actually followed. This shift was, in part, the result of suspicions that corporations like Huawei are exposed to the intervention of the Chinese government, which is believed to use providers of hardware to critical national infrastructure to interfere, disrupt or spy on foreign governments and nationals. While some countries, like the UK, regarded these risks as manageable, additional restrictions introduced by the United States in 2020 on the use of computer chips based on US designs in Huawei's equipment forced these assessments to be reviewed. A combination of the Chinese government's potential use of economic matters to influence foreign countries and intensifying Sino-US competition set the tone for policy shifts in Europe.

The potential pitfalls of dependency on China in critical infrastructure like digital communications were exacerbated by problems experienced in critical supply chains during the COVID-19 pandemic. To diversify away from China, Western European strategies towards the Indo-Pacific started to emphasise broader economic engagement with other actors. This was driven by the correlation between supply-chain diversification and national resilience and, more broadly, by the growing challenges that Beijing's authoritarian regime presented to open economies. The changing policies of three major countries – France, Germany and the UK – illustrate this in different ways.

France: the geo-economics of an Indo-Pacific state

The geo-economic considerations underpinning France's strategy in the Indo-Pacific arise from the country's overseas territories in the region and their economic importance. More than 90% of France's exclusive economic zone (EEZ) – the world's largest – is in the Indo-Pacific. The territories of French Polynesia and New Caledonia alone account for 59% of the country's 11.7 sq. km EEZ. This vast Indo-Pacific EEZ contributes to a very significant maritime industry that employs 30% more people than France's car industry and is equal in size to the aviation sector – two primary engines of French industry. In 2018, French maritime-related industrial output – including shipbuilding, energy, transport, tourism, laying sea cables and other maritime services – accounted for some €81 billion. The Indo-Pacific is also home to approximately 1.65 million French citizens, some 150,000 expats and almost 60% of the country's permanent overseas military presence.

This economic significance helps explain French President Emmanuel Macron's approach to Indo-Pacific strategy, which he first articulated in a speech delivered at Australia's Garden Island Naval Precinct in May 2018. He presented France's main objectives as the maintenance of an inclusive and stable regional environment drawing upon respect for the rule of law and rejection of the rise of any hegemonic power. Macron emphasised his interest in aligning more closely with key strategic partners like Australia, India and Japan (which all have their own Indo-Pacific strategies) and multilateral organisations, notably the Association of Southeast Asian Nations (ASEAN). For France, strong bilateral and multilateral ties reinforced the security of its overseas territories and helped tackle global challenges impeding economic prosperity and development. Crucially, France's Indo-Pacific strategy assumed an Indo-Pacific order that rested on continued US leadership.

In a subsequent speech in Réunion in 2019, Macron linked France's Indo-Pacific policy to the integration of overseas territories into the country's regional political and economic fabric. This points to a broader French concern to limit the risk of overseas territories separating themselves from the 'metropole'. French sovereignty is already contested by populations in territories like New Caledonia and, to a lesser extent, French Polynesia. In the Indian Ocean, Comoros has claims to Mayotte, while Mauritius and Madagascar contest French sovereignty over Tromelin Island and the Scattered Islands respectively. The loss of these territories would have inevitable economic and political consequences for France.

In this context, in 2018 and 2020 the French government expanded the mandate of the French Development Agency to widen participation in bilateral and regional initiatives with strategic partners on environmental protection and biodiversity. In March 2021, France became an ASEAN 'development partner' with the aim of building on the recent experience of carrying out some 170 projects within the ASEAN regional space at a total cost of €3.7bn during 2015–20. The main focus of future projects will be energy supplies, healthcare, connectivity, sustainable development of cities and water management – all themes with important implications for environmental management and prosperity.

French perceptions of China also play an important role in its renewed Indo-Pacific engagement in two ways. Firstly, within the region, the French government opposes Beijing's assertiveness in pursuing territorial claims in ways that undermine regional order. In particular, Chinese claims in the South China Sea threaten freedom of navigation, while Chinese application of core principles such as straight baselines around groups of islands, or the right of coastal states regarding innocent passage in EEZs, are inconsistent with the United Nations Convention on the Law of the Sea (UNCLOS). As French Defence Minister Florence Parly noted at the 2019 IISS Shangri-La Dialogue, this is particularly problematic for France and has led to growing concerns over Beijing's coercive behaviour at sea and how this, in turn, undermines stability and order.

Secondly, and no less significant, the COVID-19 pandemic contributed to a dramatic deterioration of French public perceptions of China.

By October 2020, 61.6% of those polled had a negative or very negative view of China, and 52.6% reported that their feeling towards China had worsened. In March 2021, diplomatic ties reached a new low point when the Foreign Ministry summoned the Chinese ambassador to France, Lu Shaye, over repeated insults and threats made against French lawmakers and a researcher on social media, as well as Beijing's sanctioning of a French Member of the European Parliament. Thus, while Macron has consistently sought to avoid an antagonistic relationship with China, the Indo-Pacific strategy adopted on his watch represents, in part, a response to a growing Chinese challenge to French interests and values.

Macron's changing approach to the Indo-Pacific has nonetheless built upon, and in some respects accelerated, a process of widening economic outreach already nurtured under his predecessor François Hollande. In recent years, France's exports to South Asia and Northeast Asia have risen more than those to any other part of the Indo-Pacific. France enjoys a favourable balance of trade with Australia, Hong Kong and Singapore, while it runs a large trade deficit (€30bn in 2017) with China. French businesses with offices and factories in the region have a turnover of €233bn, making France the European country with the largest number of companies with a regional footprint, and the second (behind Germany) in terms of volume of business. Conversely, according to data from 2018, investments in France from the region represent 14% of total investments in France, placing the region in third place in investments in France, following Europe and North America.

Germany: the challenge of a China dependency

In September 2020, Germany became the second European power after France to adopt formal 'policy guidelines' for the Indo-Pacific and in so doing ended the German government's reluctance to adopt the term. In policy terms, this emerging European alignment in vocabulary – with the publication of the guidelines just ahead of Germany assuming the European Union presidency – reflected a more coordinated effort by Paris and Berlin to initiate a process of developing an EU strategy for the region. However, Berlin's policy guidelines for the Indo-Pacific reflect different political considerations and geo-economic priorities to those of France, reflected in the 'EU Strategy for cooperation in the Indo-Pacific' document adopted in April 2021.

Unlike France, Germany's core interests are centred on its existing trade relations with the region, especially China. In 2020, German exports to China reached nearly €100bn, making it Germany's second-largest trade partner after the US. Three other Indo-Pacific countries – Japan, India and the Republic of Korea – also feature in Germany's top 25 export markets. Germany was also the largest EU exporter to ASEAN, accounting for some €22bn-worth of goods. Taken altogether, while Chinese trade ties with Germany stand in a league of their own, the Indo-Pacific as a whole represents a growth area for German trade. Germany's policy guidelines set the tone for greater diversification of ties beyond China.

Germany's Indo-Pacific guidelines place particular emphasis on Southeast Asia. ASEAN is identified as a primary partner for engagement, with the ambition to upgrade Germany's status from development to dialogue partner while seeking observer status at the ASEAN Defence Ministers' Meeting-Plus. India and, within ASEAN, Vietnam are also mentioned as significant potential partners. Some observers considered the lack of reference to other major bilateral partnerships, combined with the clear preference 'to avoid a unipolar or bipolar' regional order, as expressing ambivalence towards the shaping of regional dynamics, if not a clear reluctance to align with the US. Others stressed how this conveyed excessive caution vis-à-vis China's more assertive behaviour in the region.

On the other hand, the guidelines emphasised European, not only German, action, a theme that speaks to the German desire for greater European strategic autonomy, with reference to the EU and, to a lesser extent, NATO, as players in a stable and open Indo-Pacific. In the strategy adopted by the EU in April 2021 a similar tone emphasised cooperation by working with partners – which included ASEAN and other relevant frameworks like the Asia–Europe Meeting process.

The German focus on multilateral ties with ASEAN is in no small measure driven by the ambition to create new opportunities in the fields of connectivity and the digital economy, and by the relevance of these components of the broader field of infrastructural investments to the organisation's members. Germany also seeks to diversify investments in promising markets beyond China. With limits imposed on Chinese telecommunication companies like Huawei, the Indo-Pacific guidelines allow German industry to pursue opportunities with leading Asian equipment providers like Japan's NEC and South Korea's Samsung in 5G-related connectivity. The guidelines also indicate how Germany considers digital goods and services important not only for commercial reasons but as a source of alternatives to Chinese technologies that can ensure the shaping of standards that are likely to underwrite future prosperity across the region.

Germany's quest for greater economic diversification in the Indo-Pacific is driven by its growing concern not only about its excessive dependence on the Chinese market but about China's unfair and restrictive trade and investment practices. In 2019 the Asia division of the Federation of German Industry (BDI) published a report calling for a tougher approach towards China to protect German small and medium-sized enterprises from being overtaken by more competitive Chinese producers. German machinery manufacturers, in particular, face challenges from Chinese companies developing expertise through access to German technology and progressively pushing German competitors out of business. The new Indo-Pacific guidelines may therefore mark the beginning of a slow but steady change in Germany's approach to the region that places greater emphasis on economic opportunities in Southeast Asian markets.

The UK: the post-Brexit Indo-Pacific opportunity

The UK has conducted one of the more striking shifts in geo-economic policy towards the Indo-Pacific. In 2015, prime minister David Cameron led a large trade delegation to key countries in Southeast Asia with the aim of signalling his government's intention to invest in stronger trade ties with the region, especially Indonesia, Malaysia, Singapore and Vietnam. After the Brexit referendum in 2016, the UK deepened its attention towards the region. Until 2020, however, this was pursued under the shadow of UK trade ambitions with China. In summer 2020, this changed due to a growing consensus in London on the need for a reassessment of relations with China.

Scepticism about Beijing's initial management of the COVID-19 pandemic, coupled with China's introduction of a national Hong Kong security law in June 2020 that undermined the spirit of the 1997 Sino-British Joint Declaration, sped up the decline of UK–China relations. In July 2020, the UK eliminated 'high-risk vendors' such as Huawei from its 5G network. The 2021 National Security and Investment Act sought to rebalance the UK's desire to remain a desirable place for foreign investments with the need to protect critical areas of the national economy. It is symptomatic, for example, that the recent attempt by a Chinese-owned company to take over the UK's largest semiconductor company, Newport Wafer Fab, was reviewed by the government only after MPs raised questions about the threat to the country's high-tech future.

While the UK maintained its interest in pursuing a strong trade and investment relationship with China, London continued to harbour concerns about technological standards. British media highlighted Chinese governmental influence through multilateral institutions like the International Telecommunication Union and through the leveraging of 5G connectivity and smart-city projects in developing countries in Southeast Asia and Africa along China's Digital Silk Road. These activities allowed Beijing to promote Chinese technology standards, especially in digital connectivity, telecommunications and artificial intelligence (AI). The long-term risks of bifurcation of the internet between states that subscribe to the Chinese model and all the others would have considerable consequences for countries like the UK, which currently possess an economic edge in the field of services.

The UK's review of its economic engagement with China coincided with renewed interest in trade opportunities with the rest of the Indo-Pacific. This underpinned much of the government's post-Brexit strategy, which aimed at recalibrating trade relations east of Suez and, in so doing, aligned these ambitions with an economic agenda focused on building the economy of the future – based on a greener, more digitally connected understanding of prosperity. The Indo-Pacific region is already reshaping the landscape and composition of the UK's economic outlook. In 2019, seven of the UK's top 25 export markets were in Asia. The top three in Asia – China, Hong Kong and Japan – together accounted for some £60bn of exports in goods and services – more than the UK exported to Germany, its second-largest export market. In 2019, too, foreign secretary Jeremy Hunt reported that the UK was the largest European investor in Southeast Asia, with ASEAN trade standing at nearly US$52.2bn and over 4,000 British companies employing more than 50,000 people in Singapore alone. This data played to the strength of a key post-Brexit objective – before the COVID-19 pandemic raised serious concerns over the immediate future of global trade – one resting on the ambitious aim of concluding agreements covering 80% of British trade by 2023.

In addition to accelerating negotiations for bilateral trade agreements, in February 2021 the UK applied to join the Comprehensive and Progressive Agreement for Trans-Pacific Partnership (CPTPP). CPTPP membership would enable the UK to participate in regional debates over the development of standards and practices on trade and services, a matter of growing concern in light of China's intention to leverage its telecommunications companies to set standards in digital and AI technologies. The CPTPP has a potentially significant role to play in regard to the Regional Comprehensive Economic Partnership (RCEP) signed in November 2020, which will be the world's largest trade bloc once it enters into force. China is a member of RCEP, as are key actors in the CPTPP, notably Japan and Australia. Japan considers the CPTPP an important forum through which to develop informal coalitions to influence trade processes in the RCEP. The CPTPP could be used as a place in which consensus over trade practices and standards among key members could be used to counterbalance China's influence in the RCEP.

In the Indo-Pacific region, prosperity will depend on the expansion of connectivity – especially digital connectivity – and financial services. These are areas of UK focus, given its strengths and its concerns over

Chinese intentions to influence the development of regional standards. The 2021 Integrated Review of UK foreign and security policy placed great emphasis on 'regulatory diplomacy' to 'influence the rules, norms and standards governing technology and the digital economy'. There is great potential to leverage British expertise to develop financial practices and frameworks with key partners in the Indo-Pacific, especially Australia, India, Japan, Singapore and South Korea.

Conclusions: economic diversification as a form of resilience?

The analysis of emerging French, German and British policies towards the Indo-Pacific region offers four conclusions.

Firstly, there is growing anxiety in Europe about Chinese economic influence, but these concerns vary. In countries like the UK, Chinese investments in sectors regarded as critical to national security, especially advanced-technology firms and critical infrastructure, raise security issues. 5G networks and semiconductor firms are a case in point. As for economic cooperation with China, European companies risk providing access to cutting-edge technology to local counterparts that is then used to close the technological gap. Despite differing concerns, national strategies all aim to reduce dependency on Beijing, especially on critical supply chains. This does not mean that European countries aim to decouple economically from China. On the contrary, governments in France, Germany and the UK continue to pursue economic engagement with Beijing, albeit with greater scrutiny in sectors vital to future economic growth and national resilience.

Secondly, France, Germany and the UK regard the Indo-Pacific as a genuine opportunity. They have all adopted the 'Indo-Pacific' as a framework of interaction to engage partners across the region, with physical and digital connectivity as key pillars of prosperity. Indeed, in part to counterbalance Chinese Digital Silk Road initiatives, all the European actors view the Indo-Pacific as a region for which development of resilient digital services is both an opportunity to shape international stability – by promoting standards that do not undermine the openness of societies – and a way to enhance economic ties. The Indo-Pacific also offers opportunities to promote environmentally responsible growth, a topic of great significance in a region directly affected by climate change. Another common feature of the European approach is the increasingly shared willingness to contribute to the security of the Indo-Pacific, especially in the maritime realm, a core pillar of connectivity.

Thirdly, Paris, Berlin and London are pursuing different approaches. As an Indo-Pacific maritime state, France seeks to raise its political and economic profile through multilateral engagement on global challenges that affect the region, especially in maritime affairs. It is also enhancing long-standing bilateral relationships, especially with Australia, India and Japan. The UK is pursuing a mix of bilateral and multilateral efforts, with Australia, Japan and South Korea standing at the forefront of the bilateral dimension, and relations with India gaining increasing momentum. Multilaterally, the UK is focusing on ASEAN, an interest shared by Germany and France. The EU cooperation strategy is equally designed to engage the region through multilateral action, primarily with ASEAN.

Finally, whereas the UK has made the Indo-Pacific 'tilt' a crucial test of its post-Brexit global profile, France and Germany have inscribed their strategies towards the region within a broader European approach, one centred on the EU. Both countries share the view that the bloc has, when acting together, stronger negotiating capacity and influence – especially vis-à-vis China. The European Parliament's recent freezing of ratification of the EU–China Comprehensive Agreement on Investment, in response to Chinese sanctions on European MEPs and entities, certainly suggests this. How China responds to this will indicate how far the EU Indo-Pacific strategy will go in shaping Beijing's behaviour. What seems certain is that, for Europe, the Indo-Pacific is no longer a distant region but rather a geo-economic opportunity waiting to be seized.

The Rise of Carbon Neutrality
Is the new optimism justified?

Chinese President Xi Jinping's announcement in September 2020 that China would aim to become 'carbon neutral' by 2060 topped a year and a half of increasing worldwide climate ambition. In its annual Emissions Gap Report that November, the UN Environment Programme (UNEP) said that 'the most significant and encouraging development in terms of climate policy in 2020 is the growing number of countries that have committed to achieving net-zero emissions goals by around mid-century'. If such commitments could be achieved globally, the UNEP went on, it would be broadly consistent with the Paris Agreement's goal of keeping the global average temperature increase to well below 2°C, and ideally less than 1.5°C over pre-industrial levels.

The Paris Agreement, adopted in 2015, included a call for the world to 'achieve a balance between anthropogenic emissions by sources and removals by sinks of greenhouse gases in the second half of this century'. The resolution that formally adopted the agreement also commissioned a special report covering how to limit warming to an increase of 1.5°C. It was this 2018 report from the Intergovernmental Panel on Climate Change (IPCC), which concluded that to do so would require global CO_2 emissions to reach net zero by 2045–55 (the very beginning of the window envisioned in Paris), that set the trend towards net-zero emissions targets in motion.

By November 2020, 126 countries covering 51% of global greenhouse-gas (GHG) emissions had formally adopted, announced or were considering net-zero goals. As of June 2021, that had increased to 132 countries, most notably including the United States, as well as the European Union, covering around 65% of emissions. This was a dramatic increase in ambition over only a few years: in June 2019 such goals only covered 16% of global GDP. The global community appears to be doing the right thing at last, having exhausted all the other possibilities. But there are questions over what these targets and pledges really mean, whether countries will match these ambitions with actions in the near to medium term and whether net zero can be reached practically in the necessary time frame. Net-zero carbon by 2050 is necessary, but on its own will not be sufficient.

Carbon neutral or net zero?

The term 'carbon neutral' was the *New Oxford American Dictionary*'s Word of the Year as long ago as 2006. It is now often used interchangeably with 'net zero' or 'climate neutral', yet the terms denote different concepts and are not always used consistently in casual discourse, the media and even policy documents. Carbon dioxide is not the only GHG; methane, nitrous oxide fluorocarbons and other gases, for example, can be more potent, longer lasting or more difficult to remove from the atmosphere. Together these gases account for around one-third of the human-caused warming experienced to date, and continued to increase even in 2020, when CO_2 emissions fell due to the COVID-19 pandemic. Thus, achieving carbon neutrality at a global level (that is, ensuring that as much CO_2 is removed from the atmosphere each year as is put in) will, by itself, not halt global warming. The IPCC's various pathways to the 1.5°C goal require net-zero emissions of all GHGs by 2061–84, which will require net-negative CO_2 emissions (removing more than is emitted) to offset the reduced but still-significant other gases. In 'overshoot' scenarios, where there is significantly greater warming before the global temperature drops back down to the target, larger net-negative emissions will be needed to reduce concentrations of CO_2 in the long run.

At national, regional or local levels, carbon neutrality is even more ambiguous, since it can be achieved not just by reducing emissions or taking action to remove carbon from the atmosphere, but also by offsetting emissions against reductions made elsewhere (by buying carbon credits, for example). At the organisational or individual level, a further complication involves whether emissions from direct activities alone are taken into account, or whether the entire supply chain and after-market activities are included. In both cases, there is a risk that offsets could be double-counted, with two jurisdictions balancing the same reductions against their own emissions. The reductions, of course, only count against global warming once. Some industries, sectors and applications, such as agriculture, aviation and cement, are difficult or impossible to make carbon neutral. Others, such as military operations, might not be able to become carbon neutral without compromising effectiveness. Achieving global net-zero CO_2 by 2050 will thus require some form of CO_2 removal.

Below the global level, there is no 'one size fits all' model for time-tables or methods for achieving carbon neutrality or net-zero GHG emissions. But formal objectives must be clear about which emission sources and which gases are covered; the target date for net zero and interim targets for net reductions; whether and by what proportion the goal is to be met by reductions, removals or offsets; and how international sources of emissions such as aviation and shipping, as well as how existing carbon sinks like forests, are accounted for.

Ambitions or actions?

As of mid-2021, six European countries and New Zealand have already set net-zero emissions targets in law. Sweden was the first to do so, in January 2018, formalising a target of carbon neutrality by 2045, although it allows for international offsets to cover 15% of emissions. In June 2019, France and the United Kingdom enshrined target dates of 2050 for net-zero GHG emissions and carbon neutrality respectively. In December 2019, Denmark mandated carbon neutrality by 2050, and in June 2020 Hungary mandated climate neutrality by 2050. In May 2021, Germany adopted a net-zero target date of 2045, and in June the EU approved and adopted its objective of climate neutrality by 2050 into law. In November 2019, New Zealand set a net-zero target for all GHGs by 2050, with the notable exclusion of methane from its large farming sector. Several other countries, including the US, have introduced legislation, while another 19 have set out formal targets in policy documents or submissions to the United Nations. Net-zero targets are under discussion in a further 98 countries. Eight countries, including four EU members (Austria, Finland, Germany and Sweden) have net-zero targets earlier than 2050; two of them (Bhutan and Suriname) are already at net zero. These eight countries, however, only account for around 2% of global emissions.

Notable by their absence from the trend to net zero were G20 members Australia, India, Indonesia, Russia, Saudi Arabia and Turkey, collectively accounting for 18% of global emissions. In March 2021, Indian Energy Minister Raj Kumar Singh called global carbon neutrality by 2050 or 2060 'pie in the sky'. He was, to be sure, correctly arguing that short-term actions were at least as important as long-term goals, but he also said that developing countries wanted to continue to use fossil fuels and that rich countries 'can't stop it'. Similarly, while Australian Prime Minister Scott Morrison paid lip service in February 2021 to net zero by 2050, he declined to commit to the target without a clear path that did not involve a carbon tax: 'When I can tell you how we get there, that's when I'll tell you when we're going to get there.' Russia's draft strategy for long-term development 'with a low level of greenhouse gas emissions by 2050' would in fact entail increased emissions by 2050 and net zero as late as the end of the century. Even Russian President Vladimir Putin's call in his annual state-of-the-nation speech on 21 April for Russian emissions to be lower than the EU's over the next 30 years would only mean a 50% reduction over current annual levels by mid-century.

Part of 'how we get there' will require action on the part of the private sector and regional and local jurisdictions, whether impelled by policy-driven incentives, public opinion or self-interest. As of May 2021, 708 cities, 24 regions, 624 universities and 2,360 businesses had pledged net-zero carbon by 2050 under the aegis of the UN's 'Race to Zero' campaign, which was launched in 2019 with strict best-practice criteria for joining. Collectively, these cover nearly 25% of global emissions and over 50% of global GDP. Some multinational corporations, such as BT, IKEA, Microsoft and Unilever, have committed to net zero across their entire supply chains; Microsoft even intends to do so retroactively, offsetting all its emissions since it was founded in 1975. At the other extreme, ACI Europe – the trade association representing over 500 European airports – has a 2050 net-zero CO_2 target that covers only 2% of the emissions associated with activities that pass through its airports, since it only includes buildings and land operations, not emissions from aircraft.

All the paths to net zero by 2050, consistent with keeping global warming below 1.5°C, require that 40–60% of the emissions reductions (over 2010 levels) take place before 2030. The UNEP thus warns that, especially with regard to national net-zero or carbon-neutrality goals, the 'litmus test' will be 'the extent to which they are reflected in near-term policy action and in significantly more ambitious NDCs for the period to 2030'. These 'nationally determined contributions' (NDCs) are the formal emissions targets mandated by the Paris Agreement, initially up to 2025 but to be updated to 2030 or beyond by the UN Conference of the Parties (COP26) climate summit in Glasgow, postponed by a year to November 2021 because of the COVID-19 pandemic.

Yet as of the end of June 2021, of the G20 countries, only the UK and US had submitted new NDCs consistent with the goals of the Paris Agreement. The EU's NDC mentions the 2050 climate-neutral goal, but the 2030 commitments amount to a reduction of only 34% over 2010. Australia, Brazil, Mexico, Russia and South Korea did not increase their ambition over their original submissions. Some 101 countries, including China, had yet to submit new NDC targets at all. Given China's current high GHG emissions, by 2030 its reductions would have to be at the upper end of the 40–60% range to be consistent with the goals of the Paris Agreement, and be front-loaded into the next five years. Yet even with Xi's announced goal of carbon neutrality by 2060, China had only pledged to reach peak CO_2 emissions by 2030. Meanwhile, the G20 countries are not even collectively on track to meet their modest 2030 targets.

The road to Glasgow

The COVID-19 pandemic led to a drop in global CO_2 emissions of 6.4% in 2020, but they bounced back strongly in the second half of the year. The temporary decline offered a brief window for countries to put climate goals at the centre of any economic-recovery policy, but the pandemic also led to a slowdown in international climate negotiations, especially the postponement of COP26, as leaders were distracted by other priorities. The hiatus also meant that a new, climate-friendly administration in Washington would be involved, and indeed, offer renewed leadership in those negotiations.

During the US presidential campaign in 2020, Joe Biden promised that if elected, he would rejoin the Paris Agreement on 'day one' and would convene an international climate summit to engage the leaders of the major carbon-emitting nations within his first 100 days in office. In the event, the new president did both, rejoining the Paris Agreement on 20 January and hosting a virtual summit on Earth Day – 22 April – involving 40 world leaders, whose countries account for 80% of global emissions. On the day of the summit, the US submitted its new NDC, pledging to reduce its emissions by 50–52% by 2030, twice as much as its previous target and putting it at the forefront of the major emitters. Canada and Japan announced significantly enhanced new targets to be included in their updated NDCs. Brazil's President Jair Bolsonaro said the country was revising its net-zero carbon target from 2060 to 2050, and China announced that it would aim for peak coal use by 2025. But many of the initiatives and targets announced at the summit were symbolic, minor or reiterations of existing policy. None of the net-zero holdouts put forward new plans to reduce emissions or enhance ambition. Most significantly, Xi merely reiterated his 2020 pledge of peak carbon by 2030 and carbon neutrality by 2060.

Meanwhile, climate negotiations between some Western states and Beijing remained fraught. In late March, China declined to take part in a key British-led summit on climate and development in preparation for COP26, in what UK officials believed was a case of diplomatic arguments over human rights spilling into the climate arena. Before the Earth Day summit, Chinese Foreign Ministry spokeswoman Hua Chunying characterised Washington's rejoining of the Paris Agreement as not 'the return of the king' but 'a truant getting back to class'. Xi did not confirm his attendance at the Earth Day summit until quite late, despite a visit to China by US Climate Envoy and former secretary of state John Kerry the previous week, during which they met. Despite some encouraging statements from Xi during the summit, at a Council on Foreign Relations meeting the next day Chinese Foreign Minister Wang Yi implied that US interference with China's policies on Hong Kong, Taiwan and Xinjiang jeopardised cooperation on climate. Kerry told his Chinese opposite the 'truant' comment was 'not particularly conducive' to cooperation on climate, but called the summit 'a first step with China' and said that diplomacy would continue in the run-up to Glasgow.

Kerry has also acknowledged the concerns of China and India over the relative contributions required of developed and developing countries towards mitigation of global warming.

Part of this equity question involves the rate and degree of emissions cuts in different countries, but it also involves financial support from wealthier nations for mitigation efforts worldwide. Climate finance was second only to climate ambition at the Earth Day summit, and topped the agendas of a virtual meeting of G7 finance ministers in April and an in-person meeting of G7 foreign ministers in London in May. With the UK hosting the G7 summit in Cornwall in June as well as COP26 in November, London is using the G7 process to complement its preparations for the UN climate summit. The delivery of US$100 billion in climate finance, and new climate-finance targets for 2025, are key issues to be resolved in Glasgow, but little or no progress was made on these issues at the Cornwall meeting. Others include compensation mechanisms for loss and damage from climate change, carbon-market mechanisms, and integration of 'nature-based solutions' (the use of agriculture, ecosystems and forests to absorb carbon and protect against climate impacts) into the Paris Agreement framework.

Can we get there from here?

The various announcements leading up to and at the Earth Day summit amounted to the single-biggest reduction, at 12–14%, of the gap between what is needed to meet the 1.5°C Paris target and existing policies and ambitions. Some minor further reductions were implied by the G7 agreement in Cornwall to reduce their collective emissions by 50% of 2010 levels by 2030. But that still leaves a huge gap to be filled before COP26. Of the G20 countries, only India, Saudi Arabia and Turkey have yet to either submit or signal the content of new NDCs, and they are likely to follow Australia, Indonesia, Mexico, Russia and Turkey in maintaining or even reducing their initial commitments. Either China, the EU and the US will have to further increase their declared ambitions; or the holdout countries must be persuaded to rethink their intransigence; or some combination of both must be achieved. In most projected pathways consistent with 1.5°C warming, some countries will naturally reach net zero a decade or two before others, simply because their mix of emissions from energy, land use and so forth differs. But in the short term (to 2030), as well as in the longer term to net zero, emissions reduction is a zero-sum game. If one country fails to do its share, others must take up the slack.

The question of 'fair share' is at the heart of the global effort to mitigate climate change, whether through emissions targets or climate finance. The developed countries became wealthy by using more than their relative share of the global carbon budget since the Industrial Revolution, and the developing countries argue that they are now slamming the door behind them by trying to restrict emissions. But defining and quantifying climate equity is both diplomatically and ethically fraught. For example, by one set of fair-share metrics developed by the independent consortium Climate Action Tracker, the US should reduce its emissions by 57–63% rather than its announced 50–52% by 2030, as well as provide financing support to developing nations. Yet in terms of previous commitments and in the context of domestic US politics, Biden's policy represents a dramatic increase in ambition that may be difficult to add to further.

Even if sufficient emissions reductions can be achieved by 2030, achieving net-zero emissions by 2050 and keeping global warming to 1.5°C will also require significant removal of CO_2, whether through reforestation or planting new forests, or carbon capture and sequestration (at source, especially in bioenergy generation, or directly from the atmosphere). If the gap is not filled, an increase of 1.5°C is still possible, but would entail 'overshoot', requiring even greater CO_2 removal to balance the excess emissions. Yet nature-based solutions are unlikely to be sufficient – using afforestation alone would require planting an area the size of Brazil. Such solutions also have side effects on biodiversity and food and water security and are not necessarily permanent.

National timelines for carbon neutrality or net-zero greenhouse-gas emissions

National target dates for achieving net-zero greenhouse gases (GHG) (green) or CO_2 (yellow) emissions, or no target date (red), for the top 20 emitting countries (including the EU-27), plus the rest of the world (ROW). The area of each bar is proportional to that country's or group of countries' share of global GHG emissions. The global target-date ranges for zero CO_2 and net-zero GHG emissions represent the scientific consensus on the deadlines to keep warming below 1.5°C, rather than any formal or legal international targets.

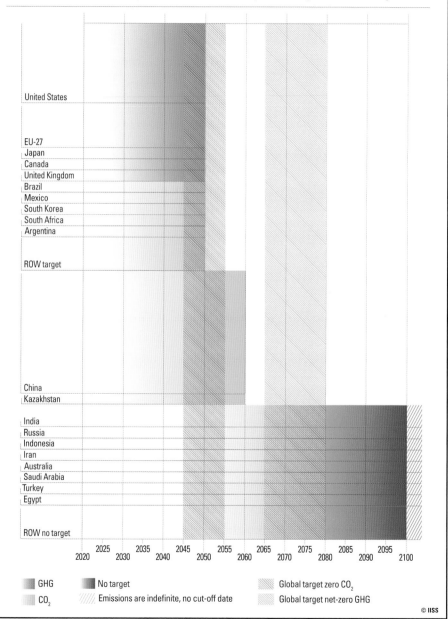

Legend:
- GHG
- CO_2
- No target
- Emissions are indefinite, no cut-off date
- Global target zero CO_2
- Global target net-zero GHG

© IISS

Sources: Netherlands Environmental Assessment Agency, 'Trends in Global CO₂ and Total Greenhouse Gas Emissions' (2020); Energy & Climate Intelligence Unit, Net Zero Tracker; IPCC Special Report, 'Global Warming of 1.5°C' (2018); UNFCCC

Engineering solutions, on the other hand, are still mostly unproven or nascent; in 2020, 40 million tonnes, or 0.1% of emitted CO_2, was captured and sequestered at source. This would have to be scaled up by more than a hundredfold by 2050 to achieve net zero.

The progress made since the adoption of the Paris Agreement is encouraging but inadequate. The Climate Action Tracker estimate for warming by the end of the century fell from 3.6°C in 2015 to 2.9°C in 2020, based on emissions trends (including the downturn caused by the COVID-19 pandemic) and new national policies. Further Paris Agreement commitments as of November 2020 brought the estimate down to 2.6°C, and net-zero targets, particularly those of China and the US, bring it down further to 2°C, within striking distance of the Paris Agreement target. But closing this last gap will not be easy, politically or practically. Roughly half the cuts required to keep warming below 1.5°C must come in the next ten years, yet current pledges and targets postpone the vast bulk of them until after 2030. Reductions of 20–23 gigatonnes of CO_2 equivalent (non-CO_2 GHGs converted into the volume of CO_2 with the same warming potential) need to be brought forward. Even then, ambitions for 2030–50 need to be ramped up. To meet their international targets, individual countries will have to adopt policies that accelerate deployment of existing low- or zero-carbon technologies and increase investment in new technologies, especially for carbon removal.

This is a daunting task, and the COP26 may be the last real opportunity before time runs out. Yet global-warming impacts fall on a continuum; the world is already feeling the effects of climate change from 1.2°C warming and 1.5°C is not a threshold between safe and dangerous. Every bit of incremental warming that is avoided counts. Despite potential stumbling blocks in the way of further increasing ambition, achieving short-term targets and developing the technology necessary for longer-term goals, the prospect of avoiding the worst impacts of climate change is brighter than at any time since the failure of the Copenhagen Climate Change Conference in 2009.

CANADA

UNITED STATES

©IISS

Drivers of Strategic Change

REGIONAL SHARE OF GLOBAL POPULATION, GDP AND DEFENCE BUDGET

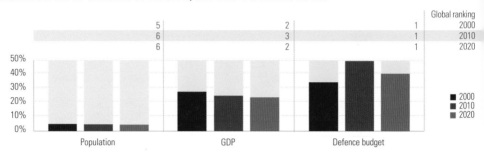

				Global ranking	
	5	2	1	2000
	6	3	1	2010
	6	2	1	2020

Population   GDP   Defence budget

■ 2000
■ 2010
■ 2020

POPULATION

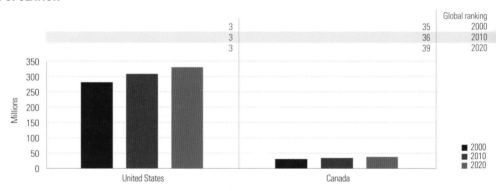

		Global ranking	
3	35	2000
3	36	2010
3	39	2020

United States   Canada

■ 2000
■ 2010
■ 2020

AGE STRUCTURE
(Percentage of national population)

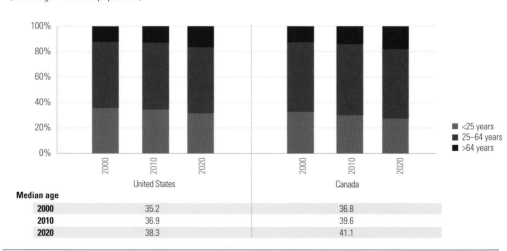

United States   Canada

■ <25 years
■ 25–64 years
■ >64 years

Median age		
2000	35.2	36.8
2010	36.9	39.6
2020	38.3	41.1

America's huge share of global defence spending is even higher than in 2000, though its share of GDP continues to fall. For a highly developed country, its population is young. But human development relative to other countries has fallen sharply. Declines in the quality of democracy and trust in government (now below 50%) reflect domestic political stress unprecedented in recent times.

GDP
(Constant 2010 US dollars)

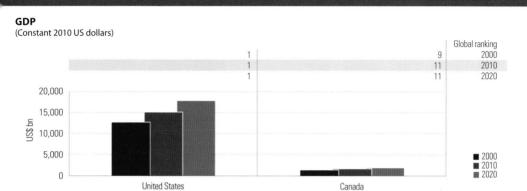

		Global ranking
1	9	2000
1	11	2010
1	11	2020

■ 2000
■ 2010
■ 2020

GDP PER CAPITA
(Constant 2010 US dollars)

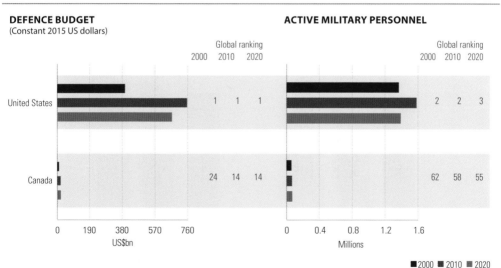

		Global ranking
10	11	2000
12	13	2010
10	12	2020

■ 2000
■ 2010
■ 2020

DEFENCE BUDGET
(Constant 2015 US dollars)

ACTIVE MILITARY PERSONNEL

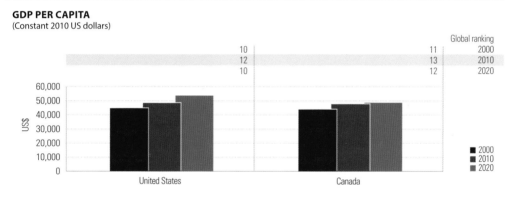

Defence budget — Global ranking

	2000	2010	2020
United States	1	1	1
Canada	24	14	14

Active military personnel — Global ranking

	2000	2010	2020
United States	2	2	3
Canada	62	58	55

■ 2000 ■ 2010 ■ 2020

For explanation of drivers and sources, see page 9

HUMAN DEVELOPMENT INDEX (HDI)
(Score between 0 and 1, where 0 denotes a low level of development and 1 a high level of development)

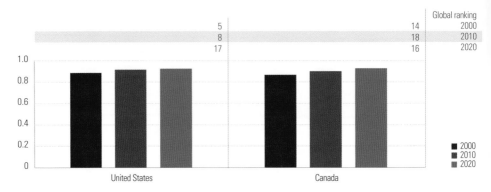

	Global ranking
5	14	2000
8	18	2010
17	16	2020

POLITICAL SYSTEM
(Score between 0 and 100, where 0 denotes no political freedom and 100 fully free)

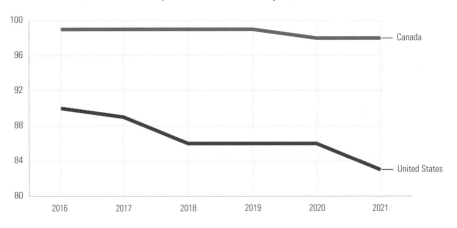

TRUST IN GOVERNMENT
(Average level of trust)

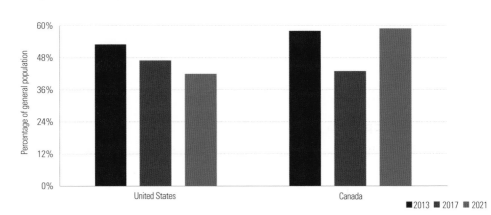

2020–21 Review

Unprecedented political turbulence marked the last seven months of United States president Donald Trump's administration. Against the backdrop of widespread social unrest and a pandemic that killed hundreds of thousands of Americans – and perhaps came close to killing the president himself – the US saw the first violent attempt to prevent the transition of executive power since the Civil War. Disputing the legitimacy of Joe Biden's victory in the November 2020 presidential election, on 6 January 2021 Trump incited his followers to storm the US Capitol in the hope of thwarting the democratic process. Although Trump became the first president to be impeached twice, he was once again acquitted thanks to ongoing protection from Senate Republicans unwilling to risk the wrath of his supporters and, as of mid-2021, his grip over the Republican Party remained secure. Although representative democracy in the US survived the challenges mounted against it in 2020–21, ongoing political and cultural polarisation suggested that its future remains uncertain.

Biden took office promising national renewal and attempts at reconciliation. While his appeal to many voters was founded on the promise of a restoration of pre-Trumpian norms of governance – and was reinforced by his appointment of many personnel who had served in earlier Democratic administrations – his domestic agenda, and budget plans drawn up to support it, appeared more ambitious than those of recent Democrat presidents.

Similarly, while Biden's foreign-policy agenda in many ways signalled a restoration of guiding principles of Barack Obama's administration – multilateralism, diplomatic engagement with Iran and US leadership on climate change – ambition and novelty were also evident, most obviously in his efforts to unite liberal democracies against the authoritarian threat exemplified by China and Russia.

US domestic politics

The COVID-19 pandemic dominated Trump's final year in office. Ineffective leadership by the executive branch, and inconsistent state policies, contributed to the highest death toll recorded by any country. As with most events in the contemporary US, the pandemic was often perceived through a politically polarised prism: Republican voters were significantly less likely to wear masks and, when they became available, to receive a vaccine. In October 2020, only weeks before the presidential election, Trump himself contracted the virus, along with a large number of his circle, many of whom had paid scant attention to infection guidelines. Despite receiving novel treatments unavailable to almost all other afflicted US citizens, his speech upon his return from the Walter Reed National Military Medical Center to the White House exhorted his compatriots not to 'let [COVID] dominate your lives'. By that point, the disease had killed over 200,000 US citizens and was yet to enter its deadliest phase. By the time Trump left office on 20 January 2021, less than four months later, COVID-19 deaths had doubled to over 414,000. While vaccination and infection rates improved substantially during the first months of Biden's administration, by June 2021 the death toll had reached more than 600,000. This colossal figure excluded the hundreds of thousands of Americans who had contracted and survived the virus, but went on to suffer the long-term effects, some crippling and possibly permanent. Yet while the US had been worst hit by the pandemic in 2020, by spring 2021 an accelerated vaccination programme meant that it was poised to enjoy a rapid economic recovery, with an expected real GDP growth of 6.4% in 2021 after a 3.5% contraction in 2020.

Despite executive policy failure in managing the pandemic, the November presidential election was tightly contested. While Biden won seven million more votes than Trump and took five states that Trump had won in 2016, including the typically Republican Arizona and Georgia, the margins in several of those states were narrow enough to require several days of vote counting before most observers were sufficiently confident to project Biden's overall victory. Biden won 306 Electoral College votes to Trump's 232 – the same margin by which Trump had defeated Hillary Clinton in 2016. Trump refused to concede defeat. He had begun his attempts to discredit the election as early as July, when he suggested delaying it due to the supposed risk of postal-voting fraud, and claimed that the election was likely to be 'rigged', echoing complaints he had made when he appeared likely to lose in 2016. Following the election, Trump's surrogates mounted numerous unsuccessful challenges to the legality of many states' votes and on 2 January 2021, Trump was recorded pressuring Republican officials in Georgia to 'find' sufficient votes to overturn Biden's victory there. On 6 January, as Congress gathered to certify the Electoral College votes, Trump urged a rally of his followers to march to the Capitol Building, arguing that 'if you don't fight like hell you're not going to have a country anymore'. Hundreds of Trump supporters stormed the Capitol and seriously assaulted numerous police officers. Five people died, including one who was shot by police while attempting to break into the House of Representatives. While most of the intruders appeared disorganised and incompetent, the mob included a core of more determined (and potentially more violent) individuals with military training, and it appeared likely that wider bloodshed was only narrowly avoided. The culmination of Trump's assault on US political norms, the riot was rich in the symbolism of a divided nation. In one of the insurrection's defining images, a Trump supporter brandished the Confederate flag in the halls of the Capitol in front of the portrait of the abolitionist senator Justin Morrill, on the very day that Georgia, the heart of the Confederacy, elected two Democratic senators (one black, one Jewish) to office, leaving control of the Senate split 50–50 between the Democrat and Republican parties. The rioters' desecration of the cathedral of American democracy, and Trump's half-hearted calls for them to desist, prompted outrage. The House impeached Trump for the second time in little over a year. While seven Republican senators voted in February 2021 to convict the former president (six more than in 2020), the vote fell ten votes short of the 67 required to convict Trump and he was acquitted.

Trump was once again protected by the reluctance of most Republicans to anger their voters, whose support for Trump remained strong. As of May 2021, 66% of Republican voters wanted Trump to stand for re-election, with 85% wanting any Republican nominee to espouse Trumpian policies. Two-thirds falsely believed that Biden's election victory was illegitimate. Reports emerged that Trump sincerely thought he would be 'reinstated' later in summer 2021 following non-existent 'audits' of supposedly fraudulent votes in the election. Congressional Republicans who displayed insufficient devotion to Trump and to the lie that he was the true victor of the 2020 election – including those with impeccable conservative credentials, such as Representative Liz Cheney – appeared to have no future in their party. In May 2021, Cheney's colleagues removed her from the post of third-ranking Republican in the House. Although 35 Republicans in the House supported a Democrat proposal to establish a bipartisan commission into the Capitol riot, along the lines of the 9/11 Commission, Republican senators blocked the initiative. Twenty-one Republican Congressmen later voted against awarding medals to the Capitol police who defended their workplace on 6 January.

Biden claimed that his presidency would reduce the temperature of US politics. In this goal, he was helped by the belated decision of social-media companies to suspend Trump's accounts after the attempted insurrection, removing one of his major platforms for incitement of violence and delegitimisation of the democratic process. In summer 2020 there had been significant social unrest over racial injustice, featuring riots, violence and the destruction of property. Biden sought to strike a fine balance between supporting racial justice while condemning associated violence and vandalism. He rejected calls by some of the Democratic left to 'defund the police', a slogan most US citizens opposed, including 72% of African Americans.

In his first six months in office, Biden also sought to pursue ambitious new policies. He recognised that he had become president in a time of convergent economic, health and political crises: a generation-defining health crisis that had prompted a historic economic crisis, coinciding with the most serious strains on US democracy since the Civil War. At the same time, these domestic challenges to the liberal, capitalist democratic order in the US overlapped with the resurging challenge of authoritarian adversaries to the democratic model and to the liberal international order. Biden's historical sensibility drew him to the analogy of the 1930s and a Democratic predecessor, president Franklin D. Roosevelt, who had also sought extraordinary measures to deal with extraordinary times. In March 2021, Biden announced a US$2.3 trillion infrastructure plan, followed by a US$1.8trn plan in April aimed at investing in education, child and family support, and tax credits for children and workers. Biden argued that this expenditure would be paid for over the following 15 years through increased taxes on corporations and wealthy individuals. By mid-2021, however, it remained unclear how Biden's plans would be reflected in congressional negotiations and eventual legislation.

US foreign policy

The most noteworthy foreign-policy development in the Trump administration's final six months was the signing of the US-brokered Abraham Accords, which ushered in the normalisation of relations between Israel, Bahrain and the United Arab Emirates. Thanks to US inducements, Morocco and Sudan later normalised relations with Israel.

Some observers wondered whether the spectacle of democracy under siege in the US would undermine Washington's traditional narrative of enshrining liberty and advancing its cause abroad. If anything, however, the attempted insurrection lent further impetus to Biden's blend of restoration and ambition in foreign policy.

In terms of restoration, Biden repeatedly reassured US allies that Trump's sullen transactionalism was gone and that 'America is back'. He expressed this in his repeated rhetorical support of NATO and the 'sacred obligation' of collective defence under its Article 5; in his freezing of Trump's planned withdrawal of 12,000 troops from Germany; and more broadly in his recommitment to a raft of multilateral efforts to address transnational challenges, which Trump had either neglected or actively undermined. Trump's withdrawal from the Joint Comprehensive Plan of Action – the agreement with Iran to restrict its nuclear programme – had particularly disconcerted European allies. As of mid-2021, it appeared likely that the US and Iran would in some fashion rejoin a nuclear agreement, although the practicalities of doing so still remained unclear. On his first day in office, Biden pledged that the US would rejoin the Paris Agreement to address climate change, later describing it as 'the existential problem facing humanity', and on 22–23 April he hosted a virtual summit of world leaders on the issue. His domestic plans to redress widespread corporate tax avoidance were reflected in his administration's brokering of a G7 agreement on a minimum corporate tax rate. Much of this was welcomed by Washington's traditional allies, although most wondered whether the pendulum might again swing back were Trump (or a fellow-traveller) to be elected in 2024.

Biden's assertions that Washington was restored to a more active international role were balanced by an element of unabashed retrenchment, at least from long-standing military entanglements. As vice president a decade earlier, Biden had argued for a lighter US military footprint in Afghanistan, more focused on counter-terrorism than counter-insurgency. Trump had declared that US forces would leave Afghanistan by May 2021, but it had remained unclear whether this would actually occur. In April 2021, Biden announced a full US withdrawal by 11 September.

Biden's foreign-policy vision appeared more overtly ideological than Obama's and was connected to his diagnosis of the challenges facing the US political and socio-economic model. By March 2021, Biden had made clear that he understood the major international dynamic as 'a battle between the utility of democracies in the twenty-first century and autocracies. We've got to prove democracy works', later pledging that 'autocrats will not win the future. America will. The future belongs to America.' Biden sought to defend democracy not only by reforming it at home but by uniting democratic states against the autocratic challenge. He claimed the G7 states were engaged in 'a contest with autocracies', and in June 2021, echoing Roosevelt's 1941 Atlantic Charter initiative, signed a 'New Atlantic Charter' with the United Kingdom. The G7 announced a 'green' democratic counter-initiative to China's Belt and Road Initiative, along with a pledge for democratic states to donate one billion COVID-19 vaccine doses to counterbalance Russian and Chinese 'vaccine diplomacy'. Days later, NATO leaders described China as posing 'systemic challenges' to the international order. In a time of crisis, these measures resembled a self-conscious effort to replicate Washington's previous triumphs over autocratic challenges and economic disaster, and its successful shaping of the post-war international order.

Biden's policy and rhetoric towards China reflected both a degree of continuity with Trump's policy and the new administration's more ideological framing of the confrontation. In March 2021, a bilateral meeting in Anchorage, Alaska, featured a heated and public verbal confrontation between top-level US and Chinese officials in which US Secretary of State Antony Blinken and National Security Advisor Jake Sullivan criticised Chinese policy on Hong Kong, Taiwan and Xinjiang, while top diplomat Wang Jiechi and State Councillor Wang Yi accused Washington of 'persuading some countries to launch attacks on China'. The Anchorage altercation signalled that Biden would continue Trump's policy of categorising China as a determined adversary – perhaps one of the few areas of bipartisan policy agreement in Washington, where there were now few exponents of the view that, as China became more prosperous, it would evolve into a 'responsible stakeholder' whose interests would broadly align with those of the US. It also underlined a break from the previous administration and to an extent from Obama's too: Biden and his team now couched the confrontation in terms of democracy's struggle against authoritarianism. Moreover, unlike Trump, Biden appeared to recognise the strategic merits of strengthening coalitions of allies against China, rather than initiating trade conflicts with these allies at the same time.

The incoming Biden administration's democracy and anti-corruption agendas, as well as Russia's attempts to interfere in two successive presidential elections against Democrat candidates, suggested that US–Russia relations were unlikely to improve. Nonetheless, Biden recognised common interests the two countries shared as the biggest nuclear powers. In late January they extended New START, one of the last major arms-control agreements, a few days before it was due to expire.

However, an early test of managing more adversarial behaviour came in late March 2021, when Russia began its biggest military build-up on Ukraine's border since 2014. At the height of tensions in mid-April, Biden both offered President Vladimir Putin a summit meeting and imposed further sanctions, including new restrictions on the purchase of rouble-denominated primary sovereign debt. As Russia began to withdraw the forces it had amassed, a senior White House official noted the administration's satisfaction with the effects of sanctions messaging on Russia. During a visit to Kyiv soon after, Blinken reaffirmed US support for Ukraine and criticised Russia's 'reckless and aggressive' actions.

At the Geneva Summit on 16 June, Biden sought to rein in Russian behaviour while avoiding a further deterioration of relations. While describing Russia as a 'great power', and Putin as a 'worthy adversary', he issued a strong warning against further cyber-hacking of critical US infrastructure.

Soon after taking office, Biden had called Nord Stream 2, Russia's nearly completed gas pipeline to Germany that bypasses Ukraine, a 'bad deal' for Europe. But in May 2021 his administration accepted that the project was a fait accompli and lifted sanctions on it. The US sought to reach agreement with Germany with the aim of reassuring Ukraine that the pipeline would not undermine its security.

Canada

Canada demonstrated superior competence to its southern neighbour in its management of COVID-19 during 2020, leaving it with a death rate around one-third that of the US. The relatively effective government response increased Prime Minister Justin Trudeau's approval ratings and political capital, although he and his government continued to face allegations of corruption or impropriety. While Canada suffered a significant economic downturn due to the pandemic, with GDP falling by about 3.3% by December 2020, this was expected to grow by over 6% in 2021. As in the US, there were indications that Canada would emerge from the pandemic with more interventionist domestic policies with higher government expenditure to address what Minister of Finance Chrystia Freeland described as 'the critical gaps in our social safety net' that the pandemic had highlighted.

In foreign policy, Trudeau welcomed Biden's presidency and the return of 'US leadership'. He stressed their shared interests, notably climate change, but also voiced his 'disappointment' at Biden's decision to revoke the permit for the controversial Keystone XL oil pipeline from Canada to the US. Canada's long-running dispute with China over the detention of Meng Wanzhou, Huawei's CFO, and China's retaliatory imprisonment of two Canadian nationals, Michael Kovrig and Michael Spavor, continued. In March 2021, it was reported that Kovrig and Spavor had been tried for espionage, but no verdicts were announced. In October 2020, Trudeau's government reacted with anger and alarm to the implicit threats made by China's ambassador to Ottawa that Canada's welcoming of Hong Kong democracy activists could affect the 'health and security' of Canadian citizens living in Hong Kong.

US–China Relations
A game of two halves?

The US–China relationship between mid-2020 and mid-2021 is best seen as a game of two halves. During the first half, which coincided with what proved to be the final phase of the Trump administration, an already fraught relationship further deteriorated dramatically. President Donald Trump, facing the prospect of defeat in his bid for re-election, redoubled his attacks on China's alleged responsibility for the COVID-19 pandemic while still holding onto the possibility that a successful execution of the Phase One trade deal negotiated with China at the end of 2018 would restore his electoral prospects. Meanwhile, Trump administration China hawks, led by secretary of state Mike Pompeo, undertook a series of anti-China measures with the apparent aim of taking the US–China relationship beyond the point of no return, creating a new reality that a Democrat administration would be unable to alter.

The first half

The overall tone of this approach was set by a series of speeches by then-national security advisor Robert O'Brien, FBI Director Christopher Wray and then US attorney-general William Barr setting out the major China-related concerns of their respective departments and culminating on 23 July 2020 in a speech on 'Communist China and the Free World's Future' by Pompeo at the Richard Nixon Presidential Library. Pompeo stated that engagement with China had been a failure and called on the free world to come together to empower the Chinese people, whom he sought to differentiate from the Chinese Communist Party (CCP), to effect change in China's behaviour.

China's Foreign Minister Wang Yi responded in a relatively restrained manner, observing that China could not allow 'a minority of US anti-China forces' to set the tone of US–China relations. But China's state-controlled media were let off the leash, launching a series of personalised attacks on Pompeo himself. The *People's Daily* published a series of op-eds under the portmanteau byline of Zhong Sheng, signifying a consensus of senior editorial – and hence Party – opinion, criticising the US system of governance and highlighting chronic US social problems including race relations and gun violence. China's 'wolf-warrior' diplomats resorted to social and broadcast media to amplify these messages while also suggesting that COVID-19 had originated in a US military laboratory. Personalised criticism was not, however, permitted to extend to Trump himself on the presumption that he might yet be re-elected.

Diplomacy, security and technology came together in ways that further damaged the relationship when, in July 2020, the US government announced the closure of China's consulate in Houston, giving the staff just 72 hours to vacate. The rationale for this decision, as explained by the assistant secretary of state for East Asia and Pacific affairs, David Stilwell, was that the Houston consulate had served as the 'epicentre' of research theft by the Chinese military in the US, with consulate staff tasking Chinese research students who had concealed their military affiliation in their visa applications, advising them on how to avoid detection and facilitating the exfiltration of stolen research material. China responded by closing the US consulate in Chengdu.

The closure of the Houston consulate was part of a wider crackdown on Chinese research students in the US with undeclared People's Liberation Army (PLA) affiliations to the point where China allegedly indicated that prosecutions of such individuals could lead to US nationals being detained in China. US academics with undeclared affiliations to Chinese universities, including under China's Thousand Talents programme, were also subject to investigation and in some cases prosecution. Meanwhile, the number of Chinese students applying to US universities fell by 99% over the previous year.

Chinese journalists working in the US were caught up in another round of a visa war that had begun in 2020 with the expulsion from China of *Wall Street Journal* staff in response to an ill-judged editorial on COVID-19 that referred to China as 'the sick man of Asia'. Chinese media organisations in the US were compelled to register as foreign missions, with a similar demand being made of Confucius Institutes, requiring them to provide details of staff and administration. This led to further journalist expulsions by Beijing, giving rise to fears that this would lead to a reduction in understanding of China at a critical period when a clear understanding of the country was more necessary than ever. Members of the CCP also fell foul of new immigration restrictions limiting access to the US to one month.

The Trump administration launched an all-out assault on China's technology ambitions that focused on, but was not restricted to, China's telecommunications national champion, Huawei. Following its success in persuading the United Kingdom to exclude Huawei from its 5G network, the US continued to exert pressure on other states to follow suit. On 29 April 2020, the US State Department announced the Clean Network initiative. The brainchild of undersecretary of state Keith Krach, this initiative was described as an effort to address 'the long-term threat to data privacy, security, human rights and principled collaboration posed to the free world from authoritarian malign actors'. In December 2020, the State Department announced that some 60 states had signed up. And while many states in the G77 group of developing countries remained committed to Huawei, a growing number of developed Western states, even if not explicitly banning Huawei from their 5G networks, took measures that effectively led to its exclusion.

At the same time, the Trump administration broadened its existing embargo on technology sales to Huawei and other Chinese technology national champions, such as the video-surveillance company Hikvision and microprocessor manufacturer SMIC, to include all products manufactured worldwide that utilised US intellectual property or equipment. This had the effect of preventing microprocessor manufacturers around the world from making sales to China and posed an existential challenge to Huawei's mobile-technology ambitions, forcing the company to refocus its efforts on becoming a leader in cloud services. This move reinforced China's conviction that the US was bent on preventing China's rise and that China would have to redouble its efforts to decouple from dependence on US technology.

While denouncing decoupling and emphasising China's commitment to globalisation and an open trading system, Chinese President Xi Jinping had in May 2020 unveiled his 'dual-circulation' economic concept to refocus the Chinese economy on domestic consumption as the priority while still engaging in the global trading system. In essence this concept could be paraphrased as 'close where we can, open where we must'. Meanwhile, China had been carefully putting together the building blocks to internationalise the renminbi with a view to reducing its exposure to possible US financial sanctions. This included plans to launch a digital renminbi.

In the aftermath of the US presidential election, Chinese officials were bracing themselves for 'a final act of madness' by the Trump administration. In the event, China's worst fears went unrealised. But in its dying days the Trump administration took a succession of further measures calculated to infuriate Beijing. These included revoking the designation of the East Turkestan Independence Movement (which seeks the independence of East Turkestan in northwest China as a homeland for the Uighurs) as a terrorist organisation; announcing a relaxation of restrictions on official dealings with Taiwan, a move with little practical but much symbolic significance; and the declassification decades ahead of schedule of the United States' Indo-Pacific strategy. This strategy, which reportedly incorporated inputs from Australia and Japan, set out plans for a regional defence strategy 'capable of but not limited to' denying China sustained air and sea dominance inside the first island chain in a conflict; defending the first-island-chain nations including Taiwan; and dominating all domains outside the first island chain. Notwithstanding Trump's own professed disdain for alliance relationships, the Indo-Pacific strategy envisaged the creation of a latticework of alliance relationships within the region designed to constrain China's freedom of action and to increase its calculus of risk. Meanwhile, the US military had engaged in an increased tempo of activity in the waters around China including conducting exercises with three carrier battle groups in the South China Sea.

During the final months of the Trump administration a series of sanctions were also imposed on Chinese officials for human-rights violations in Hong Kong and Xinjiang. Imports of cotton and agricultural produce from Xinjiang were banned, while the US Congress pressed for China's policies in Xinjiang to be categorised as genocide. In the earliest days of the administration of Joe Biden, China retaliated by imposing sanctions on senior Trump administration officials dealing with China policy and their immediate family members, all of whom were banned from entering China or engaging in business relations with Chinese companies. And China's propaganda organs revelled in the storming of the Capitol on 6 January 2021, using it as a basis to pronounce the last rites for the US democratic system of government.

The second half

The incoming Biden administration made a priority of assembling a China team made up of individuals who had extensive expertise on, or experience in dealing with, China and formed a cohesive group with long experience of working with Biden. Their other common characteristic was a tendency to hawkishness but without belligerence. Republican activists sought to portray Biden as being in hock to China by virtue of his son Hunter's business dealings there, but there was no evidence to support such allegations. On the contrary, Biden, who had referred to Xi as a 'thug' during his presidential campaign, made it clear that he would be in no hurry to reverse the actions his predecessor had taken against China. Nor did he respond to blandishments from China to undertake a reset of relations based on an expectation that the US would make concessions with China offering nothing in return.

Prior to Biden's election, China's foreign-policy community had expressed the view that, on balance, Trump's chaotic approach to policy and disdain for allies might benefit China more than Biden's approach to China, which would be more ideological but also more structured. This view was reflected in numerous social-media posts referring to *Chuan Jianguo* (literally 'nation-builder') Trump – the nation in question being China, not the US. And Biden lived up to expectations, announcing his intention to host a Democracy Summit in his first year in office that may well include Taiwan, and proclaiming his intention to restore US global leadership and repudiate Trump's unilateralism.

The Biden administration, however, struggled to contend with allies that had their own interests when dealing with China and were reluctant to be forced into making a binary choice between China and the US – and who were also inclined to hedge against the possibility of a return in 2025 to Trumpian isolationism. An early disappointment for Biden was the decision by the European Union to conclude a Comprehensive Agreement on Investment with China immediately prior to Biden's inauguration – although this was subsequently put on ice by the European Parliament as a result of reciprocal sanctions imposed by Beijing following European sanctions in relation to Xinjiang. The G7 summit held in Cornwall on 11–13 June, and the NATO summit that took place in Brussels on 14 June, further reflected the ambivalence of many US allies in relation to China – though the minimal references to China in the resultant communiqués were sufficient to draw China's ire.

Early China policy moves by the Biden administration included the announcement of a review of Pentagon strategy towards China, and the publication of White House interim national-security guidance that characterised China as being 'the only competitor potentially capable of combining its economic, diplomatic, military, and technological power to mount a sustained challenge to a stable and open international system'. US Secretary of State Antony Blinken described China as 'the greatest geopolitical challenge the United States faces in the twenty-first century'. Biden himself proclaimed his intention to prevent China from becoming the world's leading country.

The Biden administration emphasised that the key to successful competition with China lay in investment in the United States' own capabilities including physical infrastructure, technology and human capital. In the first instance this took the form of significant stimulus packages that encountered Republican opposition amid fears that they would prove inflationary. In attempting to construct a cohesive China policy, the Biden administration also had to contend with significant opposition from both Wall Street and Silicon Valley. Since opening its capital account to foreign investors in 2019, China had attracted significant US investment that it needed both to reduce high levels of domestic debt accumulated following the 2008 global financial crisis and to garner greater expertise in financial management. And while some in Silicon Valley, such as former Google chairman Eric Schmidt, argued that the technology threat posed by China made a degree of technology decoupling both inevitable and desirable, majority opinion within the US technology sector continued to favour collaboration with China for both financial and philosophical reasons.

China's own leadership, while continuing publicly to cite the mantra that the East was rising and the West was in decline, projected a stark view of US–China relations. Veteran America-watcher Yuan Peng, president of the China Institutes of Contemporary International Relations, a respected think tank and the open-source research institute for the Ministry of State Security, had since mid-2020 provided the Chinese leadership with a series of reports and briefings on US relations, highlighting the dangers China was facing. Yuan characterised the world as driven by a contest between socialism and capitalism, China versus the US, and an East–West clash of civilisations resulting in 'a more profound and complex situation than any other rise and fall of great powers in history'.

This world view was reflected in Xi's May 2021 publication entitled 'Questions and Answers on the Study of Xi Jinping Thought on Socialism with Chinese Characteristics for a New Era'. This talked of a global struggle between capitalism and socialism, which the latter was destined to win. Xi, who in a closed speech in March 2021 had described the US as 'the greatest threat to our country's development and security', spoke incessantly of the need to imbue the Chinese people with a spirit of struggle to overcome future challenges. While in this context the US was not mentioned by name, the implications were clear. There was a disconnect between this internal messaging and the message from China's diplomats about the need for coexistence. This latter message was epitomised by a statement by Wang at a virtual dialogue with the US Council on Foreign Relations in April 2021:

China–US relations are at a new crossroads. The key is whether the United States can accept the peaceful rise of a major country with a different social system, history and culture, and in a different development stage; whether it can recognize the Chinese people's right to pursue development and a better life.

The fundamental differences between the US and China went on public display at a meeting between their respective senior foreign-policy officials in Anchorage, Alaska, on 18–19 March 2021. China, clearly hoping for a reset in relations, characterised the meeting as a high-level strategic dialogue. The US, by contrast, referred to it as a one-off encounter. Normal practice is for such encounters to begin with a brief photo opportunity for the media during which the two sides exchange diplomatic pleasantries. But in response to a US statement that China's actions in relation to Xinjiang, Hong Kong and Taiwan were a threat to the rules-based international order, State Councillor Yang Jiechi delivered a diatribe in which he accused the US of Cold War thinking, abusing its military and financial power to suppress other countries, and inciting other states to attack China. He rejected US criticism of China's policies towards Xinjiang, Hong Kong and Taiwan, saying that the US, with its long record of racial injustice, had no right to adopt a high moral tone in its dealings with China. These exchanges were reportedly followed by more measured and constructive discussion in private, though few details emerged. But they laid bare the extent of profound differences between the two sides that could no longer be papered over.

A calmer atmosphere – but no real change
Following the Anchorage meeting, US–China relations appeared to settle into a new normal in which further actions by the Biden administration against China, and further criticism of the US in China's state media, went hand in hand with a measure of pragmatic cooperation. The Biden

administration, while providing no new military equipment to Taiwan, made clear its support for the island in a variety of ways, including a succession of naval transits of the Taiwan Strait intended to establish a new normal of a regular US naval presence there. And as anti-China sentiment grew within Washington, Taiwan's envoy Hsiao Bi-khim enjoyed something close to rock-star status. Congress passed the United States Innovation and Competition Act, a package of bills designed to address economic, military and geopolitical competition from China and afford greater support to Taiwan.

On 3 June 2021, Biden issued an executive order reaffirming and expanding a Trump administration measure prohibiting Americans from investing in 59 Chinese companies believed to have links to the Chinese PLA, many of them household names in China's technology sector. And faced with a media storm about the possibility that COVID-19 had leaked from the Wuhan Institute of Virology, in late May Biden ordered his intelligence community to investigate further and report within 90 days, a move that elicited a predictable Chinese response.

Although China had made clear that the US could not expect progress on specific issues in the absence of any improvement in the overall relationship, signs of progress were evident in US Special Presidential Envoy for Climate John Kerry's initial engagement with his opposite number Xie Zhenhua. US Trade Representative Katherine Tai and Secretary of the Treasury Janet Yellen both had introductory talks with Vice-Premier Liu He, China's signatory to the Phase One US–China trade deal. China's state media presented these meetings in positive terms. Ironically, given that Trump's tariffs had been the genesis of the deterioration in US–China relations, the Phase One deal had come to be almost the only area of practical cooperation between the two sides, notwithstanding the very real possibility that China may not meet its commitments under the deal. China nominated Qin Gang as its new ambassador to Washington. This seemed an unusual appointment given his lack of expertise on America. But in his previous role he had been responsible for organising Xi's foreign trips and hence, to the extent that any official at that level could claim to do so, he knew Xi's mind and enjoyed his trust. The Biden administration subsequently signalled its intention to nominate veteran diplomat Nick Burns.

Conclusion

China's leadership, preoccupied with celebrations to mark the centenary of the CCP on 1 July 2021, was keen to put a floor beneath the dramatic deterioration in US–China relations. And Biden, preoccupied with pursuing a domestic agenda in the face of unremitting hostility from the Republican Party, but also anxious for results on key issues such as climate change, was probably equally happy to see a cooling of the temperature.

But the events of the past year have laid bare the ideological gulf that has emerged between the two sides. For China, the world has become defined as a struggle between capitalism and socialism with the tide of history flowing in favour of the latter. For the US, the struggle is between liberal democracy and Chinese authoritarianism. The gulf between these two visions of mankind's future looks unbridgeable and increasingly points to a future of contestation across all realms, but with a particular focus on the struggle for technological supremacy. And the risk of actual conflict will never be far away. While the world increasingly needs international cooperation to address a growing array of challenges, the prospect of this developing between the dominant power and its major challenger looks ever more remote.

America's Crisis of Democracy
Is the country governable?

Before president Donald Trump sent insurrectionists down Pennsylvania Avenue to 'fight like hell' to compel Congress, somehow, to annul the 2020 election, there had been some previous notable assaults at the United States Capitol. The first was during the Chesapeake Campaign of the War of 1812, when British troops seized Washington and burned the Capitol Building and the White House to the ground. Over the next two centuries there were assorted shootings, bombings and other violent disturbances. At the start of this century, the 9/11 terrorist plot included a plan to fly one of the planes into the Capitol dome, which was foiled when a group of passengers aboard United Airlines Flight 93 overpowered its hijackers and crashed it into a field in Pennsylvania.

However, one attack on a much smaller scale presaged the current American crisis. On 22 May 1856, Preston Brooks, congressman from South Carolina, entered the Senate Chamber and pummelled the head of Massachusetts senator Charles Sumner with a walking cane. The provocation, as Brooks saw it, was a speech that Sumner had delivered two days prior on the specific matter of 'Bleeding Kansas' – whether the territory would be admitted as a slave state or a free state – along with more general attacks on the calumny of slavery and slaveholders, in which he took specific aim at a slave-holding cousin of Brooks.

Bleeding Sumner barely survived the attack, which inspired Ralph Waldo Emerson's lament: 'I do not see how a barbarous community and a civilized community can constitute one state.' Emerson, like most of his contemporaries, could see the enmities and contradictions that would produce, five years later, an American civil war. To understand the fractures of contemporary America, it is worth reflecting on the magnitude of that civil war, arguably the only major war to have taken place in the extended space of European civilisation for a century after Napoleon's defeat in 1815. The American Civil War lasted four years, mobilised mass armies and vast resources, and inflicted devastation and casualties (including up to 750,000 fatalities) on a scale that Europeans would not come close to suffering again until August 1914.

Civil War symbols and rhetoric were prominent in the 6 January 2021 Capitol assault, when Capitol Hill police officers were beaten with the brutality of Brooks caning Sumner, and in the events leading up to it. An iconic photo of the Capitol insurrection shows a solitary intruder holding aloft the Confederate flag. In the protests after the late May 2020 killing of a black man, George Floyd, by a white police officer kneeling on his neck, there was renewed bitter contention over the Confederate monuments still ubiquitous in the South. A month before the election, Democratic presidential candidate Joe Biden delivered a speech at the Gettysburg battlefield in Pennsylvania, invoking in both place and words the Civil War president Abraham Lincoln. 'Today, once again we are a house divided', Biden said.

Biden would soon win the presidency, but his appeal for unity was met with more division in the aftermath of the election. In Trump's first appearance in the early morning after election day – a moment that every losing presidential candidate in living memory had used for ceremonial concessions to bring the nation together – the defeated president told a White House roomful of supporters: 'this is a fraud on the American public'. Trump established himself as the first sitting president in American history to reject his own electoral defeat. The most shocking thing about his rambling speech was that, by late 2020, the words no longer shocked. Trump had been agitating his followers about non-existent election fraud for six years or so, starting with the racially charged myth that president Barack Obama had not been born in the US and was not, therefore, legitimately elected. Trump had complained about imaginary voter fraud after the 2016 election that he *won*, insisting that three million fraudulent votes prevented him from beating Hillary Clinton in the popular-vote share as well as in the Electoral College.

Candidate and president Trump's fantastical relationship with empirical truth inspired a running debate about whether his lies were just theatrically upsetting to liberal complacency, or substantially dangerous to democratic stability. The former view was famously promoted during the 2016 campaign by conservative writer Salena Zito, who wrote of then-candidate Trump, 'the press takes him literally but not seriously; his supporters take him seriously but not literally'. In the weeks after the 2020 election, members of Trump's team counselled the public to discount this refusal as theatre. 'What is the downside for humouring him for this little bit of time?', a Trump official said to the *Washington Post*, continuing:

> no one seriously thinks the results will change. He went golfing this weekend. It's not like he's plotting how to prevent Joe Biden from taking power on Jan. 20. He's tweeting about filing some lawsuits, those lawsuits will fail, then he'll tweet some more about how the election was stolen, and then he'll leave.

Epistemology and democracy

Six months after Trump indeed left the White House, the downside was manifest: a fundamental subversion of the epistemological basis of American democracy – that is, the shared assumption that votes could be counted, that both sides would acknowledge the legitimacy of that counting process and that one side would eventually acknowledge its defeat by virtue of fewer votes. This subversion, although animated by familiar racial, historical and cultural tensions, was different in character from anything in American history.

In 1860, the slave-holding southern states did not deny that Abraham Lincoln had been elected; they simply declined to remain part of the country that had elected him. Historians still cannot agree on who really won the disputed states of Florida, Louisiana and South Carolina in the election of 1876 near the end of Reconstruction; the underlying question, in any event, was not the vote count but whether the Union victors would continue to enforce full civil rights for emancipated slaves, and the compromise answer, rendered by a commission appointed to resolve the dispute, was 'no'. This compromise, reflecting, in part, the North's exhaustion with Reconstruction, meant that African Americans in the

South would be disenfranchised and oppressed for nearly a century until the civil-rights legislation of the 1960s. The presidential election of 2000 in the decisive state of Florida was an effective tie: after the US Supreme Court decision that stopped the recount, George W. Bush was ahead by 537 votes, a victory margin of 0.009%.

The narratives pushed by Trump and lawyers filing lawsuits on his behalf included claims that droves of the dead had voted in Michigan and Pennsylvania; that voting machines managed by Dominion Voting Systems had been manipulated to delete millions of Trump votes in a scheme tied to Venezuela and its president Hugo Chávez (incidentally, also dead since March 2013); and that employees of an Italian defence contractor conspired with the CIA to direct military satellites to change the results. These outlandish claims fed the conviction among a majority of Republican voters, according to opinion polls, that the presidential election was stolen.

Republicans in Congress indulged this conviction. 6 January marked the ceremonial process wherein the US vice president records electoral votes sent by the states and 'certifies' their validity, barring objection from majorities of both Houses of Congress. On this occasion, however, as the mob was breaking into the Capitol, most Republican members of the House of Representatives and a dozen Republican senators did object – or were starting to do so – before they had to flee for their lives. Upon returning to business after the insurrectionists had finally vacated the building, all the Democrats and some Republicans provided the majorities to duly confirm Biden's election.

A conceptual wall had been breached, however – an opening to the idea that an obviously fair election result might be simply overturned in the US Congress or state legislatures. Until this moment, only president Trump himself, and possibly his lawyer, former New York mayor Rudy Giuliani, appeared to believe that the vice president had the power to change the election result. Upon repetition of the idea, some millions of Trump supporters adopted the narrative. Others in the Trump entourage appeared to be mainly humouring him. The shock of the insurrection did seem to suggest to Republican lawmakers, for a few days at least, that this idea was a dangerous one. This chastening was expressed by the Republican Senate Majority Leader Mitch McConnell, who called Trump 'practically, and morally, responsible' for the 6 January insurrection, adding:

> the people who stormed this building believed they were acting on the wishes and instructions of their president, and having that belief was a foreseeable consequence of the growing crescendo of false statements, conspiracy theories and reckless hyperbole which the defeated president kept shouting into the largest megaphone on planet earth.

Clear as these words were, however, they came after McConnell had led most Republican senators in voting to acquit Trump in his second impeachment trial in February 2021. Over subsequent months it became evident that the former president was not going to fade away to take up a quiet retirement; rather, he would dominate the Republican Party and demand fealty to the myth of a stolen election.

This demand took concrete form when Liz Cheney, an arch-conservative Republican congresswoman from Wyoming and third in the House Republican leadership, refused to submit to it. She spoke against Trump's 'Big Lie', calling it a serious threat to American democracy. In consequence, there were two Republican-caucus votes to eject her from the leadership. The first, on 4 February, she won comfortably. The second, after Republican House members had had another 14 weeks to recognise the former president's continued grip on their party, Cheney lost decisively. Trump, meanwhile, promised to promote primary challenges against Cheney and other Republicans who had voted for his impeachment. And by July 2021, he was setting an even higher test of fealty to his leadership – loyal Republicans could no longer merely discount the Capitol insurrection as unimportant or irrelevant. Instead, Trump made clear, the violent insurrectionists were to be valorised for fighting – in some cases dying – to overturn a fraudulent election.

The mythology of the stolen election animated the next phase of American political conflict: in the first half of 2021, Republican state legislatures enacted 24 new laws to restrict access to voting and – most significantly – to give legislatures the power to throw out results that they might deem problematic. In other words, Trump's 6 January fantasy of simply annulling the election result could become real in 2024.

Democrats could, in theory, pass federal laws to protect against that prospect, and two major voting-rights packages were introduced, including a bill named after the civil-rights icon John Lewis (whose own head was bashed bloody in 1965, when he attempted to lead a voting-rights march across the Edmund Pettus Bridge in Selma, Alabama). But to pass these laws, Democrats would need to reform or abolish the Senate rules surrounding the filibuster, which has evolved into a supermajority requirement for most legislation that the minority party – now the Republicans – decides to oppose. And a small group of more conservative Democrats, notably West Virginia's Joe Manchin, reject such reforms as violating their commitment to 'bipartisan' comity.

The threat to democracy appeared genuine, a consequence of trends that, since at least the beginning of the century, were making elections no longer civil contests for the alternation of political power, but existential battlefields for incompatible futures. Why was one of the two major political parties driving this trend? Some argued that demographic and attitudinal change – the leftward drift of young voters; the growing share of ethnic minorities – meant that Republicans could only thrive politically by turning the constitutional levers of protection for political minorities into weapons of minority rule. A Republican candidate had won the presidential popular vote only once since 1988, yet Republicans nonetheless held the presidency for half of the three subsequent decades.

America's disparate identities, aggravated by economic grievances, have become fiercely polarising. Income disparities have grown vastly since the 1980s, mirroring disparities in cultural and economic vitality and separating cities from rural and small-town communities. These effects were sharpened by the processes of globalisation that brought American manufacturing workers into direct competition with hundreds of millions of lower-wage workers from China. The property boom of the early 2000s temporarily alleviated the most baleful consequences of this competition by giving lower-middle-class Americans seemingly easy access to housing wealth through sub-prime mortgages. But they were left worse off when that housing bubble exploded in the 2008 financial crisis.

The embrace of identity politics by significant segments of the educated and leftist young – along with university administrators and, perhaps more surprisingly, corporate human-resources departments – has arguably added a left-wing cultural illiberalism to the right's racial and political illiberalism. It has certainly heightened a climate of cultural conflict and may have contributed to a countervailing embrace of white identity.

Democratic stability and American power

The crisis of American democracy has unnerved America's allies and encouraged its adversaries. 'What happened today in Washington DC is not American, definitely', said French President Emmanuel Macron, who belongs to the former camp, on 6 January. To which Konstantin Kosachev, head of the Foreign Affairs Committee in Russia's Federation Council, in effect countered: 'the celebration of democracy is over … America no longer forges that path, and consequently has lost its right to define it. Much less force it on others.' At the same time, a Chinese foreign-ministry spokesperson compared the Capitol siege to repressed Hong Kong protests – except, she said, no one had died in Hong Kong.

The Biden administration's foreign policy is founded on the revival of American alliances, with the corollary premise that this requires a credible revival of American democracy. 'Credible' means, in the first instance, that American allies in Europe and elsewhere can be reasonably confident that the Trump presidency was an aberration and not a harbinger of the American future.

Biden himself laid out this vision during his first full White House press conference in late March 2021. America with its allies should be able to prove, Biden argued, that liberal, social-welfare, capitalist democracy will win a competition with Chinese and Russian autocracy. He was drawing on a familiar historical model. The post-Second World War

American leadership was determined to consolidate and improve on Franklin D. Roosevelt's New Deal and, indeed, export it as a 'global New Deal'. This was the plan even before rivalry with the Soviet Union intensified. In the ensuing Cold War, the liberal anti-communists who, for the most part, governed the US until the late 1960s, embraced civil rights for African Americans, enhanced and legally protected union power, and supported progressive taxation along with other fiscal and economic policies that were directed at boosting the middle class and limiting the concentration of wealth.

But this aspiration to summon the past in the service of the future will be viable only if America can transcend the disunity that, although clearly predating the rise of Trump, found a new apotheosis during his presidency. In this regard it is important to note that Republican administrations of the mid- to late twentieth century were conservative but rarely regressive. Dwight D. Eisenhower set the pattern during his two terms in 1953–61, repudiating not just the isolationism associated with senator Robert Taft, but also any serious effort to roll back the New Deal in domestic policy. Richard Nixon's 'Southern Strategy' of 1968 helped inflame resentments of the Civil War, but the domestic policies of his presidency were consistent with the orthodoxy of the time that 'we are all Keynesians now'. President Ronald Reagan launched a starker ideological attack on New Deal assumptions, and during his period in office new wealth-concentration and income disparities began and have continued to widen. Again, however, his administration's policies, enacted in concert with Democratic Congresses, were less than radical.

There are some reasons for optimism. COVID-19 vaccines are now plentiful in the US and emergence from the coronavirus scourge could renew Americans' confidence. A strong economic recovery looks likely: the pandemic produced, as economist Paul Krugman puts it, an induced economic coma rather than a balance-sheet recession as after 2008; household savings have gone up, not down, and pent-up demand for the fruits of leisure suggests a major economic expansion may lie ahead. There is reason, moreover, to expect that technological advances, such as artificial intelligence and renewable energy, will yield productivity gains.

Biden's radical centrism seems politically potent; he is a Harry Truman-style middle American who combines familiar and reassuring cultural tropes with a once-familiar social-democratic ethos. His infrastructure and spending programmes, at roughly US$4.5 trillion, are radically ambitious but generally popular. If enacted, they are likely to raise incomes. Some might argue that political dysfunction matters less than economic vitality and that America cannot be truly ungovernable while it remains rich, productive and a supplier of the global reserve currency.

But this optimism is not entirely persuasive. The crisis of American democracy, rooted in cultural and identity divisions, is unlikely to be solved even by renewed prosperity. In summer 2021, COVID-19 was surging and killing across the large swathes of America that rejected the Biden presidency and, by extension, its public-health guidance. Vaccine doses were plentiful but demand for them was falling. Variations in vaccination rates across states correlated closely with political support for Trump or Biden. The Delta variant of the virus was raging through Trump-supporting, unvaccinated populations, and Republican politicians did not try to persuade their constituents to get vaccinated.

Democratic stability cannot be taken for granted. Biden will turn 81 in 2024. As the first female and mixed-race vice president, Kamala Harris, who may succeed Biden for the party leadership, will evoke racist and misogynist opposition. Another fierce contest, not just over policy but over basic democratic rules, is likely. It is arguable that fears of democratic breakdown are overstated, and it is true that, at the crucial decision points of 2020, key Republican officials held firm against Trump's pressures and affirmed the validity of Biden's victory in their respective states. Optimists also point out that Trump failed even with the powers of an executive branch that Biden will control in 2024.

However, it emerged in August 2021 that in the weeks after his defeat Trump had pursued not just outlandish theories and frivolous lawsuits, but also a more plausible plan for nullifying the result. An ally in the Justice Department, acting assistant attorney general Jeffrey Clark, had drafted a letter calling on the legislatures of six states with the closest races to take note of 'irregularities' in their elections and therefore to convene special sessions to 'determine whether those violations show which candidate for President won the most legal votes in the November 3 election', and to replace the slate of Biden electors with Trump electors. This scheme would have exploited a constitutional anomaly – although it is an established norm that a state's electors go to the candidate with a plurality of electoral votes, the text of the US Constitution simply states that the electors be appointed 'in such Manner as the Legislature thereof may direct'. The Trump scheme failed when top Justice Department officials including the acting attorney general refused to sign the letter. But some Republican state legislators are proposing laws that would give state legislatures or presumptively Republican partisan officials greater power to decide the winner, diminishing the authority of state election officials.

The most alarming prospect is a close 2024 presidential competition with a contested outcome. Given that most Republican voters have already rejected the legitimacy of an election that was not particularly close, their potential reaction to an actual cliffhanger gives cause for concern.

The Biden administration faces daunting challenges. It is difficult to see how it can lead global cooperation against catastrophic climate change if it cannot persuade such a large share of its people to inoculate themselves against the more immediate threat of COVID-19. And it is hard to be confident in American leadership of Western democracies against authoritarian rivals when the future of its own democracy is uncertain.

Trump's Legacy for America's National-security Institutions
Can the damage be repaired?

President Donald Trump was not inclined to build consensus behind America's foreign policy. He was also wary of an entrenched federal bureaucracy, sometimes referred to as 'the administrative state', which he feared would be insufficiently obedient to him. A major casualty of these predispositions was the robust inter-agency national-security decision-making process that the US National Security Council (NSC) staff customarily supervised. Developed and steadily enhanced since the NSC's inception in 1947, the process was meant to ensure that the risks and benefits of possible US foreign and security policies and measures were systematically raised, dissected and discussed, and collective conclusions reached, to inform executive action. Brent Scowcroft, a former US Air Force general, was seen as having set the standard for exemplary NSC stewardship during the administration of George H.W. Bush – especially in steering the preparation and conduct of the 1991 Gulf War – by coordinating the recommendations of the secretary of state, secretary of defense, CIA director and other principals through a smoothly functioning NSC staff.

Trump damaged this process by discouraging his national security advisors from conscientiously and thoroughly implementing the inter-agency process. The key national-security decision-making mechanisms developed over 70 years are Deputies Committee and Principals Committee meetings. Policy options are vetted first through deputy-level officials and then through principals before being presented to the president. On fast-moving and strategically critical matters, Deputies Committee meetings can occur several times a week and Principals Committee meetings as often as once a week. During the Trump administration, meetings of both committees became very infrequent.

An atrophied inter-agency process
Rather than rely on an effective NSC process, as previous presidents had done, Trump formed a small group to dictate foreign policy. This

consisted of Trump himself, the secretary of state (Rex Tillerson in 2017–18, and Mike Pompeo thereafter) and three successive national security advisors. H.R. McMaster, Trump's first national security advisor following Michael Flynn's abortive three-week stint, was an active-duty army general and a firm institutionalist who stuck to the prevailing model of an NSC that formulated, implemented and controlled foreign policy through a proactive inter-agency process. But Trump was impatient with McMaster's conventionality, and threatened by his discomfort with Trump's transactional sensibility, impulsive policymaking by Twitter, and disruptive approaches to policy on Iran, North Korea and NATO. The White House forced him out in April 2018 and replaced him with John Bolton, a conservative ideologue and foreign-policy hawk whom Trump correctly believed would minimise the inter-agency process. This left Trump freer to, among other things, impulsively and without consultation announce the redeployment of US forces in northern Syria in December 2018, which exposed their Kurdish allies to Turkish aggression and prompted James Mattis's resignation as secretary of defense.

But Bolton eventually found Trump's foreign policy incoherent and his megalomania intolerable. In September 2019, he was replaced by Robert O'Brien, a lawyer with little experience in running a policymaking bureaucracy, who had served as chief hostage negotiator for the State Department and had publicly praised Trump's foreign policy. O'Brien refrained from challenging Trump or Pompeo, seeing himself more as a mediator or coordinator than an advocate. While he held more meetings than Bolton did, this did not translate into a robust inter-agency process.

The traditional NSC process was designed to ensure that inordinately risky foreign-policy options were not presented to the president. A telling illustration of its failure was Trump's decision to order the killing of Iranian Major-General Qasem Soleimani, commander of the Islamic Revolutionary Guard Corps (IRGC) Quds Force – arguably Iran's most powerful and venerated figure after Supreme Leader Sayyid Ali Khamenei – in January 2020 in Iraq. Initially prompted by unruly public protests against the US presence and attacks by Iranian proxies on US targets there, including one that killed a US contractor, the decision was purportedly based on intelligence that the IRGC was planning attacks on US targets in the region. While the picture of the decision-making process was not entirely clear from open sources, reliable reporting reflected a scattershot approach involving little inter-agency deliberation, with various close advisers flying back and forth between Washington DC and Trump's Florida home at Mar-a-Lago, where he made the decision. While Trump's principals framed the strike as the boldest of three possible options, and one that few reportedly considered the best, a process of full inter-agency deliberation might well have kept it from reaching Trump's desk at all.

Conditioned by Trump's impatience with process, his principals did not adequately consider several basic criteria of sound executive options. Firstly, the presented course of action should be consistent with international and domestic law. It was always clear that targeting Soleimani was arguably assassination, barred by both types of law and a classic *casus belli*, and it has made the US vulnerable to charges of criminality and hypocrisy. Secondly, proportionality is important. Assassinating the second-most-powerful Iranian official in response to demonstrations and the death of one US contractor was overkill and appeared to indicate excessive US eagerness to escalate. Thirdly, strategic context is key. While the strike was a tactical success, it impeded the strategic objectives of countering the Islamic State (also known as ISIS or ISIL) and other Sunni jihadist groups; stabilising Iraq; advancing diplomacy with Iran on nuclear and other issues; discouraging Iran from ramping up uranium enrichment; preserving intelligence and security cooperation with Iraq; and protecting American troops deployed in the region, who were subsequently targeted. Principals and deputies might also have stressed that for an administration seeking to manage great-power competition it was illogical to set the US on a path of escalation in a region it had hoped to calm so it could address more pressing strategic concerns with China and Russia.

Compromised agencies

Trump's undermining of an effective NSC-led inter-agency process was exacerbated by his choice of principals to lead the agencies central to that process.

Tillerson, Trump's first secretary of state, was the former chief executive officer of ExxonMobil. He was unschooled as a diplomat or government bureaucrat, and sought to use his corporate sensibility to streamline the State Department and make it more efficient, as a corporate raider might do with a recently acquired takeover target. Instead, he ended up isolating himself and decimating the ranks of experienced Foreign Service officers and State Department civil servants, leaving the department dispirited and understaffed. Pompeo did little to repair the damage. Hundreds of veteran diplomats retired or resigned, some the targets of partisan political purges, which diminished institutional knowledge and competence. Scores of senior positions and ambassadorships were left vacant or filled by acting officials, including 11 posts for assistant secretary and under-secretary, normally the workhorses of US diplomacy. Ethical standards diminished: seven times as many State Department employees in 2019 felt they could not report official improprieties without fear of reprisal as in 2016. Department morale probably reached a low point during Trump's impeachment trial from December 2019 to February 2020, which exposed the administration's departures from State Department protocol in pressuring Ukrainian officials to investigate presidential candidate Joe Biden and his son Hunter for corruption, and in dismissing Marie Yovanovitch – the US ambassador to Ukraine and a distinguished career diplomat – for resisting this.

In addition, the Trump administration downgraded overseas development and humanitarian assistance, proposing cuts (which were partially rolled back by Congress) to the US Agency for International Development (USAID)'s budget of more than 20% in each of Trump's four years in office in line with his 'America First' approach to foreign policy. The White House's liaison to the agency also staffed USAID with anti-Islamic and anti-LGBT political appointees, further hurting morale.

The US intelligence and law-enforcement communities were also embattled under Trump. Convinced that a 'deep state' was trying to undermine him, he rejected CIA assessments that Russia had interfered with the 2016 US election, dismissed its conclusion that Iran was adhering to the Joint Comprehensive Plan of Action constraining its nuclear programme, ignored its early warnings about COVID-19 and minimised its assessment that Russia was interfering in the 2020 election. His appointments of unqualified loyalists to positions intended for apolitical professionals undermined the integrity and professionalism of the intelligence community. They politicised the relationship between the White House and intelligence agencies, and may have impaired intelligence collection and analysis. While the CIA itself generally resisted Trump's efforts at co-optation, its leadership may have overreached in certain instances to accommodate him.

Trump supported and even cheered federal law-enforcement agencies, such as Customs and Border Protection, and Immigration and Customs Enforcement, which executed policies such as restricting immigration and securing the US border with Mexico. But from the outset of his administration, Trump targeted the FBI, the largest and most powerful federal law-enforcement agency, first dismissing its director James Comey over his refusal to back away from investigating Russian election interference, then attempting to hinder special counsel Robert Mueller's investigation of that interference, which was implemented mainly by FBI personnel. The attorney general, William Barr, who espoused the 'unitary executive' theory that accords the president substantially unchecked authority over the executive branch of government, sanitised Mueller's findings and sometimes used the Justice Department to advance Trump's personal political agenda, damaging morale and retention.

Among the primary national-security institutions, the Department of Defense was relatively stable during Trump's presidency. It largely maintained day-to-day, political–military business as usual with the United States' allies in a partially successful effort to blunt the effect of Trump's anti-alliance, and especially anti-NATO, rhetoric. The Pentagon also managed to stave off any potentially catastrophic US military action against North Korea when Trump's incendiary language made this look likely in 2018.

In addition, the Department of Defense maintained its constitutional integrity when, in June 2020, General Mark Milley, chairman of the Joint Chiefs of Staff, and Mark Esper, secretary of defense, publicly rejected Trump's attempts to involve active-duty US military personnel in the suppression of domestic civil-rights protests. On 1 June, Trump had ordered administration officials to mobilise low-flying military helicopters and military police to help law-enforcement personnel clear a path through a peaceful Black Lives Matter protest so that he could walk from the White House across Lafayette Square for a photo opportunity outside a church. Flanking him were Milley (in combat fatigues) and Esper as well as Barr and other senior officials. Trump wanted a larger deployment of troops in Washington, and the Pentagon placed a 1,600-strong rapid-reaction unit drawn from the 82nd Airborne Division and several military police units on standby near the city. Trump aides drafted a proclamation by which he could invoke the Insurrection Act of 1807, which authorises the president to deploy the armed forces domestically to suppress civil disorder when ordinary law enforcement cannot. But senior officials persuaded him not to attempt to use that authority.

Under the Posse Comitatus Act of 1878, the military cannot be used to enforce domestic civilian law unless expressly authorised by the Constitution or an act of Congress. Exceptions, including the Insurrection Act, are narrowly construed. After the Lafayette Square incident, retired and active senior US military officers made it clear that they did not believe the military should intervene against protesters and that conditions in the US did not warrant military involvement to ensure public safety and order. The pointed objections to Trump's show of military force of James Mattis (a retired four-star Marine general and former secretary of defense), Michael Mullen (a retired four-star admiral and former chairman of the Joint Chiefs of Staff), Martin Dempsey (a retired four-star general and former chairman of the Joint Chiefs) and a contrite Milley appeared to have deterred the president from further attempts to use the active-duty military, and to a lesser extent the National Guard, to advance his domestic political interests. Their statements implicitly recognised the duty of military officers to uphold the Constitution – even in the event of a direct order to the contrary. Milley told the House Armed Services Committee in August 2020 that he could 'foresee no role for the US armed forces' in the electoral process and that he would 'not follow an unlawful order'.

Other agencies did not emerge from summer 2020 untainted. Barr spuriously tried to justify the use of US forces in domestic policing roles. Moreover, through the tortuous application of federal statutes and partisan appointments, Trump effectively converted elements of the Department of Homeland Security (DHS) – originally established after 9/11 to counter foreign-sourced terrorist threats – into a domestic anti-protest strike force, downplaying right-wing extremist threats and exaggerating left-wing ones. To implement this agenda, the Trump administration drew liberally on federal agencies – including the FBI; the Bureau of Alcohol, Tobacco, Firearms and Explosives; Customs and Border Protection; the Drug Enforcement Administration; Immigration and Customs Enforcement; the US Marshals Service; the Federal Bureau of Prisons; and the hitherto obscure Federal Protective Service – with very different statutory missions and insufficient training for urban policing. The administration deployed hundreds of personnel to several American cities in unmarked vehicles and wearing combat fatigues with insignia of their affiliations obscured, affording them expansive rules of engagement. This was done largely against the wishes of state and local governments, several of which filed lawsuits or passed ordinances opposing the deployments.

In the flammable political climate, the administration overtly linked the deployments to the false claim that, if elected president, Biden would defund police forces. Trump's re-election campaign also made hyperbolic assertions that 'dangerous mobs of far-left groups are running through our streets and causing absolute mayhem'. Meanwhile, Trump condoned more disruptive and threatening actions by his supporters. In casting 'law and order' as the centrepiece of his presidential campaign and establishing a precedent for deploying a purpose-built anti-protest force, it appeared that Trump hoped to find a plausible excuse for using such a force to suppress Democratic voting through intimidation. In the event, protesters stood down and declined to provide him with that pretext. But his politicisation of domestic law enforcement at the federal level did appear to embolden his far-right supporters, whose ire over his defeat in the election culminated in the violent breach of the Capitol on 6 January 2021. Given the degree of disruption to the normal conduct of government during the Trump administration, it was unsurprising that the rate of turnover of senior White House advisers and cabinet department heads during his term exceeded that of each of the five previous presidencies.

The Biden administration's repairs

The harm that the Trump administration inflicted on the United States' national-security apparatus was extensive. By weakening the NSC-led national-security-policy and decision-making process, it removed the implicit guarantee of informed and expert bureaucratic consensus behind US government policy and action. By hollowing out and marginalising important agencies, it damaged the morale of many federal employees and prompted some to leave government, draining it of valuable talent. By instrumentalising elements of the federal law-enforcement apparatus for Trump's domestic political agenda, the administration politicised US governance to an unprecedented degree. The net results were a disorganised and enervated American national-security bureaucracy that was disconnected from the actual decision-makers and was denied the opportunity to effectively speak truth to power, and a garrisoned administration that viewed a substantial portion of the US population as its enemies. The incoming Biden administration appeared to appreciate the nature and extent of the damage and the need to address it firmly. While Trump disregarded the traditional norms of national security and governance, Biden and his team appeared committed to restoring them.

Biden's two most important national-security appointments were Antony Blinken, his secretary of state, and Jake Sullivan, his national security advisor. Both are strong Atlanticists, signalling the new administration's determination to rebuild the alliances – especially NATO – that Trump disparaged. Both officials served in senior roles at the NSC and the State Department during the Barack Obama administration, in which the NSC choreographed a notably vigorous inter-agency process and the State Department was fully empowered. Blinken focused early on boosting morale and intends to elevate professional career diplomats as opposed to political appointees. Biden also appointed Samantha Power to head USAID. As a former US ambassador to the United Nations and Pulitzer Prize-winning author, she lent gravitas and a high profile to an agency that has customarily been a bureaucratic wallflower. She has already staked out the international distribution of COVID-19 vaccines as a USAID priority and framed it as a means of re-establishing the United States' status as an indispensable nation. Sullivan, for his part, held the first all-hands NSC meeting in over a year on 28 January 2021. The new NSC reflected the centrality of the inter-agency process to policy formulation and implementation in responding to the coup in Myanmar in early February with a new sanctions package from the Treasury Department, the redirection of USAID assistance away from the Myanmar military and coordinated messaging from multiple agencies.

The administration also moved to establish better order in the federal-intelligence and law-enforcement communities. Biden chose William Burns, a career diplomat and former deputy secretary of state, to head the CIA, foremost in the constellation of US intelligence agencies. Though not an intelligence insider, Burns was widely respected, deeply versed in the inter-agency process and guaranteed to have the ear of Biden, Blinken and Sullivan. The same was true of Avril Haines, Biden's director of national intelligence, who had served as deputy CIA director and deputy national security advisor in the Obama administration. At the February 2021 Munich Security Conference, Biden proclaimed that 'America is back'. At the G7 summit in June, he won praise from European leaders for restoring American civility, cooperation and leadership after what one participant called the 'complete chaos' that Trump had wrought. But the administration's urgent tasks extended beyond bringing back experienced players and re-instituting an effective policy process. Biden acknowledged a direct connection between fixing US government and restoring America's international credibility. Thus, his administration committed itself to restoring non-partisan professionalism in a federal government in which extreme partisanship had been allowed to flourish.

Doing so crucially involves addressing far-right domestic extremism. Soon after Biden was sworn in as president, he tasked Haines with coordinating with the DHS and the FBI on a top-to-bottom assessment of the domestic extremist threat. They found that 'newer sociopolitical developments' such as the pandemic and the rise of right-wing conspiracy theories would 'almost certainly' spur violence in 2021. Furthermore, the DHS and the Pentagon in particular faced stiff internal challenges in purging their ranks of extremists whose training and expertise could make far-right groups especially formidable. Given the involvement of veterans, active-duty soldiers and law-enforcement officers in the 6 January insurrection of the Capitol, the DHS and the Justice Department also had to worry about extremists on the payrolls of state and local law-enforcement organisations. Attorney General Merrick Garland and Secretary of Homeland Security Alejandro Mayorkas made rolling back the right-wing domestic extremism that Trump had encouraged their top priority. Refocusing relevant agencies and re-energising the NSC-led inter-agency process are necessary to forge an effective policy against domestic extremism. The administration's comprehensive, multi-agency strategy for combating domestic terrorism, announced by Garland on 15 June, was a product of this process. But it was clear this would not be sufficient. Genuine bipartisanship in Congress and stronger national consensus are also crucial, but remain elusive.

MONGOLIA

NORTH KOREA

JAPAN

AFGHANISTAN

SOUTH KOREA

PAKISTAN

CHINA

NEPAL

BHUTAN

BANGLADESH

MYANMAR

TAIWAN

INDIA

LAOS

VIETNAM

THAILAND

CAMBODIA

PHILIPPINES

SRI LANKA

BRUNEI

MALAYSIA

SINGAPORE

I N D O N E S I A

PAPUA NEW GUINEA

SOLOMON ISLANDS

TIMOR-LESTE

VANUATU

FIJI

AUSTRALIA

NEW ZEALAND

©IISS

Drivers of Strategic Change

REGIONAL SHARE OF GLOBAL POPULATION, GDP AND DEFENCE BUDGET

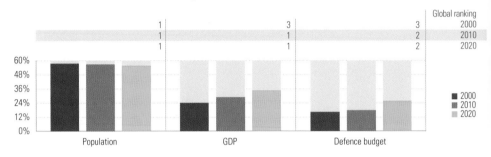

	Population	GDP	Defence budget	Global ranking
2000	1	3	3	2000
2010	1	1	2	2010
2020	1	1	2	2020

POPULATION

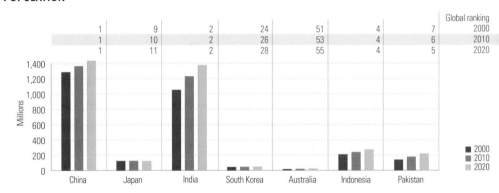

	China	Japan	India	South Korea	Australia	Indonesia	Pakistan	Global ranking
2000	1	9	2	24	51	4	7	2000
2010	1	10	2	26	53	4	6	2010
2020	1	11	2	28	55	4	5	2020

AGE STRUCTURE
(Percentage of national population)

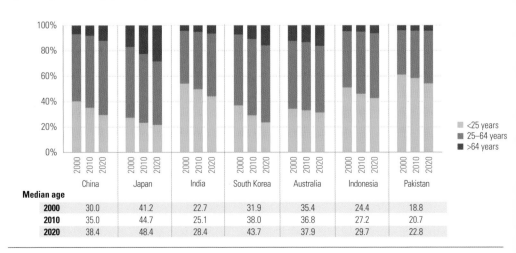

Median age	China	Japan	India	South Korea	Australia	Indonesia	Pakistan
2000	30.0	41.2	22.7	31.9	35.4	24.4	18.8
2010	35.0	44.7	25.1	38.0	36.8	27.2	20.7
2020	38.4	48.4	28.4	43.7	37.9	29.7	22.8

Legend: <25 years, 25–64 years, >64 years

Asia has the biggest GDP and population of any region. It is also the most diverse, with huge variations in power and performance between countries. China's remarkable economic growth has fuelled huge increases in defence and living standards. But prosperity has brought less, not more, freedom. With a median age now higher than America's, China will face demographic challenges.

GDP
(Constant 2010 US dollars)

	China	Japan	India	South Korea	Australia	Indonesia	Pakistan	Global ranking
	5	2	14	16	12	19	48	2000
	2	3	9	14	13	18	48	2010
	2	3	5	13	12	17	45	2020

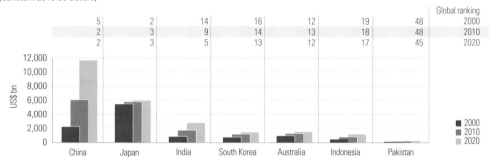

US$bn

- 2000
- 2010
- 2020

GDP PER CAPITA
(Constant 2010 US dollars)

	China	Japan	India	South Korea	Australia	Indonesia	Pakistan	Global ranking
	125	13	159	41	7	117	158	2000
	100	17	152	37	7	119	163	2010
	74	15	143	30	6	106	162	2020

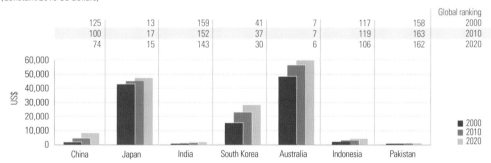

US$

- 2000
- 2010
- 2020

DEFENCE BUDGET
(Constant 2015 US dollars)

ACTIVE MILITARY PERSONNEL

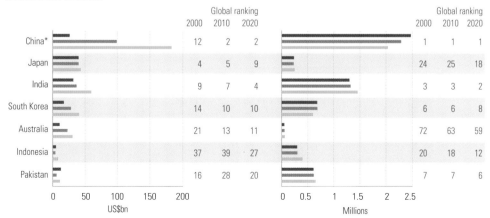

	Defence budget Global ranking 2000	2010	2020	Active military personnel Global ranking 2000	2010	2020
China*	12	2	2	1	1	1
Japan	4	5	9	24	25	18
India	9	7	4	3	3	2
South Korea	14	10	10	6	6	8
Australia	21	13	11	72	63	59
Indonesia	37	39	27	20	18	12
Pakistan	16	28	20	7	7	6

US$bn

Millions

*2000 defence budget value for China is an estimate, and may be distorted by high inflation rates.

- 2000
- 2010
- 2020

For explanation of drivers and sources, see page 9

HUMAN DEVELOPMENT INDEX (HDI)
(Score between 0 and 1, where 0 denotes a low level of development and 1 a high level of development)

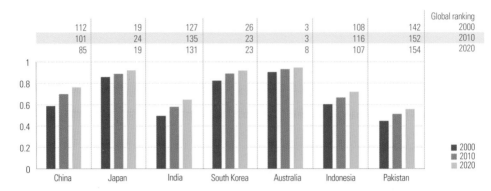

							Global ranking
112	19	127	26	3	108	142	2000
101	24	135	23	3	116	152	2010
85	19	131	23	8	107	154	2020

■ 2000
■ 2010
■ 2020

POLITICAL SYSTEM
(Score between 0 and 100, where 0 denotes no political freedom and 100 fully free)

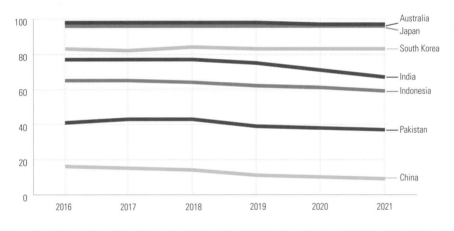

TRUST IN GOVERNMENT
(Average level of trust)

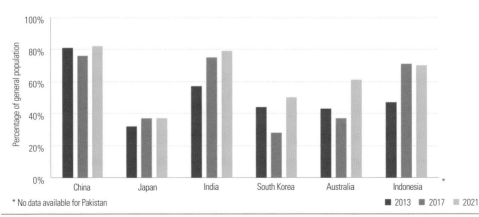

Percentage of general population

* No data available for Pakistan

■ 2013 ■ 2017 ■ 2021

2020–21 Review

Asia-Pacific

In the Asia-Pacific region, the COVID-19 pandemic preoccupied governments while strategic competition also intensified. Many official responses to COVID-19 during 2020 were widely recognised as more effective than those of their counterparts in Europe, North America and elsewhere in limiting both infection and mortality rates. By the second quarter of 2021, however, India and Malaysia had joined Indonesia and the Philippines in a group of large countries where the pandemic was essentially out of control.

At the same time, some Asian states – including Japan, Singapore, South Korea, Taiwan, Thailand and Vietnam – that had emerged relatively unscathed from the pandemic's first year were also struggling to control new waves of COVID-19 infections. The emergence of new variants of the SARS-CoV-2 coronavirus – including a particularly virulent one originating in India – partially explained the pandemic's resurgence across the region. However, official and public complacency deriving from early success, combined with the consequent failure to establish mass-vaccination programmes sufficiently quickly, also helped to explain some Asian countries' worsening COVID-19 predicament. But, assuming that publicly available data was accurate, China – where the disease apparently originated in late 2019 – stood out as an exception. While COVID-19 outbreaks continued across the country, rigorous containment measures, supplemented by a vaccination programme that ramped up from the end of 2020, limited their impact, allowing the economy to grow by 18.3% year-on-year during the first three months of 2021.

China's relative success in containing the pandemic domestically, combined with its early development of vaccines, also allowed it to engage extensively in 'vaccine diplomacy', supplying other countries that had initially found it difficult to procure supplies from Western producers. By mid-2021, Beijing had exported hundreds of millions of vaccine doses to almost 100 countries worldwide, nearly 70 of which were relatively poor nations given free supplies. In December 2020,

Indonesia was among the first countries to receive vaccines from China's Sinovac Biotech, after the same company had conducted clinical trials there; local production began the following month. During the first half of 2021, China also supplied or offered to supply vaccines in varying quantities to the other nine members of the Association of Southeast Asian Nations (ASEAN).

However, the extent to which these efforts increased China's influence in Southeast Asia was questionable. While early donations to Cambodia and Laos from February onwards may have helped maintain already close relations, elsewhere the impact was mixed. It was widely understood in Southeast Asia that Chinese vaccines were significantly less effective than their Western counterparts and, where there was a choice, many in the region preferred to avoid the former. In Myanmar, a widespread view that Beijing supported the military regime that seized power in February 2021 led to a boycott of Chinese vaccines. Similarly, in Vietnam, anti-Beijing sentiment deriving from nationalist resentment of Chinese activities in the South China Sea fuelled official and popular resistance to Chinese vaccines, though in June 2021 Hanoi approved the use of the Chinese-manufactured Sinopharm injections amid the pandemic's worsening impact on the country.

Conscious of the potential geopolitical implications of China's vaccine diplomacy, the United States and its major regional partners made strenuous efforts to compete. When US President Joe Biden met the premiers of Australia, India and Japan in virtual format for the first summit of Quadrilateral Security Dialogue ('Quad') leaders in early March 2021, a joint statement pledged their countries to – among other things – 'join forces to expand safe, affordable, and effective vaccine production and equitable access'. While the upsurge in infections in India meant that New Delhi's focus inevitably shifted towards protecting its own population rather than exporting vaccines, in early June senior US National Security Council coordinator for Indo-Pacific policy Kurt Campbell said he was 'relatively confident' that the Quad countries would produce, as planned, at least one billion vaccine doses for use across Asia by the end of 2022. In the short term, the US announced that it would donate

23m vaccine doses to Asian countries – notably Indonesia, the Philippines and Vietnam – through the international COVAX facility. During June, Japan delivered more than 1m vaccine doses to Taiwan and almost 1m doses to Vietnam; Japanese Foreign Minister Motegi Toshimitsu said his country was considering making similar donations to Indonesia, Malaysia, the Philippines and Thailand from early July. Australian Prime Minister Scott Morrison announced that his country would provide 20m doses to Asian and Pacific nations.

Intensifying strategic competition

While humanitarian motives may have partly accounted for this regional vaccine diplomacy, it also reflected more intense geopolitical contention across the Asia-Pacific. China continued to pursue its strategic goals throughout the region vigorously while the US, some of its allies and, to varying degrees, other regional states increasingly adopted counter-vailing diplomatic, economic and military measures. There was much speculation at the end of 2020 over the likely policies of the incoming US administration led by President-elect Biden towards the region. However, it quickly became clear that the political transition had only reinforced the United States' determination to stand up to the major challenge that it saw China as posing to its interests and those of regional states. Indeed, two and a half weeks after his inauguration, Biden spoke of his anticipation that there would be 'extreme competition' with China during his presidency. At the same time, some of the United States' regional partners – notably Washington's close allies, Australia and Japan – themselves also demonstrated growing resolve in standing up to Chinese pressure.

In response to growing Chinese political, economic and military pressure on Taiwan and fears that Beijing was contemplating an invasion in the medium term, the territory became an important focus for US strategic attention and for the intensifying rivalry between Washington and Beijing. While some of Washington's allies and security partners continued to steer well clear of commitments to support the US and Taiwan in the event of conflict, there were signs of incremental change on the part of key regional allies. A joint statement by Biden and Prime Minister Suga Yoshihide (who had succeeded Abe Shinzo, Japan's longest-serving prime minister, in September 2020 after the latter resigned owing to chronic illness), issued when Suga visited Washington in April 2021, 'underscored' the importance both attached to 'peace and stability in the Taiwan Strait'. Though Suga subsequently emphasised that Japan would provide only logistical support to US forces in a Taiwan conflict and would not deploy its own combat units, the joint statement fitted into a broader pattern of Tokyo signalling its support for Taiwan's freedom from Chinese intervention. The Biden–Suga statement followed similar consensus on Taiwan at a US–Japan '2+2' meeting in March, and in late May Japan and the European Union issued a statement making the same point. Behind the scenes, Japan's governing Liberal Democratic Party (LDP) Foreign Affairs Subcommittee organised the first meeting of its 'Taiwan Project Team' in February with the aim of strengthening relations with Taipei.

In Australia, governmental attitudes towards Beijing and the security threats it was widely perceived to pose to the region had become increasingly robust since revelations regarding domestic political-influence operations in 2017. Following Defence Minister Peter Dutton's assertion that a potential war over Taiwan could not be discounted, public debate erupted in April 2021 over the possibility of Australian forces supporting the US in a conflict there. While the government denied any change of policy on Taiwan, in May the Australian media reported that Canberra had stepped up its preparations for conflict over the island. While this was perhaps unsurprising given both the objective circumstances and Australia's increasingly close strategic collaboration with the US, it nevertheless highlighted the major change in the country's strategic outlook that had occurred over less than half a decade.

Chinese pressure also continued in the East and South China seas. In January 2021, Japan and several Southeast Asian countries were perturbed when the Standing Committee of China's National People's Congress passed a new law that appeared to give the China Coast Guard (CCG) new enforcement powers in all waters claimed by Beijing, including authorisation to open fire on foreign vessels and to destroy structures built on Chinese-claimed features. Tokyo's primary concern was over the implications for the Senkaku/Diaoyu islands. These are held by Japan but claimed by China, which frequently sends CCG vessels and maritime militia craft into the islands' contiguous zone and (less frequently) territorial waters. During 2020, such intrusions had continued at roughly the same historically high tempo that had prevailed since 2012, but the new Coast Guard law suggested that the Chinese challenge might intensify. Intrusions into territorial waters were indeed more frequent during February 2021 and again during April and May, and there were several incidents in which CCG vessels pursued Japanese fishing vessels near the Senkaku/Diaoyu islands. When Biden and Suga spoke in late January, only days after the former's inauguration, the new US president committed his administration to protect the islands. In March, LDP legislators proposed a revision of relevant legislation to allow the Japan Coast Guard to use force against intruders attempting to land on the Senkaku/Diaoyu islands.

In Southeast Asia, governments that claimed South China Sea features and resources appeared to grow increasingly frustrated with China's frequent failure to respect their interests. New tensions grew between Beijing and Manila over the presence from March 2021 of hundreds of Chinese fishing vessels (which Philippine authorities claimed were crewed by maritime militia personnel) near Pag-asa Island (also known as Thitu Island), the largest Philippine-occupied feature in the Spratly Islands. In early May, Philippine Secretary of Foreign Affairs Teodoro Locsin, Jr, demanded, in an expletive-laden tweet, that the Chinese vessels leave the area. Although Locsin's ministry reported soon after that it had held 'friendly and candid' talks on the South China Sea with its Chinese counterpart, within days it lodged a diplomatic protest demanding that Beijing withdraw its vessels.

Earlier, in March, Vietnam had also protested to Beijing over the presence of more than 200 Chinese vessels at Whitsun Reef. Responding to expanding Chinese activities, Vietnam strengthened its maritime militia operating from the south of the country with the aim of protecting its fishing fleet. At the end of May 2021, Malaysia also found itself on the front-line when its fighter aircraft intercepted a formation of 16 Chinese military transport aircraft that flew over its exclusive economic zone (EEZ) and into its flight information region near Sarawak State. While Beijing dismissed this as 'routine training', saying that it did not infringe Malaysia's national airspace or otherwise breach international law, Malaysia's government and many observers interpreted the incident as an unfriendly display of strength by China. Nevertheless, the perceived importance of avoiding any escalation of tension that might damage broader relations with China constrained Southeast Asian claimant states' reactions: this was clear from Philippine President Rodrigo Duterte's persistent efforts to moderate the Philippine government's posture, from Vietnam's reluctance to initiate international legal proceedings over Beijing's jurisdictional claims and activities (an idea that Hanoi had floated in 2019), and from Malaysia's generally cautious and conciliatory responses to Chinese assertiveness. Maintaining and further developing economic ties with China remained crucially important for Southeast Asian governments, but a widespread impulse to avoid alignment amid deteriorating Sino-American relations was also a significant influence on their South China Sea policies.

Concerns not to jeopardise wider links with Beijing also influenced Jakarta's posture. While Indonesia is not a South China Sea claimant state, in late 2019 and early 2020 its government and armed forces were increasingly concerned by the activities of Chinese fishing vessels supported by CCG vessels inside its EEZ near the Natuna Islands; Jakarta strengthened its military presence in the area as part of its response. However, that episode did not prevent Indonesia from agreeing with China – its largest trade partner and second-largest source of international investment – in June 2021 to create a 'platform for closer dialogue' intended to boost bilateral cooperation on COVID-19 vaccines and Belt and Road Initiative projects among other areas. Jakarta nevertheless attempted to use its largely positive wider relations with Beijing as a basis for blunting the sharp edges of China's maritime activities. In a meeting of ASEAN foreign ministers with their Chinese counterpart Wang Yi in June 2021, Indonesia's Retno Marsudi emphasised the importance for all parties of managing tensions in the South China Sea. She spoke of the need to resume talks on the Code of Conduct for the South China Sea (suspended since early 2020 because of COVID-19) and offered to host the next round of negotiations. She also encouraged all parties to comply with the existing Declaration on the Conduct of Parties, which requires 'self-restraint' in the South China Sea. However, the pro-Beijing orientation of some Southeast Asian governments (notably Cambodia's) suggested that, even if talks resumed soon, they would be unlikely to result in an agreement that would significantly restrict China's South China Sea activities.

Meanwhile, the strategic focus of the US and some of its allies and partners on the South China Sea sharpened in reaction to Chinese activities there. Recovering its deployment tempo after COVID-19 infections aboard ships temporarily undermined its operational readiness in East Asia in early 2020, the US Navy increased its presence and activities in the South China Sea, conducting ten freedom-of-navigation operations (FONOPs) there over the course of the year (compared with eight during 2019). The Trump administration also escalated its diplomatic pressure on Beijing over the South China Sea, rejecting China's 'nine-dash line' claim as unlawful, imposing sanctions on Chinese individuals linked to the reclamation and militarisation of outposts and blacklisting companies involved in expanding these 'artificial islands'. The Biden administration conducted four more FONOPs there between February and July 2021. The joint statement following the Quadrilateral Security Dialogue's virtual summit in March 2021 mentioned the importance of maintaining freedom of navigation and overflight together with the rule of international law in the maritime domain, and – more specifically – that the four powers would 'facilitate collaboration … to meet challenges to the rules-based maritime order in the East and South China Seas'. Several of the United States' European allies – France, Germany, the Netherlands and the United Kingdom – also expressed growing concern over perceived threats to maritime freedoms in Asian waters and announced plans to send warships to the region during 2021. It was expected that some of these deployments might include transits through the South China Sea.

Crisis in Myanmar

In February 2021, developments in Myanmar presented Southeast Asian governments and ASEAN with a major new challenge. Following the sweeping election victory of State Counsellor Aung San Suu Kyi's National League for Democracy in November 2020, which the leadership of the Tatmadaw (Myanmar's armed forces) viewed as a threat to its political and economic privileges, the Tatmadaw declared the election result illegitimate, overthrew the elected government, transferred power to commander-in-chief Senior General Min Aung Hlaing and imposed a year-long state of emergency. Aung San Suu Kyi and other government figures were detained incommunicado and faced criminal charges. Against the backdrop of the raging COVID-19 pandemic in the country, there was widespread civil unrest in protest of the coup and an upsurge in clashes between the Tatmadaw and ethnic-minority militias. By late April, the security forces had reportedly killed more than 700 protesters.

There was widespread international condemnation of the military takeover. China and Russia refused to support a UN Security Council resolution urging the 'restoration of democracy', but eventually a Security Council statement on 31 March called for an end to violence, military restraint, the release of Aung San Suu Kyi and other government figures, and a negotiated settlement. In Southeast Asia, some governments – notably of Indonesia, Malaysia, Singapore and eventually the Philippines – were openly critical of the Tatmadaw's seizure of power and called for ASEAN to take an active role in resolving Myanmar's political crisis. Other ASEAN member states were more reserved, and the grouping was slow to agree on a response to a challenge that was widely viewed as a test of its credibility. In late April, ASEAN convened an extraordinary Leaders' Meeting – including Myanmar's junta leader, Min Aung Hlaing – and established five points of consensus in relation to the crisis: an end to violence; constructive dialogue; facilitation of humanitarian aid; appointment of an ASEAN special envoy; and a visit to Myanmar by the special envoy to meet contending parties. In early June, ASEAN presented a list of potential nominees for the special envoy's role to the Myanmar authorities, but there was no indication of when the junta might agree to any of the nominees visiting. Meanwhile, ASEAN was as divided as ever, with several member states abstaining in a UN General Assembly vote in mid-June that overwhelmingly backed a return to democracy in Myanmar. In April, the military regime promised new elections within two years. It seemed more likely that any solution to the post-coup impasse would emerge from within rather than outside the country.

On the surface, one part of the region – the Korean Peninsula – seemed quieter in security terms than it had been since 2016–17, when the North Korean regime led by Kim Jong-un intensified its missile-testing and nuclear-weapons-development programmes. But while Pyongyang tested only two short-range ballistic missiles in March 2021, Kim's regime remained intent on strengthening North Korea's military capabilities in order eventually to secure a favourable outcome to negoti-ations with the US and intimidate South Korea and Japan. Kim promised to do exactly this two weeks before Biden took office. However, there was a glimpse of hope for a de-escalation of tension in late April when the Biden administration revealed the broad outlines of its prospective strategy towards North Korea, which contrasted with those of the two previous US administrations: according to the White House, the new policy 'will not focus on achieving a grand bargain nor will it rely on strategic patience'.

South Asia

Impact of COVID-19 in South Asia

The second wave of the COVID-19 pandemic from March 2021 contin-ued to significantly disrupt South Asian lives and livelihoods amid weak public-health infrastructure. India suffered the most cases and deaths, largely due to government overconfidence, the early easing of lockdown restrictions after a relatively moderate first wave, the emergence of the more transmissible Delta variant (first identified in India) and the absence of social restrictions at large events such as election rallies and religious gatherings. By early May, the official count of daily cases peaked at over

400,000, with the actual number assessed to be far higher. By the end of June 2021, India had recorded over 30 million cases of COVID-19, the highest after the United States; total deaths officially stood at over 400,000, although civil-society networks assessed the actual number of deaths in the range of 3.4m–4.9m. Daily cases started to reduce by late June, but the economy had contracted by 7.3% in 2020–21, India's first annual recession since 1980.

India's acute second COVID-19 wave led to a reversal of policy towards receiving foreign support. The United Kingdom was the first country to respond to India's acute oxygen requirements through the provision of oxygen concentrators, ventilators and other medical equipment. Over 50 other countries provided emergency supplies. The second wave also led to India abruptly halting its supplying of vaccines to the rest of the world, in order to prioritise its domestic requirements. From January to April, India had taken tremendous pride in publicising its vaccine diplomacy through the export of more than 66m Covishield doses to 95 countries through grants, commercial supplies and obligations to the COVAX initiative. These vaccines were manufactured in India by the Serum Institute of India (SII), the largest vaccine manufacturer in the world, and developed by Oxford-AstraZeneca. The void in the SII's commercial contracts began to be filled by supplies of Chinese and other vaccines. India's image worldwide was also hit hard by media reports and photographs of an acute lack of oxygen supplies for severely ill patients often resulting in heart failure and death.

The Delta variant also impacted neighbouring South Asian countries. In Pakistan, cases peaked in May at nearly 9,000 a day, with Pakistan's economy estimated to have contracted by 0.4% in 2020. In Bangladesh, COVID-19 cases rose rapidly to nearly 9,000 a day in late June and were expected to peak in July. However, while economies across Asia contracted, Bangladesh's economic growth was estimated at 3.8% in 2020, which was the highest growth across Asia. COVID-19 also impacted Afghanistan's fragile road map to peace, with cases rising rapidly during its severe second wave in late June.

Regional tensions

China–India tensions remained high amid aftershocks and uneasy new normal on their contested, undefined and undemarcated border. This followed the deaths in June 2020 of 20 Indian and reportedly five Chinese soldiers, the first fatalities on the border in 45 years. A February 2021 partial disengagement process focused only on the Pangong Lake area. Despite multiple rounds of subsequent military and minister-led diplomatic talks, specific friction points remained on the eastern Ladakh border, frustrating India's demand for a return to the May 2020 status quo and therefore likely stalling progress for months ahead. India's and China's militaries entrenched their year-long, unprecedented peacetime build-up using modern equipment, amid efforts to develop dual-use infrastructure to the rear. These conditions blighted prospects for any meaningful near-term political reset.

India's widening rift with China led to a growing strategic convergence with the US. This included countering China's assertive role on India's border, and its influence in the Indo-Pacific region, through strengthened defence and security ties. With India's support, the Quadrilateral dialogue (the 'Quad' – also consisting of Australia, Japan and the US) met for the first time at leadership level (in virtual format due to the pandemic) in March 2021. India also joined other G7 summit guests in signing an Open Societies Statement.

The Indian government's controversial decision in August 2019 to end the 'semi-autonomous' constitutional status of the Indian province of Jammu and Kashmir exacerbated tensions with Pakistan. In 2020, annual ceasefire violations across the Line of Control (LoC) reached their highest level since the 2003 ceasefire agreement. However, the February 2021 announcement by the Indian and Pakistan militaries of a renewed ceasefire on the LoC – initiated through 'back channel' talks – raised the prospects of a potential thaw in India–Pakistan relations.

Pakistan was expected to remain on the 'grey list' of the intergovernmental Financial Action Task Force (FATF) until October 2021 for failing to combat terrorist financing. By June, the FATF noted that Pakistan had addressed 26 of the 27 action items it required; but to be removed from the grey list, Pakistan was required to demonstrate that terror-financing investigations and prosecutions 'target senior leaders and commanders of UN-designated terrorist groups'.

Tensions between Afghanistan and Pakistan rose in May, with Afghanistan's National Security Advisor Hamdullah Mohib strongly accusing Pakistan of supporting and directing the Taliban in its rapid advance in rural areas. The Afghan government appeared confident that the Taliban would not be able to retain the territory it had taken and that a military 'stalemate' would ensue.

New Biden administration

Biden's decision to complete the withdrawal of US and NATO troops from Afghanistan by September 2021, after 20 years, marked a key feature of his administration's policy towards South Asia in the six months since it took office in January 2021. The Biden administration also increased its engagement with India to counter China's assertive role on its land border with India, through its military-logistical support in response to the Galwan border clash in June 2020, and its influence in the Indo-Pacific region, through the first Quad Leaders summit in March 2021. Climate change was a new focus. However, there was no progress on a bilateral India–US trade deal.

Taiwan
A front line in the new cold war?

For China's communist leaders, Taiwan has always represented an important piece of unfinished business. The fact that Taiwan was never under China's administrative control until the late seventeenth century, was a Japanese colony from 1895 to 1945, and has been a de facto separate state since 1949 does nothing to detract from the determination of the Chinese Communist Party (CCP) to reunify it with the mainland. The CCP sees this commitment as a major part of its claim to political legitimacy and always refers to it in Party documents and speeches as a sacred obligation.

Equally, Taiwan has always been a major factor in US–China relations. Though initially reluctant to intervene to protect Chiang Kai-shek's Nationalist regime, which made the island its base following defeat in China's civil war, United States president Harry Truman changed course in 1950 following the outbreak of the Korean War. The US then made a treaty commitment to Taiwan's defence, and until 1971 supported Chiang's claim to represent China at the United Nations.

When the US established diplomatic relations with Beijing in 1979, the question of how to preserve Taiwan's security was a major consideration. While adopting a 'One China' policy, a *sine qua non* for establishing relations with China, the US made continuing commitments to Taiwan through the 1979 Taiwan Relations Act. The Reagan administration's Six Assurances to Taiwan in 1982 reinforced this by effectively committing the US to supporting Taiwan's status quo as a de facto separate society. Formally speaking, the US no longer had a treaty obligation to assist Taiwan in the event of an attack by China. But in 1996, when China conducted missile tests in the Taiwan Strait in response to a visit to the US by Taiwan's first democratically elected leader Lee Teng-hui in 1995, the US sent two aircraft-carrier battle groups to the region to prevent the situation from escalating.

This sparked Chinese military modernisation driven by the need to keep the US out of the Taiwan Strait long enough for China to achieve military victory over Taiwan. Publicly, China has always maintained its commitment to peaceful reunification via the 'One Country, Two

Systems' formula under which it regained sovereignty over Hong Kong from the United Kingdom in 1997. It has sought to bring Taiwan into its orbit through economic integration and the exercise of soft power. But it has also set six conditions that would justify military intervention: a Taiwanese declaration of independence; significant moves in that direction; the stationing of foreign troops in Taiwan; moves by Taiwan to develop nuclear weapons; Taiwanese armed attacks against the mainland; and major outbreaks of civil unrest in Taiwan. Starting with Jiang Zemin, successive Chinese leaders have made clear that Taiwan cannot hope to postpone reunification indefinitely. Beijing has refused to rule out the use of force to achieve it.

Within these parameters Taiwan has enjoyed a long period of relative strategic stability. But in the past year, a strategic shift has brought Taiwan to the centre of a test of strength between the US and China that looks set to shape the global balance of power over the coming decades. China's Foreign Minister Wang Yi, speaking at an April 2021 Virtual Dialogue with the New York-based Council on Foreign Relations, warned: 'The Taiwan question is the most important and sensitive issue in China–US relations. … Playing the "Taiwan card" is dangerous, like playing with fire.'

China and Taiwan: different beds, different dreams

Despite Beijing's efforts to draw Taiwan closer through growing economic integration, the two sides have for some years been drifting further apart. A younger generation of Taiwanese has grown up without its parents' emotional ties to the mainland and with a growing sense of a separate Taiwanese identity. According to a July 2020 poll conducted by National Chengchi University's Election Study Center, 67% of Taiwan's population identified as Taiwanese and only 2.4% as Chinese. This generation, unlike its parents', has also grown up in the liberal democracy that emerged between 1987 and 1996 and has been repelled by signs of growing authoritarianism in China, especially after Xi Jinping's accession as CCP secretary-general in 2012. These issues were brought to a head by events in Hong Kong beginning in mid-2019, with protests against a proposed extradition bill that would enable Hong Kong residents to be extradited to China for political offences. China's uncompromising response ensured that Taiwanese President Tsai Ing-wen, whose campaign for re-election had been languishing due to Taiwan's weak economic performance, was returned to office in January 2020 with a large majority. Chinese cyber-information campaigns directed against Tsai proved not only ineffective but counterproductive. The imposition on Hong Kong on 30 June 2020 of a National Security Law enacted by China's National People's Congress rather than by Hong Kong's own Legislative Council was interpreted in Taiwan as evidence that One Country, Two Systems was a dead letter.

Unlike some in her Democratic Progressive Party (DPP) who advocate Taiwan's independence, Tsai has always eschewed such extreme positions. But on first taking office in 2016 she rejected the Cross-Strait Consensus, the informal agreement reached with Beijing in 1992 that there was only one China, with each side reserving its position on what that meant in practice. Tsai also rejected the One Country, Two Systems reunification formula on the grounds that Taiwan had never been part of the People's Republic of China and was in practice a separate state.

While Tsai's 2020 re-election was unwelcome to Beijing, even more concerning was the consequent implosion of the main opposition Kuomintang (KMT) party, which Beijing had long favoured because of its more positive attitude towards the mainland. Following its defeat, the KMT sought to distance itself from its previous stance of endorsing One Country, Two Systems and attempted, without much success, to re-invent itself to appeal to a younger electorate. Indicative of the extent of this change is the fact that in October 2020, the KMT introduced two resolutions into Taiwan's legislature calling for the establishment of formal diplomatic and military relations with the US. The fact that several months after being elected, the new KMT chairman, Johnny Chiang, had still not received the previously standard congratulatory letter from Xi also revealed the party's waning fortunes.

China's focus on developing economic links with Taiwan has been accompanied by selective economic pressure in the form of a significant reduction in levels of individual and package tourism and selective bans on Taiwanese imports. At the same time, China has sought to boost Taiwanese inward investment into the mainland through some 25 initiatives including tax credits and allowing Taiwanese companies to bid for government contracts. These initiatives have, however, failed to reverse a downward trend in Taiwanese inward investment from a high of US$14 billion in 2010 to US$4bn in 2020. Since 2016, Taiwan has sought to reduce economic dependence on China through its New Southbound Policy, which aims to enhance trading and investment links with South and Southeast Asia and Australasia. Meanwhile, a combination of the Trump administration's trade war and rising production costs in China has incentivised Taiwanese entrepreneurs to relocate manufacturing elsewhere. While Taiwanese companies still occupy a dominant role in some sectors of the Chinese economy – for example, Foxconn's manufacture of a range of electronic devices – China's economic grip on Taiwan, though still considerable, has undoubtedly weakened.

Taiwan has been further alienated by a relentless Chinese campaign to constrain its international space. This involved efforts to persuade the few countries that still have diplomatic relations with Taipei to switch allegiance to Beijing, and to exclude Taiwan from international fora. In 2021, China sought unsuccessfully to use vaccine diplomacy to encourage Paraguay to defect from Taiwan and successfully pressured Guyana not to allow the opening of a Taiwan trade office in Georgetown. China also refused to allow Taiwan to take part in the World Health Assembly (WHA), despite Taiwan's highly effective handling of the COVID-19 pandemic. The G7 pushed back, calling in its May 2021 communiqué for Taiwan to be admitted to the WHA with observer status, but to no avail.

Taiwan becomes a focus of US–China tensions

During 2020, and particularly in the latter half of the year, Taiwan came to the forefront of a US–China relationship that had deteriorated to the lowest level since before the Nixon-initiated rapprochement in 1972. The proximate causes of this deterioration were the Trump administration's trade and technology wars with China, exacerbated by the administration's high-profile criticism of China's responsibility for the COVID-19 pandemic. Starting in mid-2020, the Trump administration initiated a range of provocative actions against China that included financial sanctions and technology-sales embargoes. These included a series of high-profile initiatives in relation to Taiwan that appeared deliberately calculated to infuriate Beijing.

The Trump administration sold arms worth US$18bn to Taiwan. These included big-ticket items such as *Abrams* tanks and F-16 fighter aircraft. But sales made in the final year of Trump's presidency should significantly enhance the island's ability to mount an asymmetric response to any Chinese attack and to launch pre-emptive missile attacks against People's Liberation Army (PLA) dispositions on the Chinese mainland. These include:

- Mk 48 Mod 6 Advanced Technology heavyweight torpedoes
- Recertification of PAC-3 *Patriot* missile-defence systems
- AGM-84H SLAM-ER land-attack missiles
- RGM-84L-4 *Harpoon* Block II surface-launched missiles
- Weapons-ready MQ-9B uninhabited aerial vehicles
- Field Information Communications Systems

Military sales were accompanied by a series of diplomatic moves equally calculated to infuriate China. These began with a meeting in May 2019 between US national security advisor John Bolton and his Taiwanese counterpart David Lee in Washington and continued with a visit to Taipei in August 2020 by US health secretary Alex Azar, the first cabinet-level US official to make such a visit since 1979. At the end of 2020, US secretary of state Mike Pompeo, who in November 2020 had angered Beijing by stating that Taiwan had never been part of China, announced the end of long-standing restrictions on contacts between US officials and their Taiwanese counterparts. Pompeo's announcement was little more than a formal endorsement of practices that had evolved over time – for example, the prohibition on meeting Taiwanese officials in US government premises had long been observed in the breach – but the impact on Beijing was predictable.

The incoming Biden administration made clear that it was in no hurry to reverse the Trump administration's initiatives in relation to China, including Taiwan policy. President Joe Biden broke with precedent by inviting Taipei's Washington representative Hsiao Bi-khim to his inauguration as his personal guest, and in April 2021 sent a delegation comprising former senator Chris Dodd and two former deputy secretaries of state, Richard Armitage and James Steinberg, to Taipei. Biden also confirmed that the relaxation on US official contacts with Taiwanese counterparts would remain in place.

In an early manifestation of this new policy, the US ambassador to Palau accompanied the president of the island, one of the few states to maintain diplomatic relations with Taipei, when the latter visited Taipei in April 2021. Further evidence of a closer relationship came in the form of a visit in June 2021 by three US senators to Taipei on a US military aircraft during which they announced that the US would provide Taiwan with a substantial number of COVID-19 vaccines to combat a resurgence of the virus. Though not announcing new military sales, the Biden administration granted all the technical permissions needed to enable Taiwan to begin manufacturing eight diesel-powered submarines that are scheduled to begin entering service in 2025. These will supplement Taiwan's four existing submarines, two of which are of Second World War vintage.

The US Congress sought to enact bipartisan legislation requiring the US government to provide Taiwan with more support. The Strategic Innovation and Competition Act of 2021 identifies Taiwan as a vital national interest of the US and calls on the US government to 'advocate and actively advance Taiwan's meaningful participation in the United Nations, the World Health Assembly, the International Civil Aviation Organization, the International Criminal Police Organization and other international bodies as appropriate.'

China: carrot and stick – but a lot more stick

A key question is the extent of Chinese strategic patience. While China was still negotiating with the UK over the future of Hong Kong, Deng Xiaoping suggested that the issue of Taiwan could be left to future generations 'who may be wiser than us'. But a combination of a pro-inde-pendence lobby in Taiwan – whose ambitions have been kept in check mainly due to US pressure – and China's proclamation of two Centennial Goals, the achievement of which would logically require national reunifi-cation, has raised questions about the limits of Chinese patience.

Statements by Xi and Premier Li Keqiang in March 2021 sug-gested that peaceful reunification is still Beijing's preferred outcome. But Beijing has ratcheted up pressure on Taiwan over the past year through a set of measures that Taiwan's Ministry of National Defense refers to as 'grey-zone' activities. Most prominent has been an increase in aerial incursions by the PLA Air Force (PLAAF) and Navy (PLAN) with growing numbers of fighters, bombers, surveillance and anti-sub-marine aircraft. Now almost a daily occurrence, these have changed in strategic character by crossing the median line that has long deline-ated airspace between the Chinese mainland and Taiwan. In September 2020, a Chinese Ministry of Foreign Affairs spokesman declared that the median line did not exist. The aerial incursions serve multiple purposes: training for the PLAAF and PLAN in operations over water and in con-ducting joint operations; the creation of a 'new normal' within which elements of surprise may be concealed; intimidation of the population; and attrition of Taiwan's defence forces through the need for frequent mobilisation to monitor the incursions.

China has also carried out a major naval build-up through which, since 2015, it has launched more warships than the British navy pos-sesses. These include the amphibious assault vessels that China would need to launch a full-scale military invasion of Taiwan. The PLAN has conducted a variety of training exercises in the waters off Taiwan, which have involved its first deployable aircraft carrier, the *Liaoning*. In August 2020, China's Strategic Rocket Force test-fired two interme-diate-range ballistic missiles, a DF-26B referred to in Chinese media as a 'carrier killer', and a DF-21D into the waters between Hainan island and the Paracel Islands. These tests appeared to be part of China's anti-access/area-denial (A2/AD) strategy designed to discourage the US from coming to Taiwan's assistance.

China's military activities in the waters off Taiwan have sparked US concern. Outgoing head of the US Indo-Pacific Command Admiral Phil Davidson, testifying to Congress in March 2021, said that China could invade Taiwan within the next six years. The same month, his successor, Admiral John Aquilino, while not offering a specific time frame for a Chinese invasion, said that capturing Taiwan was China's number-one priority and that the problem was 'much closer to us than most think'. In April 2021, US Secretary of State Antony Blinken said that the US was concerned about China's aggressive moves against Taiwan and warned that it would be a 'serious mistake' for anyone to try to change the status quo in the Western Pacific by force.

These assessments appeared to be based not on any specific intelligence but on China's overall level of military preparedness and the fact that national reunification is seen as integral to the realisation of Xi's 'China Dream'. This was acknowledged by Chairman of the US Joint Chiefs of Staff General Mark Milley, who stated in June 2021 in testimony to Congress that an attack on Taiwan was unlikely in the 'near future', which he defined as within the next two years. At the Fifth Plenum of the 19th Communist Party Central Committee in October 2020, the date for the realisation of the China Dream was brought forward from 2049 to 2035, giving rise to speculation that Xi aspired to still be in power on that date and might seek to recover Taiwan as part of his legacy. A more immediate consideration for an early Chinese move would be to pre-empt Taiwan's efforts to develop the kind of asymmetric capabilities that would make this harder.

While China is building up the capabilities needed to take Taiwan by force, such an endeavour would be a huge challenge and its outcome uncertain. Taiwan's topography, with high cliffs on the western side and mud flats on the east, does not favour an amphibious assault, and ideal sea conditions are limited to April and October. A full-blown assault is therefore probably not China's first option. More likely is a continuous ratcheting up of grey-zone activities, including economic pressure – such as China's mass sand-dredging activities on Taiwan's outer islands and its March 2021 ban on imports of Taiwanese pineapples, citing 'harmful creatures' it said could threaten its own agriculture. Chinese pressure might in due course extend to occupying Taiwan's outlying islands and imposing a naval blockade around Taiwan. China's military activities around Taiwan are thus best understood as part of a continuing effort to put psychological pressure on Taiwan while seeking to deter the US. However, rising levels of military activity increase the potential for accidents and thus of escalation, giving rise to greater uncertainty.

Since 1979, US strategy in relation to Taiwan has hinged on the concept of strategic ambiguity, leaving open the question of whether it would come to Taiwan's defence in the event of a Chinese attack. This stance came under question in the dying days of the Trump administration, including through the introduction into Congress of a draft Taiwan Invasion Prevention Bill that would commit the US to coming to Taiwan's defence. There was insufficient time for the bill to be considered and its fate remained unclear. But in May 2021, Director of National Intelligence Avril Haines and National Security Council Coordinator for the Indo-Pacific Kurt Campbell both stated that abandoning the posture of strategic ambiguity would have 'significant downsides' and might increase the risk of conflict. There is no indication that the Biden administration will abandon that posture.

For the US, Taiwan has become bound up with its strategic posture in the Indo-Pacific region. Failure to come to Taiwan's assistance in the event of a Chinese attack, or an attempt to do so that failed, would fundamentally change the balance of power in the Indo-Pacific. China would be able to use Taiwan to project power beyond the First Island Chain and look to exercise control of the seas up to the Second Island Chain. Equally if not more importantly, it would have major repercussions for US alliances in the region. Military defeat is far from unthinkable. In some 18 table-top exercises conducted by the Pentagon involving a conflict around Taiwan, the US has lost every time. Such an outcome would not be fatal to the United States' status as a major power. But it would be a different power, with diminished scope and ambitions.

For the US, alliance relationships have become key to countering the threat from China, an issue that goes far beyond Taiwan. In January

2021, the Trump administration declassified its Indo-Pacific strategy years ahead of schedule. This strategy, which the Biden administration appears to have inherited, envisaged the creation of a latticework of relationships across the Indo-Pacific to inhibit China's efforts to achieve regional hegemony and increase the risks to Beijing of military action. In March 2021, US and Japanese defence chiefs agreed to close cooperation in the event of a conflict over Taiwan. Australia announced a US$270bn uplift in defence spending over the next ten years. France, Germany, the Netherlands and the UK are all planning naval deployments in the Indo-Pacific in late 2021. All but Germany will transit the South China Sea, though none is scheduled to sail through the Taiwan Strait.

Technology as a complicating factor

Technology has become something of a wild card in assessing the risk to Taiwan due to the island's unique role in producing very high-end semiconductors. The enormous costs involved in setting up the complex production process mean that most major Western technology companies have long since opted to design their own semiconductors but outsource manufacture. The Taiwan Semiconductor Manufacturing Company (TSMC) now accounts for 55% of total global production of the highest-end semiconductors, with South Korea's Samsung accounting for much of the remainder. Neither the US nor China can manufacture to this level, with China also several generations behind the US in design. The importance of TSMC's operations for Taiwan's economy is evidenced by the fact that, in the face of a prolonged drought, the Taiwanese government chose in April 2021 to divert scarce water from Taiwan's rice farmers to guarantee TSMC's continued operation.

TSMC's processes are dependent on US intellectual property, so the Trump administration was able to impose an embargo on the sale of advanced microprocessors to Chinese companies during the latter half of 2020. This dealt a serious blow to China's telecommunications national champion Huawei's ambitions to become a world leader in the provision of 5G mobile services. China responded by doubling down on efforts to develop indigenous production. It also sought to lure Taiwanese engineers to the mainland, something Taiwan tried to impede with a May 2021 decree preventing recruitment agencies from advertising such posts. Concerned about its dependence on Taiwan, the US in 2020 concluded a deal with TSMC to construct a foundry in Arizona at a cost of US$3.5bn. This is scheduled to begin production in 2024.

A global shortage of semiconductors beginning in 2020 offers a fore-taste of the consequences if TSMC's production capabilities are lost through military action. That realisation might serve as a disincentive to undertake such action. But in a worst-case scenario, China might conclude that it would more easily be able to recover from such a loss than would the US, given that it has invested heavily in the manufacture of lower-end semiconductors.

Conclusion

In an ideal world, China would prefer to rely on continuing pressure to force Taiwan to capitulate without the need for military force. But it finds itself caught up in a dynamic with the US in which both sides are effectively playing chicken over Taiwan. This has given rise to growing uncertainty and instability. Beijing will have to balance the temptation to move soon – before Taiwan has built up its asymmetric capabilities, and the US military has moved towards a posture of more dispersed and resilient deployments in the Indo-Pacific – against the risk that a military assault will either fail or will lead to a stalemate. Military conflict over Taiwan may not be imminent and may yet be avoided. But the risk of it happening has undoubtedly increased.

South Korea's Foreign Policy
Local or global?

Over the past year South Korea (Republic of Korea–ROK) has confronted its foreign-policy dilemmas with mixed success. These arise from its increasingly complex set of relationships, which can be framed as one rod and three concentric circles.

The rod is South Korea's alliance with the United States, forged in 1950 when the US led a United Nations force that saved the young ROK after it was invaded by the communist North (Democratic People's Republic of Korea–DPRK). US forces, now reduced to 28,500 personnel, have been based in South Korea ever since. While the US alliance is unquestioned in Seoul, meshing this with other key relationships – notably China and North Korea – can create challenges.

These other relationships form the three circles. The first circle is local and comprises just one state, North Korea. To liberals such as President Moon Jae-in, and two of his predecessors – Kim Dae-jung (1998–2003) and Roh Moo-hyun (2003–08), the Korean question is paramount. All have pursued peace with Pyongyang, albeit unsuccessfully. Meanwhile, the DPRK has grown from a local to a global threat: a defiant nuclear power also capable of perpetrating sophisticated cyber attacks.

This fixation on North Korea risks distracting the ROK from its broader interests. These begin, geographically, with a second circle comprising two big neighbours, Japan and China, with which South Korea has deep but difficult relations. With Japan, historical grievances prevent building the amity that shared interests should foster, and relations have worsened on Moon's watch. By contrast, South Korea treads carefully with China due to enormous trade and investment ties, though worsening US–China tensions are undermining Seoul's efforts to 'balance' between Washington and Beijing.

In recent years, Seoul has developed a third circle of strategic interests that are not local and regional, but global. The centrality of manufacturing exports and energy imports makes Seoul an enthusiast of free-trade agreements (FTAs). A founding member of the G20, South Korea was also one of four non-member countries invited to the 2021 G7 summit. Culturally, the huge success of K-pop bands such as BTS and Blackpink, and the Oscars won, respectively, by a South Korean film and a South Korean actress in 2020 and 2021, add a 'soft power' burnish to the ROK's influence and brand worldwide.

There is no consensus in Seoul on how to square these three circles, with their competing priorities. Perhaps the biggest challenge now lies in the second circle. If US–Chinese economic decoupling escalates, South Korea cannot avoid taking sides – and will choose its founding ally. Whatever the costs on the China front, this might facilitate fence-mending with a similarly placed Japan, a process that the US would encourage.

North Korea: nothing doing

Peninsular peace is Moon's priority, though this quest looks increasingly quixotic. An apparent breakthrough in 2018, with three North–South summits and two substantial accords, proved a false dawn. For over two years, since the failed summit between North Korean Supreme Leader Kim Jong-un and then US president Donald Trump in Hanoi in February 2019, Pyongyang has cold-shouldered Seoul. In June 2020, it even blew up their joint liaison office in Kaesong, just north of the Demilitarized Zone (DMZ), which the South built and paid for. Despite this gesture of contempt, Moon persisted. A reshuffle in July 2020 resulted in a new intelligence chief, national security adviser and minister of unification, all of them friendly to Pyongyang. In January 2021, Moon replaced Kang Kyung-wha, the first woman to serve as ROK foreign minister, with Chung Eui-yong, who had brokered the first US–DPRK summit in 2018. In December, the National Assembly (the legislative body of the ROK) criminalised the launching of balloons carrying propaganda into the North, bringing accusations that Moon was stifling free speech and per-secuting defectors – the main activists involved – to placate the North. Seoul retorted that such activities violated inter-Korean agreements.

None of this impressed Kim, whose seven-hour speech at the end of 2019 ignored South Korea entirely. A year later, in January 2021, at the Eighth Congress of the Workers' Party of Korea, Kim blamed the

South for the impasse in their relations and for 'raising such inessential issues as cooperation in epidemic prevention and [the] humanitarian field'. Moon had repeatedly offered aid: for an outbreak of swine fever in autumn 2019, flood damage in August 2020 and for the COVID-19 pandemic. Kim also criticised the South's arms build-up. Though disingenuous – his missile threat is the driver of the build-up – this highlights a point often overlooked. While seeking peace, Moon has not neglected deterrence, with missile development a major focus. During his presidency, defence spending has risen by 7% a year: up from 4.1% under his predecessor Park Geun-hye. Whether Seoul's actions are regarded as destabilising, or legitimate self-defence, a fresh arms race on the peninsula is troubling – but it will continue. On 25 March, after almost a year without testing, the North fired what it called a 'new-type tactical guided missile', seemingly nuclear-capable.

2021 brought hints of greater robustness and realism in Seoul. In April, Chung demanded an apology and compensation for the June 2020 destruction of the liaison office. While still reiterating its readiness to engage, Moon's government tacitly recognised that the prospect of North Korea agreeing to this was now slim. Moreover, with presidential elections approaching in March 2022, courting a disdainful Pyongyang hardly appeared a vote-winning policy for the ruling Democratic Party (DP), which hoped to retain power for a further five years even though Moon must stand down.

China: cultivating Xi

The Moon administration's approach to China has been placatory for both economic and political reasons. China is by far the ROK's largest trade partner, with Seoul running a substantial surplus; most large conglomerates (*chaebol*) and many small to medium-sized enterprises are heavily invested there. Politically, hopes of Beijing as a constructive influence on Pyongyang persisted, despite clear evidence of China breaching sanctions and sustaining the Kim regime.

Moon continued to seek a visit by the Chinese President, Xi Jinping, who last came to Seoul in 2014. This goal was widely blamed for the

South Korea's slowness to curb travel from China early in 2020, lest Beijing take offence, which made South Korea one of the first countries to be hit by COVID-19. The pandemic also thwarted summit hopes, though two other senior Chinese figures visited the country: Politburo member Yang Jiechi in August 2020, and Foreign Minister Wang Yi in November. With no substantive outcomes, each side was essentially sizing up the other's stance as US–China tensions rose. In April the recently appointed Chung visited China; his talks with Wang ran over the hour scheduled, perhaps reflecting North Korea's recent missile test.

In December, the ROK scrambled fighters when four Chinese and 15 Russian aircraft entered its Air Defence Identification Zone. This was not the first such incursion. At their regular bilateral security talks in March, China and South Korea agreed to add two new direct military hotlines to the three already operational. But given the ROK alliance with the US, military cooperation with China will remain limited to rescue operations and managing flashpoints such as illegal Chinese fishing in Korean waters.

Seoul's reluctance to offend Beijing was palpable. Unlike almost all democracies, the ROK was not among the 57 signatories in February 2021 of Canada's Declaration Against Arbitrary Detention in State-to-State Relations, prompted by an ongoing case in China. Nor did it join the 44 countries, again led by Canada, which in June sent a joint statement to the UN Human Rights Council voicing concern over abuses in Xinjiang, as well as Hong Kong and Tibet. Unlike some other US allies, the ROK has not imposed any curbs on Huawei, which in 2019 bought 17% of South Korea's electronic-components exports to China.

Official caution does not reflect public opinion. A Pew Research Center survey conducted in October found strong anti-China views, with South Koreans aged under 50 more negative (81%) than their elders (68%). Their reasons included some shared worldwide – human rights, COVID-19 – but also specific local grievances. After the ROK installed a US missile-defence system in 2017, which China vocally opposed, Beijing retaliated by restricting tourism, K-pop and other key sectors of bilateral commerce. This unacknowledged boycott caused losses to ROK firms estimated at US$7.5 billion.

Japan: fences unmended

Towards Japan, by contrast, Moon's government and most of the public share a gut suspicion, rooted in history rather than forward-looking national interest. Despite a leadership change when Suga Yoshihide succeeded Abe Shinzo as Japanese prime minister in September 2020, and talk of mending fences, 2020–21 saw no mitigation of the harm done earlier in Moon's presidency. In 2015, Park and Abe had signed an accord to 'finally and irreversibly' settle the 'comfort women' (wartime sex slaves) issue. Moon criticised this as inadequate soon after taking office in 2017, and in 2019 he closed the associated compensation fund. Separately, courts ordered Japanese firms, on pain of forfeiture of their assets in the ROK, to compensate several Koreans compelled to work for them before 1945. Tokyo retaliated in 2019 by restricting several key export items, prompting Seoul to do likewise.

Hopes that Suga could mark a fresh start were misplaced. Lacking his predecessor's authority, his popularity slumped amid many more pressing priorities, not least the Olympics and the pandemic. With nationalist ire stoked in both countries, and even moderate Japanese opinion blaming South Korea for going too far, in the absence of some substantial gesture by Moon, which was not forthcoming, Suga lacked the political capital to tackle this issue.

In late 2020, Moon appointed a new ambassador to Japan – Kang Chang-il – well known in Tokyo, and two senior ROK delegations visited. One opportunity could have been the ninth trilateral China–Japan–ROK summit, due in December, with it being Seoul's turn to host. This was postponed, however, since Suga refused to attend while the threat of seizing Japanese assets remained. Another missed chance was June's G7 summit in Cornwall, where Moon and Suga exchanged brief greetings but held no formal talks. In an all-too-typical squabble, Seoul later claimed that Suga had reneged on an agreement to meet; Tokyo denied any such plan. South Korea also talked up the possibility of a summit at the Tokyo Summer Olympic Games. Again, no meeting took place.

2021 brought contrasting, and confusing, legal verdicts. In January, the Seoul Central District Court ordered Tokyo to compensate 12 former comfort women. Yet in April a different judge rejected a similar claim, citing Japan's sovereign immunity. Similarly, a third verdict on 7 June, in one of several cases seeking compensation for wartime slave labour, in effect reversed an earlier Supreme Court judgment by ruling that law-suits were the wrong way to proceed. With the legal position thus murky and contested, strong political will on both sides – nowhere in evidence – would be needed to mend the ROK–Japan relationship.

Bad blood between its two main regional allies worried Washington, as tensions with China rose and North Korea remained a threat. Trump was insouciant, but President Joe Biden will strive to knock heads together. In one small sign of hope, having threatened to pull out of the General Security of Military Information Agreement intelligence-sharing pact with Japan in 2019, in 2020 the ROK allowed this accord to be renewed without protest.

From Trump to Biden: straightening the rod

US–ROK relations improved with the change of US president. The final months of Trump's presidency brought no progress on the two main issues: their shared quest to engage North Korea, and deep divisions over cost-sharing for the US forces in South Korea. This cost-sharing is set by accords, usually quinquennial, known as Special Measures Agreements (SMAs). Trump, ever suspicious of allies as freeloaders, sought a sharp hike in Seoul's contribution, initially demanding an exorbitant fivefold increase. The tenth SMA in 2019 covered that year only, and 2020 passed with no new agreement. One consequence was the furloughing in 2020 of 4,000 local civilian staff for two months until Seoul agreed to pay their wages.

Biden's election brought a welcome return to normality and civility. The 11th SMA was rapidly concluded just weeks into the new administra-tion, and formally signed on 8 April. It was agreed that the ROK would pay 1.1833 trillion won (US$1.059bn) in 2021, up 13.9% from 2019 and 2020, with subsequent yearly rises until 2025 matching increases in its own defence spending.

While this encouraged hopes that relations with the US would revert to their pre-Trump predictability and professionalism, it did not guar-antee plain sailing. Moon's government initially feared that Biden might turn tougher with Pyongyang, thus jeopardising the notional peace process. Several measures eased that concern, including the appointment of Wendy Sherman, an experienced negotiator seen as committed to engaging Pyongyang, as deputy secretary of state.

Yet the first bilateral '2+2' meeting of foreign and defence ministers in five years (there were none under Trump), held in Seoul on 18 March, hinted at some differences. Moon's hope of achieving the transfer of wartime operational control (OPCON) of allied forces from the US to the ROK before he leaves office next May will not be fulfilled; the 2+2 joint statement set no date for this. Compromise was evident in calling North Korea's nuclear and missile 'issues' (not threats) a 'priority': far milder language than in the statement released jointly by the Quadrilateral Security Dialogue ('Quad' – comprising Australia, India, Japan and the US) a week earlier, which robustly reaffirmed 'commitment to the complete denuclearization of North Korea'.

Such divergences were smoothed over when Biden hosted Moon at the White House in May. This was only Biden's second in-person summit (the first was with Japan's Suga in April). Both sides acclaimed this meeting as successful; Moon called it 'the best summit ever'. Its most striking aspect was an unmistakable, if still tacit, shift by Seoul on China issues. The summit produced the first joint US–South Korea communiqué to reference the South China Sea and Taiwan Strait as concerns. ROK firms also announced US$39bn in new investments in the US, clearly intended to help build alternative supply chains bypassing China in electronics, vehicles and other sectors.

North Korea loomed less large, but in May 2021, Biden appointed Sung Min as US special envoy to the country (concurrently ambassador to Jakarta), a move welcomed by Moon. Biden also pledged that any US outreach to Pyongyang would take 2018's Singapore Declaration between Kim and Trump as its basis. Unusually, as of July 2021, the North had yet to comment officially on the Biden–Moon summit. North Korean media did carry a brief critique of the US decision to lift range and payload restrictions on South Korea's own missiles that it had imposed since 1979. Moon rejoiced at recovering 'missile sovereignty'.

Hostage to sanctions: state piracy in the Gulf

Meanwhile, 2021 brought an unexpected challenge further afield, in a sharp reminder of the third circle's salience. On 4 January, Iran seized an ROK-flagged tanker, the *Hankuk Chemi*, in the Strait of Hormuz, speciously alleging marine pollution. Tehran's real motive was to pressure Seoul to release US$7bn of Iranian funds frozen in South Korean banks. This hostage-taking appeared to work: the vessel was released on 9 April, shortly before ROK Prime Minister Chung Sye-kyun visited Tehran and pledged to work on the funds issue as well as reviving the 2015 Joint Comprehensive Plan of Action (the Iran nuclear deal). Despite initial optimism, by mid-2021 there was no discernible progress. All this highlighted Seoul's readiness, largely business-driven, to maintain relations with regimes anathema to Washington; Muammar Gadhafi's Libya and Iraq under Saddam Hussein are earlier examples. During 2015–18 South Korea was Iran's third-largest trade partner. The ROK continued to buy Iranian oil until 2019, when US sanctions forbade this and also banned financial transfers, leaving Tehran's funds stranded in ROK banks. By contrast, Seoul responded firmly to February's military coup in Myanmar, condemning violence against civilians, suspending military assistance and putting other aid on hold. It remains to be seen whether this heralds a wider change in the habit of 'business as usual'.

Third circle: the world as Seoul's oyster

South Korea continued to project its economic power worldwide. An enthusiast of FTAs – it has concluded major agreements with the US (2012), China and the European Union (both 2015), among others – its more recent focus has been multilateral. The ROK was among the 15 signatories in November 2020 of the Regional Comprehensive Economic Partnership. In January 2021, Moon said he was also closely considering joining the Comprehensive and Progressive Agreement for Trans-Pacific Partnership. But here the commitment was less clear, with little sign of the necessary spadework.

Bilaterally, two big deals with Gulf states highlighted how Seoul pursues economic security. In June 2020, Qatar signed the largest-ever order for liquefied-natural-gas tankers, ordering over 100 vessels from three ROK shipyards; South Korea is Doha's top market for its gas. In August, the first of four South Korean-built nuclear reactors went onstream in the United Arab Emirates: part of a US$20bn contract, and Seoul's first success in exporting its nuclear technology.

Waning Moon: the challenges ahead

South Korean presidents are limited to a single five-year term. Moon's successor will be elected in March 2022 and take office in May. Like most presidents, Moon is likely to become a lame duck in his final year as attention shifts to the succession.

It is far from certain who will succeed him. Hitherto the electoral pendulum has swung between right and left each decade. If that pattern persists, the ruling DP may keep power for a further five years. That had looked likely, with the conservative People Power Party (PPP) yet to recover from four electoral defeats during 2016–20 and the impeachment of Park (president in 2013–17). Both Park and her predecessor Lee Myung-bak (2008–13) are serving long prison terms for corruption and abuse of power. However, the PPP's landslide victory on 7 April in mayoral by-elections in Seoul and Busan, South Korea's second city, suggested that the right might also recapture the Blue House next year.

The choice of president may affect foreign policy. The DP's two leading contenders have differing stances. Lee Nak-yon, prime minister in 2017–20 and then DP leader until March 2021, is a moderate and is well connected in Tokyo, where he spent four years as a journalist. Once the favourite, by mid-2021 he lagged behind the front runner Lee Jae-myung, governor of Gyeonggi Province, which surrounds Seoul. The latter, who is further left and more nationalist, might remain emollient towards North Korea even if this stance causes friction with Washington.

By contrast, the PPP has few 'big beasts'. The conservative front runner is currently Yoon Seok-youl, who resigned as prosecutor general in March 2021 after a lengthy battle with Moon's government over several issues. Yoon announced his presidential bid on 29 June, but had yet to join the PPP, which has rival contenders for the nomination. Any right-leaning president would be unambiguously at ease with the US alliance, warier of China and North Korea, and probably better placed to bury the hatchet with Tokyo.

Whoever enters the Blue House in May 2022, their main challenges are clear. China will loom largest, as its relations with the US worsen and pressure mounts on third countries to choose sides. That will be painful for Seoul, politically and economically, but dreams of a middle way are no longer viable. Pyongyang will remain a threat, with scant prospect of repairing inter-Korean ties. Building a future-oriented alliance with Japan would greatly benefit each nation, yet finding the political will to transcend the past will challenge them both.

These pressing local preoccupations may crowd out, but do not negate, Seoul's wider global ambitions. For a country that long saw itself as a victim and underdog – a 'shrimp among whales', as a Korean proverb has it – the symbolism and impact of being invited to June's G7 summit are hard to overstate. Even progressives like Moon could not but contrast his warm welcome in Cornwall, as earlier in Washington, with Pyongyang's endless rebuffs and China's bullying hauteur. Though the path ahead will be tricky, the ROK left has finally joined the right in fully appreciating who South Korea's true and lasting friends are.

India–China Border Tensions
What are the strategic implications for the Indo-Pacific?

Multiple stand-offs and clashes between Indian and Chinese troops in their contested western Himalayan borderland from spring 2020 sent ties between Asia's two largest countries to their lowest point since the 1962 Sino-Indian war. An uneasy militarised stalemate has followed. In response, India is moving away from its traditional posture of non-alignment in order to guarantee its strategic autonomy.

Border violence unprecedented in peacetime

On 15 June 2020 at 4,200 metres altitude, 20 Indian soldiers, including a colonel, along with at least four soldiers from China's People's Liberation Army (PLA), were killed in a mass overnight brawl in a narrow ravine. Weeks before, both sides had moved into the Galwan Valley in the eastern Ladakh region, erecting tents and digging defences. China brought in earth-moving machines. Clashes were also reported between the Indian military and the PLA further south, in Hot Springs–Gogra and Demchok, as well as around Pangong Lake. Further east, outside Ladakh, India's inhospitable northern region twice the size of Belgium, 150 troops brawled in Sikkim State's Nathu La pass, situated between Bhutan and Nepal.

By the end of summer 2020, tensions had returned to Pangong Lake. On 29 August, after Chinese troops moved into the area, Indian special forces seized the local Chushul peak overlooking regional Chinese positions. Nearby, in Mukhpari, on 7 September both sides used warning gunfire. An uneasy peace returned to the Ladakh front-line as winter set in. In January 2021, 2,500 kilometres to the east in Sikkim, another small skirmish was reported. In early May, the Indian army denied a report that Chinese and Indian patrols had 'faced off short of a clash', again in Galwan. Meanwhile, both sides kept troops facing each other in Depsang Plains, a friction point since 2013.

Throughout the year Indian and Chinese military commanders in Ladakh, at times flanked by diplomats, met to defuse tensions. These meetings may have directly contributed to preventing tensions from escalating further: by July 2020, a moratorium on patrols in a 3-km-wide zone had reportedly been agreed for Galwan. On 10 February, the two sides announced a limited disengagement agreement around Pangong Lake, covering only 20 km of the Line of Actual Control (LAC), which India considers to be 3,400 km and China 2,000 km.

The 2020 violence marked a watershed in Sino-Indian relations and was unprecedented in peacetime. The June Galwan clash was the most serious incident since 1967 and the resulting fatalities were the first on the LAC since 1975. The Mukhpari episode marked the first use of fire-arms on the LAC since 1975. The August Chushul episode led India to undertake 'pre-emptive' border action against China. India also made public the existence of its Special Frontier Force, a secret Tibetan-manned unit established after India's 1962 defeat in its limited war with China.

Origins and consequences of the clashes

India and China – which respectively claimed 38,000 and 90,000 sq. km of the other's territory – had long traded mutual accusations of encroach-ing on one another's sovereignty. Evidence suggests that China's actions and perceptions contributed most to triggering the events in Ladakh. An April 2021 assessment by the US director of national intelligence described 'China's occupation since May 2020 of contested border areas [as] the most serious escalation in decades'. This was consistent with evi-dence that Chinese forces had first moved beyond established patrolling points in Galwan and around Pangong Lake. As a result, some Indian reports estimated that China's holdings in Ladakh grew from 50–60 sq. km to 600–800 sq. km in the year to June 2021. This perception was key to India's new front-line defence stance, which one senior official of the governing Bharatiya Janata Party (BJP) called 'proactive diplomacy with strong ground posturing', and others in military circles called 'no blink-ing, no brinkmanship'. This involved countering China's perceived 'two steps forward, one step back' approach, which a former Indian national security adviser (NSA) said left China with a 'net gain of one step'. In 2020, both sides also appeared to be choosing their positions as local bargaining chips or to symbolically remind the other of the 1962 war.

China's behaviour was driven by several factors. One was the perception that Indian construction of border roads and upgrades of transport infrastructure (bridges, tunnels and the world's highest airfields) were attempts to alter the LAC in India's favour. China also opposed India's unilateral revision to the status quo in Kashmir on 5 August 2019 through the change of Ladakh's administrative status to a union territory (controlled by India, but with some Chinese territorial claims). China sought, too, to counter New Delhi's rhetorical reiteration of its claim to Aksai Chin (the Chinese-controlled sector of Kashmir that India claims is part of Ladakh) and Gilgit-Baltistan (controlled by Pakistan), the latter being a key region for the China–Pakistan Economic Corridor (CPEC). One senior Chinese analyst had deplored India's 'obsession with absolute border security'. Others cited geopolitical resentment at India's attitude and posture as a rising power in Asia, partnering with other powers to counter Chinese influence in the Indo-Pacific, warning of Indian Prime Minister Narendra Modi's 'relentless pursuit of world leadership without sufficient hard power', and insisting on 'lesson'-teaching. China might also have been encouraged to take advantage of India's distraction with the health crisis caused by the COVID-19 pandemic, which shrank the economy by a record 7.3% in the year to March 2021.

The clashes drove changes on the ground. By September 2020, tens of thousands of opposing troops, armed with heavy weaponry and possibly peaking at 50,000 on each side in Ladakh, had arrived at the border or its rear. This amounted to an increase of at least 25% in the Indian forces tasked with defending the whole border. The deployment and entrenchment of additional troops was turning the LAC in Ladakh into a dense, tense front-line increasingly comparable to the Line of Control between India and Pakistan. On both sides, the new forces comprised active and reserve military personnel rather than traditional constabulary paramilitary troops.

Both sides also built up local airpower. Fighter jets were deployed at bases close to the LAC. The PLA reportedly laid fibre-optic cables around Pangong Lake. India moved in artillery, tanks, fighter jets and helicopters. By August, both sides' equipment occupied multiple new forward positions. India's Leh airfield was reinforced with Russian Sukhoi and MiG-29 fighters, French *Rafale* fighters, and United States C-17 and C-130 transport aircraft and *Chinook* helicopters. Following a February 2021 agreement, the two militaries dismantled local bunkers and tents and moved back men, howitzers, tanks and other vehicles. But some Chinese infrastructure remained.

This militarisation tipped border management into uncharted territory. India and China previously had a modus vivendi in the absence of systematic delimitation and demarcation. In 1993–2013, five agreements created a bespoke, military–diplomatic regime to prevent friction affecting broader ties. Beijing and New Delhi used this regime's deliberate ambiguity and obfuscation to claim they could manage their differences as responsible Asian neighbours. The regime had provided face-saving and flexibility even as nationalism drove the two countries to appear strong. Assertive uses of reconnaissance vehicles, prolonged occupations and increasingly violent clashes had strained this system since the early 2010s. But from summer 2020, its mutual self-restraint principles were overtaken by more fragile political and unilateral restraints. Although local commanders reportedly used hotlines more than 1,000 times, a hotline agreed in 2013 for senior operational military chiefs did not appear to be in use. Despite three meetings at senior military level between December 2020 and June 2021, the diplomatic-led border 'Working Mechanism' produced no visible results. Unprecedented reliance on commercial satellite imagery compounded the military–diplomatic regime's growing irrelevance. Yet neither side officially acknowledged this openly. Diplomatic euphemisms rarely referred to the risk of miscalculation and inadvertent escalation. Only a few experts from both sides publicly called for new confidence-building measures and border rule-making.

Trust deficit and competition

The impact of the clashes on Sino-Indian relations was sudden and profound. At the 2018 IISS Shangri-La Dialogue, Modi had described ties with China as having more 'layers' than any of India's other bilateral relations. This breadth was central to Chinese President Xi Jinping and Modi's two informal summits in 2018 and 2019 and 18 meetings since 2014. The Galwan bloodshed appeared to come as a greater shock to India than China: this and subsequent events plunged the relationship into competition and widened the trust deficit between the two sides. India faced the difficult challenge of seeking redress for a perceived Chinese fait accompli while not wanting to admit territorial loss or intelligence failure. India would not accept normalisation unless China restored border 'peace and tranquillity' – the term India preferred to the specific territorial 'status quo' ante of April 2020. Chinese diplomacy and state media highlighted the lack of trust and damage to ties. The PLA conveyed a hard-edged border-deterrence message, releasing details of military equipment, deployments and exercises across its entire Western Theater Command. After Galwan, analysts on both sides, particularly in India, appeared to retrospectively characterise 2018–19 as a period that had been dominated by an artificial sense of mutually suspended disbelief. Chinese state media reports highlighted the fortitude and 'Karakorum spirit' of troops they described as defending the border, in apparent contrast to the 'Wuhan spirit', named after the location of the first of the two leaders' summits.

India sought an immediate answer to border developments through defence and deterrence. But it also took steps that marked a change of attitude towards the bilateral relationship, strengthening its resolve and addressing the whole-of-country power gap with China. Militarily, both countries had nuclear weapons with associated no-first-use doctrines, contributing to strategic stability. But China's military posture was strong on the border. This posed an ever-growing 'two-front dilemma' for India, given its historical defence focus on Pakistan. India's jutting shape in the Indian Ocean gave it a natural advantage for sea-control or denial strategies there against China. Yet by June 2021, India's navy had only 27 principal surface combatants and 16 submarines, compared to China's 87 and 59 respectively. As a result, India sought as much to be a 'net security provider' in the Indian Ocean, as a 'preferred security partner' able to respond first to assistance requests. To establish a broader basis for deterrence, India needed to keep up with China's economy, which was over five times larger than its own, and in most years grew at a higher rate. To address these gaps, India needed domestic defence and economic reforms and closer partnerships with the US and others.

India's most significant non-military response was its decision to proceed with trials for 5G mobile-internet technology without inviting Chinese vendors, particularly Huawei. It also banned more than 200 pieces of Chinese software for smartphones and computers; subjected public-sector contract bidders from neighbouring countries to conditional approval by its foreign and home ministries; cancelled rail and road tenders for Chinese companies; barred oil companies from using ships under Chinese flag; and reportedly held up imports of wireless technology. This drive towards economic decoupling came as India had earlier restricted investments from neighbouring countries in response to the economic shock of the pandemic. China viewed these steps to 'de-sinicise' India's economy, including implicit support for boycotting Chinese trade, as 'self-inflicted harm'. But they did little to address India's trade deficit with China.

Domestic reform efforts focused on the 'Atmanirbhar Bharat' programme to promote national economic production and consumption self-reliance without closing the economy to foreign investment and hampering export-led growth. In the defence sector, subject to national-security considerations, India raised the permitted foreign ownership stake from 49% to 74%, providing greater incentives to foreign defence companies to partner. It created and expanded an import-ban list for defence equipment. Fifteen percent of the defence-capitalisation budget was directed to the national private sector. A task force worked towards a national road map for strategic materials. Yet faced with budgetary and other constraints during the pandemic, these ambitious reforms would take years to produce their intended effects.

India also sought to accelerate military reforms and procurement. It raised the capital allocation by 18.75% in its 2021 defence budget and empowered officers below service-chief level to make procurement decisions. India was expected in 2021 to announce its military's reorganisation into tri-service theatre commands, which would eventually mirror China's 2013 reform and help reduce border asymmetries. India was reportedly repurposing an army corps away from Pakistan towards China and raising a second armoured brigade in Sikkim. It sanctioned the foreign-origin, India-built procurement of six new advanced conventional submarines. Accelerated plans to build new border roads and supporting infrastructure were driven by China's efforts to entrench militarisation and to populate and develop border regions on its side of the LAC, including through the inauguration in June of a new fast railway segment in Tibet. India's steps may have had an immediate deterrent effect on China. There was little evidence of a step change in Chinese military presence in the Indian Ocean. However, the sustainability of India's LAC operations for the national exchequer were unclear: one report estimated that they had cost around US$2.5 billion by March 2021. A cyber attack on Mumbai's power grid on 13 October 2020, though officially unattributed, was widely perceived as an unprecedented offensive by Chinese hackers.

There appeared to be little urgency on either side to revive Sino-Indian relations by diplomatic means. Separate defence- and foreign-ministerial talks in Moscow in September only led to a five-point plan of agreeing to further talks, 'quickly' disengaging, maintaining distance between troops, abiding by existing agreements and avoiding escalation.

In February, foreign ministers established a hotline, though its actual use remained undocumented. India's and China's leaders did not meet or speak during the year despite their participation in the November 2020 virtual summit of the Shanghai Cooperation Organisation (SCO). Xi wrote to Modi in April, expressing condolences for India's pandemic fatalities and offering assistance. Critics in India denounced this as insensitive, as Modi faced unprecedented domestic criticism for his handling of the health crisis. National security advisers of the two countries reportedly last spoke on 8 May 2020, and their annual talks as border negotiators and chief crisis managers failed to take place for the first time in nine years. Despite this, efforts were made to preserve chances for the leaders to re-engage personally in case the crisis worsened, ahead of Modi's in-person participation in summits from autumn 2021 and India's commitments to host leaders from the BRICS countries (Brazil, Russia,

India, China and South Africa) in September 2021 as well as the G20 in 2023. In possible anticipation, the September 2020 five-point plan revived observance of both leaders' past 'consensus' and 'guidance'. Moreover, neither Xi nor Modi accused each other or their respective countries by name: at most, Modi was reported officially to have said 'the entire country is hurt and angry at the steps taken by China at the LAC' a few days after the Galwan clash. Addressing troops, he denounced generic 'expansionism'. Throughout the period, India also withheld criticism of China on Xinjiang and continued to draw project finance from the Beijing-headquartered Asian Infrastructure Investment Bank.

Strategic encirclement and counter-encirclement

Sino-Indian border tensions significantly added to the geopolitical polarisation of South Asia and the wider Indo-Pacific region. Before 2020, both countries saw South Asia and the northern Indian Ocean as a space for competitive political and economic influence. India also saw an opportunity to build a balance of conventional deterrence to check Chinese ambitions. In 2020, India and China abandoned any pretence of cooperation in the immediate region. India sought greater inroads with neighbours concerned about China, such as Bhutan, Maldives, Sri Lanka and Bangladesh – where Modi made his first post-pandemic foreign visit in March 2021. But India faced a broad and growing disparity: it could only muster hundreds of millions of dollars in financial resources while Chinese regional investment, aid, loans and grants ran to several tens of billions. Neighbours resented having to choose between ties with India – traditionally dominated by security issues – and increasingly important economic relations with China. As a result, India stepped up counter-terrorism and maritime-security cooperation with Maldives and Sri Lanka to help insulate the region from China's and Pakistan's separate, but perceived as increasingly coordinated, actions. China in turn stepped up its de facto 'South Asia minus India' meetings, including one in April 2021 to promote its vaccine diplomacy. India's inability to honour its regional vaccine promises compounded the challenge.

Selected India–China border infrastructure

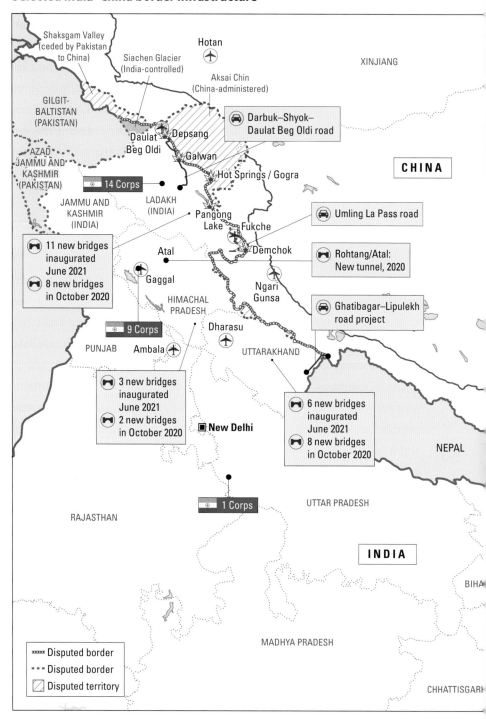

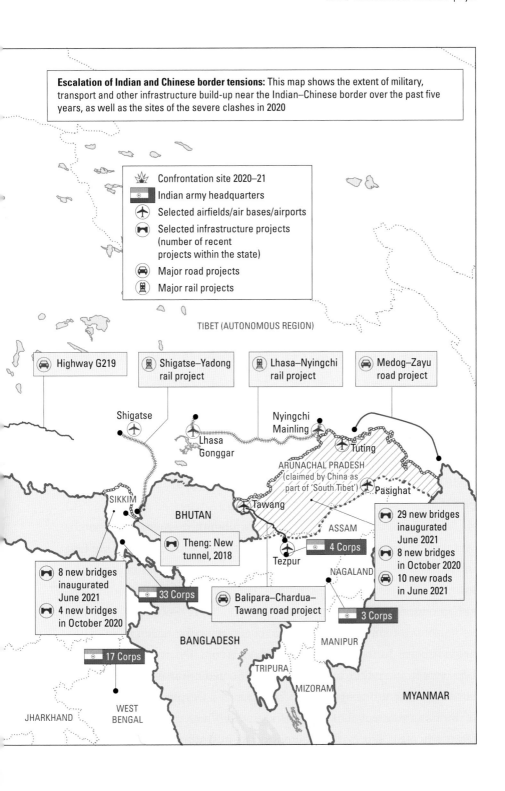

Escalation of Indian and Chinese border tensions: This map shows the extent of military, transport and other infrastructure build-up near the Indian–Chinese border over the past five years, as well as the sites of the severe clashes in 2020

Outside its immediate neighbourhood, India's external balancing was more successful. Its diplomacy traded little of the country's strategic autonomy for considerable political support from extra-regional partners. Deepening its defence-led partnership with the US coincided with greater convergence on the border issue: while in May 2020, US president Donald Trump's display of public support for India and offer to mediate the tensions had stoked Indian sensitivities, mention of those same tensions a year later by US Secretary of State Antony Blinken after a meeting with his Indian counterpart elicited no such reaction. India invited Australia to participate in the November 2020 *Malabar* naval exercise, adding a clear military undertone to the two Quad (Australia, India, Japan and the US) ministerial meetings held during the period. This paved the way for India to agree to the first Quad meeting at leadership level on 12 March 2021. Modi's India displayed its like-mindedness about China by participating in the G7 meeting hosted by the United Kingdom in June 2021. It also joined Australia in a first foreign-ministerial meeting with France, and a trilateral initiative with Japan to identify opportunities and complementarities between them for companies to diversify their supply chains away from China. It entered a 'comprehensive strategic partnership' and ten-year road map with the UK and held two summits with the European Union to reinvigorate trade talks. India also signed a Five Eyes cyber-security and cryptography statement with Japan.

As the United States' only non-treaty ally in the Quad, and a neighbour of China, India was aware that assertive diplomacy risked inviting unwelcome escalatory Chinese counter-responses. Instead of joining or forming alliances, India preferred to engage with them. While India was not an official NATO 'partner', it hosted the NATO secretary-general at its flagship international diplomatic conference (the Raisina Dialogue), held virtually during the pandemic, in April 2021. Distrust in India about US support in a wider India–China conflict fed reluctance to define the border as a front-line of the US–China contest. Despite the fact that half of India's trade passes through the South China Sea, and that India reportedly sent a navy ship there in June–July 2020, India refused joint patrols there with the US. India welcomed the Quad's implicit criticism of Chinese coercion. Some in India also supported the idea of adding a new defence and foreign ministers' meeting to the grouping but refused to see it as a potential alliance. Perhaps because of India's reservations, China did not appear to react to these moves. Chinese commentary argued that India was the weakest link in any 'mini-lateral' arrangements, particularly because of the pandemic. Yet the assumption among Chinese analysts also grew that India was committed to its partners, regardless of future developments on the border and notwithstanding disagreements or irritants.

Despite a year of heightened tensions, another limited India–China border conflict appeared unlikely. Both countries appeared to have arrested the haemorrhage of trust between them but had not set sufficiently realistic expectations of each other to normalise their relationship: the new militarised, more crisis-prone situation on the border clouded the prospects of them doing so. The pandemic also pushed India towards closer, more defence-oriented partnerships. However, with an economy heavily dependent on Chinese trade, and steady deterioration in US–China relations, India's grand strategy was likely to seek balance and engagement, even with its overbearing neighbour.

The Biden Administration's South Asia Policy
Change or continuity?

US President Joe Biden's decision to complete the withdrawal of US/NATO troops from Afghanistan by September 2021, after 20 years, marked a key feature of his administration's policy towards South Asia in the six months since it took office in January 2021. This had grave implications for the stability of Afghanistan and for ensuring the security of South Asia in the face of the threat from terrorist and extremist groups. The Biden administration also increased its engagement with India to counter China's assertive role on its land border with India and its influence in the Indo-Pacific region, while maintaining a regional focus on climate change.

Afghanistan
Policy continuation

It was widely expected that the Biden administration would continue its predecessor's policy of withdrawing US/NATO forces from Afghanistan. To determine its policy approach towards Afghanistan, within days of Biden's inauguration the White House announced a review of the Trump administration's US–Taliban peace agreement of February 2020. This agreement had aimed to withdraw most US and NATO troops in Afghanistan by 1 May 2021, with the establishment of a new intra-Afghan dialogue between nominees of the Afghan government/civil society and the Afghan Taliban in Doha in September 2020. The withdrawal of international forces was meant to take place concurrently with an intra-Afghan dialogue, stated in the US–Taliban peace agreement to start from 10 March 2020. This would have led to the final phase for the establishment of a joint mechanism to implement a permanent ceasefire. But while the Taliban and other militant groups did not attack US and NATO forces, who despite their non-combat role were potential targets as foreign troops in Afghanistan, they escalated their targeting of Afghan security forces and influential civil-society members, including prominent journalists. In May 2021, the US Chairman of the Joint Chiefs of Staff General Mark Milley stated that the Taliban had conducted 80–120 attacks a day for the past year, primarily against the Afghan security forces. United Nations Security Council reports also concluded that segments of the Taliban had not ended cooperation with al-Qaeda, despite having agreed to do so. The intra-Afghan dialogue made little meaningful progress, with the Taliban awaiting the results of the US presidential elections and refusing to discuss a permanent ceasefire. By the end of the Trump presidency, US troop levels in Afghanistan had been reduced from 13,000 prior to the February 2020 agreement to 2,500.

The Biden administration's policy review recommended a unified approach to the Afghan peace process that included all regional stakeholders and neighbours. This was planned to take the form of a UN intra-Afghan summit in Istanbul, convened by Turkey and Qatar, and scheduled for April–May, along with the foreign ministers of China, India, Iran, Pakistan and Russia to finalise a peace agreement and a road map for an inclusive government and permanent ceasefire to end the violence in Afghanistan.

Implementation and impact

On 14 April, Biden announced that the US would complete the withdrawal of all US and NATO forces by 11 September 2021, the 20th anniversary of the 9/11 terror attacks. Shortly afterwards, Biden spoke to Afghan President Ashraf Ghani to convey the US commitment to continued bilateral partnership through economic, humanitarian and security assistance. Reactions in Afghanistan were mixed. Although Ghani believed that Afghan forces would be capable of defending the country if the peace process failed, other senior governmental officials and members of the Afghan government's negotiating team in Doha expressed concern over the announcement because of the Taliban's failure to reduce violence or commit to a permanent ceasefire. In late June, Ghani and Abdullah Abdullah, chairman of the Afghan High Council for National Reconciliation, visited Washington DC to meet with Biden. During the meeting, Biden stated that although the US would still offer Afghanistan security assistance and diplomatic and humanitarian aid, the Afghans were 'going to have to decide their future, what they want'.

The Taliban considered the Biden announcement a breach of the peace agreement but did not resume attacks against US/NATO forces, preferring to await the delayed withdrawal. But its level of violence increased in May and June as the foreign troops commenced their withdrawal. The Taliban refused to participate in the planned UN-convened intra-Afghan peace summit meeting until all foreign forces had been withdrawn.

The withdrawal of the remaining 2,500 US troops and about 9,600 NATO soldiers commenced on 1 May. In late June, US officials stated that as many as 1,000 US troops, assigned to the US embassy in Kabul, would remain in Afghanistan to provide security for the US embassy and play an advisory role for the Afghan government. The US also announced continued funding, training and counter-terrorism support to the Afghan forces from a third country, although this was not named. The US troop withdrawal took place ahead of schedule and was expected to be completed by the end of August 2021.

With limited progress expected through the resumption of the peace process towards an all-inclusive transitional/interim government, the risk of an escalation of violence and another civil war in Afghanistan was high. In late June, the US intelligence community reportedly concluded that the government of Afghanistan and its capital, Kabul, could fall between six and 12 months after the withdrawal of US troops. As events transpired, this severely overstated the effectiveness of the Afghan national forces. The Taliban's rapid takeover of the country gave rise to major security concerns in South Asia and new questions about the reliability of American policy.

India

Defence and security partnership

Despite differences on tariff and trade issues, in its final six months the Trump administration focused on strengthening defence and security ties with India. This was due largely to its widening rift with China and subsequent strategic convergence with India to counter China's assertive role on its land border with India and its influence in the Indo-Pacific region. In January 2021, the US Indo-Pacific strategy, declassifying its

2018 US Strategic Framework for the Indo-Pacific, described the Trump administration's policy towards India since 2017 as seeking to ensure that 'India's preferred partner on security issues is the US', and that the 'two cooperate to counter Chinese influence', with the US offering 'support to India through diplomatic, military, and intelligence channels'.

This strategy was symbolised by the third face-to-face '2+2' US–India foreign and defence ministers' dialogue in October 2020 in New Delhi, held despite the COVID-19 pandemic. This resulted in the signing of the Basic Exchange and Cooperation Agreement for geospatial cooperation (BECA), the fourth and last of the key bilateral 'foundational agreements' on defence cooperation that the US has signed with its defence partners since 2016. Significantly, the US supplied two MQ-9A *Reaper* armed uninhabited aerial vehicles (UAVs) and cold-weather clothing to India in response to the India–China border clash in Galwan in June 2020. In the wider Indo-Pacific region, meetings of the Quadrilateral dialogue (the 'Quad' – comprising Australia, India, Japan and the US) were upgraded from senior-foreign-ministry-official to foreign-ministerial level in September 2019. In November, Australia participated in the 2020 edition of the India–US *Malabar* naval exercise, alongside its Quad partners, for the first time since 2007. In September, a US P-8A anti-submarine-warfare aircraft landed in India's Andaman and Nicobar Islands for the first time for logistics and refuelling support, signalling that the Logistics Exchange Memorandum of Agreement (LEMOA) had become operational. Signed in August 2016, the LEMOA gives the US and India access to each other's designated military facilities for supplies and repairs.

Against the background of a personal rapport between president Donald Trump and Indian Prime Minister Narendra Modi, the Trump administration did not express concerns, privately or publicly, on the curtailment of civil liberties and press freedoms by the Modi government; indeed, Trump's visit to New Delhi in February 2020 had been marked by large-scale protests against India's Citizenship (Amendment) Act. For their part, US congressional Democrats, and European states, levelled criticisms against the Modi government. This led Modi, despite Indian diplomacy's long-standing principle of ensuring bipartisan US support, to take the unprecedented step of endorsing Trump's re-election during his visit to the US in September 2019. During a Modi–Trump rally attended by 50,000 Indian Americans in Houston, Texas, Modi raised the slogan: 'In the words of candidate Trump: Abki baar, Trump sarkar' ('This time, [a] Trump government'). This was not lost on the Democrats, who in December 2019 had a brush with India's external-affairs minister when he refused to meet a Democrat congresswoman critical of India's actions in Kashmir in August 2019, leading to the cancellation of the engagement.

It was therefore with some trepidation that India's ruling political circles welcomed the new Biden administration. But India's diplomats were confident that they could re-ignite the close relationship that the Modi government had enjoyed with the Obama administration. Modi had met Biden twice when the latter was vice president, in September 2014 and June 2016. Modi was the 12th foreign leader President Biden spoke to, in February 2021. They discussed cooperation on COVID-19, a renewal of their partnership on climate change, and further cooperation to ensure a free and open Indo-Pacific, including through the Quad. US Secretary of Defense Lloyd Austin's visit to India in March was the first by a senior member of the Biden administration. While both sides highlighted the growing bilateral defence cooperation, during a press conference in New Delhi, Austin stated that he had discussed US concerns about human-rights violations with members of India's cabinet (but not with Modi), as 'partners need to be able to have those kinds of discussions'.

Policy priorities

The Biden administration focused on three issues in its first six months – cooperation in the Indo-Pacific, countering COVID-19 and climate change – which India welcomed. Highlighting the United States' commitment to the Indo-Pacific, the Biden administration raised its engagement with the Quad through participation in the first Quad Leaders' summit, held in a virtual format, in March 2021. The joint statement focused on vaccine production and distribution to the Indo-Pacific. Despite an initially delayed public response, the Biden administration provided emergency assistance to help counter India's severe second COVID-19 wave from April 2021, supplying oxygen and essential ingredients for the global vaccine supply chain. US vaccine supplies to India were also on the agenda during the visit of India's external-affairs minister to the US in late May, the first by an Indian minister since Biden became president. Subsequently, in June, the Biden administration announced that India would receive a share of the US vaccines distributed globally, to help counter its second wave. In the United States' first allocation in June, India received an unspecified share of the six million vaccines provided bilaterally by the US, and an additional share of the 7m vaccines the US provided to Asian countries through the COVAX programme. However, by the end of June, the vaccine donations by the US and via COVAX had not been sent to India, as the US was awaiting the Indian government's legal clearance for an emergency import.

US Special Presidential Envoy for Climate John Kerry visited India in April. During the US-organised Leaders' Summit on Climate later that month, Modi and Biden agreed to launch a US–India partnership on climate and clean energy. In February 2021, the US government also welcomed the Indian and Pakistan militaries' announcement of a renewed commitment to their ceasefire on the Line of Control (LoC) between India and Pakistani-controlled Kashmir.

Amid this early engagement, the timing and rationale of a US freedom-of-navigation operation (FONOP) around India came as a surprise to the Modi government. A statement issued by the commander of the US Navy's Seventh Fleet said that on 7 April, the US destroyer USS *John Paul Jones* carried out a military exercise approximately 130 nautical miles west of the Lakshadweep Islands, within India's exclusive economic zone (EEZ) in the Arabian Sea, 'without requesting India's prior consent'. Although this was consistent with Articles 56 and 58, Part V of the UN Convention on the Law of the Sea (UNCLOS) – which permits warships such freedoms in the 200-nautical-mile EEZs of coastal states – it challenged India's interpretation of UNCLOS and its own pre-UNCLOS domestic law that did not authorise such military exercises 'without the consent of the coastal state'. The Indian government responded stating that India's position on UNCLOS was that it:

> does not authorise other States to carry out in the EEZ and on the continental shelf, military exercises or manoeuvres, in particular those involving the use of weapons or explosives, without the consent of the coastal state. The USS John Paul Jones was continuously monitored transiting from the Persian Gulf towards the Malacca Straits.

Despite the media controversy the incident generated in India, this was not new: 22 US FONOPs have taken place around India in the past 30 years.

Yet the timing of the US FONOP, in the wake of India's violent border clash with China in June 2020, when New Delhi was intent on bolstering defence and security ties with the US, raised concerns in New Delhi over the perceived proclivities of the Biden administration to comment publicly on civil-liberty and freedom-of-press issues in India. Moreover, the widely disseminated public statement by the US Navy on the FONOP led to concerns in India that the US was likely to impose sanctions against India under the Countering America's Adversaries Through Sanctions Act (CAATSA) over the prospective transfer of five regiments of S-400 air-defence missiles from Russia for the Indian air force.

US engagement with India under the Biden administration will also need to include a greater focus on building US–India economic and trade ties, in addition to the focus on the continued bilateral defence relationship. Efforts under the Trump administration to reach a limited bilateral trade deal with India did not progress, and each side imposed tariffs on the other.

Pakistan
Afghanistan prism
The Trump administration had perceived Pakistan largely through the prism of Afghanistan and its plans to complete the US troop withdrawal by 1 May 2021. The Pakistani military-intelligence agency, the Inter-Services Intelligence (ISI), played a principal 'behind-the-scenes' role in

facilitating the US–Taliban peace agreement of February 2020 and the start of the intra-Afghan dialogue in September 2020 through its leverage over the Taliban/Haqqani network.

But Pakistan's close relations with China had a negative impact on US–Pakistan relations as Washington's rift with Beijing deepened. Relations were also affected by the Trump administration's closer ties with India, symbolised by its reiteration of the Kashmir dispute as a bilateral issue between India and Pakistan; and US co-sponsorship of a motion at the intergovernmental Financial Action Task Force (FATF) in June 2018 to combat terror financing, resulting in the continued 'greylisting' of Pakistan.

Relations under the Biden administration

As a consequence, the government of Prime Minister Imran Khan sought to shift the focus of Pakistan's relations with the Biden administration from a regional 'geosecurity' emphasis on China and India, to a bilateral 'geo-economic' one of enhanced regional connectivity and a peaceful South Asia. But security continued to be the primary focus of Biden's Pakistan policy. US Secretary of State Antony Blinken's first telephone call with his counterpart Shah Mahmood Qureshi focused on Pakistan's role in Afghanistan and concern over the Pakistan Supreme Court's decision in January 2021 to acquit the individuals involved in the kidnapping and murder of American journalist Daniel Pearl in 2002. US policy under the Biden administration continued to call for an end to Pakistan's support for terror groups, including groups operating in Afghanistan and those launching attacks in India. Austin expressed support for the restoration of military training of future Pakistan military leaders under the International Military Education and Training (IMET) funds.

Pakistan's engagement with the US on climate-change issues has had mixed success. Despite climate change being a significant challenge to Pakistan, Kerry did not visit the country during his visit to South Asia in April, though he visited India and Bangladesh. Although Khan was not initially invited to the US-led Leaders' Summit on Climate in April, Pakistan's climate-change minister subsequently participated as a speaker.

The Commander of US Central Command General Kenneth McKenzie met with Pakistan's Army Chief General Qamar Bajwa in February. In June, it was reported that CIA Director William Burns had made an unannounced visit to Pakistan some weeks earlier, to discuss Afghanistan with Bajwa and Lt-Gen. Faiz Hameed, the ISI director-general. In late May, Pakistan's National Security Adviser Moeed Yusuf met his US counterpart Jake Sullivan in Geneva. In late June, Khan stated that Pakistan would not allow US bases to operate in Pakistan to allow the US to conduct operations in Afghanistan. It was notable that, in his first six months in office, Biden had spoken with Indian and Afghan leaders, but not with Khan.

Bangladesh, Maldives and Sri Lanka
Outreach by the Trump administration
The Trump administration's competitive relationship with China resulted in outreach to South Asian littoral and island states not seen for many years. In September 2020, the US and Maldivian defence ministries signed a framework for the bilateral defence and security relationship to 'deepen engagement and cooperation in support of maintaining peace and security in the Indian Ocean'; India welcomed the agreement. US secretary of state Mike Pompeo visited Sri Lanka and Maldives in October 2020, marking the highest-level US visit to Colombo since 2015 and to Maldives since 2004. The January 2021 US Indo-Pacific strategy underscored its objective to 'strengthen the capacity' of Bangladesh, Sri Lanka and Maldives in order to 'contribute to a free and open order'.

Mixed progress on climate change
Climate change appeared to be the principal focus for the Biden administration's initial engagement with these three countries. Bangladesh's Minister of Foreign Affairs AK Abdul Momen made the first in-person visit to the US by a South Asian minister under the Biden administration in February 2021, although COVID-19 restrictions did not allow for a planned face-to-face meeting with Blinken. Their phone call focused on cooperation on economic, defence and climate-change issues. Following

Kerry's visit to Dhaka in April, Bangladeshi Prime Minister Sheikh Hasina participated in the Leaders' Summit on Climate, but Maldives and Sri Lanka were not invited.

The US–Maldives defence framework became operational in March, with the US army undertaking a month-long combat-training exercise with the Maldives National Defence Force. The following month, the USS *John Paul Jones* conducted a FONOP in 'the vicinity' of Maldives, to challenge its excessive maritime claim inconsistent with UNCLOS that required prior permission for foreign warships to enter its territorial sea and EEZ. Unlike in the case of India, there was no reaction from Maldives.

Prospects

The US troop withdrawal from Afghanistan was the Biden administration's single most important priority for South Asia in its first six months. A severe escalation of violence and the possible onset of a civil war in Afghanistan could result in considerable instability and significant spillover risks for Pakistan in areas adjacent to Afghanistan and an escalation of violence in Indian-controlled Kashmir through the presence of anti-India terror groups in Afghanistan. This could give rise to an Indian threat to a retaliatory attack on Pakistan, as during the Pulwama–Balakot clash in February–March 2019, and lead to the involvement of the US in a crisis-management role. However, with the United States having strengthened its relations with India compared to those with Pakistan, it may be less influential with the latter than in previous India–Pakistan crises, such as the 1999 Kargil conflict.

Alongside its climate-change and global-health agendas, relations with India will dominate long-term US engagement in South Asia. Their security cooperation will expand and deepen if US–China relations deteriorate. At the same time, human-rights violations and restrictions on civil liberties in India can be expected to complicate relations. Once US troops withdraw from Afghanistan by September 2021, the significance of Pakistan's influence over the Taliban/Haqqani network will decline for the US but not for Afghanistan.

Pakistan's deepening relations with China may become a concern for the Biden administration. A hardening of US attitudes towards China would also evoke grave concern among the smaller littoral and island states of South Asia, which seek cooperation with China on trade and investment issues for their economic development and with the US on political and climate-change issues. Their main challenge will therefore be to continue to seek to balance relations between these two economic and security superpowers.

Senior US positions responsible for South Asia continued to be filled, with the early appointment of a senior director for South Asia in the National Security Council and a deputy assistant secretary of defense for South and Southeast Asia. The nomination of Donald Lu, a senior diplomat with regional expertise, as assistant secretary of state for South and Central Asia was welcomed in the region, due to his having served in both India and Pakistan, including as deputy chief of mission in New Delhi. He is expected to be the first lead diplomat for South Asia confirmed by the Senate since 2017. But at the end of June 2021, new ambassadors to Afghanistan, India and Pakistan had yet to be nominated.

Overall, the Biden administration's initial policy on South Asia has largely been similar to that of the Trump administration. This includes a strengthening of relations with India, particularly on defence and security issues; continuing the Trump administration's focus on the withdrawal of US troops from Afghanistan without preconditions; engagement with Pakistan primarily through its role in Afghanistan; and continued relations with Bangladesh, Maldives and Sri Lanka amid increasing Chinese engagement in these countries. The most notable contrast is the Biden administration's increased engagement with the Quad, along with a new focus on climate change.

Drivers of Strategic Change

REGIONAL SHARE OF GLOBAL POPULATION, GDP AND DEFENCE BUDGET

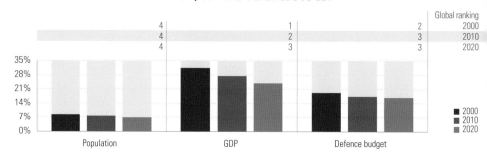

							Global ranking	
		4		1		2	2000	
		4		2		3	2010	
		4		3		3	2020	

Population — GDP — Defence budget

■ 2000
■ 2010
■ 2020

POPULATION

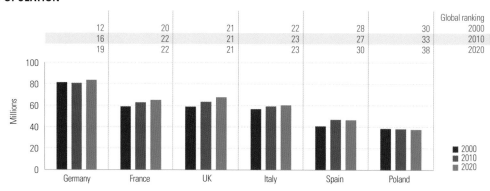

	Germany	France	UK	Italy	Spain	Poland	Global ranking
	12	20	21	22	28	30	2000
	16	22	21	23	27	33	2010
	19	22	21	23	30	38	2020

■ 2000
■ 2010
■ 2020

AGE STRUCTURE
(Percentage of national population)

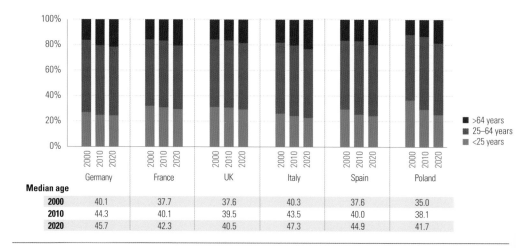

■ >64 years
■ 25–64 years
■ <25 years

Median age	Germany	France	UK	Italy	Spain	Poland
2000	40.1	37.7	37.6	40.3	37.6	35.0
2010	44.3	40.1	39.5	43.5	40.0	38.1
2020	45.7	42.3	40.5	47.3	44.9	41.7

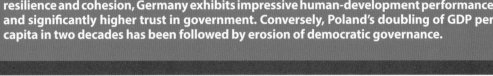

Economic, demographic and defence trends chart relative decline, particularly in active military personnel. As a rich, free continent it wields soft power. On domestic sources of resilience and cohesion, Germany exhibits impressive human-development performance and significantly higher trust in government. Conversely, Poland's doubling of GDP per capita in two decades has been followed by erosion of democratic governance.

GDP
(Constant 2010 US dollars)

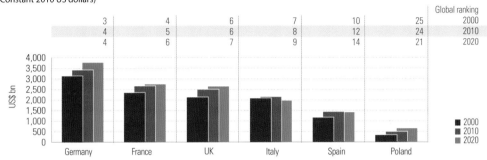

						Global ranking
3	4	6	7	10	25	2000
4	5	6	8	12	24	2010
4	6	7	9	14	21	2020

US$ bn — 4,000 / 3,500 / 3,000 / 2,500 / 2,000 / 1,500 / 1,000 / 500 / 0

Germany · France · UK · Italy · Spain · Poland

■ 2000 ■ 2010 ■ 2020

GDP PER CAPITA
(Constant 2010 US dollars)

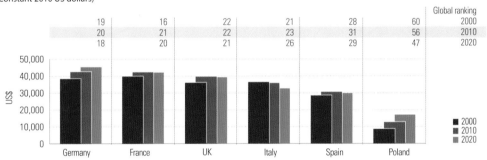

						Global ranking
19	16	22	21	28	60	2000
20	21	22	23	31	56	2010
18	20	21	26	29	47	2020

US$ — 50,000 / 40,000 / 30,000 / 20,000 / 10,000 / 0

Germany · France · UK · Italy · Spain · Poland

■ 2000 ■ 2010 ■ 2020

DEFENCE BUDGET
(Constant 2015 US dollars)

ACTIVE MILITARY PERSONNEL

	Defence Budget — Global ranking			Active Military Personnel — Global ranking		
	2000	2010	2020	2000	2010	2020
Germany	8	6	7	25	23	27
France	3	4	5	21	14	22
UK	2	3	3	27	29	34
Italy	11	11	12	23	19	30
Spain	25	18	19	34	37	43
Poland	40	25	18	26	46	44

Defence Budget axis: 0 · 15 · 30 · 45 · 60 · 75 — US$bn

Active Military Personnel axis: 0 · 50 · 100 · 150 · 200 · 250 · 300 · 350 · 400 — Thousands

■ 2000 ■ 2010 ■ 2020

For explanation of drivers and sources, see page 9

HUMAN DEVELOPMENT INDEX (HDI)
(Score between 0 and 1, where 0 denotes a low level of development and 1 a high level of development)

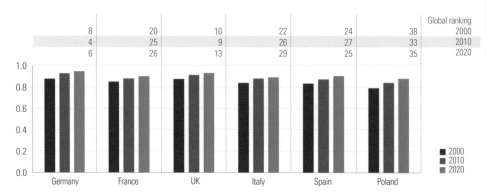

						Global ranking	
8	20	10	22	24	38	2000
4	25	9	26	27	33	2010
6	26	13	29	25	35	2020

POLITICAL SYSTEM
(Score between 0 and 100, where 0 denotes no political freedom and 100 fully free)

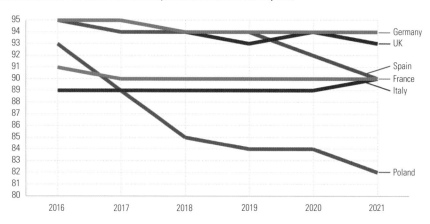

TRUST IN GOVERNMENT
(Average level of trust)

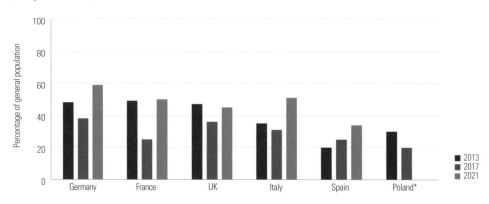

* No 2021 data available for Poland

For explanation of drivers and sources, see page 9

2020–21 Review

2020–21 was a period of fluctuating fortunes for the European Union. Under pressure to demonstrate the Union's utility in the midst of the COVID-19 pandemic, and with a slow initial vaccine roll-out undermining confidence, a €750-billion pandemic recovery fund supported by joint EU borrowing broke new ground. The management and impact of the fiscal transfers involved will determine the prospects for Europe's economic and monetary union. A Trade and Cooperation Agreement (TCA) avoided a 'no deal' outcome at the end of the United Kingdom's Brexit transition period, but ongoing negotiations over the specifics of the UK's new third-party status fuelled mutual mistrust. As the continent's struggle with anti-democratic and nationalist forces within its borders continued, transatlantic relations benefitted from a welcome reset. European attitudes towards Russia and China hardened, but individual states pursued different policies. Clearer strategies emerged for engagement with the Indo-Pacific, though questions about the adequacy of their resourcing remained.

COVID-19 response

As the second and third waves of the COVID-19 pandemic spread across Europe from late 2020, pressure mounted on EU institutions to demonstrate their utility. The European Commission seemed to have learnt some lessons from earlier squabbles between member states over personal protective equipment (PPE) and moved to improve coordination at the EU level, most notably through a joint vaccine-procurement scheme. Initially lauded as both a demonstration of the single market's buying power and a repudiation of the 'go it alone' approach pursued by the United States and the UK, the strategy was successful at least with regard to price. But delays in coordination ensured that for much of the first half of 2021, EU citizens were forced to watch as the US and UK purchased, distributed and administered vaccines at considerably faster rates. EU vaccine supplies fell behind schedule and tensions rose between EU member states over the equitable distribution within their common market of the vaccines that had been procured.

By mid-2021 the narrative was turning. Many EU member states moved ahead of schedule on the EU's objective to vaccinate 70% of all adults with at least one dose by the end of September. The EU had also reserved a further 1.8bn doses of the BioNTech/Pfizer vaccine for delivery between the end of 2021 and 2023 and appeared to be negotiating a similar mega-deal with another vaccine manufacturer. By early June 2021, the EU had exported 300 million vaccines – around the same quantity that had been delivered to EU citizens – with 2.6bn doses promised by EU producers to developing countries by the end of 2022. The development of an EU-wide digital COVID-19 certificate (to document vaccination, testing and recovery) was also under way, designed to help protect the future of the EU's passport-free Schengen Area.

European governments also agreed to provide macroeconomic support for their pandemic-hit economies. Alongside measures such as lifting limits on state aid and budget deficits, they empowered the European Commission to borrow up to €750bn (in 2018 prices) on capital markets between mid-2021 and 2026. A Recovery and Resilience Facility (RRF) entered into force in February 2020, making €312.5bn in grants and €360bn in loans available to help member states finance their resilience and recovery plans. The EU's subsequent issuance in June of its first ten-year bond resulted in one of the biggest single-tranche debt sales ever and attracted near record demand.

The EU will focus on the dispersal and monitoring of these funds, aiming to help eurozone countries return to pre-crisis output levels by the end of 2022. Although the agreement emphasised the 'temporary' nature of this new facility in order to help reassure countries like Germany that have long been sceptical of mutualising debt, this unprecedented display of fiscal solidarity could open the door to further EU-wide economic integration.

In July 2020, EU leaders agreed the EU's next long-term budget – the Multiannual Financial Facility (MFF) for 2021–27, worth €1,074.3bn in 2018 prices (including the integration of the European Development Fund). Both the MFF and RRF were designed to reinforce EU commitments to develop clearer and more ambitious agendas for common EU digital and green transitions.

Helped by the enormity of the challenge posed by the pandemic, the use of a large-scale economic stimulus by the European Central Bank proved notably uncontroversial throughout this period. Overall, generous fiscal and monetary measures helped cushion the negative impact on European economic activity, resulting in fewer lay-offs and bankruptcies than might otherwise have been expected, given the sharp contraction of economic activities caused by repeat lockdowns. Economic and fiscal policy is likely to remain supportive throughout 2021 and 2022.

Nevertheless, the crisis further highlighted divisions between member states. By May 2021, seven countries, whose combined GDP amounts to over 50% of the eurozone's total, held debt-to-GDP ratios close to or above 120% of GDP, while only eight countries had managed to keep their debt ratios below the 60% target set out in the 1992 Maastricht Treaty. Overall, eurozone debt-to-GDP ratio was expected to stabilise throughout 2021 at around 100% of GDP, some 14 percentage points higher than in 2019.

Internal tensions

Poland and Hungary spent much of the second half of 2020 trying to derail agreements on the MFF and RRF, in opposition to EU attempts to make allocations of funds conditional on adherence to democratic standards and the rule of law. Both countries continued to face proceedings under Article 7.1 of the Treaty of the European Union for alleged breaches of EU values, including attacks on the independence of the judiciary and freedom of the press. Poland and Hungary's latest assaults on these values were detailed in the EU's 2020 Rule of Law Report. Their vetoes in November of the EU budget plan forced an uneasy compromise in December that was likely to further delay links between democratic standards and EU funds and therefore hinder EU efforts to slow the erosion of these standards. Such compromises on issues of principle within the EU are likely to become increasingly problematic, not least as the Union seeks to develop its role as a promoter of an international rules-based order.

In November 2020, and in her final year in office, Angela Merkel celebrated 15 years as German chancellor. But the plaudits her government won for its handling of the first wave of COVID-19 did not survive the second and third waves, when problems with the vaccine roll-out meant that just 14.6% of the population had received one dose by early April 2021 (compared with 46.7% in the UK). Tensions between the federal and state levels increased; in March, Merkel was forced to apologise and roll back a five-day lockdown she had announced for the Easter holidays just 34 hours previously. Her government also took hits elsewhere, including from the Trump administration for Germany's refusal to abandon the controversial Nord Stream 2 gas pipeline from Russia.

In January 2021, a delayed party conference selected Armin Laschet as the next chair of Germany's centre-right Christian Democratic Union (CDU) party. In April, despite a late challenge by Markus Söder, leader of the CDU's sister party the Christian Social Union in Bavaria (CSU), the CDU and CSU confirmed Laschet as their joint candidate for chancellor in September's federal elections. By June 2021, tightening polls suggested that much of the German establishment would spend the remainder of the year distracted by a complex set of coalition negotiations. Whatever the outcome, Germany's Green party, led by its chancellor candidate Annalena Baerbock, looked set to play a key role in these negotiations and to enter government for the first time as a coalition partner.

Other leaders will likely jostle to fill the gap that Merkel's departure from the European scene will leave. French President Emmanuel Macron was expected to try to improve his European leadership credentials as he prepared for the presidential elections in spring 2022. Despite his self-proclaimed 'neither left nor right' politics, however, he would offer a fundamentally more ambitious, impatient and divisive style of European leadership than Merkel. This style would likely make it difficult for Macron to engineer the delicate behind-the-scenes compromises within the EU for which Merkel has become known. Meanwhile, Macron's own path to re-election looked far from secure; in regional and departmental elections in June his centrist party (and Marine Le Pen's far-right National Rally) failed to garner the expected support, though turnout was predictably low. The stage is set for the emergence of a third candidate and a tighter presidential race in 2022 than in 2017.

Following Merkel's retirement in September 2021, Dutch Prime Minister Mark Rutte will become one of the EU's longest-serving leaders (only Hungarian Prime Minister Viktor Orbán will have been in office longer). Rutte was re-elected in March 2021, after his government was forced to resign over a child-welfare fraud scandal. The impressive electoral performance of the liberal pro-EU D66 party offered a brief respite from the continent's growing anti-EU populism. However, the Dutch far right still achieved its best result in recent history, albeit with its 29 seats split across multiple parties.

In Italy, former prime minister Matteo Renzi withdrew his support for the coalition government of then-prime minister Giuseppe Conte in January 2021. Mario Draghi formed a cabinet of national unity that left the far-right Brothers of Italy as the sole opposition party. Fears grew that the 2023 general election could bring a populist hard-right coalition to power, should Giorgia Meloni's Brothers of Italy join forces with Matteo Salvini's League and Silvio Berlusconi's Forza Italia.

Navigating tensions with regional 'third parties'

EU member states were involved in a series of complex and tense negotiations with two close regional third parties: Switzerland and the UK. In May 2021, the Swiss Federal Council ended seven years of negotiations with the EU that had aimed to modernise their relations. Part of the reason was Swiss scepticism about 'dynamic alignment' with EU legislation and the role of the European Court of Justice. The collapse of these negotiations presented new challenges for a country that trades more with the EU than with any other partner.

Prioritising sovereignty over economics also drove the UK's determination not to seek an extension beyond 2020 of the transition agreement, under which the UK had remained part of the EU's single market and customs union after Brexit in January 2020. In late December, the UK and the EU reached a TCA that averted a 'no-deal' outcome. The deal included provisions for zero tariffs and zero quotas on all goods that complied with appropriate rules of origin. From early 2021, the trade-offs that the TCA entailed became apparent to traders and fishermen across the English Channel. But the most serious tensions arose from the implementation of the Northern Ireland Protocol (NIP), agreed as part of the EU–UK Withdrawal Agreement. In January 2021, over the EU's objection, the UK government announced a set of 'easements' that effectively suspended the required customs checks on goods arriving into Northern Ireland from Great Britain. In March, the EU formally launched legal proceedings against the UK for its alleged breach of the NIP. The rounds of mutual recriminations looked set to test the dispute-settlement systems of both the Withdrawal Agreement and the TCA.

By June 2021, concerns about the risk of violence in Northern Ireland were growing as unionist opponents of the NIP rejected it as a threat to British sovereignty and to Northern Ireland's status within the UK. The NIP featured in bilateral discussions, including with the US, at the G7 summit in Cornwall in mid-June. The EU accused the UK of reneging on an agreement that it had negotiated, signed and even lauded as a triumph, while the UK accused the EU of dangerous and 'theologically draconian' intransigence. Tensions continued over the balance of measures required to protect the peace process, the territorial integrity of the UK and the integrity of the EU's single market. A mutual lack of trust looked to be in danger of inhibiting further joint agreements; by June 2021, the EU had still not signed the already meagre Memorandum of Understanding on financial services agreed between the UK and EU in March.

Relations were further damaged by tensions over vaccine exports. The EU clumsily invoked Article 16 of the NIP in order to block the export of COVID-19 vaccines to the UK, following 'unacceptable' shortfalls in the supply of the AstraZeneca vaccine, sparking outrage in the UK government, even when the EU quickly reversed its decision. Not long afterwards, however, with tensions rising over the NIP, the UK government issued the very same threat to the EU as it considered 'all measures' to protect its territorial integrity.

External relationships

The final months of the US administration of Donald Trump were traumatic for the EU and for many of its member states. President Joe Biden's arrival in the White House led to early efforts on all sides to heal divisions. In February 2021, Trump's July 2020 decision to withdraw 12,000 troops from Germany was put on hold; the White House also quietly signalled that it would no longer make stopping Nord Stream 2 a top priority, effectively leaving the pipeline's fate to the coalition agreement that would follow the German federal elections in September 2021.

The Biden administration's early actions to rejoin the Paris Agreement on climate change and to reverse Trump's decision to leave the World Health Organization further confirmed to European partners a change in substance as well as rhetoric from the previous administration. In June 2021, a long-standing EU–US (and UK–US) dispute relating to large civil aircraft was put on hold, with an agreement secured for tariffs to be suspended for five years and a new cooperative approach worked up.

An EU–US summit held shortly before this announcement included the launch of the EU–US Trade and Technology Council. This could be an important platform to watch in 2022 and beyond, in the crafting of new rules designed to counter China's rising influence. Meanwhile, a new EU–US bilateral dialogue on China, agreed with the Trump administration in October 2020, was effectively relaunched in May 2021 with the Biden administration. While its first meeting was relatively harmonious, difficult discussions lie ahead.

Faced with the increased geopolitical and economic importance of the Indo-Pacific, Germany and the Netherlands followed France in drawing up their own Indo-Pacific guidelines in September and November 2020 respectively. The three countries then worked together to push through a coordinated EU approach, resulting in the adoption of conclusions on an EU Strategy for Cooperation in the Indo-Pacific by the European Council in April. The strategy recommitted the EU politically to the region and aimed, among other policies, to expand its security and defence dialogues and interactions there. Meanwhile, in March 2021 the UK set out its vision for its role in the world in two documents: 'Global Britain in a Competitive Age: the Integrated Review of Security, Defence, Development and Foreign Policy' and the command paper 'Defence in a Competitive Age'. These documents outlined the UK's 'tilt' towards the Indo-Pacific and were clearer than their continental counterparts in highlighting the threat to national interests posed by China's military modernisation and growing international assertiveness.

Questions arose over the resourcing of all these strategies, not least as the US focus on the Indo-Pacific would require European nations to plug more of the gaps in security provision in their immediate neighbourhood. Nevertheless, clear signals of intent were sent. In February 2021, a French nuclear-attack submarine conducted a patrol in the South China Sea and a French-led aircraft-carrier strike group departed on a four-month deployment, which would include a period in the Indian Ocean. In May, the UK's new aircraft carrier set sail to the Indo-Pacific. This deployment, which included a US Navy destroyer and a frigate from the Netherlands, represented the largest naval and air task force under British command since the Falklands War, and would last 28 weeks and include visits to 40 countries. The same month, the French navy exercised with Australian, Japanese and US forces around the US Pacific territory of Guam. Meanwhile, Germany held its first 2+2 talks with Japan in April, and in May German Defence Minister Annegret Kramp-Karrenbauer toured Guam, Japan and South Korea to promote closer defence engagement prior to the deployment of a German frigate to the region later in the year.

The EU's broader relationship with China also continued to deteriorate. EU suspicions of mask diplomacy were followed by fears that China, alongside Russia, sought advantage from the initial deficiencies in the EU's vaccine roll-out. In May 2021, Lithuania withdrew from the 17+1 forum between China and Central and Eastern European states and called on others to follow suit. A month earlier, an EU progress report assessing the dynamics of EU–China relations had called for more 'robust measures' to deal with the new challenges China posed. In presenting the criticism contained in this report to the European Council, Commission President Ursula von der Leyen and High Representative of the EU for Foreign Affairs and Security Policy Josep Borrell jointly argued:

The reality is that the EU and China have fundamental divergences, be it about their economic systems and managing globalization, democracy and human rights, or on how to deal with third countries. These differences are set to remain for the foreseeable future and must not be brushed under the carpet.

The one notable exception to this general downturn in Europe–China relations turned out to be temporary. In December 2020, pushed by Merkel as one of the centrepieces of her country's EU presidency, an EU–China Comprehensive Agreement on Investment (CAI) was finally concluded in principle. But five months later, amid mounting pushback against the deal, the European Parliament voted almost unanimously to freeze its ratification. This followed China's imposition in March 2021 of sanctions on several European entities and political representatives – measures that were in turn a retaliation against the EU's decision to join the US and UK in imposing sanctions on Chinese officials for human-rights abuses in Xinjiang. The EU made it clear that CAI ratification would not be considered while China's EU sanctions remained in place.

Nevertheless, Europe remained collectively less committed than the US to taking a confrontational line on China. Consensus on China among allies at the NATO 2021 summit was hard-won, already substantively tempered and possibly still short-lived. As Macron argued at the closing press conference: 'NATO is an organisation that concerns the North Atlantic. China has little to do with the North Atlantic. So it's very important that we don't scatter ourselves and that we don't bias our relationship with China.' The 2021 NATO communiqué mentioned China ten times but Russia 63 times. Within both NATO and the EU, it was easier to reach a consensus on Russia. Several Russian actions drove this: its poisoning, and subsequent arrest and detention, of opposition activist Alexei Navalny; its build-up of Russian troops along the border with Ukraine in April; and the disclosure of its role in an explosion at an ammunition depot in the Czech Republic in 2014.

The Elysée's enthusiasm for outreach, marked by its pursuit since 2019 of a strategic dialogue with Russia, waned temporarily after the poisoning of Navalny and the Russian backing of Belarus's brutal crackdown on mass protests following rigged presidential elections in the country in August 2020. But a meeting between Biden and Russian President Vladimir Putin in June 2021 prompted Franco-German interest in a European summit with Putin. Their joint proposal to this effect was resisted by other EU member states that favoured a tougher approach.

Sanctions remained the EU's favoured policy response to behaviour it considered unacceptable. This was true not just with regard to Russia and China; EU sanctions were also extended or strengthened against Belarus, Myanmar, Syria and Zimbabwe, as well as against entities involved in cyber crimes. In April 2021, Russia responded to two further sets of EU restrictive measures by banning outspoken European Parliament President David Sassoli, European Commission Vice President Věra Jourová (who holds the portfolio for values and transparency, and leads an EU campaign against misinformation from Russia and China) and other senior European officials from entering the country.

According to a June 2021 EU parliamentary report, relations between the EU and Turkey fell to a 'historic low point' due to continued backsliding on the rule of law and Turkey's regressive institutional reforms and hostile foreign policy. Europe's failure to exert influence on the six-week war in Nagorno-Karabakh in late 2020 undermined its role in the South Caucasus, while Turkey and, especially, Russia extended theirs.

Meanwhile, as Slovenia prepared to take over the rotating presidency of the EU for the second half of 2021, President Janez Janša – a sometimes controversial figure with a reputation for right-wing populism and unpredictable messaging – made it clear that Slovenia would lobby assertively for the further enlargement of the EU. With Bulgaria controversially blocking the accession of Albania and North Macedonia because of historical issues, this additional focus on the EU's flailing enlargement policy seemed likely to exacerbate tensions and frustrations within the EU-27.

Britain and the EU after Brexit
How far is Brexit really 'done'?

On 31 January 2020, the United Kingdom ceased to be a member state of the European Union. Brexit, in its narrow, legal sense, had been achieved. But despite UK Prime Minister Boris Johnson's claims, Brexit was far from 'done'. Some 18 months after the UK's exit, it was clearer than ever that Brexit will be a long process rather than a single event. Many of the questions that the decision to leave the EU purported to answer have not been resolved. Indeed, it is far from clear even that the deal eventually signed between the two sides can be made to work.

Brexit will have a paradoxical impact on the UK. On the one hand, the government's vision of a 'Global Britain' emerged to counter any impression that the decision to leave the EU presaged a broader withdrawal from the international scene. On the other, a reluctance to cooperate with the EU, along with the need to address pressing domestic issues – some of which arose as a result of Brexit – cast some doubt on the UK's continued ability to play the wider international role to which it aspires.

Getting to here

As crowds of Brexit supporters gathered in Parliament Square on 31 January 2020 to celebrate the end of UK membership of the EU, most would have been unaware of the fact that the first two cases of COVID-19 in the country had been confirmed the same day. The latter was to have a significantly greater short-term impact than the former, not least because, as its membership ended, the UK entered a 'transition period' – to last until 31 December 2020 unless both sides agreed to extend it – during which the UK remained part of the EU's single market and customs union. Trading relations between the UK and the EU were therefore not affected the day after formal membership ended.

On 2 March 2020, negotiations began on a treaty to regulate future relations between the UK and the EU. The talks were disrupted as COVID-19 spread and the UK followed continental countries into lockdown. It took the two sides several weeks to decide on a format for online negotiations and, even then, political leaders were overwhelmed by the need to respond to the pandemic. Consequently, many observers assumed that the UK government would decide to take advantage of the possibility of an extension of up to two years to allow more time to secure an agreement.

That assumption, however, proved ill-founded. Having stated its determination not to extend the transition period in its manifesto for the 2019 election, and enshrined this in law via the EU (Withdrawal Agreement) Act 2020, the government stuck to its guns, and the 30 June deadline to request an extension came and went. As the UK emerged from the first lockdown, the government needed to negotiate a deal with the EU within six months that would determine its future relationship with its nearest and largest trading partner.

Progress was far from smooth. In early September 2020, the UK announced its intention, in the words of Secretary of State for Northern Ireland Brandon Lewis, to 'break international law in a very specific and limited way'. The initial version of the Internal Market Bill gave the UK government the ability, should no trade agreement be agreed with the EU, to overrule elements of the Protocol on Ireland/Northern Ireland.

The Protocol had been agreed as part of the EU–UK Withdrawal Agreement in October 2019 to address the specific problems created for the island of Ireland by the decision to leave the EU. That decision raised the spectre of a border between the Republic of Ireland and Northern Ireland – something that both the UK and EU were committed to avoiding. This left two options: either the UK as a whole remained within the EU customs union and single market – obviating the need for border checks – or Northern Ireland was to have a special status, leaving it within the customs union and subject to EU rules where necessary to preserve the 'all-island economy'. The Johnson government had no intention of committing the UK to continue to follow EU rules and so the second option was chosen, and the Protocol was born.

Perhaps unsurprisingly, then, the EU reacted angrily to the threat by the UK to renege on the agreement while the ink on the prime minister's signature was barely dry. Brussels accused the UK government of unilaterally altering parts of a bilaterally agreed international treaty, and hence of breaking international law. Fears that the stand-off might prevent a successful completion of talks were allayed when the government later withdrew the offending clauses of the Bill.

However, the incident left a bad taste and undermined trust between the two sides – a theme that EU negotiators have subsequently been keen to stress. On 16 October, Johnson stated that the country should prepare for a no-deal outcome unless the EU adopted a 'fundamental change of approach'.

As the December deadline approached, the two sides remained at loggerheads over issues ranging from fisheries to the 'level-playing-field' arrangements that would allow the EU to impose penalties if Britain weakened its regulatory standards. The Johnson government attempted to make good on its commitment to 'take back control' and defend British sovereignty, while the EU was quick to block any suggestion that a third country could undercut the standards of the single market.

Interim deadlines – the final European Council summit and the European Parliament's final plenary session of 2020 – came and went. Despite some talk of a provisional agreement that would avoid a hard border in Northern Ireland, the rhetoric from both sides turned from cautiously optimistic to simply cautious. In early December, Johnson warned UK businesses to prepare for World Trade Organization rules, and the EU published its own no-deal contingency planning.

In those final fraught weeks, it appeared that exiting the EU with no deal in place was a real possibility. And yet, on 24 December, the two sides finally secured an agreement that was subsequently signed on 30 December. The UK government struck a victorious tone, declaring the UK a sovereign state once again. From the EU there came more of a relieved sigh, as the EU's chief negotiator Michel Barnier conceded that the clock was 'no longer ticking'. Compromises from both sides on access to fisheries and state subsidies seemed remarkable, though scenes of gridlock at Dover as a result of COVID-19-related trade disruption in mid-December may have served as a sign of things to come for Johnson and thus a catalyst for speedy agreement. 2021 began with a UK–EU deal in place. But though Brexit may now have been 'done', it was still not over.

Uncertainties

Surprisingly, more than five years since the UK's 2016 referendum, it is still not entirely clear what the ultimate nature and impact of Brexit will be. Uncertainty is inherent in the nature of the 30 December Trade and Cooperation Agreement (TCA), which was deliberately silent on several key policy areas. Uncertainty also stems from the fact that implementing an agreement is often far trickier than negotiating it. Both sides are coming to realise this as they try to negotiate a means of making the Northern Ireland Protocol work.

In line with the TCA, key issues such as the ease with which the two sides could exchange data and the degree of access to the EU market that UK financial-services firms would enjoy were to be dealt with separately in the months following the signing of the agreement. At the end of June 2021, the European Commission issued two 'adequacy' decisions for data flows between the UK and the EU. While this guarantees data flows in the short term, the European Parliament and Council of Ministers can ask the Commission to withdraw them at any time.

As for financial services, in April, the two sides announced that a memorandum of understanding would be signed to create a 'stable and durable' basis on which to build cooperation in financial services. However, there is still no sign that the EU is in any hurry to grant the equivalence status to UK financial-services rules that would allow easier access to the EU market for financial-services firms – not least given the apparent determination of the UK chancellor to make the most of the UK's new-found regulatory autonomy to increase the competitiveness of the City of London.

Perhaps most important of all is the uncertainty over the implementation of the Withdrawal Agreement, and particularly the Protocol on Ireland/Northern Ireland. From virtually the moment it came into (provisional) effect, tensions arose between the UK and the EU, with the former accusing the latter of an unnecessarily legalistic approach to implementation, while EU officials voiced their frustration at UK reluctance to act on a text it had negotiated, signed and urged Parliament to ratify.

Things came to a head on 3 March when the UK announced its intention unilaterally to extend grace periods relaxing checks on British supermarket suppliers and other businesses trading in Northern Ireland until October. In response, the EU launched a formal legal action for breaches under EU law and accused the UK of acting in defiance of the good-faith provision contained in the Withdrawal Agreement. In June 2021, the EU agreed to a request from the UK government to extend the grace period on shipments of chilled meats from Great Britain to Northern Ireland in return for the UK agreeing to remain aligned with EU food-production rules and standards for that period.

The need for most checks has therefore been temporarily alleviated, but the issue has not been resolved, merely postponed. As the end of the extended grace period approaches in October 2021, the two sides will again face off over whether the EU will be willing to implement the protocol in a more 'sensitive' way, or whether the UK will agree to continue to abide by EU animal- and plant-health rules in the future.

What next?

Brexit within the UK

Brexit has helped to fundamentally reshape electoral politics in the UK. At the December 2019 election, Johnson effectively assembled a 'Leave' coalition. Nearly four-fifths of those in favour of leaving the EU in December 2019 backed the Conservatives. Post-2019, Conservative voters – comprising those in traditional Tory shires but also formerly Labour-backing 'Red Wall seats' – share very few policy preferences, particularly when it comes to economic policy. They are, however, united by their conservative social values. Continuing to mobilise voters around this cleavage will therefore be key to maintaining Johnson's coalition of support. This will have significant implications for the future of UK–EU relations.

The pandemic will serve to disguise the impact of Brexit on the UK economy. While most of Europe remains under lockdown and travel between countries is actively discouraged, the full economic ramifications of leaving the single market and customs union will remain unclear. Yet Brexit will continue to affect the UK's economic performance. Modelling suggests not only a significant impact on GDP over the medium term (a reduction of 7.6% of UK GDP over 15 years, according to the government's own analysis) but also that the economic consequences of Brexit will exceed the medium-term impact of the pandemic.

The politics and economics may, however, pale into insignificance should Brexit have implications for the territorial integrity of the UK that some expect. The 2016 referendum and subsequent political instability have destabilised politics in Northern Ireland, leading to sustained talk of the possibility of a 'border poll' on potential unification with the Republic. Meanwhile, the apparent determination of the government to refuse a second referendum on Scottish independence has further stoked tensions with the Scottish National Party government. While a referendum is hardly a foregone conclusion, and a victory for independence far from inevitable even if one were held, the preservation of the Union will nevertheless be a major – if not the major – challenge confronting the UK government for some time to come.

The UK–EU relationship

At the same time, and not least because of the coalition on which Johnson's parliamentary majority is based, tensions between the UK and the EU are likely to continue. The UK government has already revelled in picking unnecessary fights – such as its initial refusal to grant the EU ambassador in London the full diplomatic status accorded to other ambassadors. As for the EU, the UK's status as a third country and economic competitor equally provide little incentive for compromise. Just as the UK government remains keen to promote the benefits of its independence outside the EU, the EU has an undoubted interest in Brexit being seen to fail.

The dispute over vaccine production provided an early example of how things might play out. The UK government used the development of its vaccine programme as an opportunity to laud the benefits of its new-found sovereignty, while in late January the Commission took the unprecedented step of attempting to activate Article 16 of the Northern Ireland Protocol, which prevented the transport of vaccines across the Ireland–Northern

Ireland border. The chain of events was hardly reassuring for those anxious to see closer ties re-established between the two sides.

Foreign and security policy – which the UK refused to incorporate into the TCA – remain something of a special case. On the one hand, this may not prove to be all that significant, as EU agreements with third countries tend to be relatively thin: observer status, or the right to be consulted, may make a difference at the margin but little more. On the other hand, London is clearly unwilling to engage in meaningful cooperation with the EU itself. The 2019 Conservative manifesto did not contain a single reference to maintaining security cooperation with the EU but did mention bolstering several other 'alliances and institutions that help project our influence and keep us safe: the UN and the UN Security Council; NATO; the Commonwealth; Five Eyes; the G20; the G7; and the World Trade Organization'.

While Johnson has stressed that Euro-Atlantic security remains a national priority, cooperation with the EU has not figured as an aspect of his foreign policy. Cooperation with European allies has occurred bilaterally, or via small groupings of member states, such as the E3 (the UK, France and Germany). Some in London hope that the visit by German Chancellor Angela Merkel at the beginning of July 2021, which followed the signing of a joint declaration stressing a variety of shared foreign- and security-policy interests, will serve as a model for bilateral cooperation with other member states.

Ultimately, the nature of the EU–UK relationship will continue to be shaped as much by events as anything else. On certain issues, such as combatting climate change, sanctions policy or tackling the global pandemic, there are clearly advantages for the UK to working with the EU rather than with individual member states. However, a new crisis requiring military intervention on, say, the scale of the Libyan conflict, would quite possibly lead to enhanced cooperation with individual European states.

Paradoxical outcomes

On the one hand, the UK government has been at pains to stress that the UK will be an active participant in international politics. 'Global Britain' has been the key phrase in an important year in UK foreign policy, as the UK chairs the UN Security Council, holds the presidency of the G7 and co-chairs the UN Climate Change Conference (COP26) with Italy. Confronting a plethora of challenges – dealing with China, Iran and Russia, strengthening multilateral institutions, and addressing the climate crisis, inter alia – implies that the UK will continue to assert itself internationally and to work closely with allies.

On the other hand, the politics of Brexit account for a marked reluctance on the part of the UK to work closely with the EU. It remains to be seen how effectively the Johnson government can manage to combine international activism with a refusal to collaborate closely with the bloc on its doorstep. Ultimately, the kinds of challenges that confront it might prove to be the crucial factor. While the EU plays only a limited role in military matters, it is hard to envisage how the UK might limit itself to cooperating with member states in areas that fall directly within EU competences such as sanctions or climate change.

An active foreign policy, moreover, will depend on the government enjoying sufficient bandwidth to focus on international affairs. In 2022, the Johnson government will have to manage the ongoing economic and practical fallout of Brexit while also being preoccupied by recovery from the health and economic impacts of the pandemic. The economic effects of the UK's new loose relationship with the EU will reveal themselves as the recovery from the pandemic gathers pace, plausibly making the transition back to normal politics more painful for the Conservative Party. On top of which, the rumbling tensions caused by the determination of the Scottish government to press for another independence referendum will occupy much time and attention in both Westminster and Whitehall.

In sum, perhaps the biggest question for those interested in the UK's international ambitions is whether the government will have the space and time to engage meaningfully with the outside world, or whether Global Britain will fall victim to the requirements of post-Brexit and post-pandemic policy.

EU Defence Ambitions and Capabilities
Can it do better in a more dangerous environment?

The European Union is sometimes seen as a 'postmodern power' whose global influence rests on its political values, economic strength and power to set regulatory standards rather than on its military strength. Yet it now faces a world less secure than at any time since EU integration developed in earnest in the 1980s. Hard power is once again a currency that matters in its neighbourhood. Does the EU have this in sufficient quantity? If not, what are its prospects for gaining it?

Integration efforts

EU security and defence cooperation is not new: it has been an area of integration for more than 20 years. Pushed forward by France and the United Kingdom, the EU began to form what is now known as the Common Security and Defence Policy (CSDP) in 1999. It adopted its first security strategy in 2003, the same year it began to conduct crisis-management operations, of which six military and 11 civilian ones were ongoing in spring 2021. In June 2021, plans emerged to launch a military training mission to Mozambique later in 2021. The 2009 Treaty of Lisbon included a solidarity clause that commits member states to assist each other in cases of terrorist attacks or for disaster-response purposes, and an assistance clause that requires member states to assist each other in cases of armed aggression with all means in their power – a far-reaching commitment.

In 2016, the EU published a global strategy for foreign and security policy, and in 2019 the European Commission set up a Directorate-General for Defence Industry and Space. In 2020, work on a so-called 'Strategic Compass' began, which is due for completion in 2022 and aims to provide political guidance on security and defence matters for the next ten years. In this process, the EU and its member states have done both better and worse than many commentators realise. While proponents of the EU process of defence cooperation often exaggerate its achievements, it is equally common for those unconvinced of the overall undertaking to assume the worst in terms of performance.

The central promise of the EU as a security actor has remained the same since the late 1990s and is essentially twofold: firstly, because the EU provides a multilateral forum that can theoretically bring to bear political, diplomatic, development, economic, as well as civilian and military crisis management on a set of problems, its potential offer is more comprehensive than that of other organisations, such as NATO. Secondly, by collaborating in the EU framework, member states should be able to lower the transaction costs of working together on security and defence issues and might on occasion reap efficiency gains and economies of scale.

The central problem for the EU as a security actor has also remained remarkably constant: the gap between the expectations EU rhetoric creates and the EU's actual military ability remains significant. EU institutions can only hope to achieve effect in security and defence terms if member states provide effective capabilities – because the EU as an institution does not own or command them – and if member states have a shared political agenda to deploy resources for common objectives – because their security policies remain driven by distinct national priorities.

Evolving international context

What has changed radically is the international context in which the EU operates and to which its aspirations need to correspond. While the mid- to late 1990s provided the inspiration for the EU's civilian and military crisis-management efforts, today the EU and its member states must chart a path that protects the foundations of their prosperity and security in an era of great-power competition that could lead to military conflict. At the same time, challenges to security in Europe's southern and eastern periphery remain plentiful. Thus, threat vectors range from stability risks such as regional conflicts or international terrorism with primarily indirect and non-existential impact, to systemic conflict and armed aggression with direct and potentially existential effects on European security.

This evolution of the international context is reflected in the security and defence initiatives the EU has been pursuing since 2016, when its current foreign- and security-policy strategy was published. The strategy, entitled 'Shared Vision, Common Action: A Stronger Europe', stated its five priorities as the security of European citizens; state and societal resilience to the east and south; integrated conflict and crisis management; cooperative regional orders; and progress on global governance. It called for defence collaboration to become the default mode of member states and introduced notions of deterrence, full-spectrum defence and the protection of the EU, which suggested an expansion of the crisis-management agenda of the early 2000s, even though these new ideas remained largely undefined at the time.

In the wake of the 2016 strategy, the EU launched several initiatives to propel the agenda of closer defence collaboration forward. In December 2017, a process called Permanent Structured Cooperation (PESCO), foreseen in the Treaty of Lisbon, was launched, which provides a framework within the EU for member states to work together on capabilities. It comprises two core elements. Firstly, a set of legally binding commitments on participating member states (currently 25 EU member states, with Denmark and Malta the exceptions) include real-terms increases to defence spending and defence-investment spending that are reviewed in the form of annual national implementation plans. The second element is a set of projects that groups of member states pursue across a range of capability areas. At the end of 2020, the number of projects stood at 46, ranging from training centres to land systems, maritime, air, space, cyber and enabling capabilities.

A companion initiative is the Coordinated Annual Review on Defence (CARD), which aims to harmonise defence-planning assumptions among EU member states. One of the mechanisms through which CARD is meant to achieve this is by identifying opportunities for collaboration among member states based on their national planning assumptions and inviting member states to pursue them. A first report on CARD presented in November 2020 identified some 55 opportunities. Finally, the European Defence Fund (EDF), an EU-level budget for defence R&D and capability development was announced in 2016, with the full programme agreed in 2020. These initiatives are designed to provide political and financial incentives for closer defence collaboration with a view to generating better capabilities.

European strategy and autonomy

The current European Commission, led by former German defence minister Ursula von der Leyen, which took office in late 2019, refers explicitly to geopolitical ambition for the EU, and to the need to become fluent in the language of power. Vice-President of the Commission and EU High Representative of the EU for Foreign Affairs and Security Policy Josep Borrell also promoted the view that at a time of intensifying great-power rivalry between the United States and China, the EU should chart its own course, independent of these two competitors, in a bid for European strategic autonomy.

The 2016 global strategy twice mentions strategic autonomy as being important for Europe's ability to act effectively in the pursuit of peace and security. While the strategy itself does not define what this would amount to, it seems reasonable to assume that it entails the independent definition of political positions and decisions to pursue them, the existence of capabilities to implement those decisions, and the means to generate and create those capabilities.

Strategic autonomy is not a concept that is specific to security and defence, but it occupies an especially significant position in this policy arena. In the last five years it has gained currency in Europe primarily for four reasons. Firstly, security and defence came to be interpreted as a policy area in which the EU could deliver for citizens who had become somewhat wary and even sceptical of the process of European integration – not least in the wake of Brexit. 'Protecting Europe' thus became a valuable task politically. Secondly, the UK's exit from the EU itself meant that one of the voices that could usually be relied upon to dampen thoughts of a more ambitious role for the EU in foreign affairs had left the stage, making it easier for the more aspiring members to be heard. Thirdly, threat perceptions changed with the growing recognition that Russia had become a direct and acute challenge to the very foundations of Europe's security order, operating within European societies to try to weaken them and changing borders by force. In the long run, a threat also loomed in China's ambitions for a leading global role that might undermine the rules-based order for which the EU stands and on which the prosperity of its member states is based. Finally, the election of Donald Trump as US president in 2016, and his subsequent deprecation of European allies, suggested to Europeans that the United States' security guarantees might not be as iron-cast as had long been assumed. This was compounded by the sense that, irrespective of who occupies the White House, the Indo-Pacific has clearly emerged as the geopolitical priority for the US.

On the face of it, the EU should have the strength to be a major geopolitical player. In constant 2015 US dollars, the combined defence spending of the EU-27 rose by more than 20% from US$172 billion in 2014 to about US$207.5bn in 2020. More than 1.3 million soldiers serve in member states' armed forces. In 2021, the EU's member states could draw on 64 heavy transport aircraft, a growing number of combat-capable uninhabited aerial vehicles (UAVs), just under 1,000 fighter/ground-attack aircraft, more than 4,000 main battle tanks, three aircraft carriers, nearly 50 submarines and several space-based intelligence assets. Leaving aside the US, a natural partner and treaty ally to nearly all EU member states through NATO membership, the EU as a whole is outgunned on a number of indicators by both China and Russia, but EU capacities are nonetheless significant.

However, aggregate data on spending and equipment neither reflects usable capability nor provides easy international comparisons. China and Russia have highly opaque defence budgets and spend more on defence than they report. Furthermore, comparing spending based on market exchange rates – while allowing for international comparisons – underestimates the purchasing power of China's and Russia's defence spending. EU member-state defence spending is fragmented, in parts duplicative and in general less efficient than it would be if it were controlled by a single government. The same goes for equipment inventories, which feature significant numbers of obsolete platforms – among armoured vehicles, for example – and are marred by a multitude of equipment types that complicate working together effectively on operations.

Changes in defence spending and selected military capabilities of the US, China, Russia and the EU member states, 2014–20

On an aggregate level, the 27 EU member states command significant military expenditure and capability, even compared to major powers such as China, Russia and the United States. In the past five years, EU members have made progress on some capability gaps, such as air transport. Other areas, such as uninhabited combat aerial vehicles or electronic-intelligence aircraft, remain weak. But these are national assets: mobilising them for multinational action via the EU remains as difficult as when the EU's Common Security and Defence Policy (CSDP) was created over 20 years ago.

The data also illustrates a shifting international context and military-modernisation trends, notably the expansion of China's military capability and the collapse of Russian–Western political and security relations after Russia's intervention in Ukraine in 2014.

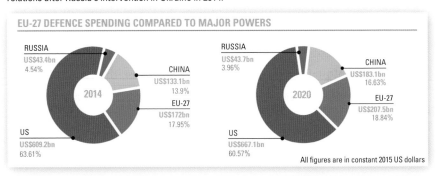

EU-27 DEFENCE SPENDING COMPARED TO MAJOR POWERS

2014
RUSSIA US$43.4bn 4.54%
CHINA US$133.1bn 13.9%
EU-27 US$172bn 17.95%
US US$609.2bn 63.61%

2020
RUSSIA US$43.7bn 3.96%
CHINA US$183.1bn 16.63%
EU-27 US$207.5bn 18.84%
US US$667.1bn 60.57%

All figures are in constant 2015 US dollars

SELECTED CAPABILITY INDICATORS

AREA	EU-27	US	RUSSIA	CHINA	
Personnel (Active Military)	1,362,160	1,433,150	771,000	2,333,000	2014
	1,345,660	1,388,100	900,000	2,035,000	2020
Heavy Transport Aircraft	5	285	132	16	2014
	60	274	132	42	2020
Uninhabited Combat Aerial Vehicle – Heavy	2	433	0	0	2014
	16	498	0	12+	2020
Electronic-Intelligence Aircraft	5	53	36	11	2014
	5	51	35	17	2020
Fighter/Ground-attack Aircraft	1,164	2,485	326	801	2014
	970	2,541	459	1,017	2020
Maritime Patrol Aircraft/ Anti-submarine Warfare Aircraft	68	170	53	3	2014
	61	123	51	17	2020
Attack Helicopters	257	908	290	150	2014
	304	885	414	276	2020
Main Battle Tanks	4,657	2,785	2,809	6,540	2014
	4,189	2,509	3,300	5,650	2020
Infantry Fighting Vehicles	5,800	3,086	4,750	3,550	2014
	5,859	3,419	6,450	6,710	2020
Aircraft Carriers	3	10	1	1	2014
	3	11	1	2	2020
Frigates	80	14	7	48	2014
	75	21	15	46	2020
Submarines	47	74	56	70	2014
	49	68	49	59	2020
Satellites	21	124	74	68	2014
	26	141	106	132	2020

© IISS

Source: IISS Military Balance+, accessed August 2021

The result, in terms of usable military capability for the EU-27, is that the whole is less than the sum of its parts. In fact, even if the military level of ambition for EU crisis-management operations, originally defined in 1999 for achievement by 2010, were to remain unchanged and not raised further, internal assessments conducted by the EU Military Staff in 2019 suggested that it would remain out of reach until the end of the 2020s. An independent assessment conducted by the IISS and the German Council on Foreign Relations (DGAP) in 2018 reached similar conclusions.

Marginal improvements

The question is whether the recent policy initiatives (PESCO, CARD and the EDF) and the latest round of EU strategising – embodied in the work on the Strategic Compass – will change this picture significantly. While it is still early days, at this point the balance of probabilities is that improvements will be marginal. PESCO, an initiative with real potential, risks falling victim to core weaknesses in the EU's approach to defence. Because it is a bottom-up process into which member states insert their projects, there is no singular purpose. Some projects simply reflect what member states would have done anyway; others focus on less-than-critical requirements; and a few actually focus on solving recognised and prioritised capability shortfalls. The commitments that PESCO entails have yet to live up to their binding intention. For decades, EU member-state governments have tended to meet in Brussels and agree wide-ranging obligations, only to forget about them when they return to their respective capitals. As Sven Biscop, an astute veteran of European defence analysis, observed in 2020, the '25 participating Member States … could implement all [PESCO] projects and still be not much more capable than they are today'.

CARD has only just completed its first proper cycle, but it is already obvious that national defence-planning processes remain stubbornly national. In some quarters in Brussels, there is an assumption that in order to focus on EU ambitions, national-defence planners just need to learn more about EU-level processes and better understand their potential benefits. This is an optimistic assumption. EU planning documents and capability-development plans are already referenced in many national-level documents. The issue is not so much information flow, but rather that for many governments, the EU's military level of ambition, as currently expressed, is only one part, and often not the dominant part, of the national-security puzzle. Some governments will focus on significant national requirements, while others will look to NATO. Most will also look to the EU, but not for their primary cues. Review documents released by the EU at the end of 2020 also suggested that the integration between CARD and PESCO was still lacking.

The EDF, approved in April 2021 and aligned with the 2021–27 multi-annual financial framework for the EU, will have a budget of €7.95bn to cover that period. Of this, some €5.3bn will be earmarked for co-financing collaborative capability development with the remainder going to collaborative defence research. While in total this is almost 40% less funding than was originally mooted for the EDF, it still represents a notable influx of defence-investment funding dedicated to collaborative work. Some effects of the EDF are likely to be long term and will flow from the way the money is actually spent and the regulations associated with it. Given that demand for project funds is likely to exceed the money available under the EDF, in allocating funding the European Commission will need to make choices between funding a small number of larger and structurally important projects – which would likely favour the more developed defence-industrial bases of a small number of member states – and funding a larger number of smaller projects – that would likely involve more member states and small and medium-sized enterprises.

In addition, the rules governing third-party participation are likely to make effective collaboration with non-EU companies, and with EU-based companies controlled by non-EU entities, difficult to achieve, as they either prevent (in the case of non-EU participants) or limit (in the case of entities controlled by non-EU participants) access to EDF funds and classified information related to these projects and control the intellectual-property rights generated through collaboration. A likely side effect of the EDF will therefore be an increased role for the European Commission as a regulator in the European defence market.

The Strategic Compass initiative will also need to strike a fine balance between member-state positions. An early indicator was the classified shared-threat analysis commissioned in the framework of the Compass in 2020. Words matter – the exercise was deliberately styled a shared *analysis* of threats, not an outright shared *assessment* of threats. The latter could reasonably have been expected to include some form of prioritisation and options on how to address the different threats – steps that seem to be absent from the analysis because it was decided at the beginning of the process that member-state positions were too diverse to allow for a proper assessment.

While the details are not in the public domain, it is thus entirely possible that all member states agree entirely with the threat analysis but continue to have very different ideas about the ranking of threats and what to do about them. At the time of writing, it was unclear to what extent this first step of the Strategic Compass generated a genuinely expanded set of shared assumptions among EU governments. This will matter for the four agreed areas that will form the elements of the Strategic Compass: crisis management, resilience, capabilities and partnerships. In all these areas, the Strategic Compass initiative will need to underline, develop and bring to fruition the theoretical promise of EU action: comprehensive policy responses, based on efficiency and effectiveness gains generated by cooperation. Those holding the pen will need to write both ambitiously and realistically. It is therefore likely that the outcome will be only limited improvement in EU security and defence policy, rather than a major breakthrough.

If this is the outcome, the recent EU security and defence initiatives will confirm the dominant pattern of the past 30 years: in the face of external pressures, existing mechanisms and instruments for EU security and defence cooperation have been found wanting, which has led to limited and insufficient adaptation. This gradual evolution is frustrating and almost certainly too slow considering the rapid change that now characterises, and will continue to shape, the international security environment. EU security and defence policy cannot be much more than EU member states want it to be.

CHAPTER 8
Russia and Eurasia

RUSSIAN FEDERATION

BELARUS

UKRAINE

DOVA

GEORGIA

ARMENIA

AZERBAIJAN

KAZAKHSTAN

UZBEKISTAN

TURKMENISTAN

KYRGYZSTAN

TAJIKISTAN

©IISS

Drivers of Strategic Change

REGIONAL SHARE OF GLOBAL POPULATION, GDP AND DEFENCE BUDGET

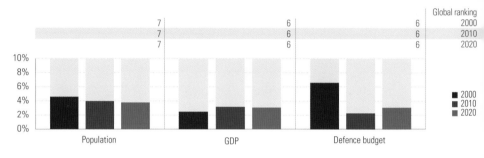

	Global ranking		
Population	7		2000
	7		2010
	7		2020
GDP	6		2000
	6		2010
	6		2020
Defence budget	6		2000
	6		2010
	6		2020

■ 2000
■ 2010
■ 2020

POPULATION

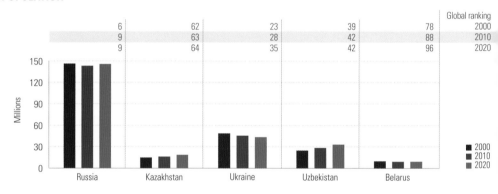

Global ranking	Russia	Kazakhstan	Ukraine	Uzbekistan	Belarus
2000	6	62	23	39	78
2010	9	63	28	42	88
2020	9	64	35	42	96

■ 2000
■ 2010
■ 2020

AGE STRUCTURE
(Percentage of national population)

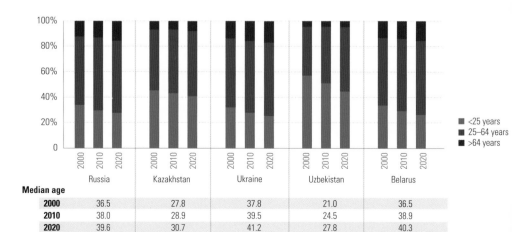

■ <25 years
■ 25–64 years
■ >64 years

Median age	Russia	Kazakhstan	Ukraine	Uzbekistan	Belarus
2000	36.5	27.8	37.8	21.0	36.5
2010	38.0	28.9	39.5	24.5	38.9
2020	39.6	30.7	41.2	27.8	40.3

GDP
(Constant 2010 US dollars)

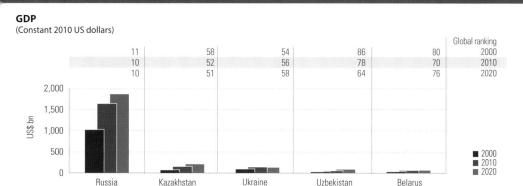

					Global ranking
11	58	54	86	80	2000
10	52	56	78	70	2010
10	51	58	64	76	2020

US$ bn — Russia, Kazakhstan, Ukraine, Uzbekistan, Belarus

■ 2000 ■ 2010 ■ 2020

GDP PER CAPITA
(Constant 2010 US dollars)

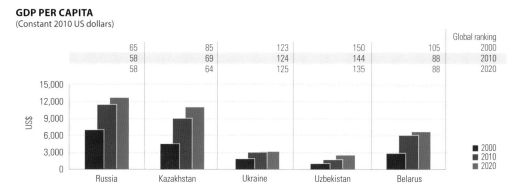

					Global ranking
65	85	123	150	105	2000
58	69	124	144	88	2010
58	64	125	135	88	2020

US$ — Russia, Kazakhstan, Ukraine, Uzbekistan, Belarus

■ 2000 ■ 2010 ■ 2020

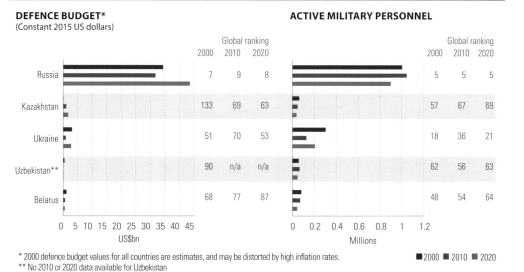

DEFENCE BUDGET*
(Constant 2015 US dollars)

	Global ranking		
	2000	2010	2020
Russia	7	9	8
Kazakhstan	133	69	63
Ukraine	51	70	53
Uzbekistan**	90	n/a	n/a
Belarus	68	77	87

0 5 10 15 20 25 30 35 40 45
US$bn

ACTIVE MILITARY PERSONNEL

	Global ranking		
	2000	2010	2020
Russia	5	5	5
Kazakhstan	57	67	69
Ukraine	18	36	21
Uzbekistan	62	56	63
Belarus	48	54	64

0 0.2 0.4 0.6 0.8 1 1.2
Millions

■ 2000 ■ 2010 ■ 2020

* 2000 defence budget values for all countries are estimates, and may be distorted by high inflation rates.
** No 2010 or 2020 data available for Uzbekistan

For explanation of drivers and sources, see page 9

HUMAN DEVELOPMENT INDEX (HDI)
(Score between 0 and 1, where 0 denotes a low level of development and 1 a high level of development)

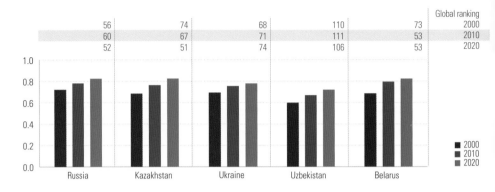

POLITICAL SYSTEM
(Score between 0 and 100, where 0 denotes no political freedom and 100 fully free)

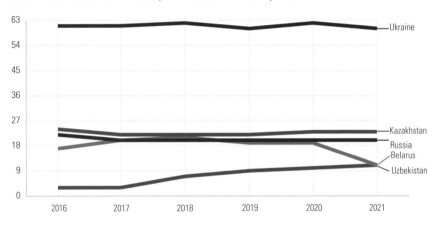

DOMESTIC APPROVAL RATING FOR PRESIDENT VLADIMIR PUTIN, AND ASSESSMENT OF THE CURRENT STATE OF AFFAIRS IN RUSSIA

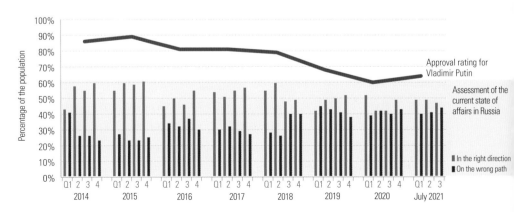

For explanation of drivers and sources, see page 9

2020–21 Review

2020–21 was a geopolitically turbulent year in Eurasia, with war between Azerbaijan and Armenia, regime change in Kyrgyzstan, the biggest protests of Alexander Lukashenko's long rule in Belarus, a major Russian military build-up, a border conflict in Central Asia and the election of a strongly pro-European Union president in Moldova. A new phase of more severe and concerted repression began in Russia, epitomised by the poisoning of opposition leader Alexei Navalny. Russia's relations with the United States and Europe continued to deteriorate, with the West imposing further sanctions in response to a range of Russian actions.

Sputnik V: diplomacy abroad, reluctance at home

In August 2020 Russia registered Sputnik V, the world's first COVID-19 vaccine, albeit before phase III trials had been completed. The vaccine became publicly available in early December. By July 2021, 31 countries – notably in Latin America – had ordered the vaccine or agreed to produce it domestically. But the authorities found it harder to persuade their own citizens to accept it as scepticism about its safety hindered take-up. Official messaging was ambiguous. President Vladimir Putin was reportedly vaccinated in March 2021, though unlike many other national leaders, he did not receive his vaccine publicly. Only in June 2021 did he confirm that he had received Sputnik V and advise the population to be vaccinated. By this point, the spread of the Delta variant was causing Russia's worst wave of COVID-19 fatalities. Excessive mortality figures suggested that the total death toll had reached 475,000, the fourth highest in the world. But Russia's vaccination rate in June of 12% remained one of the lowest in the developed world. So severe was vaccine reluctance that the push by several regions for mandatory vaccinations for health- and service-sector workers spurred a market for fake vaccination certificates. Most other post-Soviet countries had even lower vaccination rates: apart from the Baltic states, only Azerbaijan and Kazakhstan outperformed Russia.

Russia's tightening screws

The acute impact of COVID-19 compounded chronic systemic underperformance, pushing real incomes down to their lowest level in a decade. However, many elites were shielded. The share of Russia's national income owned by billionaires increased substantially, reaching over one-third of Russia's GDP – the highest proportion of any country. In response to inflation, which reached 6.5% in June, the authorities not only raised interest rates but imposed price controls and export tariffs on basic foodstuffs for the first time in the post-Soviet period. Labour shortages arose as many migrant workers returned to Central Asia during the pandemic. As a consequence, the idea of using prisoners to work on infrastructure projects, as in Soviet times, was revived, notably on the Baikal–Amur Mainline railway.

A series of laws implemented constitutional amendments that had been approved in a referendum in July 2020. These included provisions allowing Putin to remain in office until 2036. In September 2020, the ruling United Russia party won all 18 governor elections but lost its overall majority in local legislatures in Novosibirsk, Tomsk and Tambov. Opposition leader Navalny's 'Smart Voting' strategy appeared to play a role in this. Nonetheless, political opposition looked weak after the referendum. Despite this, a new and more intense era of repression set in from summer 2020. The Russian authorities had long allowed limited dissent and opposition, and even found it useful to do so to monitor public moods and provide a limited safety valve for discontent. But the limits of toleration narrowed sharply. Any politics not controlled by the Kremlin was increasingly treated with suspicion, prosecuted and suppressed. Repression rather than dialogue defined state–society relations more than ever.

Civil-society groups and independent media faced growing repression. The 2012 'foreign agent' law, which imposes onerous and costly restrictions on individuals and organisations that receive foreign assistance, was extended and applied even more widely, often forcing them to disband or cease their activities. Online news portals including Meduza and VTimes (which was forced to close) were targeted. Among other cases, defence journalist Ivan Safronov was charged with treason and his lawyer subsequently arrested; the editors of a student magazine, *Doxa*, were placed under house arrest; and some employees were dismissed even for expressing online support for the opposition.

Broader restrictions against foreign influence were imposed on the education system. In pursuit of efforts to develop a 'sovereign internet', the authorities tested Russia's capacity to disconnect from the global internet. In March, Roskomnadzor, the state communications regulator, slowed down Twitter and warned it and other major social-media platforms to remove content it deemed undesirable. Russian courts subsequently imposed fines on them.

On 9 July 2020, Sergei Furgal, governor of the far eastern region of Khabarovsk, was arrested and charged with contract killings he had allegedly ordered as a businessman in 2004–05. For several months, large local demonstrations were held in support of him.

Navalny's poisoning and return

The most significant events of the year centred on Navalny, whose anti-corruption campaign, effective use of social media and organisational talents had long made him a thorn in the Kremlin's flesh. On 20 August 2020 he fell violently ill on a domestic flight. After doctors in Omsk saved his life following an emergency landing, he was allowed to leave the country while still in a coma for treatment in Berlin. Tests conducted by the Organisation for the Prohibition of Chemical Weapons showed that he had been poisoned with Novichok, the military-grade nerve agent used in the attempted murder of Sergei and Yulia Skripal in Salisbury in 2018. After his recovery, Navalny extracted details of his poisoning by impersonating a Russian official and phoning one of the operatives responsible. Research by the investigative website Bellingcat on the Navalny case and suspected poisonings of other figures confirmed the ease with which sensitive personal data could be bought from Russia's leaky institutions.

Navalny returned to Russia on 17 January 2021 and was immediately arrested, sparking demonstrations across the country that led to the arrest of more than 11,000 protesters over the month that followed.

A video that Navalny had made was released, detailing the lavish palace that Putin had built for himself in Gelendzhik, on the Black Sea. In February, Navalny was sentenced to two and a half years in IK-2, one of Russia's harshest penal colonies. Soon after, he went on a 24-day hunger strike in protest of his treatment. In June, Navalny's Anti-Corruption Foundation (FBK) was designated an 'extremist' organisation, forcing it and its network of regional offices to disband. Public approval of Navalny's actions fell to 14%. If Navalny had calculated that his return to Russia would spark wider protests or change, the initial outcomes did not appear to vindicate this.

By June 2021 Putin's popularity was 66%, up from the historic low of 59% in April 2020, but still far below the 80%+ ratings he had enjoyed for four years after the annexation of Crimea in 2014. Approval of the United Russia party fell to a low of 27% – though this was still more than twice as high as the approval ratings of either of its closest rivals, the Liberal Democratic Party and the Communist Party. As preparations for parliamentary elections in September 2021 – the last important political test before the presidential elections in 2024 – got under way, the influence of the *siloviki* (security officials) looked stronger than ever. Russia appeared to be reviving its harshest form of authoritarian rule in over three decades. The major question was how much more restrictive this would become.

Foreign policy

Putin and incoming US President Joe Biden agreed a five-year extension to the New START nuclear treaty in January 2021, a few days before it was due to expire. This extension, which Russia had long sought, symbolised the continuing shared interest of the two biggest nuclear powers in preserving elements of strategic stability. Putin also took part in a virtual summit on climate change that Biden hosted in April, and subsequently expressed greater public concern than before about the threat that global warming presented to Russia.

Such cooperation was the exception. In other policy areas, Russia's relations with the West continued to deteriorate as a series of security and human-rights developments fuelled distrust and sanctions. Some incidents involved espionage. In December 2020, the US announced that Russia was behind a sophisticated cyber attack and data breach of SolarWinds, a major supplier of business software to government and private companies. In April 2021, the Czech government announced that the Main Intelligence Directorate (GRU), Russia's military intelligence service, was responsible for an explosion in the town of Vrbětice that blew up stored ammunition and killed two people in October 2014. These revelations led to further sanctions on Russia, as did Navalny's poisoning and subsequent imprisonment.

Russian military actions also prompted Western alarm and punitive responses. In early 2021, Russia exerted concerted pressure on the EU. High Representative Josep Borrell was repeatedly humiliated during a visit to Moscow in February, including by the expulsion of three EU diplomats. Soon after, Foreign Minister Sergei Lavrov threatened to cut off relations with the EU if it imposed sanctions on 'the most sensitive areas' of the economy. In late March, Russia began its biggest military build-up on its border with Ukraine and in occupied Crimea since 2014, evoking grave alarm in the US and Europe. On 22 April, Defence Minister Sergei Shoigu announced that forces would be withdrawn, but that weapons and equipment would remain in place.

At the height of the crisis, Biden invited Putin to a summit meeting. This took place in Geneva on 16 June. It was Putin's first foreign trip since the pandemic began, indicating the high priority he placed on the optics of engaging with Biden as an equal. The two countries agreed to return their respective ambassadors, who had been withdrawn due to rising tensions in the previous months. Apparently satisfied with the meeting and his press conference afterwards, Putin praised Biden after the summit as 'shrewd' and 'professional'.

There was one further moment of military tension on 23 June when the British destroyer HMS *Defender* passed close to Crimea en route from Odessa to Batumi. Russia, seeking to reinforce its unrecognised claims to the waters around the peninsula, issued warnings to the ship and flew fighters close to it. Its claim to have fired warning shots as well was denied by the UK Ministry of Defence.

Despite a series of damaging developments in relations with the US and Europe, Russia secured a major long-term objective as the Biden administration accepted the nearly completed Nord Stream 2 gas pipeline as a fait accompli. This pipeline will supply gas to Germany via a maritime route bypassing Ukraine, and aims both to strengthen Russia's influence in Europe and to weaken Ukraine.

In May 2021 Russia began its two-year chairmanship of the Arctic Council. Its stated priorities included responsible governance and sustainable development. An early initiative was to seek to revive military talks that had ended after Russia's annexation of Crimea.

The role of Russian mercenaries in Africa was highlighted by a United Nations report documenting abuses they had carried out in the Central African Republic. Russia suffered an apparent setback to its plans to extend influence in Africa when Sudan announced it was reviewing an earlier agreement to lease a naval base in Port Sudan for 25 years. Elsewhere, Russia stood out in seeking close ties with, and arms sales to, the military junta that came to power in a February coup in Myanmar. Despite large-scale repressions, Deputy Defence Minister Alexander Fomin visited on 26 March and Moscow hosted the leader of the junta, Min Aung Hlaing, in June.

Unprecedented protests in Belarus

In presidential elections held on 9 August 2020, Belarus's authoritarian leader Alexander Lukashenko sought a sixth term in office. Although the main opposition candidates had been arrested or left the country, the wife of one of them, Svetlana Tikhanovskaya, was allowed to stand and ran a spirited campaign. Peaceful protests erupted after official results declared Lukashenko the winner with over 80% of the vote. These were suppressed with extreme brutality, provoking further outrage that spread across the country. In the weeks that followed, unprecedented demonstrations filled the major towns and cities.

For a time, it appeared that the Lukashenko regime could fall. Despite a difficult relationship with Russia, exacerbated before the election by the arrest in Minsk of 33 mercenaries of the Russian state-linked Wagner

Group, Lukashenko appealed to Putin for support. Putin agreed to create a 'law-enforcement reserve' to intervene if he deemed it necessary, and new loans to keep Belarus financially stable. Gradually, Russian support, Lukashenko's grip on Belarus's elites, and the scale and brutality of the riot police and other repressive organs intimidated most of the opposition off the streets.

Western countries imposed sanctions on Belarus. Refusing to recognise Lukashenko's re-election, they instead began to meet Tikhanovskaya, whom the authorities had forced out of the country under extreme duress. State persecution of civil society and journalists intensified. On 23 May, Belarus forced down a plane overflying its airspace in order to detain Roman Protasevich, an opposition internet journalist. This incident led to further sanctions and deepened Belarus's estrangement from the West. With no prospect of restoring legitimacy at home, and no alternative to Russian financial support of Belarus's largely unreformed economy, Lukashenko found himself more dependent on Putin than ever. The key question was what price Putin would demand as he sought to exploit this opportunity to extend Russia's influence.

War and crisis in the Caucasus

From September to November 2020 Azerbaijan fought a six-week war against Armenia to regain much of the territory of the Nagorno-Karabakh enclave that it had lost in the early 1990s. Turkish military assistance, especially the provision of uninhabited aerial vehicles (UAVs), played a key role in Azerbaijan's victory. However, Russia played an adroit diplomatic role in ending the conflict, marginalising both Turkey and the Organization for Security and Co-operation in Europe (OSCE), and extending its own influence by securing the presence of its troops as peacekeepers on the ground. The conflict marked the biggest geopolitical shift in the region since Russia's intervention in Ukraine in 2014. Despite Armenia's disastrous performance in the war, Prime Minister Nikol Pashinyan won re-election in June.

In Georgia, the governing Georgian Dream party won an unprecedented third term in power in parliamentary elections on 31 October under a new electoral system. This sparked protests in Tbilisi that lasted several weeks. Alleging election fraud, the opposition United National Movement (UNM) boycotted parliament. In February 2021, a police raid on the UNM headquarters, and the arrest of its head, Nika Melia, triggered a political crisis. In April, President of the European Council Charles Michel mediated an agreement between the main political parties to resolve it. The UNM ended its boycott of parliament in May. It was not clear, though, how stable this compromise would be.

Ukraine's twin challenges of Russia and corruption

In local elections on 25 October 2020, Ukrainian President Volodymyr Zelensky's Servant of the People party won the highest percentage of the vote (17.6%) but failed to win any mayorships in the largest cities. Independent, non-party candidates performed well.

The Zelensky administration stepped up efforts to curb Russian political influence. In February 2021, the authorities closed down three TV channels linked to Viktor Medvedchuk, Ukraine's most influential pro-Russian politician and oligarch, and froze his financial assets. These moves were one likely cause of Russia's subsequent escalation in tensions. A ceasefire that had largely held since July 2020 broke down and was followed by Russia's military build-up on Ukraine's eastern border. Ukraine's army refused to be provoked by attacks on the demarcation line. Zelensky struck a defiant tone during the crisis. Putin did not accept his offer to meet. In May, Medvedchuk was charged with treason and placed under house arrest.

Struggles over corruption and the role of oligarchs continued. On 1 July 2020, National Bank of Ukraine governor Yakiv Smolii resigned, citing 'systematic pressure' against the bank's reform agenda. A wave of senior-staff resignations in June 2021 drew attention to the difficulties of maintaining reform momentum. In October 2020, the Constitutional Court annulled reform legislation and curbed the powers of the National Anti-Corruption Bureau of Ukraine (NABU). The Ukrainian parliament restored NABU's powers and in March 2021 Zelensky moved to dismiss the Court's chairman, Aleksandr Tupytsky, and another judge.

The IMF remained deeply concerned about the course of reform. On 5 March, the US imposed sanctions on the influential oligarch Ihor Kolomoyskyi for 'involvement in significant corruption'.

Moldova's pro-EU president

On 24 December Maia Sandu became the first female president of Moldova, having defeated pro-Russian incumbent Igor Dodon, who had been backed by Putin, in elections in November. After her victory, Sandu, a former prime minister who ran on a pro-EU platform, declared her intention to be 'president of European integration' and called for the withdrawal of Russian troops from the separatist region of Transdniestr. In response, Russia warned that such moves would risk 'serious destabilisation'.

Sandu inherited a parliament led by Dodon's Socialist Party, which sought to frustrate her reform programme and reduce her powers. A protracted power struggle ensued, which Sandu resolved in April 2021 by dissolving the legislature, paving the way for elections in July.

Central Asia

In Kyrgyzstan, disputed elections held on 4 October 2020 ignited public protests that led to the overthrow of the government, as similar protests had done in 2005 and 2010. President Sooronbai Jeenbekov annulled the results and imposed a state of emergency in Bishkek, the focus of the protests, but failed to quell them. On 15 October he resigned, in order, he said, to avoid bloodshed. Parliament appointed Sadyr Japarov as acting president. During the protests, Japarov had been freed from prison, where he was serving a sentence for kidnapping. In January 2021 he was confirmed as president in a landslide election victory.

In late April 2021 a dispute over irrigation water on the Kyrgyzstan–Tajikistan border escalated into severe clashes that involved security forces. Over 50 people died, the majority of them Kyrgyz. This incident highlighted the larger issue of unresolved border issues among Central Asian states.

US plans to withdraw from Afghanistan raised concerns in Central Asia and beyond about the threat of instability. As Eurasia approached the 30th anniversary of the break-up of the Soviet Union in late 1991, events of the past year and those unfolding to its south showed a region continuing to evolve in unpredictable ways and faced with external security challenges reminiscent of the 1990s.

A Belarusian Spring in Autumn
How much has changed, and what next?

Following fraudulent elections on 9 August 2020 in which Alexander Lukashenko sought a sixth consecutive term in office, Belarus erupted in protests that mounted the biggest ever challenge to his 26-year rule. Lukashenko's ruthless use of force, his ability to prevent elite defections and his successful appeals for Russian assistance helped to keep him in power. But his methods contributed to further, and irretrievable, loss of domestic legitimacy. Together with security-service efforts to detain and silence dissidents beyond Belarus's borders, they also left the country more isolated from the West than ever. The uncertain future of the regime has important strategic implications for Russia, the European Union and NATO.

Early signs of turbulence

Only Lukashenko's first election in 1994 had been free and fair: subsequent ones were neither, reflecting the authoritarian nature of the regime he built. Some earlier elections, notably in 2006 and 2010, had been stress points for the regime, propelling events into a predictable political cycle: mass protests on election night led to a forceful crackdown that in turn led to Western sanctions that were gradually eased until the next post-election crackdown began the cycle again. But even before the August 2020 election day, there were signs that this time events might prove more volatile.

Several forces had combined to raise disillusion with Lukashenko's long rule to unprecedented levels. One was the emergence of a new generation for which his Soviet style of authoritarianism held no appeal. Years of underperformance by Belarus's largely unreformed and state-dominated economy compounded this. A third factor was Lukashenko's disastrous mishandling of the COVID-19 pandemic. Like other strong-men leaders, he failed to protect his country from this viral invasion, deprecating its threat and even insulting its victims. This had two effects: it further drained support from him, including among traditional supporters; and it prompted civil society to mobilise to fill the vacuum left by his leadership. Demonstrating a remarkable capacity for self-organisation in a highly repressive environment, civic groups supported medical staff through 3D printing of essential equipment, crowdfunding and other innovative grassroots forms of cooperation. This experience helped to embolden and build capacity for civil society.

In the weeks leading up to the election, simmering discontent in the streets was reflected in new and more forceful resistance to police attempts to break up demonstrations. Even more significant was the decision of three prominent figures to run against Lukashenko: Viktor Babariko, the long-serving chairman of major bank Belgazprombank; Valery Tsepkalo, former head of the Minsk Hi-Tech Park, a major economic success story; and Sergei Tikhanovsky, a popular video blogger. As members of the elite with substantial regime ties, Babariko and Tsepkalo promised to be far more formidable opponents than the dedicated but relatively unthreatening opposition leaders whom Lukashenko had allowed to take part in previous elections. While their intention to stand carried inherent risks, it conveyed both the extent of concern in some elite circles about the course that the country was taking, and a degree of confidence that they could do so without fear of reprisal.

The latter calculation proved wrong. Tikhanovsky was arrested in May and detained. Babariko was arrested in June on charges of embezzlement and later sentenced to 14 years in prison; and Tsepkalo left the country out of concerns for his safety. Following her husband's arrest, Tikhanovsky's wife, Svetlana Tikhanovskaya, decided to stand as a candidate. Seeing no threat in a housewife and former teacher lacking any political experience, the authorities accepted her registration and permitted her – against her own expectations – to run against Lukashenko.

This repression united the opposition. Tsepkalo's wife, Veronika, and Babariko's campaign manager, Maria Kolesnikova, joined forces with Tikhanovskaya. The three women appeared together at several rallies during a spirited and energetic election campaign that attracted large crowds of supporters. Then, and in the months that followed, the prominent role that women played in the protests became one of their most distinctive features.

But the most dramatic pre-election development was very different in nature. On 29 July, 33 members of the Russian Wagner Group, the 'private military company' closely linked to the GRU, Russia's military intelligence service, were arrested in the capital, Minsk. Belarusian security officials claimed they were 'planning terrorist acts'. This incident underscored the tense state of Belarusian–Russian relations. Long fractious, these had deteriorated further in recent years due to Russia's attempts to turn the dependence of Belarus's largely unreformed economy into political leverage.

A dam burst of protest

Official results of the election gave 80.1% to Lukashenko and 10.1% to Tikhanovskaya. These radically implausible figures were further undermined when, at great risk to themselves, several election officials released true tallies showing that Tikhanovskaya had won the most votes in their polling stations. Mass protests began in the streets of major cities, not only Minsk, and were met with extreme violence and mass arrests by the riot police. Harrowing evidence of brutality began to accumulate, including screams recorded from outside the notorious Okrestina prison in Minsk. Those subsequently released reported meticulous and sadistic torture, including sexual violence, that in some cases caused life-changing injuries. Several people died on the streets and in prisons, or were found hanged – as was an exiled activist, Vitaly Shishov, in the Ukrainian capital Kyiv in August 2021. When Tikhanovskaya went to the Central Election Commission to lodge a formal protest against the result, she was detained there and told that if she did not leave the country immediately, her children would become orphans. Facing this apparent threat to her life, she crossed the border into Lithuania to continue her campaign for new and free elections in exile.

Rather than intimidating the population as the authorities intended, these actions ignited further outrage. Peaceful protests began to sweep across the country, taking in many smaller towns as well as cities.

Long-banned opposition symbols were suddenly ubiquitous, notably the white-red-white flag that had been created for the short-lived Belarusian National Republic in 1918 and was revived after the break-up of the Soviet Union in 1991 before being outlawed by Lukashenko. Civil-society groups proved adept at using social media to coordinate demonstrations. In some cities the protests grew so large that, for a time, the riot police ceased trying to break them up, and on occasion even lowered their shields.

As protests swelled, Lukashenko sought to appeal to what he believed to be his core supporters. On 17 August, he visited the large state-owned military Minsk Wheeled Tractor Factory, but was met – to his evident astonishment – by the same chants of *'ukhodi!'* ('leave!') that were heard on the streets. A week later, state television showed him with a Kalashnikov rifle in his hand and his young son Nikolai by his side, apparently organising a defence of his presidential palace. So great were the opposition crowds that Lukashenko's official inauguration as president took place in secret the following month. In a brief change of tactics, on 10 October he visited a group of prominent political detainees in prison, including Babariko and Tikhanovsky, and spoke to them for several hours. But this produced neither a comprise with, nor division of, the opposition. Nor did it have any impact on the protests.

The regime recovers

Yet despite this unprecedented popular challenge to his rule, Lukashenko neither ceded power nor fled the country, as many other dictators have done in the face of sustained national protests. By the end of 2020 he appeared to have secured his position, at least in the short term. Three factors enabled him to achieve this.

Firstly, the experienced and well-resourced Belarusian security services learned to intimidate most of the protesters off the streets through a process of tactical adaptation. In particular, they calibrated their violence in ways sufficiently severe and targeted to instil fear without further fanning the flames of wider outrage. In addition, members of the Coordination Council, the opposition leadership group set up after the protests began, were forced abroad or arrested, hindering the movement.

Secondly, Lukashenko succeeded in preventing significant splits or defections within the elite – usually a necessary condition for fundamental change. His highly personalistic form of rule, even by authoritarian standards, helped him achieve this – in particular, the absence of a formal party structure that could incubate factionalism, and regular reshuffles of key political and security heads that continued during the protests. There were signs of disquiet in state structures, but with few exceptions – notably, some resignations from the Ministry of Foreign Affairs and from the police and other security structures, some of whom set up an opposition group, BYPOL – this was not openly expressed. Rare attempts at local level to engage with protesters, notably in the western city of Grodno, were punished.

Thirdly, after initial hesitation Russia threw its weight behind Lukashenko. The Kremlin did not immediately take a position on the protests. Several media outlets and some prominent voices, notably veteran politician Vladimir Zhirinovsky, condemned the regime's brutality. Lukashenko publicly appealed to President Vladimir Putin for support, claiming that if forces of democratic change succeeded in Belarus, they would spread to Russia. On 27 August, Putin backed Belarus's embattled leader, endorsing his outlawing of the Coordination Council as unconstitutional and announcing the creation, at Lukashenko's request, of a 'law-enforcement reserve' that would intervene if Putin considered it necessary. Senior Russian officials subsequently painted the protests as Western-inspired and enabled.

The pre-election tensions of the Wagner Group incident were forgotten as Belarus and Russia found common cause as authoritarian neighbours. An intense series of exchanges followed, including visits by a Russian government delegation led by Prime Minister Mikhail Mishustin, Defence Minister Sergei Shoigu, head of the Foreign Intelligence Service Sergei Naryshkin and Secretary of the Security Council Nikolai Patrushev. Lukashenko visited Putin in Sochi on 14 September. Despite awkward body language that reflected evident exasperation at Lukashenko's entreaties, Putin agreed to lend Belarus US$1.5 billion. Russia provided other support, including journalists to replace those who had resigned from Belarusian state television in protest, as well as analytical and intelligence advice.

This support reassured Lukashenko, staved off an early financial crisis and added to the regime's actual and potential repressive capacity. It also escalated a domestic crisis about the future of Belarus's governance into a geopolitical contest between Russia and the West. The Belarusian opposition had been careful not to provoke Russia, emphasising its wish for a constructive relationship with Russia and unsuccessfully seeking a meeting with its embassy in Minsk. No EU flags were flown in the protests. But Russia viewed the prospect of democratic change as inherently threatening, for two reasons.

Firstly, the Kremlin worried about the wider implications of democratic regime change in a strategically important country that bordered three EU and NATO member states as well as Ukraine. Even if the leadership of a free Belarus would be sincere in its wish for good relations with Russia – which would accord with the preferences of most Belarusians – it would almost certainly seek a better relationship with the West too, undermining Russia's aspirations to subordinate Belarus within some form of de facto 'union state'. Secondly, and even more fundamentally, the peaceful removal of a veteran authoritarian ruler in a neighbouring eastern Slavic state after an election would be an unwelcome precedent for Putin ahead of the 2024 presidential election in Russia, preparations for which increasingly dominated domestic policies. This meant that the Kremlin saw the prevention of democratic change in Belarus as an essential interest.

As Lukashenko re-established control, the question then became what price Russia had extracted for its support – or, indeed, whether it had been able to secure any quid pro quo. For while Lukashenko could look nowhere but to Russia for support, it was not clear whether Russia had any alternative, at least in the short term, to backing Lukashenko if it was to avert a collapse of his regime. Their dependence was thus mutual, locking them even more tightly into a distrustful embrace.

There were signs, though, that Russia was exploring more significant longer-term outcomes than the acceleration of long-established integration 'road maps' to which Lukashenko paid lip service in early

2021. On 2 March, the two countries signed a five-year strategic defence agreement for the first time. Four days later, a new pro-Russian party, Soyuz (Union), held its first congress in Minsk. Lukashenko revived vague plans – reportedly at Russia's behest – for constitutional reform. These initially promised to disperse some power away from the highly autocratic presidency. On 11–12 February, he elaborated these at a rare meeting of the All Belarusian People's Assembly, a hand-picked gathering of the elite at which Lukashenko sought to consolidate his control. But the signs were that these changes would be cosmetic. It appeared unlikely that Lukashenko would willingly compromise his domination of the regime he had built. The details will become clearer ahead of the constitutional referendum now planned for early 2022.

The West responds and the regime escalates

Western countries quickly condemned the repression. In a series of coordinated steps, the United States, United Kingdom and the EU imposed sanctions on individuals and entities responsible for repressions. On 18 January 2021, Belarus also lost its status as co-host of the ice-hockey championships for what the International Ice Hockey Federation described as 'safety and security issues'. Western countries refused to recognise the election of Lukashenko. Instead, several European leaders and, in July 2021, US President Joe Biden, met Tikhanovskaya. They did not recognise her as the legitimate president, as she did not claim this status for herself. Rather, she called for free and fair elections that would allow the people to choose who would govern them.

Previous post-election crackdowns on human rights in Belarus had been followed by limited relaxation and improvement in relations with the West. The scale and severity of the violence this time made it inherently unlikely that this pattern would be repeated. Not only did persecution of civil-society groups and journalists intensify, but Belarus escalated actions beyond its own borders for the first time. On 23 May 2021, the authorities forced a commercial Ryanair flight overflying Belarusian airspace en route from Athens to Vilnius to land in Minsk, by issuing a false bomb alert and sending up a MiG-29 fighter to escort it down. The purpose of this operation was to detain Roman Protasevich, an opposition internet journalist, who played an important role in coordinating protests and disseminating news from Belarus from abroad. Soon after his arrest, and under evident psychological and physical duress, Protasevich made a tearful confession of plotting against the government on Belarusian state television. The Ryanair incident violated international aviation rules and led to further, more severe Western measures, including sectoral sanctions and a ban on the use of Western airspace and airports by Belarusian carriers.

Protasevich's detention was significant for two reasons. Firstly, it suggested that the regime, despite its apparent restoration of control, was far from confident of its prospects and was prepared to go to unprecedented lengths to silence even a single dissenter. Secondly, the regime was now prepared to reach beyond its borders to protect itself, putting at risk over 100 passengers on an international flight. The planning of the operation almost certainly involved the presence of the KGB (the Belarusian security service) in Greece, an EU member state. In sum, the regime was prepared to pose an international threat, not just a domestic one, in order to stay in power.

This defiance of Western opinion escalated. On 24 May, the day after it forced down the Ryanair jet, Belarus expelled all Latvian diplomatic staff in retaliation for Latvia's replacement of Belarus's official flag with the banned white-red-white flag in the capital, Riga. Latvia responded in kind, expelling all Belarusian diplomats. In June, Belarus began flying in migrants from Middle Eastern countries, notably Iraq, and immediately sending them to its borders with Lithuania and Latvia. By late July over 3,000 migrants had crossed these borders, compared to 81 in 2020, imposing financial strains on the receiving countries. This operation, conducted at some cost to the authorities, did not benefit Belarus in any way: its sole purpose appeared to be to inflict costs on its EU neighbours. The country, it seemed, had given up any pretence of interest in the eventual improvement of relations with the West.

Into uncharted territory

While Lukashenko still held power as the first anniversary of the election approached, everything about the circumstances of his rule had changed significantly and probably irreversibly. Domestically, he enjoyed little legitimacy: only a minority supported him, and fewer still with any enthusiasm. No one had rallied spontaneously to support him: a couple of pitiful and short-lived state-organised demonstrations only brought this home. After 27 years in power, he offered no reason for obedience beyond the appeal of fear. He still commanded the obedience of state structures that administer this fear. But the optics of major events such as the All Belarusian People's Assembly suggested limited enthusiasm even among elites, especially outside the security organs.

The regime is unlikely to regain any significant degree of popularity. Neither its recent brutality, nor the collective experience of having defied it even for a few weeks, are likely to be forgotten. Nor can prosperity substitute for freedom: the chronic economic problems that helped fuel discontent will almost certainly get worse as Western sanctions bite and talented young people, especially in the IT sector, leave the country.

In the absence of popular legitimacy, the question of elite cohesion becomes more important than ever. Lukashenko's increasingly erratic and impulsive decision-making, which is imposing growing costs on the state to protect the regime, will test this. A new factor is the revelation that Belarusian 'cyber-partisans' had extracted huge quantities of data from the Ministry of Internal Affairs in mid-2021. Probably the biggest hack of any state's security systems to date, it included personal data of KGB officers and other security personnel. From July 2021, the cyber-partisans began to release these details with the aim of holding accountable those responsible for state repression.

Belarus's international position is also more anomalous than ever. It is becoming not just the last dictatorship, but the only pariah, in Europe. Even the communist states of Eastern Europe sought a degree of engagement with the West during the Cold War. With the exception of Albania under Enver Hoxha (who died in 1985), it is hard to think of a regime that has been as actively hostile to the rest of the continent as Belarus is now. And Albania lacked Belarus's educated and globally connected population.

Belarus's strategic position, and the contest of values within it, mean that Russia and the West will continue to follow developments closely and seek to influence them. Russia seeks to bolster the regime while increasing its influence within it. Its chief advantages are the close ties it enjoys with the regime, especially the security services, its military strength and Belarus's financial dependence on it. Its chief dilemma is how to pursue its goal without alienating either the population or part of the elite in ways that trigger adverse outcomes for it, as it did in Ukraine after 2014.

The West now seeks, to an extent it did not before August 2020, a free and democratic Belarus. Its chief advantages are the support for this goal among a majority of the population and the West's own still largely untested capacity to exert economic and psychological pressure on the regime. Its chief dilemma is how to pursue its goal without driving the regime into genuine subordination to Russia.

The only certainty of this complex and fluid situation is that events will be hard both to predict and to manage. The astonishing outpouring of peaceful protests last autumn surprised even those who took part in them. Further surprises may follow.

The Changing Security Landscape of the South Caucasus
What are the implications of the second Armenia–Azerbaijan war?

In autumn 2020, a 44-day war between Armenia and Azerbaijan dramatically changed, at great human cost, the status quo that had persisted in the South Caucasus since the mid-1990s. Azerbaijan recovered large parts of territory it had lost to the Armenians more than a quarter of a century before; Armenia was defeated on the battlefield and lost its de facto control of the disputed territory of Nagorno-Karabakh; and Russia deployed a peacekeeping force in Karabakh itself, giving it 'boots on the ground' in the region for the first time since the Soviet era.

The new war confirmed that the Armenian–Azerbaijani conflict over the highland territory of Nagorno- (or 'mountainous') Karabakh, the longest running of all the ethno-territorial disputes in the former Soviet space, remains the most bitterly contested. At its heart is an almost insoluble conundrum regarding the status of the region of Karabakh (as it is often known), which for hundreds of years has had an Armenian majority but is also important to Azerbaijan and was allocated to Soviet Azerbaijan in 1921 as an autonomous district. Since the dispute broke out under Mikhail Gorbachev in 1988, when the Karabakh-Armenians campaigned to join Soviet Armenia and Soviet Azerbaijan strongly resisted, this dispute has been central to the national projects of Armenia and Azerbaijan, with both seeking to build a nation at the expense of the other.

The war of 1991–94, conducted as the Soviet Union broke up, resulted in an Armenian victory. The Armenians took full control of Nagorno-Karabakh and captured, either wholly or partially, seven Azerbaijani districts outside the autonomous region, whose entire civilian population, consisting of more than half a million people, fled or were expelled. The ceasefire of 1994 froze the situation on the ground, but there were no peacekeepers and international diplomacy failed to close the gap between the almost incompatible positions of the two sides. The efforts of the French, Russian and US mediators – the so-called 'co-chairs' of the Organization for Security and Co-operation in Europe (OSCE) Minsk Group – to mediate a solution had been desultory, at best, for a decade.

Fighting broke out on 27 September 2020. The situation had been tense for more than two months following several days of skirmishes on the international border between Armenia and Azerbaijan in July. Azerbaijan was publicly frustrated by the reluctance of Armenian Prime Minister Nikol Pashinyan to engage with the framework document under discussion in negotiations mediated by the Minsk Group co-chairs – the so-called 'Basic Principles'. This evidently encouraged Baku to explore its military options.

The Azerbaijani leadership started the conflict at a time when it believed it could reset it in its favour quite rapidly. The weather was still good and there were several weeks before winter conditions would make fighting more difficult on the high ground in Karabakh. The COVID-19 pandemic constrained international diplomacy and the dispatch of senior officials to the region to urge a ceasefire. Another factor may have been the US election campaign distracting Washington. The Trump administration had been relatively disengaged in the South Caucasus and its reaction to growing tensions was weak. Two days before fighting began, the US embassies in Armenia and Azerbaijan put out a travel advisory warning US citizens not to travel to outside the capital cities of the two countries, but the State Department did not issue a statement to the parties to the conflict urging restraint.

Critical to Azerbaijan's eventual victory was direct military support from Turkish President Recep Tayyip Erdogan, which helped break the two-decade stalemate. This was a sharp break with Ankara's previous policy on the conflict, which had been to offer political support for Azerbaijan but press for a peaceful resolution of the dispute. Azerbaijan also cashed in on years of petro-diplomacy, fuelled by oil and gas exports and lobbying, by receiving support from Pakistan and also from Israel, which has long seen Azerbaijan as a friendly ally in the Muslim world and a regional counterweight to Iran.

For more than a decade, Turkish officers had trained the once-derided Azerbaijani military to new NATO standards. According to some reports, Turkish military advisers were present in Baku, helping direct the operation from September. Azerbaijan deployed Turkish *Bayraktar* TB2 uninhabited aerial vehicles (UAVs), and the Israeli *Harop*, Orbiter and *SkyStriker* loitering munitions, to considerable effect. Azerbaijan was able to limit the use of ground troops while these drones destroyed Armenian armour and defences, enabling its forces to make rapid progress in the regions south of Karabakh. There is strong evidence that Turkey also recruited more than 2,000 mercenaries from Syria to fight for Azerbaijan – although Baku and Ankara continue to deny this.

The Armenian side, along with many international experts, had assumed that its control of the high ground and rings of defences built up over many years would protect it against a new Azerbaijani offensive. The reality proved very different. Azerbaijani tactics delivered swift results. The Armenian military not only lost territory but was unable to rotate its men. After the ceasefire, the de facto leader of the Karabakh-Armenians Arayik Harutyunyan said that morale had collapsed and troops were sick with COVID-19 and other illnesses.

By 16 October, after fierce fighting, Azerbaijani forces had captured the Armenian-majority town of Hadrut, inside Nagorno-Karabakh. On 22 October, Azerbaijan announced that it had reconquered the Armenian-held portions of its frontier with Iran along the Araxes river. Azerbaijani forces then appeared to be moving to cut off the so-called Lachin corridor, the road that connects Armenia with Nagorno-Karabakh.

In the last few days of October, attention turned to the hilltop town of Shusha (known to Armenians as Shushi) in the heart of Karabakh. It is often said: 'He who controls Shusha controls Karabakh'. The town overlooks the whole of the territory. It is also symbolically significant in Azerbaijan, being the birthplace of its most famous composers and musicians, the site of two eighteenth-century mosques and the only town in Nagorno-Karabakh that had an Azerbaijani majority during the Soviet era.

When Azerbaijani forces achieved the impressive feat of capturing Shusha on 8 November, they were close to cutting off the region's main city of Stepanakert and had a clear prospect of capturing the whole of Armenian-administered Nagorno-Karabakh and driving out its ethnic

Armenian population. Estimates of the population of the territory ranged between 100,000 and 150,000. A large proportion had fled to Armenia during the conflict, but many had stayed behind. There was a serious risk of even greater bloodshed and that Armenia might try to deploy Russian-made long-range *Iskander* missiles against Azerbaijan, a step it had not taken hitherto in the conflict. There is evidence that one was fired against Baku on 9 November but did not hit its target.

At this critical point, the Russians decisively intervened. On 9–10 November, Pashinyan, Azerbaijani President Ilham Aliyev and Russian President Vladimir Putin signed a Russian-brokered ceasefire to end a conflict that had claimed more than 7,000 lives. The vast majority of these were young army conscripts who were not born at the time of the 1991–94 conflict.

The trilateral agreement confirmed a decisive Azerbaijani military victory. A complete swing of the pendulum entirely reversed all the Armenian gains and conquests from the previous war. As a result, Azerbaijan recovered all seven districts it had lost in 1992–94, with the exception of the narrow Lachin corridor. It also captured around one-third of Armenian-administered Karabakh, forcing around 30,000 ethnic Armenians from their homes.

The statement ended more than 25 years of what had seemed an almost permanent equilibrium on the ground and a desultory negotiating process, presided over by the OSCE Minsk Group, which had failed to deliver results. The agreement also inserted Russia into the heart of the conflict zone for the first time. As soon as it was signed, Russia almost instantly began to deploy a 1,960-strong peacekeeping force to Karabakh.

Despite its military alliance with Yerevan and the commitments of the Collective Security Treaty Organization to the Republic of Armenia, Moscow had kept strict neutrality during the conflict. There was speculation that Russia had deliberately turned a blind eye to Azerbaijan re-igniting the conflict, regarding the Armenians as too inflexible and wanting to see a more balanced status quo emerge in which Azerbaijan would receive most of its occupied territories back and Russia would play a more central role. Talking to journalists after the ceasefire agreement,

Putin suggested that the Armenians might not have lost so much territory had Pashinyan agreed to the ceasefire that he proposed on 19–20 October.

Winners and losers

The war dramatically changed the fortunes of the two main actors in the region, Armenia and Azerbaijan, and of the two most important neighbours, Russia and Turkey.

Azerbaijan's recapture of the seven districts around Nagorno-Karabakh will make possible the return of half a million internally displaced persons who had been expelled by Armenian forces. This process will take several years, however, as it requires demining, reconstruction and phased resettlement at a cost of several billion dollars. The reconstruction of the territories is now being presented as a national-unity project for Azerbaijan.

Azerbaijan's victory was a personal triumph for Aliyev, whose popularity skyrocketed as a result. Despite being in office since 2003, the president had lived in the shadow of his father and predecessor Heydar Aliyev, but has now ensured his legacy as the liberator of lost lands. Since the conflict, Aliyev has consolidated his authoritarian rule by further harassing and marginalising his political opponents.

Armenia was plunged into turmoil by its military defeat in November 2020. It not only lost territory to Azerbaijan and faced mass displacement of its population, but relived old traumas as Azerbaijan received the support of Turkey, which it still holds responsible for the killing of more than 1m Armenians in 1915–16, a massacre that US President Joe Biden recognised as 'genocide' in April 2021. Several issues keep the conflict smouldering for the Armenian side. One is the continued detention of Armenian captives in Azerbaijan. As of late June 2021, a little under 200 Armenian prisoners of war were reported to be in Azerbaijani captivity. Yerevan said they were prisoners of war, while Baku maintained that they did not qualify for this status, having been taken captive after the 9–10 November ceasefire. Many international bodies, such as the European Parliament and the US State Department, have called for the captives' release on humanitarian grounds.

A second issue is border demarcation between Armenia and Azerbaijan. As Soviet-era maps were never exact, all post-Soviet countries had to go through this process, sometimes quite painfully, but this never happened between Armenia and Azerbaijan because of the first Karabakh conflict. With Azerbaijan regaining control of territories adjoining Armenia after the latest conflict, the issue became extremely contentious. On 12 May, Azerbaijani forces moved 3.5-kilometre into an area that most maps showed to be part of southern Armenia, sparking a new mini crisis. On 20 May, a new Russian-led border-demarcation commission was announced. A third issue is Azerbaijan's expulsion of 30,000 Armenians from their homes in recaptured territories. Some of these were internally displaced inside Karabakh, while others fled to Armenia.

The reputation of Pashinyan, who came to power on a wave of people power in Armenia's peaceful Velvet Revolution of 2018, was severely undermined by Armenia's defeat, his personal handling of the crisis, and his refusal to confer with other members of the political and military elite both during the war and in agreeing Armenia's capitulation to Azerbaijani demands. In the 20 June election called in the aftermath of the conflict, Pashinyan nevertheless campaigned on domestic issues and managed to secure re-election against an opposition dominated by old elites and still distrusted by much of the population.

Russia scored a strategic success by taking the driving seat in the diplomacy of the conflict for the first time, and therein marginalising Western countries. Under the terms of the ceasefire, Russia gained the right to deploy the 1,960-strong peacekeeping force to protect the new 'Line of Contact' around the much-reduced territory of Armenian-administered Nagorno-Karabakh. This fulfilled a long-standing ambition, which Russia failed to achieve in 1994 when the first conflict ended, to deploy Russian peacekeepers to the conflict zone. As the Karabakh mission is resupplied via both Armenia and Azerbaijan, the deployment also provides Russia with a new link to its military base in Gyumri in Armenia.

Russia's new role in Karabakh differs from the one it plays in other post-Soviet conflict zones, however. It must work with both sides and is more engaged in a classical peacekeeping operation while also carrying out demining, humanitarian assistance and construction. Moscow must tread carefully; it is there nominally to protect the Armenians of Karabakh and is effectively making itself their new patron, replacing Yerevan. But it is also there with the consent of Baku and must work closely with the Azerbaijani government. Russian has now been approved as a second official language inside Karabakh itself. However, this is not South Ossetia, where Russia is in full control, in defiance of its internationally recognised parent state, Georgia. The Russian peacekeeping force operates in Karabakh with the consent of Azerbaijan. The ceasefire agreement provided for a Russian military presence in Karabakh for five years, with the possibility of extension unless vetoed by another party to the agreement. This gives Azerbaijan bargaining power with Moscow as the two countries negotiate over the future of Russia's presence.

Turkey asserted itself in the South Caucasus militarily for the first time in 100 years. Erdogan reaped domestic rewards for his support of Azerbaijan, the Turkic country that can claim the closest kinship with Turkey. Aliyev invited him to share the limelight at Azerbaijan's victory parade on 10 December 2020. However, Erdogan's post-conflict ambitions – notably, for the OSCE Minsk Group to be dissolved and for Turkey to be given equal status to Russia as a mediator – did not materialise. Nor did Turkey get to deploy peacekeepers – only around 50 observers in a largely symbolic mission near the town of Aghdam outside Karabakh itself.

Theoretically, the new realities allow for normalisation of relations between Armenia and Turkey, which have had no diplomatic relations since Armenia became independent in 1991, and no open border since 1993 when Turkey closed it after Armenia captured Azerbaijan's Kelbajar region. Now that Armenian forces have left the occupied Azerbaijani regions, the impediments to establishing official relations have been lifted. However, if resistance to normalisation came primarily from Turkey in the past, now it comes from Armenia, furious at Turkey's role in the 2020 war.

The outcome of the conflict has also sharply reduced the influence of international organisations and Western countries. Since 1994, mediation of the Karabakh conflict had formally been the preserve of the co-chairs of the Minsk Group of the OSCE. From 1997 these were France, Russia and the United States. Russia was always the most active member, but for many years the other two were also influential and played a balancing role. For more than a decade, however, Russia has been the principal member and Russian Foreign Minister Sergei Lavrov the only important foreign actor mediating between Baku and Yerevan.

The descent into a second war, and Russia's emergence as the unrivalled power broker in the region, was a defeat for multilateral diplomacy and for Western engagement. The Minsk Group co-chair format continues formally. However, the co-chairs have been almost invisible since the 9–10 November ceasefire, while France's open support for Armenia during the conflict has ruled it out as a trusted mediator in Azerbaijani eyes. Moreover, the mediators' chief task of resolving the political dispute between the two countries by coming up with a new formula for the status of the disputed region of Nagorno-Karabakh looks as impossible as ever.

New transport routes and other neighbours

The aftermath of the second Armenia–Azerbaijan war also promised to change the region by opening up transport routes that had been closed for nearly 30 years. After a meeting of Armenian, Azerbaijani and Russian leaders in Moscow in January 2021, a trilateral working group was set up to facilitate new transport projects. This fulfils a joint Azerbaijani–Russian–Turkish agenda to link the road and rail networks of all three countries. Since the Black Sea railway route via Abkhazia was cut in 1992, Russia has not had a direct rail link to Armenia, Turkey or northwestern Iran. It hopes now to have one via Azerbaijan.

The ceasefire declaration commits Armenia and Russia to build transport communications between western Azerbaijan and the Azerbaijani exclave of Nakhichevan, via Armenia. This link, which would reconnect Azerbaijan's two separated territories, is Baku's highest domestic priority. Armenia fears a loss of its sovereignty and has been pushing for the reopening of a northern route, over which it would have more control, which would run from northwest Azerbaijan to the northern Armenian town of Ijevan, then on to Yerevan and Nakhichevan.

The new projects are viewed nervously in both Georgia and Iran, which share borders with Armenia and Azerbaijan. For the past three decades Iran was left an awkward bystander to this conflict and to major developments in the South Caucasus as a whole. With a large Azerbaijani minority in the north of the country, it now faces the challenge of a more assertive Azerbaijan. It has sought assurances that the new Azerbaijani–Turkish transport routes would not restrict its access to Armenia and has redoubled its commitment to Armenia as a northern route.

Georgia has always tried to tread carefully around the Karabakh conflict, so as not to offend its neighbours and to avoid inflaming tensions between its own large minority Armenian and Azerbaijani populations. However, the deployment of the Russian peacekeeping force is a cause for new apprehension in Georgia, as it now sees Russian troops deployed in four locations in its immediate neighbourhood: in Abkhazia, Armenia (Gyumri), South Ossetia and now Nagorno-Karabakh. Georgia also fears that new transport routes bypassing it may reduce its status as the main transit hub of the South Caucasus. These fears may be premature: infrastructure is already in place, especially the Baku–Tbilisi–Kars railway, opened in 2017, which cut journey times and increased freight transit across the region. Azerbaijan and Turkey have a vested interest in that route; it will take them some time to build a viable alternative.

Georgia's main connection to Russia remains the Lars–Kazbegi road across the mountains of the Greater Caucasus. Trade and transit are often restricted because of bad weather and the whims of Russian customs officials and border guards. If non-Georgian traders and travellers begin to use the easier Azerbaijan–Russia north–south route, Georgians who want to trade with Russia may be more vulnerable to future Russian restrictions at the border. Georgia may need to reconsider the Anaklia deep-water port project, stalled since early 2020, and look again at reopening the railway beside the Black Sea through Abkhazia. This would not only reconnect Armenia, Georgia and Russia, but serve as a new transit route for Turkey, Ukraine and other countries.

Prospects

While the 9–10 November ceasefire declaration ended bloodshed, it was merely a 'statement', not a peace treaty. One of the core issues of the Armenian–Azerbaijani conflict – the status of the territory of Nagorno-Karabakh and the rights of its Armenian inhabitants – remains disputed. Aliyev has repeatedly declared the Karabakh conflict 'resolved' and ruled out any territorial autonomy for the Armenians of Karabakh. The Armenians, in turn, maintain their long-standing support for its secession from Azerbaijan. In the meantime, Karabakh is isolated, as Azerbaijan refuses to allow access to any international organisations except the International Committee of the Red Cross.

Lavrov said in June 2021 that discussions on the Karabakh status issue should be postponed for several years while more immediate questions are tackled. Moscow is more interested in consolidating its new military foothold in the region and opening up transport routes than in seeing a permanent peace deal that nullifies its new role as essential broker between Baku and Yerevan. Continuing deadlock serves Russia's interests.

However, Russia's new role brings with it the burden of responsibility. In the Caucasus, local politics and informal armed actors have long had the potential to destabilise the geopolitical designs of bigger powers. If things go wrong, both sides will blame Moscow. As a June 2021 International Crisis Group report observed, 'Russia's peacekeepers have found themselves mediating disputes over mundane matters from access to water to stray cows, without a clear mandate for how to handle tensions along the front'. This may be why Russia has not abandoned either multilateral diplomacy in the form of the OSCE Minsk Group, or bilateral cooperation with Turkey in the new ceasefire-monitoring centre.

The dream of regional economic connectivity that flickered into life in November 2020 faded somewhat in 2021 in the face of continued Armenia–Azerbaijan confrontation. New transport infrastructure will be difficult without Armenia's support. Georgia, meanwhile, looks at the new post-war realities to its south with suspicion and will want to see its interests heeded in any cross-regional projects. The 2020 Armenia–Azerbaijan war left many issues unresolved and created new challenges.

Uzbekistan: Testing the Mirziyoyev Agenda
How are domestic reforms and more cooperative diplomacy faring?

September 2021 marked the fifth anniversary of Shavkat Mirziyoyev's ascent as president of Uzbekistan, following the death in office of the long-serving Islam Karimov. Karimov had been president during the entire post-Soviet period, and before that the first secretary of the Communist Party of the Uzbek Soviet Socialist Republic. After the break-up of the Soviet Union in 1991, Karimov consolidated his authority and maintained a firm grip on the economic, political and societal levers of control. He pursued a highly repressive domestic policy with an abysmal human-rights record. In foreign and security policy, Uzbekistan often stood apart from other countries, and shied away from multilateral organisations and security agreements. Other than during 2001–05, when Uzbekistan briefly had a 'strategic partnership' with the United States in support of the latter's efforts in Afghanistan, foreign military forces have not been based on Uzbek soil. A high degree of economic autarchy matched Karimov's aversion to international cooperation.

As prime minister during the last 13 years of the Karimov presidency, Mirziyoyev well understood the challenges facing the country. On becoming president, he immediately began announcing reforms, impressing upon Uzbek citizens and foreign observers that change was afoot via speeches, public declarations and social media. While remaining carefully respectful of his predecessor, Mirziyoyev also established his reputation as a leader willing to take on a bureaucracy that had ossified in the later years of the Karimov presidency. Mirziyoyev's administration framed his reforms as part of Uzbekistan's 'third renaissance', connecting them to past periods of intellectual and economic growth in the region: the eleventh and twelfth centuries of Bukhara, and the Timurid period of the fifteenth and sixteenth centuries. So far, the reforms have brought innovation and modernisation, but minimal liberalisation. Despite the COVID-19 pandemic, this pattern continued in 2020–21.

Challenges on the domestic front

Mirziyoyev's latest economic reforms, especially in monetary, trade and manufacturing policies, have focused on a gradual acceptance of international standards. For example, Uzbekistan's use of child labour and forced adult labour in the cotton industry has long attracted international criticism. In January 2021, the International Labour Organization reported that systemic forced labour and child labour had come to an end, although some non-governmental organisations (NGOs) still highlight poor working conditions and other negative practices in the industry. Privatisation policy has also developed. Throughout 2020, several state-run businesses, including the iconic Hotel Uzbekistan, were offered up for foreign ownership.

During the past year, the Uzbek government implemented a monetary policy with the aim of increasing tax collection, reducing reliance on external hard-currency borrowing, and eventually creating a freely convertible Uzbek som. Nearly 43% of the US$6 billion of tax revenues in the fiscal year 2020–21 came from indirect taxes, primarily value-added taxes. In 2020, the government borrowed US$5.5bn on the international market, a figure expected to fall below US$5bn in 2021. According to the IMF's 2021 country report on Uzbekistan, this decline in international borrowing has caused inflation to rise slightly, but still within a manageable range of 10–13% over the last year. In all, the country has managed to weather the international economic shock of COVID-19, sustaining a GDP growth rate of 1.6% in 2020, with a forecast rate of 4.8% for 2021.

Regional trade also held at a respectable US$36bn, with China (20%) and Russia (19%) the most significant trade partners. The four neighbouring Central Asian states (Kazakhstan, Kyrgyzstan, Tajikistan and Turkmenistan) collectively represent another 20%, with Turkey accounting for just under 9% of trade. Germany, South Korea, Switzerland and the United Kingdom are also important trade partners. Uzbekistan remains dependent on international prices of the cotton, gas and strategic minerals it exports.

Uzbekistan's semi-autarchic economy has been less severely affected by COVID-19 than some other countries. Trade fell by 14% in 2020, but this was a less traumatic drop than that of neighbouring states. Trade is rebounding slightly in 2021, given the higher price for raw-material exports. But remittances from Uzbek citizens working abroad have been adversely affected. In 2019, more than 900,000 Uzbeks worked in Russia, Turkey and other countries, sending home over US$8bn in remittances (nearly 15% of Uzbekistan's GDP). It is too early to determine the net losses from the past year, but there is no question that remittances have declined in 2020–21 and unemployment will increase as travel to Russia is limited.

International organisations and media applauded the new monetary policy as well as efforts to address the economy through modest privatisation, but also cautioned against over-optimism. In September 2019, *Forbes Magazine* highlighted the potential of the US$1.7bn international business and trade hub being built in Tashkent, made easier with measures such as floating the currency-exchange rate, lifting capital controls and more enhanced privatisation of state-owned properties. In addition, Uzbekistan has received more than US$7bn in foreign direct investment during the past five years, with three of these years having the highest per annum investment since 1992. But questions remain about the limits of reform. Western companies and governments questioned whether human-rights issues would be addressed in an open and transparent manner, and whether comprehensive reform would address pervasive corruption.

With respect to human and political rights, much work needs to be done. During the late Karimov years, Uzbekistan was regularly given some of the lowest scores of any country on economic, political and civil freedoms. In 2016, the year of Karimov's death, Freedom House's 'Freedom in the World' report gave Uzbekistan a score of three out of a possible 100, ranking it as one of the most unfree countries in the world. Under Mirziyoyev this score has moved to only 11 out of 100 in the 2021 report. Freedom House's 'Nations in Transit' report – which evaluates the state of democracy in 29 countries in the region stretching from Central Europe to Central Asia – gave Uzbekistan a democracy score of 1.25 out of seven for 2021, again earning it a place in the list of 'consolidated authoritarian regimes'. Early in his tenure, Mirziyoyev released an undeclared number of political prisoners, closed the infamous Jaslyk prison and reviewed the criminal-justice system, as well as the rights of speech and assembly. Presidential elections are scheduled for December 2021. While it is too early to tell who will compete against him, it is certain that Mirziyoyev will seek re-election. It is also expected that the registered political parties will field candidates to run against him, although the identities of these candidates were unknown as of mid-2021. Amnesty International and Human Rights Watch have acknowledged gradual improvements over the past five years but remain critical of Uzbekistan's overall human- and political-rights performance.

Under Mirziyoyev the state has also begun to ease its pressure on civil society, with the government promoting the inclusion of some NGOs and international institutions. In 2018, legislation was passed to streamline NGO registration, and taxes and fees for NGO registration were reduced in January 2020. The Uzbek government claims there are now more than 10,000 NGOs in the country, although perhaps 70% have some state connection, with a smaller percentage 'self-initiated'. Because funding remains a perennial problem, these latter organisations find it difficult to survive, as exemplified by groups like Oltin Qanot, a youth organisation, which must compete with the state-run Youth Union of Uzbekistan. Foreign news organisations, such as the US broadcaster Voice of America, gained the right to register and return to the country in 2017. Blocks on internet access to international media were lifted in May 2019. During the past year, more reporting was allowed on controversial issues within the country. For example, when a dam collapsed near Sardoba (along the Uzbekistan–Kazakhstan border) in May 2020, it was reported that more than 70,000 Uzbek citizens were displaced by flooding, causing significant economic and environmental damage. The media fallout in the subsequent months pressured the government to address issues previously not discussed in such public fora. Whether this was an isolated incident or a sign of greater transparency remains to be seen. International organisations cite the above developments as proof of progress.

The COVID-19 pandemic has tested Uzbekistan. The country closed its borders and air links in March and April 2020. During late summer 2020, COVID-19 cases averaged 500–800 per day, though officially reported deaths were unusually low, often below ten per day. With limited opportunities for testing, it is likely that cases were underreported. As the second summer of the pandemic began, there was hope that vaccines – whether from China or Russia – would allow life to return to normal. As of July 2021, over 3.6% of Uzbekistan's population had been fully vaccinated, and more than 6.2% had received their first dose. Thus far, more than 3.5 million doses have been administered, primarily the Russian vaccine Sputnik V.

Cautious multilateralism remains a priority

In terms of regional relations, Mirziyoyev's priority is to develop stronger engagement with Uzbekistan's immediate neighbours. His first trips abroad after taking office were to Turkmenistan and Kazakhstan in March 2017, and his first meetings were with his regional counterparts, in both bilateral and multilateral settings. Mirziyoyev signalled that Uzbekistan would now settle differences with its neighbours and create conditions for cross-border cooperation, trade and security. Obstacles to transit and trade between Uzbekistan and Kazakhstan were subsequently lifted. Moreover, Uzbekistan and Tajikistan began to cooperate on the Rogun Dam, and the spectre of conflict between the two appeared to recede. The focus of the past year was on strengthening ties within Central Asia and the broader Eurasian space, while Uzbekistan bided its time to develop longer-term strategies with other states beyond the region, such as Turkey, Iran and countries in South Asia. Uzbek Foreign Minister Abdulaziz Komilov reinforced these messages in a series of virtual and in-person meetings with his counterparts throughout 2020 that were held more frequently than before. In February 2021, he visited Tajikistan, Kazakhstan and Afghanistan, focusing on regional trade, water management and regional security cooperation. Considering the violent border clash between Tajikistan and Kyrgyzstan in April 2021 in Tajikistan's Vorukh exclave, such cooperative efforts by Tashkent are more important than ever. A meeting of the chief executives of the Uzbek, Tajik and Kyrgyz provinces that comprise the shared Fergana Valley on 23 April 2021 reflected this effort.

Uzbekistan's relations with Russia remained strong. Early in his tenure, Mirziyoyev met with Russian President Vladimir Putin and signed several bilateral agreements on security-related issues. In 2020, Uzbekistan participated in several multilateral and bilateral security exercises and exchanges. Some analysts speculated that Uzbekistan might go so far as to join the Collective Security Treaty Organization (CSTO) or the Eurasian Economic Union (EEU). While it gained observer status in the EEU in December 2020, in mid-2021 there was no sign that it intended to become a full member of either organisation in the immediate future.

Relations with China remained characterised by high-level visits and statements of mutual respect. However, no significant agreements were made in 2020–21, other than continuations of earlier, ambitious programmes of infrastructure development and transit support for Turkmen gas going to China. As China is framing its engagement with Central Asia in terms of its Belt and Road Initiative (BRI), bilateral engagement ends up being part of multilateral projects. The BRI's Central Asian efforts began in 2015, so Mirziyoyev has had to manage relations with a more regionally active China than Karimov did. In mid-2021, there were approximately 50 specific BRI-related projects in Uzbekistan, most focusing on developing transit links for regional efforts, or local industrial-enhancement efforts. But these projects account for less than 5% of all BRI-related investment projects in Central Asia, with significantly more taking place in Kazakhstan and Kyrgyzstan, the countries China deems essential to the 'middle route' of the BRI network to Europe. Uzbekistan–China technology and security cooperation includes the 'safe city' initiative, launched in 2017, with a case study by Huawei to develop a comprehensive 'Safe Tourism' programme in Bukhara. This was enhanced by an April 2019 agreement between Uzbekistan and China under which up to US$1bn would be used to install state-of-the-art video and facial-recognition technology, as well as better connectivity with and among police officers, especially in key cities such as Tashkent and Samarkand. Such projects were given special attention in 2020, which Mirziyoyev declared the 'Year of Development of Science, Education and the Digital Economy'. More important is the fact that these efforts allow for greater surveillance capability, skills that are part of the Chinese Digital Silk Road.

There has been an uptick in relations with the US in the past year. Although the administration of Donald Trump viewed relations in transactional terms, engagement with Uzbekistan did improve. A new US Strategy for Central Asia, released by the US National Security Council in February 2020, set out how the US could effectively engage with the region considering the inevitable military departure from Afghanistan. While it reiterated approaches used by past administrations, it couched efforts in more modest and achievable terms. Absent were claims about helping to transform the region in terms of democratisation, human rights and market liberalisation. Rather, the new strategy focused on stability and transparency – and on how the US could manage ties with countries in the region. The Trump administration continued the C5+1 format, created under the Barack Obama administration, for summits bringing together all five former Soviet republics in Central Asia with the US. The administration of Joe Biden has followed suit, seeing it as a logical vehicle through which to engage with Central Asia.

The Afghanistan conundrum

Managing the consequences of events in Afghanistan is a high priority for Tashkent. Uzbekistan had been supportive of Ashraf Ghani's government in Kabul. Mirziyoyev's speech to the United Nations General Assembly in September 2020 outlined measures that Uzbekistan would take to assist in the future development of Afghanistan. Uzbek officials highlighted the rail link between Termez in Uzbekistan and Hairaton in Afghanistan, opened in August 2011 as part of the US–NATO Northern Distribution Network, as evidence of this commitment. Extensions of this line to other cities in Afghanistan were proposed in meetings with Afghan counterparts in late 2020 and early 2021. Trade with Afghanistan remained relatively modest, but officials expressed interest in expanding it.

Security cooperation with the US included several visits in both directions and, from March 2020, a US–Uzbekistan–Afghanistan trilateral security dialogue. Afghanistan was a major focus of the C5+1 meeting in Tashkent on 15–16 July 2021. The collapse of the Ghani government has created major uncertainty in Central Asia. Sharing a heavily guarded 156-km border with Afghanistan, Uzbekistan's concerns about instability are especially acute. Even before the Taliban's takeover, it had conducted joint military exercises with neighbouring Tajikistan, which shares a much longer border with Afghanistan, and Russia.

A troubling year ahead?

Looking ahead, Uzbekistan faces four challenges. The first is not unique to the country: how will it handle the COVID-19 crisis and the necessary return of the country to normalcy? As a double-landlocked country in a region known for poor connectivity, it is imperative that the movement to open the country to the global economy, which Mirziyoyev began in 2016, gets back on track. On 29 December 2020, Mirziyoyev outlined to the Oliy Majlis (the parliament of Uzbekistan) how the country had 'passed the test' of managing COVID-19, though he acknowledged that much work was still needed. As of mid-2021, the World Bank had provided US$295m to assist in pandemic-related issues. International travel and trade, largely curtailed in 2020–21, is slowly ramping up, especially cross-border trade within Central Asia. With three of Uzbekistan's five neighbours – Kazakhstan, Kyrgyzstan and Tajikistan – in the EEU, the country will inevitably face complications in manoeuvring through this organisation's regulations.

Secondly, domestic dynamics need to be managed. While the official discourse focuses on opening and liberalisation, Uzbekistan remains a centralised and authoritarian political system. Even if things improve more than expected in the coming year, an expectations gap could easily arise, where popular demands for political and economic change outstrip limited progress. If the government fails to address these demands, discontent could find solace in radical political Islam. To date, the spectre of extremism has been managed, but a renewed expression of it combined with the return of fighters from Syria and other conflicts could be a toxic mix.

Thirdly, managing the risks posed by the return of the Taliban to Kabul remains a paramount foreign-policy concern for Tashkent. If a regional solution can be found, Uzbekistan is likely to play a key role. The US Department of Defense views Uzbekistan as a cooperative partner if the return of a security presence in Central Asia is required. Tensions elsewhere in the region may mean that Tashkent will have to address concurrent challenges. The second Nagorno-Karabakh war between Azerbaijan and Armenia in September–November 2020, the October 2020 post-election violence in Kyrgyzstan, and the border clash between Kyrgyzstan and Tajikistan in April 2021 all suggest that the neighbourhood is unsettled. It remains to be seen if these actors can set aside their differences to focus on the Afghanistan security challenge.

The final challenge is how Uzbekistan will be able to balance the influence of outside powers. The past year underscored Mirziyoyev's commitment to greater regional and global engagement while maintaining Uzbekistan's autonomy in any great-power competition. Early speculation that Uzbekistan would become much closer to Russia under Mirziyoyev has proved ill-founded, despite Moscow's wish to see Uzbekistan more engaged in both the EEU and CSTO. If China's BRI provides meaningful development within Central Asia, pressure will mount on Uzbekistan to participate more fully in the transregional schemes or risk being isolated. The US and European Union have focused more on specific areas of transactional cooperation in the past year. It remains unclear how the West's military disengagement from Afghanistan in 2021 will affect its relations with Uzbekistan. Each of these four challenges requires deft handling and favourable circumstances. Failure in any one area could cascade into others. In short, the coming year will require an agile and responsive government in Tashkent.

CHAPTER 9

Middle East and North Africa

TURKEY

Caspian Sea

Mediterranean Sea

TUNISIA

MOROCCO

SYRIA

LEBANON
ISRAEL

IRAQ

IRAN

JORDAN

KUWAIT

ALGERIA

LIBYA

EGYPT

BAHRAIN

QATAR

WESTERN
SAHARA

SAUDI ARABIA

UAE

OMAN

Red Sea

YEMEN

Arabian Sea

©IISS

Drivers of Strategic Change

REGIONAL SHARE OF GLOBAL POPULATION, GDP AND DEFENCE BUDGET

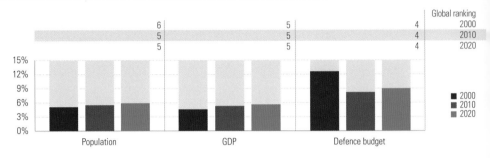

			Global ranking
6	5	4	2000
5	5	4	2010
5	5	4	2020

Population / GDP / Defence budget

■ 2000
■ 2010
■ 2020

POPULATION

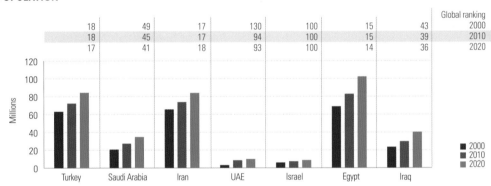

							Global ranking
18	49	17	130	100	15	43	2000
18	45	17	94	100	15	39	2010
17	41	18	93	100	14	36	2020

Millions

Turkey / Saudi Arabia / Iran / UAE / Israel / Egypt / Iraq

■ 2000
■ 2010
■ 2020

AGE STRUCTURE
(Percentage of national population)

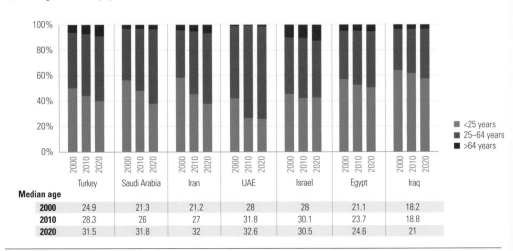

■ <25 years
■ 25–64 years
■ >64 years

Median age	Turkey	Saudi Arabia	Iran	UAE	Israel	Egypt	Iraq
2000	24.9	21.3	21.2	28	28	21.1	18.2
2010	28.3	26	27	31.8	30.1	23.7	18.8
2020	31.5	31.8	32	32.6	30.5	24.6	21

Defence spending is high relative to population and GDP. Many countries face a potentially combustible mix of a young population, low economic growth and declining freedom (from already-low levels). Most hydrocarbon exporters have raised their budget-balancing oil-price assumption above the recent US$40–70 price range. Only Saudi Arabia has bucked this trend.

GDP
(Constant 2010 US dollars)

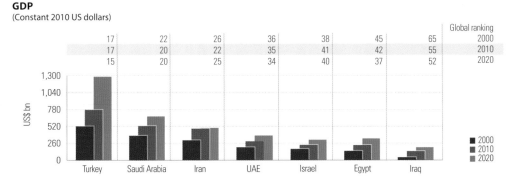

Global ranking

2000	17	22	26	36	38	45	65
2010	17	20	22	35	41	42	55
2020	15	20	25	34	40	37	52

US$ bn: 1,300 / 1,040 / 780 / 520 / 260 / 0

Turkey · Saudi Arabia · Iran · UAE · Israel · Egypt · Iraq

■ 2000 ■ 2010 ■ 2020

GDP PER CAPITA
(Constant 2010 US dollars)

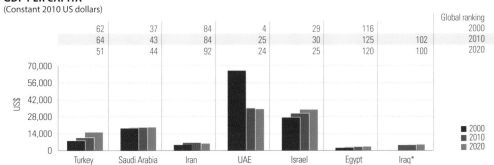

Global ranking

2000	62	37	84	4	29	116	
2010	64	43	84	25	30	125	102
2020	51	44	92	24	25	120	100

US$: 70,000 / 56,000 / 42,000 / 28,000 / 14,000 / 0

Turkey · Saudi Arabia · Iran · UAE · Israel · Egypt · Iraq*

* No 2000 data available for Iraq

■ 2000 ■ 2010 ■ 2020

DEFENCE BUDGET
(Constant 2015 US dollars)

ACTIVE MILITARY PERSONNEL

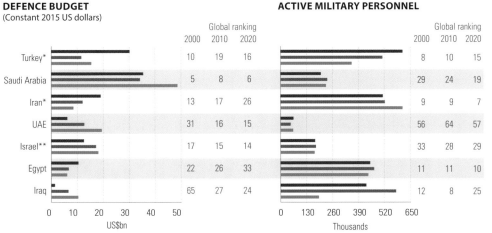

| | Global ranking | | | | Global ranking | | |
	2000	2010	2020		2000	2010	2020
Turkey*	10	19	16		8	10	15
Saudi Arabia	5	8	6		29	24	19
Iran*	13	17	26		9	9	7
UAE	31	16	15		56	64	57
Israel**	17	15	14		33	28	29
Egypt	22	26	33		11	11	10
Iraq	65	27	24		12	8	25

0 10 20 30 40 50
US$bn

0 130 260 390 520 650
Thousands

*2000 defence budget values for Iran and Turkey are estimates, and may be distorted by high inflation rates.
**No 2020 data available for Israel. 2019 data is therefore used in place of 2020 data.

■ 2000 ■ 2010 ■ 2020

For explanation of drivers and sources, see page 9

HUMAN DEVELOPMENT INDEX (HDI)
(Score between 0 and 1, where 0 denotes a low level of development and 1 a high level of development)

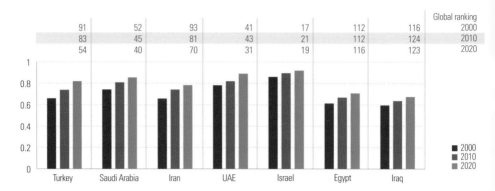

							Global ranking
91	52	93	41	17	112	116	2000
83	45	81	43	21	112	124	2010
54	40	70	31	19	116	123	2020

POLITICAL SYSTEM
(Score between 0 and 100, where 0 denotes no political freedom and 100 fully free)

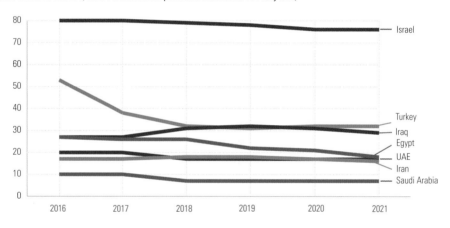

FISCAL BREAKEVEN OIL PRICES (2016–21)

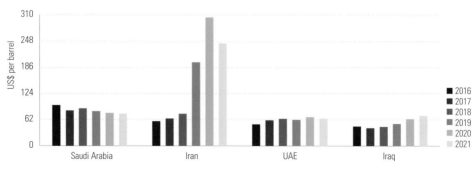

Average spot crude price 2015–20, US$/barrel Dubai dated

2015	2016	2017	2018	2019	2020
$51.22	$41.02	$53.02	$70.15	$63.71	$42.41

For explanation of drivers and sources, see page 9

2020–21 Review

The past year saw a relative, if tentative, easing of tensions in the Middle East as local powers adjusted to the stress and cost of the COVID-19 pandemic; to fatigue and frustration on various battlefields; and to a new United States administration bent on taming conflicts. However, the sources of regional competition and instability remained largely unaddressed.

COVID-19

The COVID-19 pandemic exacted an economic toll on all Middle Eastern and North African states except Egypt. In 2020, regional GDP declined by 3.9% but this drop was unevenly distributed, significantly affecting economies exposed to oil prices, tourism and transport and dependent on remittances from abroad. A rebound was expected in 2021 but was likely to be uneven and dependent on vaccination rates, macroeconomic policies and oil prices.

The pandemic highlighted the gap in healthcare capabilities and financial resources between the rich Gulf states and most other countries in the region. In countries such as Iraq and Jordan, the lack of medical equipment and mishaps at derelict hospitals illustrated the dire conditions of state institutions, while vaccination rates remained low due to limited availability of vaccines. Iran was particularly affected, with a death toll among the highest in the region and low vaccination rates due, in part, to the regime's rejection of Western vaccines. Most countries sought to acquire vaccines directly, but also depended on COVAX, the international vaccine facility, because of their limited influence and financial means. Israel distinguished itself by the speed with which it vaccinated its population. Having offered favourable terms to the Pfizer pharmaceutical company, its government conducted a rapid inoculation of its population, which allowed an early reopening of the country.

In contrast, the Gulf states secured vaccines early from several suppliers and implemented policies to keep their economies afloat. But there was little coordination among them on health measures or economic recovery plans. Saudi Arabia imposed the toughest travel regime, suspending the annual pilgrimage to Mecca and banning arrivals from most countries, while the United Arab Emirates (UAE), highly dependent on tourism and international business, relaxed its travel rules, thus exposing itself to new waves of infections.

The pandemic also generated new interest in health and vaccine diplomacy. Bahrain and the UAE were among the first countries to acquire and deploy the Chinese Sinopharm vaccine, even before it was validated by the World Health Organization. The UAE positioned itself as a hub for vaccine production and deployment: a joint Chinese–Emirati venture began producing Sinopharm in the country, with the intent of distributing the vaccine regionally and globally. Bahrain announced that it would produce the Russian Sputnik V vaccine. In contrast, Saudi Arabia deployed only Western-made ones.

Waning conflicts?

In two of the region's most intense conflicts, the Second Libyan Civil War and the Syrian civil war, levels of violence were considerably lower during the year.

Prospects to de-escalate and possibly resolve the civil war seemed brighter in Libya. By the second half of 2020, the daring attempt by eastern warlord Khalifa Haftar to capture Tripoli with the backing of the UAE and Russia had failed. His mostly Islamist rivals mounted a vigorous defence of the city and its United Nations-backed government, receiving considerable military assistance from Turkey. This setback and the fear that Turkey and its local allies would push their advantage generated concern in summer 2020 that Egypt would intervene. This did not happen as Cairo, already concerned by the filling up of the Grand Ethiopian Renaissance Dam (GERD) and other regional challenges, was reluctant to jump-start a ground operation. Ankara, too, felt overstretched, given rising tensions in the Eastern Mediterranean and its involvement in the Nagorno-Karabakh and Syrian conflicts. As a result, the front line stabilised along the Sirte–Jufra axis, although oil facilities and ports remained contested. UN and Western reports about the level of Emirati, Russian and Turkish violations of the UN arms embargo created reputational damage for all three countries.

This fragile stalemate provided an opening for the revitalisation of UN mediation, facilitated by the fatigue and de-escalation of regional powers and renewed engagement by the US and European governments, notably through the so-called Berlin Process. This resulted in a UN-brokered political agreement in early 2021 that established a new government recognised by eastern and western political factions. Abdul Hamid Dbeibeh, a businessman from the city of Misrata, took over as prime minister and rapidly obtained regional and international acceptance. Sensitive matters linked to oil exports, state spending and security reform remained unresolved; the agreement also called for the departure of foreign forces, which had not happened by mid-2021. Elections scheduled for late 2021 were expected to foster political jockeying and brinkmanship.

In contrast, and even as international attention receded, Syria's conflict remained volatile. While the government managed to restore nominal control over 70% of the country, its actual power was challenged by the proliferation of militias, the lack of a stabilisation strategy and its weakened sovereignty.

The Syrian battlefield remained crowded and complex, with fragile arrangements sustaining de facto ceasefires and a struggling UN process. In the northeast, the Kurdish-led administration found relief in the continued presence of US troops – which Donald Trump had once sought to fully withdraw – as they provided protection from the Syrian Armed Forces of President Bashar al-Assad, as well as from Iranian, Russian and Turkish forces. Israel continued a bombing campaign aimed at eroding the military infrastructure of Iran, which nonetheless remained determined to maintain its presence. In northern Syria, Russia and Turkey were locked in a complex dynamic combining cooperation and confrontation. The Assad regime, arguably the weakest of these actors, nevertheless benefitted from these rivalries.

The economic and social situation within regime-held areas deteriorated. The government proved unable to design a reconstruction strategy or mobilise resources from its allies Russia and Iran. Lebanon's financial crisis further debilitated Syria's economy. In summer 2020 the Caesar Syria Civilian Protection Act, a comprehensive set of US sanctions, came into force, deterring foreign investors and traders and limiting any economic re-engagement of Syria by Arab and other states. Economic degradation and the human cost of the COVID-19 pandemic put additional pressure on humanitarian agencies as international funding also dried up. Regardless, in a show of defiance the regime ran a presidential election in May 2021 that Assad won handily. Western and several Arab states decried the election as unfair and unfree, but China, Egypt, Russia and other states argued in favour of Assad's full reintegration into the international community.

The US–Russia–Turkey dynamic remained central to Syria's future. Even as the incoming US administration of Joe Biden gave Syria policy low priority, it remained focused on the potential for greater spillover of the conflict, which could result in new refugee flows, destabilisation of the Kurdish-run region and the return of the Islamic State, also known as ISIS or ISIL. The prospect of a large humanitarian crisis in northern Syria grew as Russia sought to block the renewal of UN authorisation to transport humanitarian assistance across the Turkish–Syrian border. Moscow tried to use its influence at the UN Security Council to compel Western and Middle Eastern states to endorse the regime's sovereignty and to provide assistance through Damascus, much of which has been diverted.

Yemen's complex war showed no sign of abating. The core conflict between the Houthi movement and a variety of rivals, most notably the internationally recognised Aden-based government, continued. By 2021, the country's fragmentation appeared to be in such an advanced stage that a comprehensive political settlement seemed highly unlikely despite intensifying UN mediation efforts. Taking advantage of the military failure and fatigue of Saudi Arabia, the Houthis made advances throughout the country. The main axis was towards the government stronghold of Marib, which sat at the intersection of strategic routes and hosted major oil installations. The prospect of its fall, which would deal a debilitating blow to the anti-Houthi coalition, prompted an intense defence of the city by Saudi airpower and resistant tribes, inflicting heavy casualties on the Houthis.

The government appeared weaker than ever: it relied on a coalition of bickering tribal, political and military interests and was challenged by UAE-backed southern secessionists, while its dependency on Saudi political support and funding led many Yemenis to disparage it. Riyadh attempted to shore up the government's authority by brokering a reconciliation agreement in 2019, but tellingly, it took a further agreement, in December 2020, for the proposed unity government to be formed. On the ground, a proliferation of militias only nominally supporting the government created a war economy and a patchwork of zones of influence that called into question the country's unity.

Conscious of the military setbacks and immense reputational damage of its involvement, Saudi Arabia sought de-escalation of the conflict, announcing unilateral steps such as the suspension of airstrikes and offering a ceasefire in early 2021. Sensing weakness and conditioning any acceptance of a ceasefire on Saudi concessions, the Houthis refused to reciprocate. Instead, they intensified missile and uninhabited-aerial-vehicle (UAV) attacks against Saudi territory.

The Biden administration sought to recalibrate the US relationship with Yemen. It suspended Yemen-related military assistance to Saudi Arabia, appointed a special envoy for Yemen and reversed the Trump administration's designation of the Houthi movement as a terrorist organisation. However, the lack of responsiveness of the Houthis to US and Saudi overtures demonstrated to Washington its limited leverage.

It remained uncertain whether US–Iranian nuclear diplomacy, revived by the Biden administration in spring 2021, would translate into de-escalation in Iraq, Syria or Yemen. Despite ample evidence to the contrary, Iran insisted that it had no influence over the various militias operating in these countries and denied transferring weapons and missiles to them.

Continuous slides

Elsewhere in the Middle East, state weakness remained a primary driver of fragmentation and competition. In spring 2021, arrests of senior Jordanian figures exposed fractures in the Hashemite Kingdom. Prince Hamzah bin Al-Hussein was accused of fomenting dissent, together with disgruntled tribal chiefs, former officials and a junior royal, against his half-brother, King Abdullah II bin Al-Hussein. Jordan's geopolitical position had weakened during the Trump administration, which broke with previous US governments by downgrading the relationship with Amman in favour of more accommodating and aligned Gulf states. Amman felt that Trump's dismissiveness of Palestinian national demands would affect its interests and security. The Abraham Accords, which in the autumn of 2020 normalised relations between Israel and four Arab states, including the UAE and Bahrain, after significant US encouragement and pressure, undercut Jordan's focus on achieving Palestinian statehood through Arab leverage. Jordan also worried that Saudi Arabia could displace it as the protector of Islamic holy sites in Jerusalem. With the conflict in Syria unresolved, Iraq struggling to stabilise, Iranian and Russian forces at its borders and an intransigent Israeli policy under prime minister Benjamin Netanyahu, Jordan was particularly uneasy. Its economy, dependent on declining foreign aid and remittances and facing a massive refugee burden, also faced difficulty. While political dissent had been subtly managed for decades, the prospect of well-connected members of the elite conspiring to weaken the king's authority was particularly worrisome. Abdallah could, however, count on strong backing from Europe, Israel and the US, as well as domestic security services that maintained cohesion and loyalty.

Lebanon's free fall accelerated during the year. An explosion that destroyed the Port of Beirut and parts of the capital on 4 August 2020 appeared to epitomise decades of pervasive corruption and mismanagement. The government of Hassan Diab resigned, but his replacement, Saad Hariri, was unable to form a new cabinet due to political bickering over its composition and the respective powers of the president and prime minister. This political vacuum made the management of the economic crisis even harder and the cohesion of the security forces became a matter of concern. Political factions, the most organised and resilient of which was the militant Shia Hizbullah, began to prepare for the potential collapse of the country amid concern that violence would erupt. A senior Hizbullah commander was found guilty by an international tribunal of having organised the assassination of former prime minister Rafik Hariri in 2005. COVID-19 exacerbated this crisis. By mid-2021, the Lebanese pound had lost over 90% of its value in two years, over half of the population had fallen below the poverty line, and bank deposits and credit lines were inaccessible.

The situation in Iraq was similarly grave. Mustafa Al-Kadhimi, prime minister since May 2020, lacked a loyal base and was constrained by the power of parties that resisted any political or economic reform, compounding the challenges of low oil prices and a bloated public sector increasing public deficits. Iran-backed militias remained determined to expel US forces assisting the Iraqi security forces defeating the Islamic State. Their political and military strength repeatedly forced the Iraqi security forces to back down from confrontation. The protest movement struggled to maintain momentum. Assassinations of prominent activists and professionals by militias keen on protecting their hold on the state demoralised protesters. Failure to investigate these killings demonstrated the government's weakness.

The Trump administration threatened a full pull-out of Iraq in 2020 to protest against militia attacks but retracted its threats as this would have benefitted Iran. Attacks against US military targets increased in 2021 even as the US and Iran resumed nuclear negotiations. It was unclear whether Tehran encouraged these attacks to pressure the US or whether militias acted on their own.

New US administration, new regional approaches

The Trump administration's priorities had been to maintain warm relations with Gulf states, notably Saudi Arabia and the UAE, isolate Iran and promote Israel's regional political and economic integration. In the administration's final months, it approved massive arms sales to Saudi Arabia and the UAE, including a package of F-35 aircraft and advanced UAVs to the UAE. It also achieved two notable diplomatic breakthroughs: the Abraham Accords and the formal end to the Gulf rift that had pitted Saudi Arabia and the UAE against Qatar since 2017. Saudi Arabia appeared keen to move on despite Qatar having not met any of the 13 conditions listed by Riyadh and allied states. The reconciliation was sealed during a Gulf Cooperation Council summit in January 2021 and was followed by growing political and economic exchanges, although relations between Qatar and the UAE remained frosty.

The Biden presidency signalled a shift in tone and priorities. The US recalibrated relations with Saudi Arabia and resumed nuclear diplomacy with Iran, the kingdom's main geopolitical rival. Biden also released an intelligence finding that implicated the Saudi leadership in the 2018 assassination of prominent Saudi journalist-turned-critic Jamal Khashoggi and imposed sanctions on several officials. Crown Prince Muhammad bin Salman Al Saud was not subjected to sanctions, illustrating Washington's interest in maintaining a cordial relationship with Riyadh.

Biden's focus on reviving nuclear diplomacy with Iran met with mixed reactions. While nations such as Qatar and Oman were supportive, Saudi Arabia and the UAE worried this would lead to a relaxation of US attitudes towards Iran. To assuage such fears, the US Department of State aimed to conduct a dialogue with Iran over its missile programme and support for regional militias. In April 2021, Saudi and Iranian officials met for the first time since 2016 in Baghdad to discuss regional de-escalation. The UAE had already opened channels with Iran in 2019. These talks failed to produce tangible results but were seen as preferable to active enmity.

Prospects for diplomatic breakthroughs were low, however, especially with the end of the Rouhani presidency and the victory of the hardliner Ebrahim Raisi in the June 2021 elections. Raisi, a protégé of Iranian Supreme Leader Sayyid Ali Khamenei, won an election with the lowest turnout in decades, a sign of popular dissatisfaction with the Iranian political system. But he was seen as the best-placed candidate to succeed Khamenei and drew support from the hardline clergy as well as the ascendant Islamic Revolutionary Guard Corps. Contrary to Rouhani, who hoped that the nuclear deal would lead to better political and economic relations with Western countries, Raisi opposed such engagement and hoped to solidify relations with China and Russia.

However much the US sought to extricate itself from Middle Eastern conflicts, the escalation of tensions in Iraq and the May conflict in Gaza showed it remained tied to the region. The Biden administration conducted several raids in Iraq and Syria against Iranian-backed militias in retaliation for escalating attacks aimed at driving US forces out of both countries. This attracted congressional criticism and embarrassed the Iraqi government.

The May 2021 war in Gaza highlighted the United States' enduring partnership with Israel. The conflict began when Palestinian families faced ejection from their houses, and escalated as Israeli security forces faced mounting protests. Hamas, the Islamist movement in control of Gaza, began firing missiles into Israel, compelling a large-scale Israeli air campaign. The conflict, which caused hundreds of mostly Palestinian casualties, occurred just as Israel faced a domestic crisis. In March, Israel had held its fourth legislative election in just two years and Netanyahu's political rivals allied to form a government that was announced in June. The new cabinet, headed by far-right politician Naftali Bennett who will be succeeded by centrist Yair Lapid in 2023, adopted policies on Iran and the Palestinians similar to Netanyahu's but was markedly different on domestic matters as well as in tone. Despite growing calls from the Democratic Party's progressive wing to loosen ties with Israel, Biden offered strong support throughout the conflict. He did, however, re-establish ties with the Palestinian Authority, which the Trump administration had cut off, and provided much-needed humanitarian assistance.

Egypt was a prominent beneficiary of the Gaza conflict. Its influence with Israel and leverage over Hamas were essential in brokering the ceasefire. Biden's May 2021 phone call with Egyptian President Abdel Fattah Al-Sisi, a leader he had previously shunned, was widely interpreted as acknowledgement of Egypt's regional importance. Seeking US support to prevent Ethiopia from filling the GERD, Cairo in turn sought to improve this relationship.

Turkey struggled to rebuild relations with Washington. Ankara hoped that converging interests in countering Russia and stabilising northern Syria could support this. But its expected deployment of the Russian S-400 *Triumf* air-defence system led to US sanctions on Turkish officials in December 2020. Tensions over the fate of the Kurdish militia in Syria also continued to mar relations.

Beyond the conflicts in the region, the US was increasingly focused on countering China's growing presence in the Middle East. Chinese investments in infrastructure and provision of technology were seen as posing long-term risks to the US military presence and influence. In particular, growing relations between China and the UAE, which has in recent years ordered modern US aircraft and deployed other sensitive US technology, became a matter of concern.

Restoring the Iran Nuclear Deal
Can Iran's nuclear hedging be constrained by diplomacy, or merely legitimised?

'Maximum pressure'

Having unilaterally withdrawn from the Joint Comprehensive Plan of Action (JCPOA), known as the Iran nuclear deal, in May 2018, in his last year in office former United States president Donald Trump applied ever-tougher economic sanctions against Iran. His stated objective was to coerce it into accepting tighter and longer-lasting limits on its nuclear programme and into accepting other US demands concerning its missile and regional activity, which are often referred to as Iran's 'malign behaviour'.

Trump's policy of 'maximum pressure' certainly created economic pain, keeping Iran in recession for a third year running and exacerbating the toll taken by the country's 1.3 million confirmed cases of COVID-19 in 2020, which led to over 56,000 fatalities in a nation of 85m. Oil sales, which had topped 2.5m barrels per day (bpd) prior to the reimposition of sanctions, fell to half a million bpd in mid-2020 before inching up slightly (though Iran may have shipped more under the radar). Iran's currency, the rial, continued a precipitous fall, losing over 50% of its value in the first nine months of 2020.

Yet maximum pressure failed to force any policy changes. To the contrary, Iran responded defiantly, moving further and further away from its obligations under the JCPOA. By the end of May 2021, Iran had accumulated 16 times the amount of enriched uranium the deal allowed. It also sought to strike back in asymmetric ways. In September 2020, the US intelligence community claimed that Tehran had considered assassinating Lana Marks, the US ambassador to South Africa. The following month, John Ratcliffe, the director of national intelligence, claimed that Iran sought to interfere in the 2020 US presidential election.

In past years, less egregious cases of nuclear non-compliance forced Iran into diplomatic isolation. In 2020, however, it was the US that found itself isolated. Secretary of state Mike Pompeo's attempt in August to extend a UN ban on conventional arms trade with Iran that was set to expire in October under the terms of the JCPOA found support from only one other member of the Security Council, the Dominican Republic. Pompeo's effort to then restore all pre-2015 UN sanctions was dismissed by UN Secretary-General António Guterres and many UN member states on grounds that the US, having withdrawn from the deal, could not exercise the rights of membership that would have allowed it to invoke a 'snapback' mechanism.

But the Trump administration had other cards to play, especially extraterritorial sanctions. These could effectively prevent third parties from doing business with Iran by threatening to block their access to the US economy and even the US dollar. All such secondary sanctions that had been applied in previous years over Iran's nuclear activities had been lifted in 2016 under the JCPOA. The deal, though, did not remove other, non-nuclear-related sanctions. Trump muddied the distinction between the two. In addition to re-invoking all US nuclear-related measures, he layered new sanction designations on the Central Bank of Iran and other financial institutions under the guise of counter-terrorism (claiming these institutions were funnelling cash to Hizbullah, for example) and other non-nuclear concerns. Sanction designations freeze all US assets controlled by the entities in question, prohibit US citizens from associating with them, and create a chain of guilt by association for third parties.

In the final months of 2020, the Trump administration added a flood of new counter-terrorism sanctions to entities pivotal to Iran's economy, including the Ministry of Petroleum, the National Iranian Oil Company and the entire financial sector. Iranian Foreign Minister Javad Zarif and the Supreme Leader's office were blacklisted for good measure, raising concerns that the administration did not, in fact, seek to negotiate a better deal. Then-US special representative for Iran Elliott Abrams admitted that the purpose of the new sanctions was to bind the hands of the incoming Biden administration by increasing the political cost of lifting measures that would impede restoration of the JCPOA. By the end of 2020, the Trump administration had blacklisted over 1,500 Iranian entities. Some of these measures would have been applied by any US administration, such as those relating to the Iranian government's alleged interference in the US election and to human-rights abuses committed during a crackdown on protesters in November 2019. But most appeared to have ulterior motives, as Abrams acknowledged. Hawks called the flurry of measures a 'sanctions wall'.

Although US pressure did not extend to kinetic attacks, Iran's nuclear infrastructure suffered several strikes that were widely presumed to have been conducted by Israel. On 2 July 2020, an explosion and fire partially destroyed a centrifuge production plant in Natanz. On 27 November, Mohsen Fakhrizadeh, the veteran head of Iran's nuclear-weapons development work – which appears to have been on hold since 2014 in accordance with a hedging strategy to keep capabilities and personnel available for ramping up when deemed necessary – was killed in a road ambush near Tehran. Then on 11 April 2021, nine months after the first attack on Natanz, the main enrichment facility at the plant was hit by a power blackout that knocked several thousand centrifuges out of commission. In response to both cases of sabotage, Iran ramped up uranium enrichment in other ways.

Following the assassination of Fakhrizadeh, the Iranian parliament passed a nuclear law mandating the use of more advanced centrifuges, the production of 20% enriched uranium (a level that is theoretically weapons-usable), the manufacture of uranium metal (a dual-use technology necessary for bomb production) and restrictions on inspections by the International Atomic Energy Agency (IAEA). Iran's own coercion efforts sought to force the incoming Biden administration to lift Trump's sanctions.

Compliance for compliance

During the 2020 election campaign, presidential candidate Joe Biden promised to return to the JCPOA if Iran restored the nuclear limits to which it had committed under the deal. He did not say Iran would have to move first, but his initial moves as president and statements by his top aides seemed to suggest this. Biden announced that Trump's maximum-pressure policy was over and took symbolic steps, such as removing strict travel limits on Iranian diplomats in New York and revoking a travel ban that primarily impacted Iranian citizens. He also brought back several former officials from the administration of Barack Obama who had helped negotiate the nuclear accord, including Robert Malley, who was named as special envoy for Iran.

Yet Biden kept all economic sanctions in place during the first 100 days of his tenure. Even a request from Seoul to release some of the US$7 billion Iranian oil revenues frozen in banks there in exchange for Iran releasing a South Korean oil tanker detained on dubious charges was not acted upon. Biden had more pressing priorities in addressing the double health and economic crisis brought on by the COVID-19 pandemic and in getting his key nominations past an evenly balanced Senate. He also wanted to avoid the domestic opprobrium that would come from making unilateral concessions and by appearing too eager to return to the deal. His envoys also needed to consult with Israel, Saudi Arabia and other regional partners before removing any sanctions.

Conservative lawmakers and pundits nevertheless accused Biden's team of 'squandering leverage' by offering to lift Trump-era sanctions without demanding concessions from Iran that went beyond JCPOA limits. Some critics insisted that Iran should release several US–Iran dual citizens whom it had detained on highly questionable grounds over the previous few years. Other hawks wanted Iranian concessions on issues such as its missile development, its support for violent non-state actors and its poor human-rights record. Further demands would have required an extension of the 11–15 years under which Iranian enrichment is constrained under the JCPOA and a reduction of the nuclear activity allowed within Iran. In other words, Biden's opponents wanted him to return to the policy of his predecessor under which no sanctions would be lifted unless Iran met a dozen demands laid out in May 2018 by Pompeo. Biden's supporters countered that the former team had failed to coerce Iran into accepting even one of those demands, and that leverage was discarded when Trump removed the benefits that Iran was promised for meeting US demands.

In an illustration of how fraught relations had become, during Biden's first weeks in office the US was engaged in retaliatory conflict with the Iran-backed Kataib Hizbullah militia in Iraq. The action started on 15 February when US forces in Erbil sustained multiple rocket attacks that killed a civilian contractor. Ten days later, Biden ordered limited airstrikes against Kataib Hizbullah facilities on the Iraq–Syria border. Then on 3 March, ten rockets were fired against Iraq's Ayn Al Asad air base where US forces were stationed, with unclear attribution.

Negotiations on restoring the JCPOA were delayed by Iran's refusal to meet with US counterparts, even in a multilateral setting, until sanctions were lifted. In early April, European partners finally arranged for 'proximity talks', under which the other parties to the JCPOA – China, France, Germany, Russia and the United Kingdom as well as the European Union – met sequentially in Vienna with the Iranian and US delegations.

The issue of sequencing was overcome rather quickly, with all parties implicitly agreeing to the principle of simultaneity under a 'compliance for compliance' approach. But a US proposal for a step-by-step JCPOA return, which had appeared to find favour with Iranian president Hassan Rouhani, was rejected by Supreme Leader Sayyid Ali Khamenei. In an address marking the Iranian New Year on 21 March 2021, Khamenei insisted on the US lifting all sanctions upfront. He also said that Tehran was in 'no hurry' to revive the JCPOA.

It was also agreed early on that the scope of talks would be limited to the JCPOA. In his election pledge to restore the deal, Biden had also said he would pursue discussions on missiles, Iran's regional activities and other issues of concern. At times, his administration implied that any agreement on restoring the nuclear deal would be contingent on Iranian willingness to engage in follow-on talks on these measures. As the spring wore on, however, this insistence faded. Likewise, the Biden administration postponed its stated intention to make the JCPOA 'longer and stronger' (e.g., by extending the time limits).

The crux of the talks concerned the scope of the sanctions to be lifted. In early April, the US announced that it would remove those sanctions that were 'inconsistent with the deal' – that is, sanctions imposed on non-nuclear grounds that would prevent Iran from resuming trade in oil and other key commodities. The phrase came from a clause in the JCPOA that required the US (as well as EU member states) to 'refrain from any policy specifically intended to directly and adversely affect the normalisation of trade and economic relations with Iran inconsistent with their commitments' laid out in the accord.

In other words, the Biden administration would dismantle Trump's sanctions wall on Iran's automotive, energy, finance, insurance and shipping sectors. Yet some other sanctions would remain, such as those imposed in response to Iran's human-rights record. One sticking point was whether the Islamic Revolutionary Guard Corps (IRGC), a four-letter word for both sides of the American political aisle, would continue to be blacklisted.

Iran, for its part, continued throughout the spring to insist that 'all' sanctions be lifted, and that it would have to verify that this measure had been taken before it would return to the JCPOA. Iran's negotiators would need to find a way to define 'all' that would not require the US to remove measures that were clearly outside the ambit of the talks. The Biden administration itself had even put Iranian human-rights abusers on the Treasury blacklist. Meanwhile, Iran further upped the ante in April by beginning to enrich small amounts of uranium to the 60% level, close to weapons grade.

Iran sought to impose time pressure on the talks by insisting that its December 2020 nuclear law to partially restrict IAEA inspections would be implemented if sanctions were not soon lifted. The parliament had insisted that this provision come into effect by 21 February, a deadline that was twice extended in negotiations between Iran and IAEA Director General Rafael Grossi. Many Western media outlets misinterpreted the law to mean that Iran would expel inspectors, when they would actually remain in country. What the law did, rather, was suspend certain IAEA verification rights, including the 'additional protocol', which provided for more intrusive monitoring mechanisms. Under the deals with Grossi, for four months Iran committed to collecting tapes of continuous surveillance activity and turning them over to the IAEA upon sanctions relief. Expiration of the second extension on 24 June left the IAEA in limbo, uncertain as to when it would be able to review the tapes. Meanwhile, talks on restoring the JCPOA remained stalled throughout June.

Obstacles

Other IAEA-related matters posed a peril for the talks and for the lon-
gevity of any restored deal. In 2019, inspectors detected anthropogenic,
or human-made, uranium particles at a warehouse in the Turquzabad
district of southern Tehran that had not been declared to the agency as
being nuclear-related. The agency found Iran's explanations about the
uranium to be 'not technically credible'. In March 2021, Grossi reported
to the agency's board that Iran had still not adequately answered questions about apparent nuclear activity at four separate undeclared sites.
The activity in question appeared to pre-date the JCPOA, and thus
would not be a violation of the accord. Failing to report nuclear activity
at any time is, however, a potential violation of Iran's basic safeguards
agreement with the IAEA and could result in new Security Council penalties if not resolved. This issue promised to darken prospects for Iran's
future reconciliation with the US and other Western countries.

Domestic politics also threatened the talks in both Tehran and
Washington. Iranian hardliners did not want Rouhani and his team, who
are seen as moderates, to gain any foreign-policy credit in the run-up to
the presidential election on 18 June. Amidst an onslaught of criticism by
JCPOA opponents, Zarif, who led in opinion polls as the preferred candidate from the moderate ranks, fell victim to the leaking of an oral-history
tape in which he complained about Iran's decision-making structure, the
oversized role of the IRGC and Iran's relations with Russia – an indiscre-
tion that put him at odds with Khamenei.

US hardliners, such as former national security advisor John Bolton,
also seized on the tape to attack Zarif. For them, it was evidence that he
did not represent the real decision-makers in Iran and was thus an unre-
liable negotiating partner. Republican lawmakers insisted that if Biden
did revive the JCPOA, they would undo it again when they next came
to power. In the meantime, they sought to construct legislative hurdles,
including invoking the 2015 Iran Nuclear Agreement Review Act, which
requires certification of full Iranian compliance with the terms of the
JCPOA if sanctions are lifted. Sanctions proponents at the Foundation
for the Defense of Democracy and other right-wing think tanks warned

that any foreign company that did business with Iranian entities that had been subject to counter-proliferation designations would face retroactive penalties in the future. During the Trump presidency, most third-party companies avoided the complications of the Iran market, even for non-sanctionable sales of food and medicine, because of the lack of financial channels and the political danger. Even if sanctions on Iranian banks are lifted again, foreign firms are likely to continue to be prudent.

Many observers had expected that Iran might seek to wrap up the negotiations shortly after the election, which, as expected, was won by hardline jurist Ebrahim Raisi after all prominent rivals were disqualified by the Guardian Council, a powerful body of senior jurists. Striking a deal while Rouhani was still in power would saddle him with all blame for the concessions Iran would have to make, while reserving the benefits of the sanctions relief that would come with implementation for the next president. The Iranian political establishment appeared to be stuck in a non-compromise mode.

Although the agenda of the proximity talks in Vienna in spring 2021 was limited to the nuclear issue, the talks had a knock-on effect on two non-nuclear issues. In early May, a state-run Iranian television channel reported that four Iranian Americans detained in Iran on spying charges would be traded for four Iranians held in the US for sanctions violations and the release of US\$7bn in frozen Iranian funds. Although both the Iranian and US governments denied the report, communications had clearly advanced on a detainee swap to accompany a nuclear deal, just as had been the case in 2016 when the JCPOA was first implemented. Yet talks on this issue also stalled.

In other non-nuclear-related developments in May, news emerged that Iranian and Saudi officials had been meeting in Baghdad to discuss the ongoing war in Yemen. Saudi Crown Prince Muhammad bin Salman voiced support for better relations with Tehran. With Washington no longer wedded to antagonism with Iran, Arab leaders had reason to reduce the state of enmity.

Israeli leaders drew the opposite conclusion. Israeli prime minister Benjamin Netanyahu, who six years earlier had tried to derail Obama's diplomacy with Iran by directly appealing to the US Congress, may have sought to derail Biden's plans by directly confronting Iran with kinetic attacks. But while the 11 April explosion at Natanz did not cause Iran to walk away from the talks, it did contribute to Iran's decision to enrich uranium to 60%, just as the assassination of Fakhrizadeh spurred the December legislation on abandoning JCPOA commitments. Israel did not seek a green light from Biden for either attack and indicated that it would not do so for future strikes. With Biden returning to Obama's policy of accepting uranium enrichment in Iran, Israel has become more determined to take steps of its own to combat what it considers to be an existential threat. Assassinations, cyber attacks and bombings with faint fingerprints look set to continue if diplomacy appears incapable of blocking Iran's path to a nuclear weapon.

Such kinetic actions set back Iran's capacity in the short term, but risk driving its nuclear-development programme towards further secrecy and weapons intent in the longer term. The unknown variable is the degree to which Iran's determination to acquire nuclear-weapons capability is already fixed. Judging that Iran will not abandon a latent weapons capability, Biden and his European partners believe that Iran's nuclear hedging can be best contained through diplomacy. Whether restoring the JCPOA buys time to address fundamental animosities or simply legitimises an unstoppable quest for nuclear weapons will be history's judgement.

The Abraham Accords
How important are they?

The Abraham Accords, a series of agreements signed between Israel, the United States and four Arab countries in 2020–21, were a major development in the politics and diplomacy of the Middle East. They both reflected and reinforced longer-term foreign-policy realignments in the region.

The Accords comprised an overarching declaration of support for the establishment of diplomatic relations between Israel and its neighbours in a spirit of peace and tolerance, and four individual agreements involving the Arab signatories. These were: a treaty of peace and normalisation between Israel and the United Arab Emirates (UAE); a declaration of peace and diplomatic relations between Israel and Bahrain; a joint declaration by Israel, Morocco and the US that Morocco would establish diplomatic relations with Israel, and that the US would recognise Morocco's sovereignty over the disputed territory of Western Sahara; and a declaration by Sudan that it welcomed progress made in establishing diplomatic relations between Israel and others in the region – but did not specify whether Sudan itself planned to establish such relations.

The agreements between Israel, Bahrain and the UAE, signed just ahead of the US presidential election in November 2020, were motivated primarily by the desire for a united front against shared security threats – above all, from Iran, and to some extent the Muslim Brotherhood. While US diplomats had encouraged this rapprochement since at least the time of the Barack Obama administration, it gained new impetus under president Donald Trump as his son-in-law and Middle East envoy Jared Kushner pushed Arab countries to recognise Israel – both to put pressure on Iran and to record a symbolic foreign-policy success for US domestic audiences. As part of these efforts, the US had brought Gulf countries and Israel together at a 2019 conference in Warsaw, hosted jointly with Poland, with Kushner engaging in intensive shuttle diplomacy.

Israel, Bahrain and the UAE did not agree to cooperate only at the behest of one US administration. They share a longer-term concern that the US might not continue to provide them with support against a growing range of state, non-state and hybrid security threats. All three countries were troubled by US policy towards the Arab uprisings a decade ago, and by US failure to prevent the fall of Egyptian president Hosni Mubarak in 2011. Since then, they have joined forces to lobby the US on regional issues. Above all, they have coordinated their advocacy in the US to oppose, or impose new conditions on, the Joint Comprehensive Plan of Action (JCPOA) with Iran. The Gulf Arab countries were also aware that establishing relations with Israel, accompanied by pledges to hold interfaith dialogue and encourage religious tolerance, would help their reputation in the US.

Yet the Accords do not just represent a defensive arrangement among countries pushed into the same camp by common threat perceptions and an eye to US opinion. The leaders' motivations also include economic and security 'pull' factors: Israel, Bahrain and the UAE are all small, high-income states that seek to exert international influence well beyond their size and seek a basis for cooperation on shared economic interests, combining Israel's strengths in technology and R&D with Gulf Arab capital and experience of energy, trade and logistics. Israel and most Gulf countries had already pursued, informally and quietly, diplomatic and security contacts and cooperation for some years. But substantial programmes of trade and investment are harder to take forward in the absence of formal relations.

The Accords are expected to open up new areas of trade and investment and so contribute to reshaping regional geopolitics. Abu Dhabi is reportedly planning to invest in an Israeli offshore gas field in the Eastern Mediterranean, which would give it a direct interest in a sub-region facing a variety of maritime border disputes (including those between Greece and Turkey, and Israel and Lebanon), but may further increase tensions between the UAE and Turkey. Some areas of economic and technological cooperation have defence and security implications. Israel and the UAE both pursue space programmes and share interests in artificial intelligence, robotics, cyber and high-tech surveillance; in March 2021 they agreed to collaborate on an anti-drone system.

The addition of Morocco and Sudan to the Accords, in December 2020 and January 2021 respectively, reflected different dynamics. Both North

African countries had more specific and transactional reasons for signing. As a quid pro quo, Sudan had secured its removal from the US black-list of state sponsors of terrorism, which was vital to securing financial assistance for the fragile and impoverished country during its transition to civilian rule. Morocco obtained US recognition of its sovereignty over the disputed territory of Western Sahara, breaking with the long-standing international consensus that there should be a referendum on self-determination for the territory. Neither country was willing to hold a public ceremony with Israeli officials to mark the establishment of diplomatic relations because of considerable popular opposition at home.

By contrast, for the UAE and Bahrain, the optics of signing a high-profile diplomatic agreement in Washington DC were important, especially in the run-up to the highly polarised US presidential election. The Accords not only boosted their relations with the Trump administration but were welcomed by Democrats at a time of growing congressional criticism of Gulf human-rights records. But the Accords were contentious in the region, especially as they were signed with Benjamin Netanyahu, an Israeli prime minister long opposed to a Palestinian state, and with a US administration that was no longer on speaking terms with the Palestinians.

Palestinians conspicuous by their absence

One of the most striking elements of the Abraham Accords is how little they had to say about the Palestinian issue. The agreements were feted as a bold move towards peace, but the signatories had never been at war with one another. Technically, the Accords ended the respective Arab countries' boycotts of Israel, rather than any inter-state conflicts. Their claim to be peace agreements rested on wider perceptions of an over-arching Arab–Israeli conflict and of tensions between major world faiths.

Yet such perceptions were exaggerated. The Gulf states had not been enemies of Israel before the Abraham Accords. There had been earlier efforts to leverage mutual interest in economic and technological coop-eration to smooth the path to Arab–Israeli peace. At the time of the Oslo Accords in 1993–95, Oman and Qatar agreed to host Israeli trade mis-sions, which were closed after the second Palestinian intifada broke out in 2000. Oman also established a centre for Arab–Israeli cooperation on water and desalination research. There were successive efforts to involve Gulf states in an 'economic track' for peace to support a negotiated two-state solution. In the 2000s, Tony Blair, the envoy of the United Nations Quartet on the Middle East peace process (comprising the UN, the US, Russia and the European Union), involved Gulf investors in a West Bank investment conference to improve Palestinian living conditions. But the economic track was never enough to overcome the political impasse.

Furthermore, while the Gulf states maintained an official boycott of Israel, in 2002 they had signed the Arab Peace Initiative (API), endorsed by the Arab League, under which all Arab states (except Jordan and Egypt, which already had relations with Israel) offered to recognise Israel in return for a negotiated two-state solution with a just solution for refugees. The Abraham Accords marked a departure from this Arab consensus by separating relations with Israel from the Israeli–Palestinian issue. For this reason, the Palestinian leadership and public strongly rejected the Accords.

Annexation abandoned?

The first country to sign the Abraham Accords, the UAE, was able to link its agreement to a positive step for the Palestinians. Israel agreed to suspend plans to annex large swathes of the West Bank, an action that would likely have put a viable Palestinian state permanently out of reach. The plans had been endorsed by the Trump administration, which had announced in November 2019 that the US would no longer consider Israeli settlements to be illegal. For its part, the UAE publicly stated that Israel would need to choose between normalisation with Arab countries and annexation of Palestinian land; it could not have both.

For Netanyahu, the UAE's offer of an olive branch contributed to a complex cost–benefit calculation that also reflected domestic priorities and pressure from other countries. It provided him with a face-saving way to climb down from his pro-annexation position and declare a different victory. Indeed, polling in Israel suggested that the Accords with the UAE were much more popular with the Israeli public than outright annexation of Palestinian lands in the West Bank.

However, Palestinian leaders argued that the UAE had no authority to negotiate on their behalf and that it had cut the price of normalisation by offering diplomatic relations in return not for a negotiated political settlement, but merely for refraining from causing a deterioration of the status quo. Palestinians also contended that de facto creeping annexation of West Bank lands was happening anyway. Polling in June 2021 indicated that most Palestinians already thought the two-state solution would never be implemented. Where a previous generation had seen an agreement in principle on a two-state solution as a realistic goal, the younger generation born after the Oslo Accords increasingly viewed it as a mirage.

This remains a critical strategic issue for the future of the conflict. Younger Palestinians are increasingly sceptical of the paradigm of Palestinian statehood within which Fatah orients itself. A growing civil-society movement argues that Palestinians should adopt a non-violent struggle for equal rights within a single state. Palestinian and Israeli political leaders oppose this for different reasons. Palestinians do not want to give up on statehood; Israeli leaders (and most of their public) reject a one-state solution, as the demographics of the combined territories of Israel, the West Bank and Gaza would prevent Israel from preserving a Jewish majority and thus its founding ambition to be both a Jewish state and a democracy. However, Netanyahu had repeatedly said that he would never countenance a Palestinian state. Naftali Bennett, who succeeded him as prime minister in June 2021 and is a former head of a settler council, has long rejected the two-state solution and in early 2021 insisted that he would never make a peace agreement with the Palestinians. International diplomacy therefore hit an impasse: the international community remains committed to a two-state solution and does not want to promote a one-state solution over Israeli objections, but also does not see any current credible political pathway to a two-state one.

It is in this context that the signatories of the Abraham Accords decided to pursue their own bilateral objectives with Israel – and related benefits for their relations with the US – rather than wait for a wider regional peace agreement. Since the UAE signed the Accords, and Israel made its apparent concession on annexation, there has been a striking absence of even symbolic concessions to the Palestinians, with neither a regional peace conference, nor even Arab–Israeli cooperation to assist the Palestinians in fighting the COVID-19 pandemic.

Palestinian political shifts

The Accords – and the urgent humanitarian needs created by COVID-19 – initially shocked Palestinian leaders into revisiting the need for national unity across the bitter and polarised Hamas–Fatah divide. Intra-Palestinian talks began shortly after the signing of the Abraham Accords. In late 2020, Palestinian President Mahmoud Abbas said he would authorise presidential and legislative elections in 2021. These were long overdue: the last presidential election was held in 2005. However, in April 2021, Abbas postponed the elections indefinitely, saying it was unclear whether Israel would permit Palestinian residents of East Jerusalem to vote – although Israel had not yet taken any public position on this. Hamas described the move as a 'coup' against its agreements with Fatah. Nonetheless, Abbas faces little international pressure: since Hamas's victory in legislative elections in 2006, the US, Israel and many other countries had preferred not to see further Palestinian elections. But the Palestinian Authority was badly weakened by the failure to renew its mandate with its population, most of whom are under 30 and have never had a chance to vote.

The Palestinian leadership's perception of the UAE's signing of the Abraham Accords was coloured by the view that Abu Dhabi was backing one of Abbas's personal rivals, Mohammed Dahlan, a former Fatah head of preventive security who had been residing in Abu Dhabi for some years as an adviser to its government while personally disbursing aid to the West Bank and Gaza. Dahlan, a former prisoner who learned Hebrew in Israeli jails, has generally been perceived by Israeli officials as one of the more palatable Palestinian leaders. He formed a new political movement, the Democratic Reformist Current, to compete in the expected Palestinian legislative elections in 2021, before they were indefinitely postponed. Other well-known Fatah figures including long-time prisoner Marwan Barghouti, and Yasser Arafat's nephew Nasser Al-Kidwa, along with a number of Fatah political leaders from Gaza who had been thrown out by Hamas in 2007 but were allowed back in during the run-up to the elections were also willing to challenge President Abbas.

Palestinian criticism of the Accords was weighed carefully by other Arab countries that came under heavy pressure from the outgoing Trump administration to sign them. Kuwait has an active civil society and parliament that are strongly opposed to normalisation with Israel. Although Oman has a history of contacts with Israel, and hosted Netanyahu's first visit to the Gulf in 2019, it has not wanted to normalise relations with Israel at the expense of diplomatic ties with the Palestinians. Saudi Arabia would be the most significant prize for Israeli and US diplomacy, given its claim to Islamic leadership. But it is more constrained than the smaller Gulf states, not least because the king is more sceptical of normalisation with Israel than the crown prince.

Regional reactions

Iran and Turkey criticised the Accords, underlining the fact that the non-Arab Muslim states were among the most vocal backers of the Palestinians. Iran condemned the agreement as a 'betrayal', with president Hassan Rouhani warning the UAE not to 'give Israel a foothold' in the region. Iran was likely to have concerns that direct cooperation between Israel, the UAE and Bahrain could shift the military balance in favour of the smaller Gulf Arab states. For its part, Turkey called the Accords 'hypocritical', despite its own long-standing relationship with Israel. Jordan and Egypt were relatively quiet. Both had long-standing peace agreements of their own with Israel, which were intended to lead to broader regional peace that did not materialise, and valued their relations with the Gulf states. However, both were concerned that the Accords undercut their interests and diplomatic standing. In particular, Jordan was concerned that Saudi Arabia or the UAE would challenge its historical role as the overseer of the holy sites in Jerusalem, from which the monarchy derived legitimacy and prestige.

In principle, the Arab countries that now have relations with Israel could help to broker a wider Arab–Israeli peace linked to the two-state solution and the end of the occupation. This may be an angle that the administration of Joe Biden seeks to pursue. But while suggesting that it would continue pushing for rapprochement and recognition between Israel and other Arab states, the US appeared unwilling to expend much diplomatic capital on the Israeli–Palestinian conflict. There was no indication that any other major international actor would prioritise this.

The Accords' commitment to people-to-people contacts and interfaith dialogue was widely welcomed. Images of a rabbi blowing the Jewish *shofar* in Dubai resonated around the world, especially at a time when anti-Semitism and other religious hatreds are being stirred by conspiracy theories, extremists and online disinformation. But there has so far been no related work to reduce the on-the-ground tensions over the sharing of sacred space in Jerusalem. Rather, an invitation to Emiratis to visit Jerusalem's Al-Aqsa mosque prompted Palestinians to highlight their own difficulties in exercising their rights to worship there. During Ramadan in 2021, new restrictions were placed on worshippers at the mosque, ranging from a total entry ban on West Bank Palestinians who had not received a COVID-19 vaccine – supplies of which were tightly limited in the West Bank – to the cutting of the wires of the mosque's speakers by Israeli police to ensure the sound of Muslim prayers would not disturb an Israeli Memorial Day ceremony at the Western Wall, a sacred Jewish site below the mosque.

Renewed violence shows limits, but also resilience, of the new alignments

The UAE and Bahrain moved quickly to establish embassies in Tel Aviv, appoint ambassadors and establish direct flights. In the UAE, there was little open disapproval of government policy, while in Bahrain, where civil society is more active, the Accords met with some criticism. But the political opposition's ability to mobilise was limited. There were few protests in Morocco.

Sudan faced a more difficult balancing act. Forging ties with Israel was sensitive for a country navigating transition from a self-styled Islamist regime to civilian rule. While the country's urgent need for development assistance was a key motive, its decision was likely influenced by its friends in the region. The chairman of the transitional governing council and commander of the army, Abdel Fattah al-Burhan, is close to Egypt, while the deputy chair of the transitional council, and former commander of the paramilitary Rapid Support Forces (previously known as the Janjaweed), Mohamed Hamdan Dagalo (Hemeti), is close to the UAE. Nonetheless, Sudan signed its 'Abraham Accords declaration' in Khartoum with a visiting US official and without an Israeli signatory, reflecting the delicacy of the issue for the country.

The escalation of violence in Israel and Palestine in May 2021 illustrated both the resilience of the Accords and the lack of progress in resolving the Israeli–Palestinian conflict and occupation. At the beginning of Ramadan, tensions flared as Israeli authorities limited gatherings around the Old City of Jerusalem and pressed ahead with plans to evict Palestinian families from Sheikh Jarrah, a neighbourhood in occupied East Jerusalem. As footage emerged of Israeli forces damaging the Al-Aqsa mosque and tear-gassing worshippers, Bahrain and the UAE issued a joint statement calling for Israeli restraint. Hamas launched an unprecedented number of rockets into Israel to position itself as the 'defender' of Al-Aqsa and claim leadership of the Palestinian cause. Israel responded with air raids. In 11 days of fighting, at least 12 Israelis and 253 Palestinians were killed, including two Israeli and 60 Palestinian children.

Once Hamas entered the fray, the Gulf countries shifted their tone, calling for calm rather than focusing on Israel's actions. The conflict and diplomatic embarrassment it caused did not appear to have affected the strategic rationale that underpinned the Bahraini and Emirati decision to seek normalisation. There was a flurry of tweets on Gulf social-media platforms, likely to have been state-sanctioned, criticising the Palestinians and praising Israel.

In June, as Netanyahu left office after 12 years as prime minster, he noted his ability to both befriend Gulf leaders and say 'no' to the US president on issues such as the Iran nuclear deal. This positioning of an Israeli leader as someone who could work with key Arab states and stand up to the US – rather than the other way around – underlined the foreign-policy realignments under way in the region.

The Future of Islamic Insurgencies
Have they passed their peak?

For nearly half a century, Islamist insurgency has been a persistent feature of the political landscape of the Middle East. From al-Takfir wa'l-Hijra in Egypt in the 1970s to the Armed Islamic Group in Algeria in the 1990s, and from al-Qaeda in Iraq in the 2000s to the Islamic State (also known as ISIS or ISIL) today, armed groups espousing varying forms of Islamist ideology have sought to unsettle states and seize power in the name of re-establishing God's law on earth. The high point of this history was ISIS's ascendancy in Iraq and Syria during 2014–16, when the group controlled a swathe of territory the size of the United Kingdom and ruled over millions of people, raising taxes, providing security and administering its own form of justice. In response, the United States and its partners set about building a coalition of dozens of countries and local militias to roll back ISIS's gains, and in 2019 the coalition succeeded in defeating its project in Iraq and Syria.

In the wake of ISIS's territorial defeat, some observers have speculated that Islamist insurgency, and Islamism more generally, have passed their peak. The Islamist wave that hit the Middle East in the 1960s, so the argument goes, may be coming to an end due to the bloody excesses of ISIS and to disillusionment with the brief period of Muslim Brotherhood rule in Egypt (2012–13). Some even point to the emergence of a new secularising trend in the Middle East as evidence of the waning appeal of political Islam. Nonetheless, evidence continues to accumulate that Islamism and Islamist insurgency remain a potent force in the Middle East. As the events of the past year show, armed groups raising the banner of Islam continue to wreak havoc across the region, sustained by a host of political and economic dynamics conducive to prolonged insurgency. While some groups are weakened and attacks are down in some areas, the trend is not so pronounced as to suggest continuous decline.

ISIS versus al-Qaeda

Most Islamist insurgent activity in the Middle East belongs to the militant Sunni transnational movement known as *al-tayyar al-jihadi* ('the jihadi movement'). Since 2014, the jihadi movement has been divided between adherents of the two jihadi blocs, ISIS and al-Qaeda. In June 2014, fresh from its conquest of about one-third of Iraqi territory, ISIS declared itself the restored Islamic caliphate, claiming the legal authority to rule over all the world's Muslims and deeming all other jihadi groups, including al-Qaeda, invalid. This created an enduring rivalry between ISIS and al-Qaeda that continues to this day, though ISIS currently has the upper hand in the Middle East. Upon its announcement of the caliphate, ISIS, seeking to expand its presence beyond Iraq and Syria, declared the establishment of local affiliates, or 'provinces', in various countries, including Egypt (in the Sinai Peninsula) and Libya. Al-Qaeda, for its part, maintains affiliates in Syria, Yemen, Somalia and the Sahel, among other places.

Today, both ISIS and al-Qaeda function largely as insurgent groups, though both aspire to the administration of territory. ISIS continues to posture as the restored caliphate, even though it no longer controls significant territory. Its leader is an Iraqi former imam known as Abu Ibrahim al-Hashimi al-Qurashi (a *nom de guerre* – his real name is Amir Mohammed Abdul Rahman al-Mawli al-Salbi), who took over as caliph upon the death of Abu Bakr al-Baghdadi in October 2019 and is believed to be hiding in the Iraqi desert. The leadership transition has not yet had a discernible effect on the group's general trajectory. Al-Qaeda presents itself as a loyal subsidiary of the Islamic Emirate of Afghanistan (the Afghan Taliban). Its leader remains the Egyptian veteran jihadi Ayman al-Zawahiri, who has been identified as living in eastern Afghanistan, though other sources assert that he has recently died. The respective leaderships of the two groups set the broad direction of their organisations but have little direct command and control over the day-to-day operations of their various parts and affiliates.

Iraq and Syria

Iraq and Syria remain hotbeds of ISIS insurgent activity, though the number of attacks and casualties claimed by the group declined somewhat over the past year. Well before ISIS lost its last territorial foothold in Iraq and Syria in March 2019, when it was driven from the Syrian border town of Baghouz by the US-led coalition, it was already shifting its strategy from one of holding territory to one of insurgency. This was a development anticipated by ISIS's own spokesman, Abu Muhammad al-Adnani, in a speech in mid-2016, in which he predicted that the group may well be driven from its strongholds and forced into the desert, only to wage guerrilla warfare and come back stronger than before. In short, ISIS's strategy for both Iraq and Syria is focused on 'exhausting' the enemy through a relentless spate of hit-and-run guerrilla-style attacks. Once the intended exhaustion is achieved, then its 'soldiers' can go back to seizing and holding territory.

Insurgent attacks in service of this strategy continued at a steady pace during July 2020–June 2021, when ISIS claimed a monthly average of 106 attacks in Iraq and 46 in Syria. These numbers represented 6% and 35% decreases, respectively, over the same period the preceding year. Most were small-scale assaults – ambushes, assassinations or bombings – directed against security forces and government and tribal officials. In Iraq, most attacks targeted the Iraqi security forces, including the army, local police and the Shi'ite-dominated militias known as the Popular Mobilisation Units (PMU), now nominally operating under the umbrella of the Iraqi Armed Forces. In Syria, the attacks focused on the Syrian military and its Iranian allies and their militias, as well as the Kurdish-dominated Syrian Democratic Forces (SDF), a US-supported militia that controls most of the territory east of the Euphrates river.

In both countries, attacks were heavily concentrated in rural areas, though there were several notable exceptions. One was a double suicide bombing in a Baghdad market in January 2021, which killed more than 30 civilians. According to the United Nations, ISIS boasts some 10,000 active fighters in Iraq and Syria, though this number is probably inflated. Iraqi intelligence estimates a number in the low thousands. Attack data shows that ISIS remains a potent, if not ascendant, threat in Iraq and Syria. While not poised to re-establish control over substantial territory any time soon, its insurgent capabilities remain intact and it will continue to be able to exploit the complex political and security environments of each country. In Iraq, the slow pace of reconstruction in formerly ISIS-controlled areas, and the heavy presence of the PMU (perceived as tied to Iran's expanding influence in the country), breed resentment in Sunni communities.

In Syria, the authority of the SDF east of the Euphrates is generally unpopular with the majority Sunni Arab population, while to the west of the Euphrates the Syrian army is too weak to control all the territory under its nominal authority. ISIS enjoys some control over Syria's central desert despite the presence of Syrian forces backed by Russian air support. With the Syrian civil war at a stalemate, this situation is unlikely to change soon. Also noteworthy in Syria is the presence of the sprawling detention facility in al-Hol, in the area under SDF control. The facility holds more than 60,000 men, women and children who once lived under ISIS, many of whom continue to identify with the group. Security at al-Hol is weak and many detainees, most of whom are from Iraq and Syria, have escaped. The facility remains a liability, particularly as a prison break could add fuel to the insurgency.

Elsewhere in Syria, the Islamist group Hayat Tahrir al-Sham (HTS) has established itself in northwestern Idlib province, ruling over some 3m people (most of them displaced from other parts of the country). While formerly affiliated with al-Qaeda, HTS has since turned against its former parent organisation and even imprisoned many al-Qaeda loyalists on its territory. The new Syrian al-Qaeda affiliate, Hurras al-Din, is barely able to function on account of such pressure. HTS is now more concerned with governance than insurgency and has even made entreaties to the US in the hope of being removed from the US list of foreign terrorist organisations. In 2019, the Syrian regime began an offensive to reassert authority over Idlib, but the move was blocked by Turkish forces, which intervened to prevent yet another surge of Syrian refugees into Turkey. As elsewhere in Syria, the battle lines around Idlib are unlikely to shift in the near future, and so the HTS 'statelet' is set to persist. The case of HTS can in one sense be seen as the triumph of Islamist insurgency – military accomplishments translated into political gains – though more radical jihadis see its evolution (i.e., its abandonment of al-Qaeda and new-found reliance on 'secular' Turkey) as a betrayal of the bedrock principles of jihadism.

North Africa

Before Iraq and Syria became the centre of Islamist insurgency in the region, North Africa was the most important area of activity. During the 1990s, jihadi groups were simultaneously active in Algeria (in a full-scale civil war), Egypt and Libya, carrying out numerous attacks on security forces and other targets. In the turmoil unleashed by the Arab Spring beginning in late 2010, jihadi actors re-emerged in force in Tunisia, Libya and Egypt. While the threat has largely been contained, it has not been totally defeated, and insurgent activity persists in these countries to varying degrees.

In Egypt, insurgent activity is mostly restricted to the Sinai Peninsula, specifically in the far north, a thinly populated area some distance from the tourist destinations on the Red Sea. The insurgency in Sinai broke out in 2011 amid the chaos wrought by the Arab Spring and came to be dominated by the jihadi group Ansar Bayt al-Maqdis. In 2014, the latter pledged allegiance to ISIS, rebranding itself as the group's 'Sinai Province' (Wilayat Sinai). Since then, the so-called Sinai Province has been one of the most continuously active ISIS franchises, carrying out regular attacks on Egyptian security forces, tribal elements accused of supporting and collaborating with security forces, and Christians. After some extraordinary attacks in the mid-2010s, including the bombing of a Russian civilian aircraft and the November 2017 assault on the al-Rawda mosque that left more than 300 people dead, the Egyptian military stepped up its counter-terrorism operations in 2018, vowing to eradicate the militants from the area. Sinai Province attacks have since slowed but continue at a steady pace. During the past year, the group claimed responsibility for 182 attacks and 402 casualties. As in Iraq and Syria, these numbers are slightly down – 17% and 23%, respectively – from the preceding year. In addition, Sinai Province regularly posts images and videos of its operations online, including grisly executions of those it has taken captive. The UN estimates that it has 500–1,200 fighters.

ISIS also claims a presence in Libya and Tunisia, though attacks in these countries have been only sporadic in recent years. In 2016, the group's 'Libya Province' took control of a strip of land on the Mediterranean around the city of Sirte but was later routed by local and foreign forces. Despite occasional attacks, the franchise has not been able to recover. The ceasefire reached between the warring parties in the Libyan civil war in October 2020 has further aided counter-terrorism efforts there.

Algeria has long been the home of al-Qaeda's North African franchise, al-Qaeda in the Islamic Maghreb (AQIM), which has operated under that name since 2007. Previously known as the Salafist Group for Preaching and Combat, the group has been waging a low-level insurgency against the Algerian state since the mid-1990s and was still quite active in the 2000s. In recent years, it has shifted its focus further south to the Sahel region; it no longer poses a serious threat in Algeria and has not carried out a major attack in the country since 2016.

Arabian Peninsula

Saudi Arabia, like Libya, was the site of a disquieting level of ISIS activity in the mid-2010s but also managed to neutralise the threat. Between mid-2015 and mid-2016, there was on average one ISIS attack every 12 days, targeted at Saudi security forces and Shia Muslims. Since then, however, the militant networks have been disrupted and attacks have ceased almost entirely. In the past year, ISIS claimed only one attack in the kingdom.

Yemen, the site of a protracted civil war that broke out in 2014, is home to several active Islamist insurgent groups. The first and most successful is the Zaydi Shia movement known as the Houthis (Ansarullah), which took control of much of northern Yemen, including the capital Sana'a, in late 2014. The Houthi takeover prompted the Saudis and Emiratis to intervene on behalf of the Yemeni government of President Abd Rabbo Mansour Hadi, though they have not been able to achieve their objective. The Houthis are ideologically and materially linked to Iran, and their rise marks the success of another Iranian-backed Shia Islamist movement in the Middle East. The Houthis' main opponents, the Saudi- and United

Arab Emirates-backed Yemeni security forces – with the Saudis providing airstrikes – supporting either Hadi's government or the secessionist Southern Transitional Council, have repeatedly failed in their efforts to dislodge the Houthis from their northern stronghold.

The other Islamist insurgent groups in Yemen are the local franchise of al-Qaeda, al-Qaeda in the Arabian Peninsula (AQAP), and that of ISIS, known as its 'Yemen Province'. Once regarded as al-Qaeda's strongest and most threatening franchise, AQAP has suffered severe setbacks in recent years and remains a shadow of its former self. The group was initially successful in exploiting the security vacuum left by the 2011 Yemeni revolution and the civil war that followed, seizing control of Mukalla, Yemen's fifth-largest city, for more than a year between 2015 and 2016. Since then, however, AQAP has been decimated by increased military pressure from the US and the Saudi-led coalition and found itself in a prolonged confrontation with ISIS's Yemen Province. The latter, which has never been as successful as its al-Qaeda counterpart, has likewise been severely weakened over the past few years. When not fighting each other, both groups have staged attacks on the Houthis and Yemeni forces. In the context of the Yemeni civil war, neither is a particularly strong actor, though neither is a spent force. If one is to experience a revival, it is likely to be AQAP, which has long-standing connections to Yemen's tribes and greater financial resources.

Beyond the Middle East

The general picture that emerges is one of persistent but not reinvigorated Islamist insurgency. In Iraq and Syria, as well as in the Sinai Peninsula, ISIS jihadis continue to carry out insurgent operations, though at a slightly lower rate than in the preceding year. In all three areas they remain a capable threat with devoted followers committed to a long-term strategy of exhaustion. Elsewhere in the Middle East, North Africa and the Arabian Peninsula, the jihadi threat has receded considerably, though the Houthis' consolidation of power in Yemen, with the support of Tehran, marks an Islamist success of another kind. With regard to jihadism in particular, the picture is certainly brighter than it was in 2014–16 during the height of ISIS's territorial project. But it is too soon to tell whether the decline in insurgent activity over the past year is the beginning of a longer-term trend or merely a reflection of the ebb and flow of a long struggle.

The picture becomes more worrisome when one looks beyond the Middle East, where Islamist insurgencies have wavered or stagnated, to Africa and Central Asia, where they have found considerable success in recent years. In the Sahel region of Africa, including in Mali, for example, local branches of ISIS and al-Qaeda compete for control of territory. In Nigeria, ISIS's 'West Africa Province' (ISWAP) is increasingly powerful and possibly set to eliminate its rival Boko Haram. In Somalia, the al-Qaeda-linked al-Shabaab carries out almost daily attacks against security forces. There are also active jihadi factions loyal to ISIS in central and eastern Africa – insurgencies in the Democratic Republic of the Congo and Mozambique are being waged in the name of ISIS's 'Central Africa Province' – though some analysts cast doubt on this link. In Central Asia, the Taliban's rapid takeover of Afghanistan has created major new uncertainty and alarm. The Taliban's own greatest rival may turn out to be another Islamist group, ISIS's 'Khorasan Province' in eastern Afghanistan.

All this should give pause to those who assume that Islamist insurgency has passed its peak and is headed inevitably towards decline. Militant Islamism, particularly of the kind associated with al-Qaeda and ISIS, continues to thrive across much of the Islamic world.

CHAPTER 10

Sub-Saharan Africa

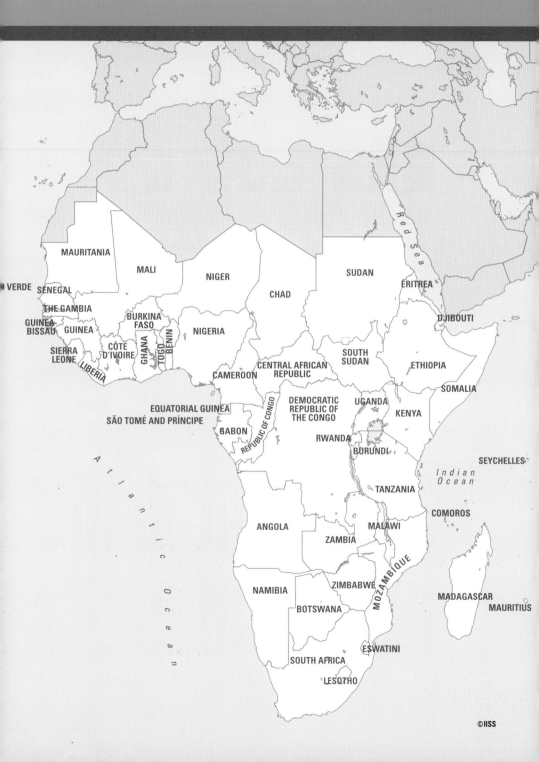

©IISS

Drivers of Strategic Change

REGIONAL SHARE OF GLOBAL POPULATION, GDP AND DEFENCE BUDGET

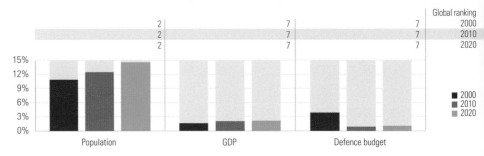

	Global ranking	
Population: 2, GDP: 7, Defence budget: 7		2000
Population: 2, GDP: 7, Defence budget: 7		2010
Population: 2, GDP: 7, Defence budget: 7		2020

Legend: ■ 2000 ■ 2010 ■ 2020

POPULATION

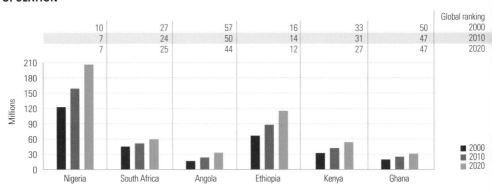

	Nigeria	South Africa	Angola	Ethiopia	Kenya	Ghana	Global ranking
2000	10	27	57	16	33	50	
2010	7	24	50	14	31	47	
2020	7	25	44	12	27	47	

Legend: ■ 2000 ■ 2010 ■ 2020

AGE STRUCTURE
(Percentage of national population)

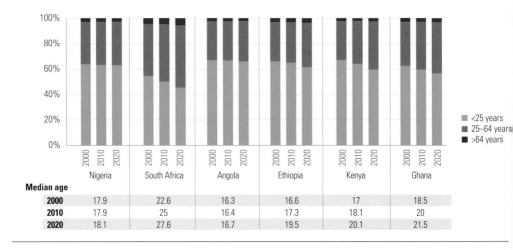

Legend: ■ <25 years ■ 25–64 years ■ >64 years

Median age	Nigeria	South Africa	Angola	Ethiopia	Kenya	Ghana
2000	17.9	22.6	16.3	16.6	17	18.5
2010	17.9	25	16.4	17.3	18.1	20
2020	18.1	27.6	16.7	19.5	20.1	21.5

Africa's young, large population has the potential to fuel a 'demographic dividend' of growth or a 'youth bulge' of conflict. Larger economies like South Africa and Nigeria have struggled to raise living standards. Ethiopia, a standout economic success, is now racked by civil conflict. A notable success story is the region-wide growth of secondary education, auguring well for future growth and development.

GDP
(Constant 2010 US dollars)

	Nigeria	South Africa	Angola	Ethiopia	Kenya	Ghana	Global ranking
	41	31	71	109	81	83	2000
	30	29	64	96	84	81	2010
	27	31	62	74	73	69	2020

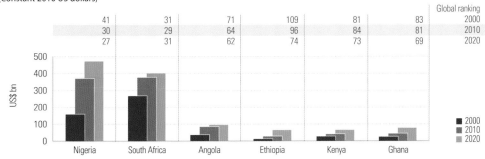

Legend: ■ 2000 ■ 2010 ■ 2020

GDP PER CAPITA
(Constant 2010 US dollars)

	Nigeria	South Africa	Angola	Ethiopia	Kenya	Ghana	Global ranking
	143	71	118	187	155	141	2000
	135	79	112	192	162	142	2010
	142	86	128	180	154	134	2020

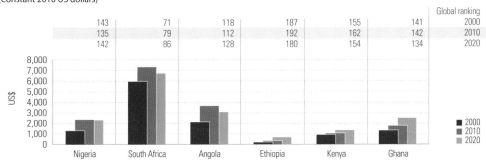

Legend: ■ 2000 ■ 2010 ■ 2020

DEFENCE BUDGET
(Constant 2015 US dollars)

ACTIVE MILITARY PERSONNEL

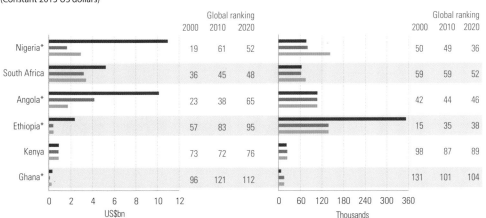

Defence budget Global ranking:

	2000	2010	2020
Nigeria*	19	61	52
South Africa	36	45	48
Angola*	23	38	65
Ethiopia*	57	83	95
Kenya	73	72	76
Ghana*	96	121	112

Active military personnel Global ranking:

	2000	2010	2020
Nigeria*	50	49	36
South Africa	59	59	52
Angola*	42	44	46
Ethiopia*	15	35	38
Kenya	98	87	89
Ghana*	131	101	104

*2000 defence budget values for Nigeria, Angola, Ethiopia and Ghana are estimates, and may be distorted by high inflation rates. ■ 2000 ■ 2010 ■ 2020

For explanation of drivers and sources, see page 9

HUMAN DEVELOPMENT INDEX (HDI)
(Score between 0 and 1, where 0 denotes a low level of development and 1 a high level of development)

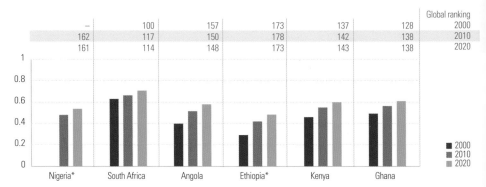

*No 2000 data available for Nigeria

POLITICAL SYSTEM
(Score between 0 and 100, where 0 denotes no political freedom and 100 fully free)

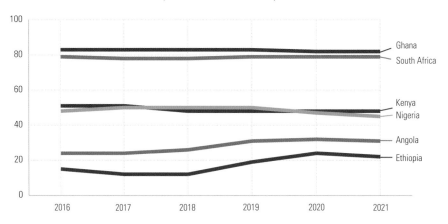

PERCENTAGE OF CHILDREN IN EDUCATION (GROSS)*

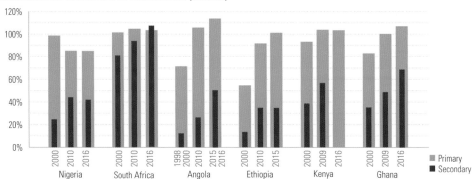

Primary data for Angola 2000 is from 1998. Primary data for Angola 2016 is from 2015. Primary and secondary data for Ethiopia 2016 is from 2015. Primary and secondary data for Kenya 2010 is from 2009. Secondary data for Kenya 2016 not available. Primary and secondary data for Ghana 2010 is from 2009.

* The data shows gross enrolment, which can exceed the population of the age group that officially corresponds to the level of education because of repeaters or late enrollers. Therefore some values are greater than 100%

2020–21 Review

As elsewhere in the world, the COVID-19 pandemic – and governments' responses – was a key determinant of sub-Saharan Africa's political and economic environment over the past year. Death rates remained well below the levels in Western and most Asian states – possibly reflecting the relative youth of the population, lack of comorbidities and climate. Most governments in the region also imposed measures ranging from social distancing to full-scale lockdowns. This rapid action appeared to play a major role in limiting the first wave of infections in many African countries.

Most restrictions were gradually lifted during the second half of 2020, in part reflecting growing social tensions (given the key role played by informal-sector activity in many African states), but also COVID denialism in countries such as Tanzania. However, the emergence of local and more infectious variants, notably in South Africa, required their reimposition, although these measures were generally less stringent than those imposed in early 2020. Meanwhile, access to vaccines remained a pressing issue. Most countries in the region were reliant on the World Health Organization (WHO)-led COVAX initiative, doses acquired by the African Union (AU), or donations of Chinese or Russian vaccines. COVAX will cover only 20% of the population of eligible countries, well below the levels deemed necessary for herd immunity. Logistical and financial constraints, and vaccine hesitancy, have further constrained the roll-out of vaccination programmes. Continued restrictions may be necessary well into 2022 – particularly given the emergence of new variants against which some vaccines are less effective – with potentially negative implications for economic activity and social stability.

Nearly 20 sub-Saharan African states held national elections between July 2020 and June 2021. Incumbents performed well in almost every case. In some instances, this reflected genuine popular support for the government's handling of the COVID-19 pandemic, or of economic performance over the course of the preceding term. In others, however, long-standing presidents and ruling parties made the most of their privileged access to state media and funding, and the relative underdevelopment of opposition groups, while several incumbents sought to circumvent presidential-term limits. Meanwhile, legislative elections in Chad and Ethiopia were postponed from 2020 to 2021 because of the pandemic.

There were contrasting election experiences in two of the largest economies in West Africa, Côte d'Ivoire and Ghana. In Côte d'Ivoire, incumbent President Alassane Ouattara was declared the winner of the October 2020 presidential election with some 94% of the vote. The election was controversial on several grounds. Ouattara had served as president since 2010 and had initially said that he would not contest the poll. However, following the unexpected death of his chosen successor, Amadou Gon Coulibaly, just three months before the vote, he decided to stand again. This prompted opposition accusations that he was exceeding the two-term limit. While Ouattara maintained that the approval of a new constitution in 2016 allowed him to reset the term limit, several opposition parties boycotted the vote.

The election was particularly sensitive because incumbent president Laurent Gbagbo's refusal to step down in 2010 – in the face of a victory for Ouattara, then the opposition candidate – had led to a five-month civil war. However, while some 85 people died in unrest following the 2020 presidential election, there was no large-scale violence, in part because Ouattara engaged in reconciliation with opposition politicians. As a result, all major political parties competed in the March 2021 legislative elections, including the Ivorian Popular Front (FPI), which had boycotted all elections for a decade. Opposition groups did not offer a coherent policy platform, while the ruling Rally of Houphouetists for Democracy and Peace (RHDP) campaigned on strong economic performance prior to the COVID-19 downturn and secured a strong legislative majority.

Ghana's presidential election in December 2020 was much closer, with incumbent President Nana Akufo-Addo securing 51.6% of the vote, only just ahead of his main rival, John Mahama, with 47.4%. The opposition rejected the outcome, citing irregularities, but the Supreme Court upheld the result. The margin was even narrower in the legislative election held at the same time, with both the ruling New Patriotic Party (NPP) and opposition National Democratic Congress (NDC) securing 137 out of 275 seats. The NPP secured the slimmest possible majority following the announcement by the single independent MP that he would cooperate with the ruling party, but the parliamentary arrangement presents clear challenges to policymakers.

In Ethiopia, the ruling Prosperity Party (PP) is expected to secure a substantial victory in the June 2021 elections, the results of which have yet to be declared (in part because voting in some areas was delayed until September). The vote was the first electoral test for Prime Minister Abiy Ahmed – appointed in 2018 following the resignation of Hailemariam Desalegn – and for his partial relaxation of the ruling group's dominance of the political scene. The elections were contested by more than 45 political parties, as well as a substantial range of independent candidates. However, while notably more free than previous elections – in the 2010 and 2015 elections, the ruling Ethiopian People's Revolutionary Democratic Front (EPRDF), the precursor to the PP, won 91% of the seats in parliament – opposition parties continued to operate at a substantial disadvantage, since constraints prior to 2018 meant that they had had little time to build up national operational structures or funding. In addition, most opposition groups remained small and ethnically or regionally based, somewhat limiting their national appeal. The results of the election are unlikely to address the increasing ethnic tensions in Ethiopia, notably in Tigray, where postponement of the August 2020 national elections prompted accusations that Abiy was using the pandemic to hold onto power beyond his constitutionally mandated term (which ended in September 2020). The Tigray People's Liberation Front (TPLF) – a dominant member of the former ruling coalition, but strongly opposed to the PP – held a regional election that federal authorities did not recognise. In November 2020, tensions in Tigray escalated into civil conflict, ethnic violence and allegations of human-rights abuses by Ethiopian troops. The United States and the Ethiopian Orthodox Church described these events as genocide. Moreover, the federal authorities failed to maintain control of Tigray, as the TPLF retook Mekelle, the provincial capital, at the end of June 2021. The federal government attempted several face-saving measures, including the declaration of a unilateral ceasefire, and announcement that troops had been 'redeployed' ahead of the declaration of election results, but the TPLF remained determined to drive all federal forces out of Tigray, and Eritrean forces back into that country.

Improved outlook under Biden, and US reorientation towards the Horn

The election of Joe Biden as US president in November 2020 prompted optimism about a fresh start for US–Africa relations, with Biden's overt multilateralism offering a strong contrast to Donald Trump's detachment (or even outright hostility). While Biden has chiefly focused on domestic priorities so far, his administration has started to outline foreign-policy goals, notably in a March 2021 speech by US Secretary of State Antony Blinken. Several of the aims outlined will have a direct or indirect impact on US–Africa relations. These include efforts to tackle COVID-19 and improve global health security; revitalise ties with allies and partners, including in Africa; and renew democracy – although Blinken specifically ruled out 'costly' military interventions or efforts to overthrow authoritarian regimes.

The Biden administration has placed new emphasis on democratic governance and human rights in sub-Saharan Africa. In March, Blinken described acts carried out in the Tigray region as 'ethnic cleansing', an allegation the Ethiopian authorities strongly denied. In the same month, Biden sent Senator Chris Coons, a long-standing ally, to Ethiopia to meet Abiy as well as AU representatives, to convey the president's 'grave concerns' over the humanitarian crisis in the area. In April, Blinken appointed Jeffrey Feltman, a former US ambassador to Lebanon and subsequently under-secretary-general for political affairs at the United Nations, to the newly created position of US special envoy for the Horn of Africa.

US interest in the strategically important Horn area had hitherto focused on Djibouti, which hosts Camp Lemonnier, the only permanent US base in Africa and host to around 4,000 joint and allied forces, military and civilian personnel. This will remain important, particularly given development work at China's nearby naval base. In April, US Africa Command (AFRICOM) head General Stephen Townsend stated that construction of a new pier meant that the Chinese base was now able to host aircraft carriers, assault carriers or nuclear-powered attack submarines. Feltman's stated initial priorities included volatility in Ethiopia, including the conflict in Tigray; escalating tensions between Ethiopia and Sudan; and the dispute with Egypt and Sudan around the filling of the Grand Ethiopian Renaissance Dam (GERD). The US joined other mediators, including the AU, in seeking an agreement that would address Egyptian and Sudanese concerns about the impact of GERD on the flow rates of the Blue Nile. With Ethiopia, Egypt and Sudan all fully occupied with domestic concerns, an escalation into outright military confrontation remained unlikely.

Although not highlighted as an early priority, the new special envoy will also have to tackle challenges in another Horn state, Somalia. In December 2020, Trump ordered the withdrawal of some 700 US troops based in Somalia, which was completed in mid-January 2021. Most were relocated to neighbouring states to continue efforts to tackle the threat posed by the al-Shabaab Islamist insurgent group. However, the draw-down had a deleterious impact. Townsend told a Senate Armed Services Committee hearing in April that 'the repositioning of forces out of Somalia has introduced new layers of complexity and risk … Our understanding of what's happening in Somalia is less now than it was when we were there on the ground.' The timing was particularly difficult given an uptick in domestic instability in Somalia over the holding of presidential elections. A March attempt by incumbent President Mohamed Abdullahi Mohamed (popularly known as 'Farmaajo') to extend his term by two years – to allow for the holding of one-person-one-vote, rather than, as in the past, indirect clan-based, elections – led to substantial splits within the security forces, enabling al-Shabaab to ramp up attacks.

Further complicating the situation, Biden had pledged to cut back on drone strikes, a controversial strategy with a high risk of collateral damage that had been heavily used in Somalia by the Trump administration. There is a clear risk that reduced use of drone strikes, and the removal of US troops, will enable al-Shabaab to increase its public presence and movement – particularly if the Somali government remains focused on its own political divisions – and it seems unlikely that the US will amend its position in the near term. In early February, Biden instructed the US Department of Defense to conduct a 'global posture review', examining the location and magnitude of US troop deployments worldwide. This has yet to be completed, but Somalia is likely to be a substantially lower priority than the larger Horn of Africa states, or continued support for multilateral military initiatives such as efforts to tackle Islamist terrorism in the Sahel. France leads counter-terrorism efforts in the latter, and is likely to remain a dominant player, notwithstanding French President Emmanuel Macron's June 2021 announcement that *Operation Barkhane* would end in its current form, and that French troops in the region would be cut over the course of several years. (Macron announced that the operation would be replaced by a new international coalition with 'significant' French contributions and leadership, and the US is likely to continue to take a supportive rather than active role.) Biden has yet to name a US envoy to the Sahel to replace Trump appointee J. Peter Pham, despite Macron's announcement, as well as serious new instability in the area following the death of long-standing Chadian president Idriss Déby (reportedly while visiting troops battling a rebel incursion) in April.

China using soft power to bolster links after a testing period

The COVID-19 pandemic created various challenges for Sino-African relations. Chinese trade and investment flows, on which many sub-Saharan states remain reliant, were dislocated by the imposition of lockdown measures within China, as well as supply-chain disruptions arising from virus-containment measures imposed globally. In the early part of the pandemic, China's image was also damaged by videos circulated on social media showing discrimination against Africans in some Chinese cities.

Subsequently, however, China undertook a diplomatic and economic offensive across the continent to show itself as a reliable partner and tackle criticism of its initial handling of the virus. This initially involved offers of medical assistance, by both state and private-sector entities, and the deployment of Chinese medical workers. Most high-profile was the offer of doses of the Sinovac and Sinopharm vaccines to African states otherwise reliant on the COVAX initiative or doses secured through the AU. Although there were questions over the efficacy of the vaccines – particularly against the local variant in South Africa – China sought to contrast its offer of assistance with perceived 'vaccine nationalism' by Western states.

While the COVID-19 pandemic and its socio-economic impact were the primary focus of China–Africa cooperation over the past year, China also continued to bolster economic and security links. For example, a free-trade agreement (FTA) with Mauritius came into effect on 1 January. While ten sub-Saharan African countries have bilateral investment treaties with China, this is the first FTA, and offers a potential model for future trade and investment agreements in the years ahead. The economic benefits are heavily weighted towards Mauritius, which gained immediate duty-free access to the Chinese market for more than 7,500 products, and a commitment from China to import 50,000 tonnes of sugar a year (a welcome boost following the end of the European Union sugar-quota regime in 2014). From China's perspective, the FTA offers a stepping stone into Southern and East African markets, and the fact that it pre-dated a similar agreement with India, a significant geopolitical rival of China, is a bonus.

The FTA is also consistent with China's growing focus on the strategically significant Indian Ocean region, through which almost two-thirds of global oil trade is routed. Townsend told the Senate Armed Service Committee: 'We know the Chinese desire a network of bases around the globe. My concern is the greatest along the Atlantic coast of Africa.' According to Townsend, China is looking to set up a base in Tanzania, with which it conducted naval joint military training in March. Tanzania is potentially attractive, being located near enough both to heavily trafficked parts of the Indian Ocean and to the Mozambique Channel. China had cultivated particularly strong links with president John Magufuli, who died in March 2020. A substantial strategic reorientation under his successor, Samia Suluhu Hassan, appears unlikely.

China's overarching economic and security policy towards Africa will be outlined at the next tri-annual Forum on China–Africa Cooperation, due to be held in Senegal in September 2021. However, US officials will continue to flag the challenge arising from the potential development of military bases along Africa's eastern coast.

Russia appears to suffer a setback in Sudan

Meanwhile, Russia's ambitions for a naval presence in East Africa appeared to have suffered a setback, with reports in late April that Sudan had suspended plans for Russia to open a naval logistics base in Port Sudan. Russia denied this. It already had access rights to the port, and in November 2020 had announced an agreement to establish a naval base including a logistics centre – with the capacity to host up to 300 personnel and four naval units, including nuclear-powered vessels – for 25 years (renewable in ten-year periods), as well as the right to use Sudanese airports and airspace to support the base. In exchange, Sudan would receive weapons and military equipment free of charge, while Russian military advisers would be sent to train Sudanese forces.

If established, the Port Sudan facility would be Russia's first naval base in Africa and only its second (after Tartus in Syria) outside the former Soviet Union. The rationale behind the base was clear: a base in Sudan would allow it to flex its military capabilities and influence from the Indian Ocean to the Red and Black seas. Russia had been attempting to set up a base in the area for some time. A plan for a base on the Yemeni side of the Bab el-Mandeb Strait was abandoned because of the war in Yemen, while talks with Djibouti fell through after the Djiboutian authorities agreed to provide only a small area in an unfavourable location, and the construction costs – estimated at US$1 billion – were deemed prohibitive. However, the initial negotiations on the Sudan base were conducted with Omar al-Bashir, the long-standing Sudanese president who was overthrown by the military in April 2019. The transitional government that succeeded him has been seeking rapprochement with the West instead. In December 2020, the US Congress removed Sudan from the US State Department's state sponsors of terrorism list, on which it had been placed in 1993, effectively clearing the way for the country to seek international financial assistance, and the following month the US agreed to provide a US$1bn bridging loan to enable Sudan to clear arrears on debts owed to the World Bank.

Russia is comparatively poorly placed to provide substantial funding for the Sudanese regime. If confirmed, the suspension of Russia's plans for a base will undermine a major achievement of President Vladimir Putin's Africa policy, as formulated at the first Russia–Africa Summit in 2019, when Putin placed strong emphasis on military cooperation and pledged US$20bn in investment without conditionality. With Russia continuing to deploy state-linked military contractors on the continent – most recently in Mozambique since 2019 to tackle a growing Islamist insurgency in the north of the country – such cooperation is likely to be a key facet of the second Russia–Africa Summit, due to be held in 2022.

Sudan's Slow-motion Revolution
Will transition lead to stability and growth?

Sudan is roughly half-way through the transition programme established following the ousting of its 30-year president, Omar al-Bashir, in a *coup d'état* in April 2019. The new authorities have taken substantial steps in some areas of reform and are starting to reap the rewards in terms of improved international standing. However, economic challenges – exacerbated by the impact of the COVID-19 pandemic – persist, while relations with subregional states such as Ethiopia have proven to be testing. While the most likely scenario is that presidential and parliamentary elections will go ahead – though potentially somewhat later than the planned completion date of December 2022 – it remains possible that the military will seek to hold on to power, leading to substantial public unrest and renewed international isolation.

A gradual move from autocracy to democracy

Following the coup, and further civilian protests, a transition agreement was signed in July 2019 by a coalition of opposition groups, the Forces of Freedom and Change (FFC) and the Transitional Military Council (TMC) that succeeded Bashir. Under its terms, a sovereign council (SC) is due to hold power for 39 months, with the presidency of the SC shifting from the military to civilians after 21 months. The scheduled transition period is due to end in December 2022, with parliamentary and presidential elections returning the country to democratic civilian rule. Such rule is very much the exception in Sudan: between independence in 1956 and Bashir's seizure of power in 1989, there were five attempted or successful military coups. Although Bashir made the transition from leader of a military coup to civilian president, his rule was consistently criticised as undemocratic (while he continues to face charges at the International Criminal Court of crimes against humanity, war crimes and genocide).

This tumultuous political history, and the need to create executive, legislative and judicial institutions and procedures – and secure a comprehensive peace agreement, including with disparate armed rebel groups prior to elections – are among the stated factors in the agreement of a relatively long transition period. However, the TMC was initially reluctant to share power with civilians and did so under substantial external pressure and amid worsening domestic social unrest. Given this, civil-society groups have expressed concern that the military seeks a long transition period to further entrench its power, thwart the necessary reform of a rentier system from which military interests benefit and potentially renege on the agreed transition.

Some substantial successes on political priorities

The transitional cabinet that took office in September 2019, after a further period of negotiation, set out an ambitious list of key priorities for the transition period, including the pursuit of 'comprehensive peace', reform of state institutions, the establishment of a 'balanced' external policy, tackling corruption, greater provision of social care and efforts to tackle long-standing macroeconomic imbalances. The transitional government has achieved several high-profile successes, most notably the signing of peace agreements with rebel groups. In September–October 2020, the transitional government signed agreements with the Sudan People's Liberation Movement–North (SPLM–N), a rebel group that controls substantial swathes of territory in Blue Nile and South Kordofan states, and with the Sudan Revolutionary Front (SRF), an alliance of rebel groups operating in the states of Blue Nile, Darfur and South Kordofan. The deals, under which all sides agreed to cease hostilities, were hailed as potentially ending years of conflict in the Blue Nile, Darfur and South Kordofan regions (in Darfur alone, a large-scale ethnic conflict in 2003 left some 300,000 people dead and 2.5 million displaced). The agreements were clearly over-optimistic, given persistent ethnic tensions and ongoing conflicts over access to land and water in the various states – for example, in January 2021, the UN High Commissioner for Refugees (UNHCR) reported that 250 people were killed and more than 100,000 displaced in renewed intercommunal clashes in Darfur. Nonetheless, the agreements are significant, not least because they entail the integration of rebel groups into mainstream politics, with rebel leaders to be given three seats in the SC and one-quarter of the seats in the cabinet and parliament.

The 300-member transitional parliament has yet to be established. But in February 2021, three members of the SRF were appointed to the SC, and a new transitional cabinet including four appointees from former rebel groups (as well as members of other opposition parties) was announced. Notably, Gibril Ibrahim, the leader of the Justice and Equality Movement (JEM) – at one stage a major Darfuri rebel group – was appointed finance minister. Ibrahim, and the freshly appointed foreign-affairs minister, Mariam al-Mahdi, are civilian technocrats, and could therefore bolster the civilian element of the transitional government (which includes the SC and the appointed cabinet members), amid continued tensions with the military component and allied pro-Islamic parties.

Several issues have sparked tensions. In December 2020, General Abdel Fattah al-Burhan – the current chairman of the SC – announced the creation of a Transitional Partners Council (TPC), a 29-member body including members of the FFC, the military wing of the SC and the council of ministers. This was rejected by Prime Minister Abdalla Hamdok, amid concerns over the proposed inclusion of Mohamed Hamdan Dagalo (Hemeti), deputy commander of the Rapid Support Forces (RSF), a controversial paramilitary organisation accused of violent crackdowns on pro-democracy supporters during the 2019 protests. The scope of executive powers conferred on the TPC also raised concerns. Burhan's initial proposal that the TPC be given the power to resolve disputes between the partners in the transitional agreement prompted criticism from the cabinet that this could potentially undermine the transitional parliament. It was subsequently agreed that the TPC would coordinate and resolve differences between the various elements of the transitional government, but on a consultative basis and without infringing on the powers of the SC or the cabinet. Nonetheless, the dispute underscores continued concerns among civilian political groups over the power of the military.

The military elements of the transitional government won a significant dispute in October 2020 over the normalisation of relations with Israel. This was a major point of contention between the military and civilian wings of the SC. The civilian transitional authorities had criticised a February 2020 meeting between Burhan and Israeli prime minister Benjamin Netanyahu in Uganda on the grounds that Burhan had not sought cabinet approval and that his reported agreement to pursue normalisation of ties was outside the transitional government's mandate. Underscoring the continued sensitivity of the issue, Haidar Badawi, the foreign-ministry spokesperson, was dismissed by the acting foreign minister, Omar Qamar al-Din, in August 2020 after stating that Burhan 'put Sudan on the right track with his meeting with the Israeli prime minister' and that Sudan was 'looking forward to concluding a peace agreement with Israel'.

However, Burhan and his allies argued that improved relations with Israel could facilitate the transitional government's key foreign-policy goal – Sudan's removal from the United States' list of state sponsors of terrorism, to which it had been added in 1993 when the US accused Sudan of hosting various Islamist militant groups as well as al-Qaeda leader Osama bin Laden. Normalisation of relations with Israel was not a stated precondition for removal. However, improved relations between Arab states and Israel was a clear priority for the US government in the second half of 2020 under president Donald Trump, with the US brokering the Abraham Accords with Bahrain and the United Arab Emirates (UAE). Sudan's decision to follow suit was by no means universally popular domestically and was opposed by several major political parties, pro-democracy activists, Islamists and much of the youth population.

However, normalisation was backed by Saudi Arabia and the UAE, the prime financial supporters of the Sudanese military (committing US$3 billion in aid in April 2019, just after Bashir was overthrown). With the civilian elements of the transitional authorities lacking a clear plan for Sudan's removal from the terrorism list, the military view prevailed. This had the intended effect: in October 2020 Trump announced that the US would remove Sudan from the list once Sudan had paid US$335m in compensation to US victims of terrorist attacks carried out by groups based in Sudan during the Bashir regime. Following the transfer of funds – covering Sudan's alleged involvement in bombings of US embassies in Kenya and Tanzania (in 1998) and an attack on the USS *Cole* in Yemen (in 2000) – Trump signed the order removing Sudan from the list, a decision that was welcomed by both the military and the civilian wings of the regime. On the same day, Sudan signed an official agreement normalising relations with Israel, although it did not officially accede to the Abraham Accords until January 2021.

The economy remains the biggest challenge – and potential threat

The chief potential benefit of the removal from the US list is economic, since Sudan's inclusion had effectively prevented the country from securing debt relief, loans from the IMF and other international financial institutions, and substantial Western investment. Long in debt distress, Sudan was unable to fulfil its financial obligations and needed to restructure its foreign debt. According to the World Bank, Sudan's external debt stock was equivalent to 198.9% of its GDP at the end of 2019, and the country's large arrears on debt repayments to the IMF, World Bank and African Development Bank left it unable to secure new concessional financing while it remained on the US terrorism list.

Sudan underperforming as an investment destination

Sudan's effective exclusion from the international community, particularly from the oil and gas sectors, has also acted as a constraint on investment. According to the UN Conference on Trade and Investment, foreign direct investment (FDI) into Sudan totalled US$7.1bn between 2014 and 2019 (the most recent available data). In contrast, investment in neighbouring Egypt and Ethiopia totalled US$44.2bn and US$18.5bn respectively. Lack of investment exacerbated years of mismanagement under the Bashir regime and contributed to persistent economic underperformance. GDP has grown by an average of only 0.13% a year since 2005, while inflation was an estimated 163.3% in 2020. Revitalising the economy is probably the greatest test for – and potential threat to – the transitional government. The Bashir regime change was effectively triggered by an economic crisis that became a political crisis, and an ongoing failure to improve economic activity and living standards could lead to renewed political upheaval.

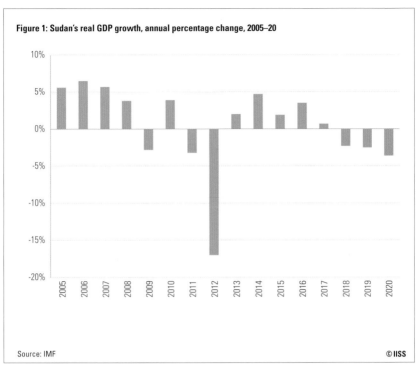

Figure 1: Sudan's real GDP growth, annual percentage change, 2005–20

Source: IMF ©IISS

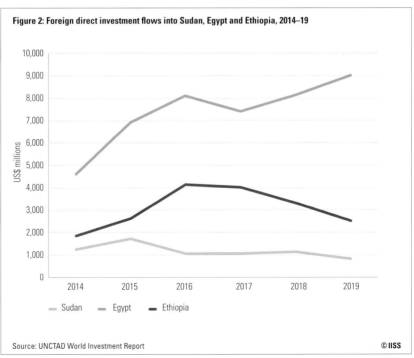

Figure 2: Foreign direct investment flows into Sudan, Egypt and Ethiopia, 2014–19

Source: UNCTAD World Investment Report ©IISS

While the authorities face substantial challenges, they are also making clear progress. The IMF was not able to provide financial support, even after Sudan's removal from the US state sponsors of terrorism list, because of arrears on existing debt. However, in March 2021 Sudan announced that it had cleared its debt arrears to the World Bank (thanks to a US$1.15bn bridging loan from the US). In May it did so with the African Development Bank (via a US$425m bridging loan from Ireland, Sweden and the United Kingdom), and at a conference hosted by France on 17 May, Paris Club members agreed to clear Sudan's arrears to the IMF. France announced a US$1.5bn bridging loan to clear such arrears, as well as approving clearance of Sudan's US$5bn debt to France. Germany pledged to settle US$110m of Sudan's IMF liabilities, offered to provide debt relief of around US$476m and pledged with Italy to write off US$1.8bn of dual debt. Norway agreed to waive US$100m of bilateral debt. These steps should enable Sudan to reach 'decision point' on debt relief under the IMF and World Bank heavily indebted poor countries (HIPC) initiative by the end of 2021. Sudan has also been making progress on another HIPC condition – the establishment of a track record on policy and reform implementa-tion. In pursuit of this, in June 2020 Sudan agreed a 12-month programme with the IMF. This unfunded programme is designed to help the transi-tional government tackle macroeconomic imbalances and boost 'inclusive' growth by increasing social spending. Sudan has successfully completed two reviews of the programme, meaning that it is expected to reach deci-sion point for debt relief under HIPC in June. In addition, Saudi Arabia – Sudan's third-largest creditor, to which it owes some US$4.6bn of debt – announced in May that it would press for sweeping debt restructuring at a creditors' conference in Paris. It would likely take two to three years to reach HIPC 'completion point' and this would be subject to continued reforms. The potential rewards are substantial, however, since HIPC relief would enable Sudan to clear nearly all its external debt and gain access to the large-scale funding for necessary expenditure on infrastructural devel-opment and social spending.

However, adjustment measures have proven painful and politically contentious, particularly given the additional challenge of the global

COVID-19 pandemic. In February 2021, the Central Bank of Sudan devalued its core exchange rate from SDG55:US$1 to SDG375:US$1 in an attempt to narrow the gap between the official and black-market exchange rates. Although not a full float of the Sudanese pound, the IMF welcomed the devaluation as reducing distortions in the economy. However, devaluation will also serve to accelerate inflation that has been rising since late 2019, prompting the authorities to declare an 'economic state of emergency' in September 2020. The government continues to struggle to tackle the issue – in part because of flooding in the country, which has undermined agricultural production, driven up food prices and further damaged supply chains already dislocated by COVID-19. By April 2021, inflation had risen to an all-time high of 363.1% year-on-year.

Economic challenges fuel political unrest

Accelerating inflation, scarce basic commodities and deteriorating living conditions sparked riots in multiple cities in February, prompting seven Sudanese states – East Darfur, North Darfur, South Darfur, West Darfur, North Kordofan, West Kordofan and Sennar – to impose curfews and declare a three-month state of emergency. Government offices were targeted in the protests, with rioters setting fire to facilities including the secretariat of West Kordofan State in Al-Fula and the headquarters of the local government and state radio and television in El Daein, the capital of East Darfur. While the transitional government sought to attribute the unrest to disgruntled supporters of Bashir and his dissolved National Congress Party (NCP), local media outlets described the unrest as the 'revolution of the hungry' and pointed to numerous previous demonstrations against deteriorating economic conditions. Underscoring the challenge for the authorities, some protesters demanded that Hamdok's government resign, while others called for 'a correction' in the course of the revolution.

Worsening socio-economic conditions present a clear risk to social stability, particularly given other reforms such as the removal of fuel subsidies, the lifting of electricity prices and the planned expansion of the tax base by 60%. In mid-June there were protests in the capital, Khartoum, following the government's decision to raise fuel prices by between 93% and 128%. Previous attempts to remove or even reduce subsidies, particularly on food staples, regularly sparked street protests and led successive governments to revoke planned reform. These issues have proved highly significant before: the protests that eventually led to the coup against Bashir were prompted by his decision to lift bread subsidies. Persistent instability, driven in part by subsidy reform, could potentially delay the transition programme. Burhan may cite unrest as a reason for the military to hold on to chairmanship of the SC.

External tensions could also be used as a pretext for delaying the completion of transition to civilian rule. In particular, there is a clear risk of continued volatility on the border with Ethiopia. There have been periodic tensions between the two states over the fertile al-Fashaga triangle for years, notwithstanding a compromise agreement in 2008. However, the situation deteriorated in late 2020 as a result of the conflict in Ethiopia between federal troops and forces loyal to the state authorities in Tigray. According to the UNHCR, between early November and mid-February more than 61,000 people – most of them Tigrayan – crossed the border into eastern Sudan, heightening risks of disputes over resources in the area. There has also been a series of armed clashes between Ethiopian and Sudanese troops along the border, while in early May Sudan claimed sovereignty over Ethiopia's Benishangul-Gumuz region, where the Grand Ethiopian Renaissance Dam (GERD) is being constructed. The GERD is a major source of tensions between Ethiopia and Sudan (as well as Egypt) and in April the Sudanese foreign-affairs minister wrote to UN Secretary-General António Guterres and the UN Security Council claiming that Ethiopia's failure to agree a legally binding arrangement on the dam threatens regional peace and stability. Sudan's letter also focused on the risks associated with Ethiopia's planned second filling of the dam in the third quarter of 2021, stating that this could undermine critical Sudanese water infrastructure.

In this sensitive domestic and international political environment, the military may seek to retain chairmanship of the SC well beyond the scheduled 21 months, or retake power from civilian leadership should political stability deteriorate. Any such move would be likely to lead to substantial protests – and a violent attempted crackdown by the military – while any elections held under military leadership would probably be neither free and fair, nor widely accepted by the international community. This would leave Sudan cut off from international funding once more, and heavily reliant on traditional Middle Eastern allies such as Saudi Arabia. At present, however, Sudan's general direction of travel does appear to be towards reform (albeit gradual) and re-engagement with the international community. The most likely scenario, therefore, is that parliamentary and presidential elections will take place, either in December 2022 or relatively soon thereafter, and that this will lead to a new political dispensation, since the long-dominant NCP has largely been marginalised.

However, democracy is not deeply rooted in Sudan. Any new civilian administration will face fierce resistance to its efforts to challenge the political and business interests of the military and of those who thrived under the Bashir regime. This will be all the more difficult given the relative lack of experience of the new political groups, suggesting that further periods of instability are highly likely.

Ethiopia's Conflict in Tigray
Will the centre hold?

The situation in Ethiopia may now be as serious as at any time since the end of the Italian occupation in April 1941, when British-led forces and Ethiopian fighters entered Addis Ababa to reinstate the emperor, Haile Selassie. This ended the threat of Italian colonialism and restored the sovereignty of the Ethiopian state. Ethiopia has faced many challenges since then. Among them were the invasion by Somalia (July 1977–March 1978), in which Ethiopia could have lost the eastern region of Ogaden, and the long war with Eritrea (September 1961–May 1991), after which Eritrea become an independent state in 1993. Challenging as these events were for the government in Addis Ababa, they did not threaten the integrity of the state itself. Yet just one day after the war in the northern region of Tigray erupted on 4 November 2020, senior US diplomats, including two former secretaries of state for African affairs, Johnnie Carson and Chester Crocker, warned that the conflict could lead to 'the fragmentation of Ethiopia', which would be 'the largest state collapse in modern history'.

Origins of the crisis

The root cause of the fighting in Tigray, and in other parts of Ethiopia, is the ethnic tension that has been brewing ever since the foundation of the Ethiopian empire by emperor Menelik II, who ruled from 1889 until 1913. Expansion from the traditional areas of imperial domination, the highlands of what European travellers termed 'Abyssinia', into the southern and eastern lowlands created modern Ethiopia. The country more than doubled in size, incorporating many ethnic and religious groups that had not previously been part of Ethiopia. In acquiring a strong Muslim minority, the empire was no longer predominantly Christian (according to a July 2021 estimate, 31.3% of the Ethiopian population is now Muslim). The largest ethnic groups were no longer Amhara or Tigrayan, but Oromo. The Oromo were treated as second-class citizens, and sometimes as slaves, until at least the 1930s. Tensions within the empire, together with the famine of 1973–74, led to the overthrow of emperor Haile Selassie in

1974. The military regime that replaced him was in turn overthrown by a combination of Tigrayan and Eritrean rebels in 1991. Eritrea became independent two years later, while the Tigrayans became the dominant force within the Ethiopian government. Under their visionary but authoritarian leader, Meles Zenawi, the Tigray People's Liberation Front (TPLF) took control of the country by dividing it into nine ethnic-based regional states and two federally administered city states in 1995. Through the Ethiopian People's Revolutionary Democratic Front (EPRDF), which they controlled, the Tigrayans managed to dominate politics, even though they made up no more than 7% of the population.

The system of ethnic federalism that the Tigrayans established gradually eroded as their ability to control regional parties broke down. The regions themselves became increasingly powerful with the creation of paramilitary forces answerable to the regional authorities and not the central government. Clashes between regions became more severe as ethnic groups campaigned for the return of neighbouring areas they claimed their ancestors had once controlled. Disputes over territorial control escalated across Ethiopia. By 2018, the Ethiopian populace had tired of rule by the Tigrayan minority, whom they regarded as corrupt and self-serving. Matters came to a head in 2018 when a series of demonstrations by Oromo youth (partly sparked by the mishandling of land issues around Addis Ababa) contributed to a change of government, and an end to Tigrayan domination. After protracted and bitter discussions in the EPRDF council, on 27 March 2018 Abiy Ahmed was elected chair of the ruling coalition following the surprise resignation of Hailemariam Desalegn. With that, Abiy became the prime minister of Ethiopia, a decision endorsed by parliament on 2 April 2018.

As prime minister, Abiy was unusual for two reasons. He could claim Oromo ancestry (this was the first time an Oromo had led the country), and he was neither Orthodox Christian nor Muslim (the two main religions). As an evangelical Christian, he believed his vision for his country was divinely inspired. His aim was to re-centralise control, but he has faced resistance from the ethnically based regions created by the Tigrayans. The conflicting land claims remained unresolved by the

Conflict in Tigray, 2020–21

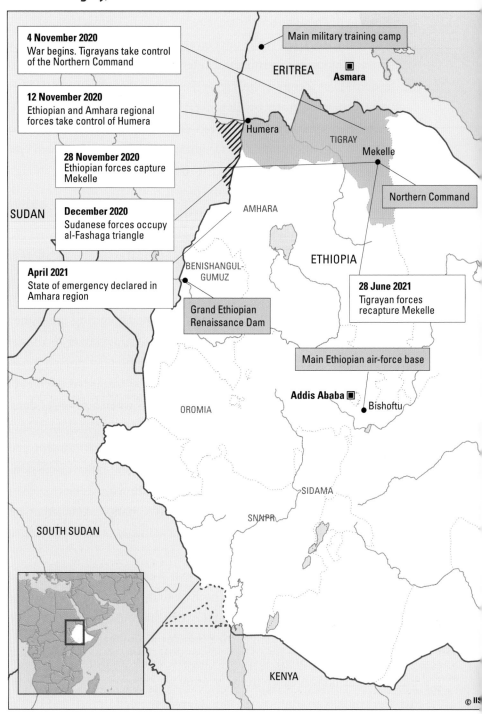

4 November 2020
War begins. Tigrayans take control of the Northern Command

12 November 2020
Ethiopian and Amhara regional forces take control of Humera

28 November 2020
Ethiopian forces capture Mekelle

December 2020
Sudanese forces occupy al-Fashaga triangle

April 2021
State of emergency declared in Amhara region

Main military training camp

ERITREA

Asmara

Humera

TIGRAY

Mekelle

Northern Command

SUDAN

AMHARA

ETHIOPIA

28 June 2021
Tigrayan forces recapture Mekelle

BENISHANGUL-GUMUZ

Grand Ethiopian Renaissance Dam

Main Ethiopian air-force base

Addis Ababa ■

Bishoftu

OROMIA

SIDAMA

SNNPR

SOUTH SUDAN

KENYA

© IIS

Strengths of armed forces in Tigray conflict, November 2020 to July 2021

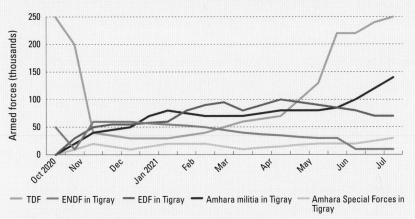

Source: Robert Wade. Approximate numbers based on analysis of open-source material.

➡ Tigray Defence Force (TDF)

This initially comprised Tigray Special Forces and the Tigray militia and totalled around 250,000 armed personnel. The number grew as the conflict began, then fell dramatically as the ENDF, Amhara forces and the EDF attacked. From February 2021, more Tigrayan civilians joined, spurred by atrocities and ethnic cleansing. By July, estimated TDF strength was 250,000–500,000. It is doubtful that Tigray could equip and sustain more than 250,000.

➡ Ethiopian National Defense Force (ENDF)

45,000–60,000 troops had long been deployed in Tigray, with some (but not their equipment) redeployed elsewhere after the 2018 Ethiopia–Eritrea agreement. As conflict began, many ENDF forces withdrew into Amhara and Eritrea, leaving around 10,000 in place to fight the Tigrayans. In mid-November 2020, ENDF forces re-entered Tigray with Amhara and Eritrean forces, but from January 2021 suffered losses to the Tigrayan insurgency. After a series of tactical defeats in June, and a government-declared ceasefire, the ENDF substantially withdrew from Tigray.

➡ Eritrean Defence Forces (EDF)

The EDF supported initial ENDF attempts to close the Sudanese border with Tigray. In mid-November 2020, EDF divisions conducted a series of offensives with the ENDF in Tigray. As the TDF strengthened its operations from May

2021, EDF forces withdrew north. By July 2021 most had withdrawn to a buffer zone on the Ethiopian side of the Ethiopia–Eritrea border and on the Ethiopia–Sudan border.

➡ Amhara militia

From 3–4 November 2020, the Amhara militia moved into western Tigray with Amhara Special Forces and the ENDF. Its presence grew as the Tigrayan population was forced out of western Tigray, enabling seizure of land and property. With TDF victories over the ENDF, and TDF declarations that it would recover western Tigray, in late June 2021 the Amhara militia was deployed to defend what it saw as reclaimed Amhara land.

➡ Amhara Special Forces (SF)

These were initially deployed, with the militia, into western and southern Tigray, with some moved to other areas in mid-December. Numbers fluctuated with further redeployment into the Oromo Special Zone of Amhara and Oromia proper in March and April 2021. Since TDF victories in June 2021, the Amhara SF have redeployed to the front in western and southern Tigray/northern Amhara.

Oromia SF / Afar SF / Somali SF / Sidama SF

There are rumours that Oromia SF provided reinforcements to ENDF units in early 2021. Since TDF victories in late June, some SF from other regions of Ethiopia have been deployed to Tigray.

change in government. The Amhara, for example, demanded the return of large areas of western Tigray. Amhara officials argued that lands amounting to about one-quarter of Tigray were taken from them during the years when the TPLF dominated the central government. Other ethnic groups made similar claims.

Abiy began a series of rapid reforms. He released political prisoners, freed journalists and lifted the state of emergency, while repairing relations with neighbouring countries. The most significant development was his ending of the 'no-war, no-peace' confrontation with Eritrea, which had continued since the border war of 1998–2000. His visit to the Eritrean capital, Asmara, in July 2018 was marked with jubilation and was followed by a reciprocal visit by Eritrean President Isaias Afwerki to Addis Ababa. Abiy was awarded the Nobel Peace Prize in 2019 for his efforts and hailed as a visionary leader. The Norwegian Nobel Committee expressed its hope that the prize would 'strengthen Prime Minister Abiy in his important work for peace and reconciliation'.

At the time of the peace deal with Eritrea – formally signed in Saudi Arabia on 16 September 2018 – few of the discussions behind it were made public. But the course of events since then suggests that two points underpinned the agreement. Firstly, the Ethiopian and Eritrean leaders saw the Tigrayans as their major obstacle to progress and agreed that their leadership should be eliminated. Abiy's hostility towards the Tigrayans was rooted in their long hold on power (1991–2018). They were widely seen as having taken more than their share of resources for their home region, and as dominating the Ethiopian military and security services. This made them too powerful to ignore. Abiy put in place a series of measures to weed them out of state structures. Isaias's hatred of the Tigrayans (and the TPLF in particular) was even more long-standing and visceral. The Eritrean People's Liberation Front (EPLF) that he led had both cooperated with, and fought against, the TPLF since the 1970s. Their differences were deep-seated, ideological and political. After the 2018 peace deal, it became increasingly evident that the leaders of Eritrea and Ethiopia were determined to rid themselves of the Tigrayans, who were entrenched in their northern stronghold along the Eritrea–Ethiopia border.

Secondly, the Ethiopia–Eritrea agreement was extended to incorporate Somali President Mohamed Abdullahi Mohamed (popularly known as 'Farmaajo'). The Eritrean and Ethiopian leaders drew the Somalis into what became a regional partnership designed to control the future of the Horn of Africa. In January 2020, Eritrea, Ethiopia and Somalia held their third trilateral meeting. They proposed forming a new regional bloc, referred to as the 'Horn of Africa Cooperation'. The new bloc could be linked to Saudi Arabia's wider ambition to extend its influence in the Horn of Africa – it announced the launch of the 'Council of the Arab and African States bordering the Red Sea and the Gulf of Aden' in January 2020. This new Arab–African alliance has eight members: Djibouti, Egypt, Eritrea, Jordan, Saudi Arabia, Somalia, Sudan and Yemen. The Council was created as a competitor to the other regional bloc, the Intergovernmental Authority on Development (IGAD), which Eritrea has long distrusted. The Tigrayans were not party to the wider regional relationship.

The outbreak of conflict

The groundwork for the war in Tigray was laid well in advance. On one side of the conflict was the Ethiopian government and its armed forces, Eritrea and Somalia, together with Amhara regional forces. In July 2020, Abiy made an unprecedented visit to Eritrea's main military training camp. In October 2020, Isaias visited the Ethiopian air-force headquarters. The Tigrayans responded to these apparent preparations for war by blocking the removal of heavy weapons from their border with Eritrea and refusing to allow a senior commander to be replaced in the Ethiopian National Defense Force (ENDF) Northern Command, which is based in the Tigrayan regional capital, Mekelle. To bolster its troops, Ethiopia withdrew some of its peacekeeping forces from Somalia in mid-November 2020, and from the disputed Sudanese border region known as the al-Fashaga triangle. Against the Ethiopian government and allied forces stood the Tigrayans, with many of the troops and weapons of the powerful Northern Command of the ENDF.

The war in Tigray erupted on 4 November 2020. The Tigrayans took control of the Northern Command, seizing weapons in Mekelle and attacking troops that did not defect to their side. Some Ethiopian soldiers fled into Eritrea, where they were looked after by local villagers until they could be rearmed and resupplied by the Eritrean government. Meanwhile, the Ethiopian air force attacked Tigrayan targets, while Ethiopian and Amhara forces launched a powerful offensive on the town of Humera, on the tripoint of Sudan, Eritrea and Ethiopia. It is the gateway to Sudan, and both Addis Ababa and Asmara were determined to cut the Tigrayans' ties to Sudan which could have acted as a conduit for supplies. Eritrean artillery and troops joined the battle, and the Tigrayans were soon forced out of the area. Eritrean troops crossed into Tigray from the north, while Ethiopian forces also attacked from the southeast and east. By 29 November, Mekelle was surrounded and within hours it had fallen. Abiy announced that its capture marked the end of the army's operations, tweeting that military operations in the Tigray region had been 'completed and ceased'.

This was a wildly inaccurate assessment. The Tigrayans had pulled their troops out of Mekelle and, after a period of disorganisation, began a powerful guerrilla campaign from Tigray's rugged hills and mountains. By April 2021, Abiy had to admit that far from the war being over, his forces were bogged down in 'difficult and tiresome' fighting on eight fronts. In March, after denying for months that any Eritreans were involved in the war, Abiy was also forced to concede that they were. The United States and the European Union repeatedly called for the Eritreans to withdraw and for unrestricted access to Tigray for humanitarian agencies. The federal authorities failed to maintain control of Tigray, as the TPLF retook Mekelle at the end of June 2021 and remained determined to drive all federal forces out of Tigray, and Eritrean forces back into that country.

International and humanitarian response

The first diplomatic attempts to end the war were made by the African Union (AU) a few weeks after the start of the conflict, with South African President Cyril Ramaphosa reaching an agreement with Ethiopian President Sahle-Work Zewde to appoint mediators in the conflict. Former president of Mozambique Joaquim Chissano, former president of Liberia Ellen Johnson Sirleaf and former president of South Africa

Kgalema Motlanthe were asked to act as special envoys of the AU entrusted to facilitate negotiations between parties to end the conflict in Ethiopia. The Ethiopian presidency is a significant but largely ceremonial position, and it almost immediately became apparent that it had overstepped the mark. Abiy swiftly rejected the mediation offer on 21 November 2020, saying that Ethiopia was engaged in an internal law-and-order operation that did not require outside assistance.

The international community has since attempted repeatedly to halt the Tigray war. The United Nations offered its good offices. The EU sent Finnish Foreign Minister and EU envoy Pekka Haavisto on two missions to the region. US President Joe Biden and Secretary of State Antony Blinken have made resolving the conflict a priority. The president sent a personal envoy, Senator Chris Coons, to Ethiopia in March 2021 in an attempt to bring about a ceasefire, but without any clear result. This was followed by the appointment of a special envoy for the Horn of Africa, Jeffrey Feltman, who was dispatched to the region in May 2021. The Feltman mission was asked to resolve the dispute over the Grand Ethiopian Renaissance Dam (GERD) on the Blue Nile – which is of grave concern to Egypt and Sudan – as well as the war in Tigray. So far none of these diplomatic interventions have borne fruit, but in late May Biden issued a statement making it clear that he was not prepared to let the matter rest and sent Feltman back to the region in another attempt to reach a settlement.

In the meantime, humanitarian agencies have had only limited access to Tigray. By March 2021, the Famine Early Warning Systems Network was reporting that much of the region was in a Phase 4 emergency – one level below famine. Some observers suggested that starvation was being used as a weapon of war. Large areas of northern Tigray are inaccessible because they are controlled by Eritrean troops, while large areas of central Tigray cannot be reached because of the fighting. Towards the end of April 2021, even the Ethiopian government-appointed interim authority in Tigray warned of the threat of famine on an 'unprecedented' scale. The UN reported that half of all Tigrayan women screened were acutely malnourished. In May, the US Agency for International Development (USAID) said that getting aid into the worst-hit areas was now a matter of life and death, while in early June, the UN World Food Programme estimated that 5.2 million people, equivalent to 91% of Tigray's population, needed emergency food assistance as a result of the conflict.

Reports have emerged of several atrocities and widespread sexual abuse. In April, Robert Mardini, director-general of the International Committee of the Red Cross (ICRC), said the organisation's staff in hospitals and clinics in the region were hearing first-hand of extreme sexual violence. 'Those reports are extremely horrific, very shocking … I haven't heard such terrible accounts for more than two decades in the humanitarian sector', said Mardini, who had closely followed the civil wars in Syria and Yemen when he headed the ICRC's Near and Middle East division in 2012–18.

Further conflicts facing Ethiopia

As the war entered its sixth month, voices of dissent began to be heard. The head of the Ethiopian Orthodox Church, Abune Mathias, denounced what he described as a 'genocide' against the people of Tigray. It was a message he had been attempting to deliver to the outside world for several months but complained that he was under house arrest and faced censorship. In May 2021, the *Addis Standard* published a lengthy opinion piece arguing that the time had come to open a dialogue with the Tigrayan resistance. At the time of writing there was no suggestion that this path would be taken, but while the war continued with little sign of reaching a conclusion, mainstream Ethiopians began to question Abiy's strategy.

On 21 June 2021, after two postponements, Ethiopians went to the polls in a general election. This passed off peacefully but was marred by the fact that the war in Tigray prevented the election being held there, while conflicts in other regions meant that about one-fifth of polling stations were closed. Voting was delayed in 110 of 547 constituencies. Abiy appeared set for a victory, since the two main Oromo parties had refused to participate after their leaders were imprisoned and supporters attacked.

Although the Tigray war is the most serious challenge that Abiy's government faces, it is by no means the only one. In September 2020, just before the war erupted, the International Organization for Migration

(IOM) reported that more than 1.8m Ethiopians were internally displaced. The assessment, carried out in 1,200 villages, put conflict as the primary reason for displacement (around 1.2m) followed by drought (just over 350,000).

Tigray is not the only region in which there has been unrest. Clashes between rival ethnic groups over land and resources frequently cause conflict. There have been clashes between the Amhara and the Oromo, and a state of emergency was declared in the Amhara region in April 2021. There has been fighting in the western region of Benishangul-Gumuz involving four ethnic groups. Tensions between the Afar and the Somalis have led to attempts to reach a negotiated settlement, but none of these issues have been resolved. Abiy's attempts to claw back control from the regions and re-establish a centralised state could spark off further clashes.

Concerns in the international community are now widely shared. The fear is that the war in Tigray will consume Ethiopian resources, eroding its strong recent record of economic growth. If the conflict cannot be ended, families in the rest of the vast country will become increasingly restive about their children being sent to die on a front line in a region many have never visited. Tensions with Egypt and Sudan over the Nile waters also pose real risks. Egyptian President Abdel Fattah Al-Sisi has threatened none too subtly that he might use force if Ethiopia refuses to reach a deal on the use of the Nile. Sudan and Egypt recently renewed their military ties. A dispute with Sudan over the al-Fashaga triangle, where there have already been clashes between Sudanese, Ethiopian and Eritrean forces, could also escalate.

Ethiopia has been an important Western ally in the Horn of Africa. With so many crises to contend with, and Abiy apparently driven by a visionary zeal, there are concerns that Ethiopia could erode as a state. Ethiopia's withdrawal of its forces to redeploy them to the conflict in Tigray has already undermined the war against Islamist groups in Somalia. Ethiopian peacekeepers in South Sudan have also been recalled. These are only the first developments that reduce regional stability. If the Ethiopian state proves incapable of ruling this huge multi-ethnic country, the consequences will be felt across the entire region.

France's African Intervention
Is Gulliver tied up in the Sahel?

In 2021 France continued to be the strongest force on the ground in the western and central Sahel, where it has been conducting its most important military operation in Africa since the end of the Algerian War in 1962. But it has found itself involved, somewhat unwillingly, in a situation that would have been unthinkable barely 15 years ago. Developing an effective strategy for conducting its operations will prove difficult for France.

From absence to a light footprint

France has remained a military power, albeit a reactive one, in sub-Saharan Africa since most of its colonies in the region gained independence in 1960. With permanent bases there and intervention forces on standby in France that the president of the Republic can commit whenever he wishes, the French army has become the rapid-reaction force of the continent. For this reason, France has been called 'Africa's policeman'. But its role has not extended to all its former colonies – only those that have signed bilateral defence agreements.

For a long time, though, this did not apply to the Sahel–Saharan strip due to the proximity of Algeria, which was hostile to any French military presence in the area, as well as to the initial choices of the states in this region. The only exception was the 1978–79 air raids from the French base in Dakar, Senegal, to support Mauritania against the rebel Polisario Front. Apart from this, France's most significant operation on the continent was in Chad, the first country allied to France that faced the threat of being overrun by a pro-Libyan organised rebellion. Responding to calls by several successive Chadian presidents, France intervened and fought almost continuously from 1968 to 1987. While French forces remained in Chad after this period, France scaled down its military activity in the region. It no longer wanted to intervene on the front line, preferring to support African or European Union operations 'from behind'.

When Nicolas Sarkozy was elected French president in 2007, sub-Saharan Africa ceased to be a strategic priority for France. Its bases in

Dakar and Abidjan, Côte d'Ivoire, were reduced to 'regional training hubs', and the end of the French military presence in Chad and thus in the Sahel was considered for 2014. The initial cause of France's return to the region was the arrival in northern Mali of the Algerian Salafist Group for Preaching and Combat (SGPC), which in 2007 became al-Qaeda in the Islamic Maghreb (AQIM). AQIM intended to fight France in the Sahel with assassinations and, above all, a major campaign to take Western hostages, in the heart of a region prone to instability from regular Tuareg autonomous revolts in Mali and Niger since independence, and growing trafficking of drugs and people.

As a consequence, Sarkozy decided to increase France's involvement in the region but with a 'light footprint'. In cooperation with the United States, France launched a 'Sahel plan' in 2009 to help local armies fight non-state armed groups. A small, discreet special-forces unit, called 'Sabre', was added to try to free hostages by force when possible. Only Mauritania and, to a lesser extent, Niger really cooperated with France and, in the first case, managed to effectively resist the jihadist movement. Relations with Mali remained difficult and ambiguous, with Bamako reproaching France for its part in the 2011 military intervention in Libya against the regime of Muammar Gadhafi and especially for its sympathy for Tuareg autonomy. Paris in turn was exasperated by Mali's failure to tackle AQIM.

The extent of Mali's weakness finally became apparent in early 2012 when the National Movement for the Liberation of Azawad (MNLA) drove the Malian Armed Forces (FAMa) out of northern Mali and took over the main towns there. Criticising the government's inaction and corruption, a group of soldiers staged a coup on 22 March 2012 that ousted the president, Amadou Toumani Touré, and further paralysed the country. A coalition of forces – AQIM, Ansar Dine (a Tuareg jihadist movement created by Iyad Ag Ghali) and the Movement for Oneness and Jihad in West Africa (MUJAO), a Malian movement of mixed ethnicities from the Gao region – took advantage of the situation to turn against the MNLA and took its chance to take control of the north of the country.

Conflict in the Sahel and French intervention

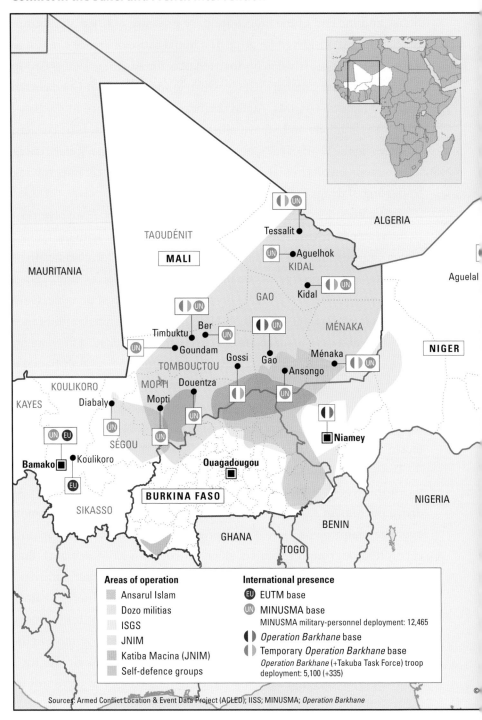

Areas of operation

- Ansarul Islam
- Dozo militias
- ISGS
- JNIM
- Katiba Macina (JNIM)
- Self-defence groups

International presence

- **EU** EUTM base
- **UN** MINUSMA base
  MINUSMA military-personnel deployment: 12,465
- ◖ *Operation Barkhane* base
- ◖ Temporary *Operation Barkhane* base
  Operation Barkhane (+Takuba Task Force) troop
  deployment: 5,100 (+335)

Sources: Armed Conflict Location & Event Data Project (ACLED); IISS; MINUSMA; *Operation Barkhane*

France in the Sahel: key decision points

● **January 2013–July 2014**
French-led *Operation Serval* to combat Islamic militants in Mali

● **August 2014**
French-led *Operation Barkhane* is launched with wider mandate for operations across the Sahel. Initial deployment of 3,000 troops

● **April 2017**
G5 Sahel Joint Force (FC-G5S) comprising forces from Burkina Faso, Chad, Mali, Mauritania and Niger is created, with headquarters in Bamako. French deployment increases to 4,500 troops

● **January 2020**
Pau summit: France and the G5 Sahel countries agree a four-pillar strategy. French deployment increases to 5,100 troops

● **March 2020**
French-led Takuba Task Force of 2,000 European and African soldiers under *Operation Barkhane* is launched

● **February 2021**
France–G5 Sahel summit in N'Djamena focuses on reinforcing local armed forces, governance and development aid

● **10 June 2021**
French President Emmanuel Macron announces the end of *Operation Barkhane* over the next two years

Conflict-related fatalities in Burkina Faso, Mali and Niger, 2012–20

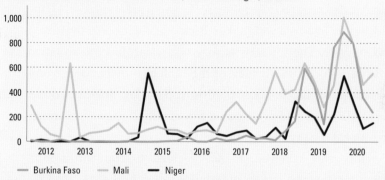

Source: ACLED. Event types: battles; violence against civilians; explosions/remote violence

French attitudes towards military intervention in Mali

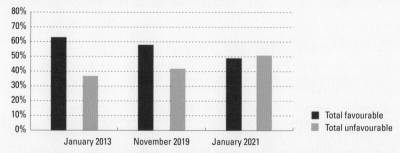

Source: IFOP for *Le Point*. Conducted by self-administered online questionnaire of a representative sample of 1,021 French people aged 18 and over on 12–13 January 2013; 1,004 people on 18–19 November 2019; and 1,004 people on 5–6 January 2021

The unexpected start of the war

Considering the threat that this situation could pose to both neigh-bouring and allied states, and perhaps to Europe, Sarkozy's successor as president, François Hollande (elected in 2012), decided to increase France's involvement much more than his predecessor had. The French plan was to support the Economic Community of West African States (ECOWAS) and its African-led International Support Mission to Mali (AFISMA), which would protect the south of Mali while the FAMa were being reconstituted with the help of the EU Training Mission in Mali (EUTM–Mali). This plan was practically accepted when a jihadist offen-sive in central Mali to take over the city of Mopti changed the context radically once again.

Faced with general helplessness and at the request of the Malian interim government, on 11 January 2013 Hollande decided to engage French forces in direct large ground combat against the enemy for the first time in Africa since 1980. *Operation Serval* was a great success. All the towns held by the jihadists were taken back and their bases destroyed by the end of May. The military victory was clear, but the situation remained uncertain. To the dismay of the Malian provisional govern-ment and indeed all the political parties in Bamako, France had not fought the MNLA, and had even joined forces with it to gain control of the city of Kidal at the expense of the FAMa.

Once victory was achieved, France decided to maintain a mili-tary presence in Mali and to join with other forces in the so-called G5 Sahel countries (Burkina Faso, Chad, Mauritania and Niger) to set up *Operation Barkhane* in August 2014. Its objective was to contain the activ-ity of armed groups, known as 'armed terrorist groups', at a low threat level until the local armed forces could carry out this mission themselves within the framework of a restored state authority. It was a risky bet. France's resources in the Sahel were reduced to half those of *Operation Serval*; France was simultaneously engaged in several other operations around the world; and it continued to reduce its defence budget and human resources. These reduced forces could not prevent the return of enemy armed organisations.

The other three foreign forces operating in Mali also had many shortcomings. Despite considerable resources, the United Nations Multidimensional Integrated Stabilization Mission in Mali (MINUSMA), established in 2013, has no direct effect on the enemy groups. EUTM–Mali only provides training to the FAMa, which is essential but superficial compared to the scale of what needs to be done. The G5 Sahel Joint Force (FC-G5S), created in 2017 to coordinate the action of local armies around the border areas with a common headquarters in Bamako and dedicated battalions, is above all a coalition of weaknesses that has little impact on the enemy. In the absence of strong political will, the local forces most at risk in Burkina Faso, Mali and Niger were hindered by structural problems and progressed less quickly than the jihadist groups.

Since 2015 it has not been possible to halt the deterioration of the situation. Despite the Algiers Agreement of 2015 between the government in Bamako and 14 armed groups, the conflict in northern Mali against the separatists remained frozen. New jihadist organisations emerged in new spaces, such as the Macina Liberation Front (FLM) in central Mali, which eventually joined forces with AQIM, Ansar Dine and Al Mourabitoun to form the Group to Support Islam and Muslims (JNIM) in 2017. The Islamic State in the Greater Sahara (ISGS) also emerged and expanded into the 'three borders' (Burkina Faso, Mali and Niger) area of the weak countries and particularly into northern Burkina Faso with another jihadist group, Ansarul Islam. All these organisations succeeded in establishing themselves on a growing scale, both by force and by offering alternative administration and justice. As a result, self-defence militias have also multiplied, sometimes with the support of the governments of Mali and Burkina Faso but without any real oversight. They are fuelled by the growing socio-ethnic tensions and make the situation worse through their exactions.

2019 was a black year for the conflict. The number of violent incidents doubled compared to the previous year. Local armies suffered heavy blows from jihadist groups and found themselves on the verge of collapse. At the same time, the image of France, accused simultaneously of helplessness and association with corrupt regimes or controversial armed organisations, deteriorated. However, it took the death of 13 French soldiers in a helicopter collision on 25 November 2019 to prompt a strong reaction from Paris.

Breaking the deadlock

Leaders of the G5 Sahel countries met Hollande's successor, President Emmanuel Macron, at a summit held in Pau, France, in January 2020 and noted the deterioration of the situation, the weariness of public opinion in France and the Sahel, and the de facto failure of the adopted strategy. However, the idea of a military withdrawal seemed impossible, as the French force had become the keystone of the entire security system in the region. Without *Operation Barkhane*, which was by far the most powerful military force in action, it was likely that jihadist organisations would overcome the armies of Burkina Faso, Mali and Niger, with consequences that are difficult to imagine. At the same time, *Barkhane* could not function without the logistical support of MINUSMA and the material assistance of US and European allies. From a diplomatic point of view, after having sought to share the Sahelian burden with its European partners, it seemed that backing out was not an option. France found itself hampered by the multiple links it had forged with multiple players, unable to leave but also unable to continue with the same course of action.

The Pau summit decided that operations should continue along the same strategy, but with greater efforts and resources. A new structure, the 'Coalition for the Sahel', was created to better coordinate the efforts of all stakeholders in the region. The coalition was based on four pillars: fighting against terrorism; strengthening the capabilities of the G5 Sahel states' security forces; supporting the return of the state and administrations in the region; and providing development assistance.

In the first pillar, France committed an additional 600 soldiers – bringing the total forces in *Operation Barkhane* to 5,100, twice the number initially deployed – as well as new technical resources such as three armed *Reaper* drones. Paris also asked local states to commit more of their armed forces on the ground in cooperation with French forces. As a result of this effort, pressure on the enemy grew much stronger, albeit at the cost of the lives of 13 more French soldiers by January 2021. The ISGS, the priority enemy group, itself in conflict with the JNIM, did not manage to carry out any major attacks during the year following the Pau summit and its influence was considerably reduced. At the same time, important JNIM cadres were killed in 2020, including Abdelmalek Droukdel, the long-standing leader of AQIM, in June.

However, the second pillar of the new coalition's strategy, the build-up of local forces, has produced results much more slowly, despite the establishment of a new joint headquarters for *Barkhane* and the FC-G5S as well as increased resources and scope of action of the EUTM operation. While operations conducted in close cooperation and coordination with French forces have been effective, local forces remained as fragile as ever when they faced the enemy alone. Worse still, reports of abuses by the national armed forces of Burkina Faso, Mali and Niger against their own populations rose to their highest levels in 2020. For the first time the number of such abuses exceeded those perpetrated by the jihadists. They have been carried out with impunity and no accountability. Effective control of the terrain and protection of the population – the cornerstones of success in such operations – are therefore not improving. Two-thirds of Mali's territory is outside Bamako's authority. It is shared between armed groups that signed the Algiers Agreement and the JNIM, which is becoming more and more established in the centre of the country. The Burkinabe state no longer controls the north of the country against the ISGS and Ansarul Islam. Niger and Chad are in a better situation but are under pressure on several fronts from enemies that are not otherwise targeted by France, such as Boko Haram.

Barkhane is sand

France has weakened the hold of armed groups on the Sahel, but remains bogged down, particularly as the structural instability of the region has sometimes created new opponents. The past year has been full of unexpected and mostly negative events. On 9 August 2020, the ISGS murdered six French nationals in Kouré, near Niamey, the Nigerien capital, an area supposedly controlled by the authorities. Above all, difficult political transitions have resulted from a sometimes-contested democratic process, or a more violent event such as the coup in Mali in August 2020 that ousted President Ibrahim Boubacar Keïta to install a transitional government. Some of these political changes have also led to changes in local governments' relationships with armed groups and initiation of dialogue in Mali with Iyad Ag Ghali and Amadou Koufa, the leader of the FLM, despite French reluctance. In October 2020, Bamako's release of 200 JNIM prisoners as a sign of goodwill was very badly perceived by Paris despite the corresponding release of Sophie Petronin, the last French hostage in the region.

One year after the Pau summit, a France–G5 Sahel summit in N'Djamena in February 2021 reviewed the progress of the war. Contrary to what many had thought, France is not reducing its military effort. It is also carrying the development of the Takuba Task Force, which was formed by a French initiative in 2018 and became operational in 2020 under the command of *Operation Barkhane* to assist local forces run by teams of special forces from several European countries. It currently comprises 2,000 African and European troops, from the Czech Republic, France, Estonia and Sweden. Given that local military units seem to perform well when supported by foreign forces, it is hoped that this will put additional pressure on the enemy groups, starting in Mali. EU countries are quite heavily involved in MINUSMA and the EUTM, but as members of Takuba some seem willing to engage in combat as well. This is a major development among European countries. The arrival in February 2021 of a Chadian battalion to reinforce the FC-G5S in the three borders area is also an important development. Unfortunately, this unit carried out abuses of the local population that immediately offset its undeniable military contribution.

The N'Djamena summit focused on the other pillars – reinforcement of local armed forces, governance and aid for economic development – policy areas where France has little influence. After being put on hold following the coup in Bamako and the COVID-19 pandemic, the EUTM–Mali operation resumed at the end of 2020 and underwent significant expansion to extend training to the FC-G5S and eventually to Mali's neighbouring countries. However, the handover of responsibility for local security to local armies, referred to as 'Sahélisation', is at a stand-still largely because it does not address the structural problems of these armies to any great extent.

It is not possible to re-establish the authority of the state and its governance, nor to make a real contribution to economic development, if the population is not protected by firmly established security forces on the ground. However, in order to ensure that these local units are stronger than the enemy in the long term – that is, without the direct support of foreign forces – a properly staffed and well-paid administration is essential. An effective justice system that punishes unethical behaviour and monitors the use of resources to ensure transparency is also needed. But these essential preconditions of military success are also sensitive. By trying to achieve them, France risks accusations that it is violating Mali's sovereignty.

France is currently fully engaged in a conflict that is costing more than €1 billion a year in civilian and military expenses, and has claimed the lives of 57 soldiers since 2013. Yet it does not control the parameters of this conflict. For the first time since the start of the operation in Mali, polls carried out in January 2021 indicated that a majority of French people oppose its extension, one year before the 2022 presidential election, and at a time when France, like many other countries, is experiencing a serious health and economic crisis. The deaths of more French soldiers will accelerate the erosion of public opinion. Every alleged or real blunder – such as the January 2021 airstrike on the Malian village of Bounty, in which France is accused of causing the deaths of more than 20 civilians – will tarnish its reputation. Every unexpected political event, such as the death of President Idriss Déby in Chad in April 2021, or the latest *coup d'état* in Mali on 24 May 2021, when Colonel Assimi Goïta took power, will create new uncertainty.

The French army is more than ever the strongest force on the ground, but it is a vulnerable force. It is unlikely that *Operation Barkhane* can continue in this way beyond the next two years, but there is no question of withdrawing. On 10 June, Macron announced the gradual transformation of *Operation Barkhane* over the next two years. The ground forces will be withdrawn from the most critical zone in Mali. But France will maintain its capacity to put pressure on the enemy through air and special forces. It will also retain the ability to intervene again as it first did in January 2013. This will be a more economical way for France to fight a war that is likely to be long and to undergo further changes.

CHAPTER 11

Latin America

BERMUDA

MEXICO

BAHAMAS

CUBA

DOMINICAN
REPUBLIC

HAITI

BELIZE   JAMAICA   PUERTO RICO

HONDURAS

GUATEMALA   DOMINICA

EL SALVADOR   NICARAGUA   BARBADOS

COSTA RICA   TRINIDAD AND TOBAGO

PANAMA   VENEZUELA

GUYANA   FRENCH GUIANA

COLOMBIA   SURINAME

ECUADOR

PERU   BRAZIL

BOLIVIA

PARAGUAY

CHILE

URUGUAY

ARGENTINA

Falkland Islands   ©IISS

South Georgia

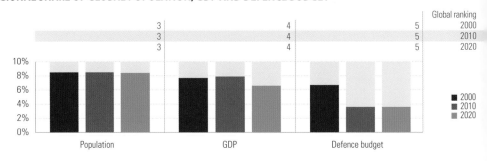

Drivers of Strategic Change

REGIONAL SHARE OF GLOBAL POPULATION, GDP AND DEFENCE BUDGET

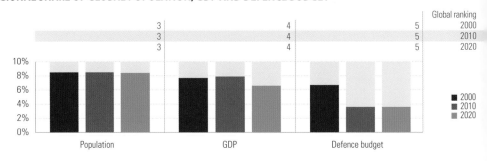

		Global ranking	
			2000
			2010
			2020

	Population	GDP	Defence budget
2000	3	4	5
2010	3	4	5
2020	3	4	5

POPULATION

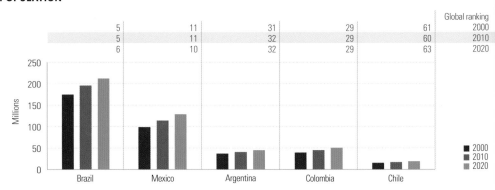

	Brazil	Mexico	Argentina	Colombia	Chile	Global ranking
2000	5	11	31	29	61	
2010	5	11	32	29	60	
2020	6	10	32	29	63	

AGE STRUCTURE
(Percentage of national population)

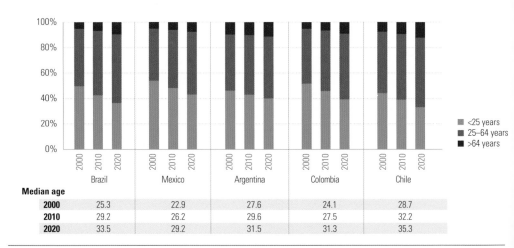

■ <25 years
■ 25–64 years
■ >64 years

Median age	Brazil	Mexico	Argentina	Colombia	Chile
2000	25.3	22.9	27.6	24.1	28.7
2010	29.2	26.2	29.6	27.5	32.2
2020	33.5	29.2	31.5	31.3	35.3

This region exhibits more continuity than any other. Most countries show little variation in their relative level of major power resources over the past 20 years. One exception is defence budgets: many have fallen in absolute as well as relative terms, with Colombia the major exception. Despite this, Brazil's armed forces, as well as Colombia's, have increased significantly.

GDP
(Constant 2010 US dollars)

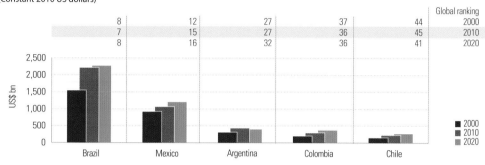

					Global ranking
8	12	27	37	44	2000
7	15	27	36	45	2010
8	16	32	36	41	2020

US$ bn — 2,500 / 2,000 / 1,500 / 1,000 / 500 / 0

Brazil · Mexico · Argentina · Colombia · Chile

■ 2000 ■ 2010 ■ 2020

GDP PER CAPITA
(Constant 2010 US dollars)

					Global ranking
59	58	61	83	56	2000
60	67	65	86	55	2010
65	68	72	84	54	2020

US$ — 14,000 / 11,200 / 8,400 / 5,600 / 2,800 / 0

Brazil · Mexico · Argentina · Colombia · Chile

■ 2000 ■ 2010 ■ 2020

DEFENCE BUDGET
(Constant 2015 US dollars)

ACTIVE MILITARY PERSONNEL

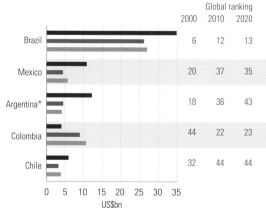

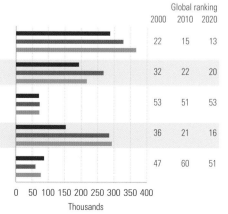

	Global ranking		
	2000	2010	2020
Brazil	6	12	13
Mexico	20	37	35
Argentina*	18	36	43
Colombia	44	22	23
Chile	32	44	44

0 5 10 15 20 25 30 35
US$bn

	Global ranking		
	2000	2010	2020
Brazil	22	15	13
Mexico	32	22	20
Argentina*	53	51	53
Colombia	36	21	16
Chile	47	60	51

0 50 100 150 200 250 300 350 400
Thousands

* 2000 defence budget value for Argentina is an estimate, and may be distorted by high inflation rates.

■ 2000 ■ 2010 ■ 2020

For explanation of drivers and sources, see page 9

HUMAN DEVELOPMENT INDEX (HDI)
(Score between 0 and 1, where 0 denotes a low level of development and 1 a high level of development)

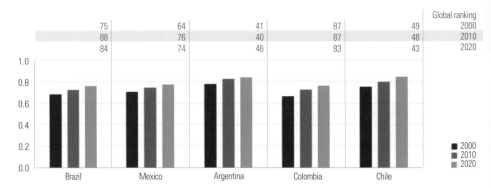

					Global ranking
75	64	41	87	49	2000
88	76	40	87	48	2010
84	74	46	83	43	2020

■ 2000
■ 2010
■ 2020

POLITICAL SYSTEM
(Score between 0 and 100, where 0 denotes no political freedom and 100 fully free)

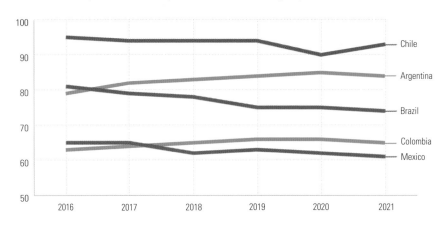

TRUST IN GOVERNMENT
(Average level of trust)

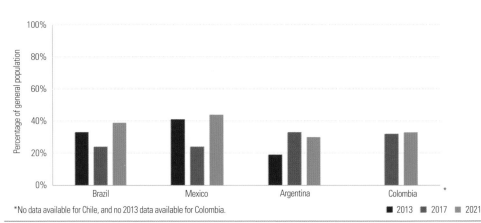

*No data available for Chile, and no 2013 data available for Colombia.

■ 2013 ■ 2017 ■ 2021

For explanation of drivers and sources, see page 9

2020–21 Review

Latin America will arguably emerge as the region most severely affected by the COVID-19 pandemic. A combination of factors – First-World disease burdens (particularly major COVID-19 risk factors, such as diabetes and hypertension), underfunded health systems, high levels of labour precarity, weak state capacity to enforce sanitary measures such as lockdowns, and underdeveloped social safety nets – created a perfect storm of vulnerabilities. These were exacerbated during a deadly second wave of the pandemic, by which time few governments could afford to return to the strict economic shutdowns implemented during the first wave.

Latin America also faced the world's steepest economic contraction, with the IMF estimating that regional real GDP fell by 7% in 2020. The hardest-hit countries were those that rely on tourism and trade, such as those in the Caribbean, while Mexico and Peru suffered most among major economies. The region also faced considerable reversals in socio-economic development. In March 2021, the UN's Economic Commission for Latin America and the Caribbean (ECLAC, or CEPAL in Spanish) estimated that the number of poor people in the region swelled to 209 million in 2020, a poverty rate of 33.7% of the population. This was an increase of 22m compared to 2019, resulting in levels of poverty not seen in the last two decades. ECLAC's report also observed deterioration in income inequality and labour participation, particularly among women.

Despite the region's weak social-protection mechanisms, most governments made extraordinary efforts to prevent further hardship. ECLAC estimated that nearly half the region's population benefitted from these emergency measures, which included direct income support for households and businesses, financial support for health systems, as well as liquidity support in the form of capital injections, asset purchases, debt assumptions and guarantees. According to the IMF, in the year March 2020–21 direct-income-support measures alone reached over 8% of 2020 GDP in Brazil and Chile, over 7% of GDP in Peru and over 4% of GDP for the region as a whole. Mexico was an outlier in this respect, spending a mere 0.7% of GDP, which may partly explain why its economic contraction was more severe than those of its peers. Overall, however, the scale of the region's fiscal measures was well in excess of those implemented during the 2008–09 global financial crisis and much larger than what might have been expected given the fiscal space available.

The downside to providing this support was that the region's economies suffered considerable fiscal deterioration between 2019 and 2020, with the combination of extra spending and loss of revenues resulting in many countries adding over 10% of GDP to their debt levels. Even in Mexico, with its paltry spending, debt stock worsened by over 7% of GDP. Even though the region's economy is set for a relatively strong rebound in 2021–22, making up for the fiscal losses during the pandemic will take much longer and may force countries with smaller fiscal space to undertake consolidation measures that could impact longer-term growth.

Second and third waves

As with many other parts of the world including the United States and Europe, Latin America endured a far deadlier second wave of the COVID-19 pandemic in the latter part of 2020 and early 2021. Due to more limited fiscal resources and lockdown fatigue, this proved much more difficult to contain than the first wave. Mexico was one of the earliest countries in the region to experience a surge in cases and deaths in late 2020, which peaked in late January 2021. Meanwhile, the emergence of a new P.1 variant, first identified in Manaus, Brazil, caused a massive spike in that country in March–April, with more than 4,000 daily deaths recorded during its peak. The response of Jair Bolsonaro's government was widely seen as ineffective, with state governments scrambling to take measures in the absence of federal support. The greater transmissibility of the P.1 variant, as well as its ability to evade previously acquired immunity, resulted in a spike in cases across South America, with almost all major countries reporting record daily deaths during April–May (in contrast to Mexico, where cases and deaths declined continually after the January peak).

The second wave coincided with the region's vaccination campaigns, which had mixed success. Chile has been notable as one of the global leaders in vaccine uptake, with 55.9% of the population receiving at least one dose by the end of May, a higher proportion than the US and all European countries except for the United Kingdom. However, there was some controversy over its reliance on less-effective Chinese vaccines, which was believed to be the reason why its daily new cases continued to surge in April–May. On the positive side, the vaccines were effective at keeping hospitalisations and deaths lower than during the first wave. Large gaps in vaccine uptake were also evident: while most middle-income countries in the region had provided at least 15–25% of their populations with at least one dose by June 2021, this figure fell to below 10% or even 5% among the lower-income countries, which will rely mostly on global vaccination schemes like COVAX (which has so far been notably under target) and donations from wealthy countries.

The political impact of the pandemic varied. In most countries, the public was largely forgiving of its leaders even in the face of poor public-health responses. Most of the region's most unpopular leaders, such as Ecuador's Lenín Moreno and Chilean President Sebastián Piñera, were highly unpopular before the pandemic, while the popularity of others – like Colombian President Iván Duque – slumped for non-COVID-19 reasons. Some, like Mexico's Andrés Manuel López Obrador, escaped largely unscathed despite widely publicised policy failures. By and large, the pandemic does not appear to have left a lasting political impact, with voters being far more sensitive to bad economic policies and leaders' misdeeds.

There were two major exceptions. Argentina's Alberto Fernández suffered a sustained decline in popularity from the start of the pandemic. But Brazil's Bolsonaro could prove to be the pandemic's biggest political victim, given the severe slump in his popularity during the country's deadly second wave, which took the death toll up to 500,000 by mid-June. This led to an outbreak of large-scale protests, particularly during May and June 2021. Although Bolsonaro's supporters also staged numerous rallies in support of the president, his declining popularity and the outbreak of social unrest triggered a notable shift in support to his likely main 2022 election rival, Luiz Inácio 'Lula' da Silva of the Workers' Party. Lula has been ahead of Bolsonaro in every major national poll since mid-March and has a commanding lead of as much as 10–20 percentage points in some of the more recent ones.

2019 protests leave their mark on 2020

Latin America entered the pandemic with lingering political discontent, which in 2019 had led to some of the largest protests in the region's history. This discontent continued to manifest itself in numerous ways, notably in anti-establishment voting tendencies in elections during 2020–21.

Peru experienced some of the most dramatic political changes in the region. In September 2020, president Martín Vizcarra was subject to a 'motion of permanent moral incapacity' by Congress over his alleged cover-up and obstruction of justice in a case involving irregular payments to an entertainer (known as the 'Richard Swing affair'). Had it passed, this would have removed Vizcarra from office. He survived the vote, but barely a month later, in October, he faced a similar motion following revelations of illicit payments made to him by various construction companies during his time as regional governor of Moquegua. He renounced the presidency on 9 November, and was succeeded by the president of Congress, Manuel Merino. Many saw Merino's accession as unconstitutional (and even as a *coup d'état* in disguise). It triggered a wave of violent protests that forced Merino to step down just five days later, on 15 November. His replacement by Francisco Sagasti managed to defuse popular unrest (not without a few minor scandals) and lay the groundwork for the 2021 elections.

In Peru's elections on 11 April 2021, a socialist rural teacher, Pedro Castillo, and long-time right-wing contender, Keiko Fujimori, earned the right to face each other in a run-off on 6 June. The two populists from opposite sides of the spectrum fought a very close race, with Castillo emerging narrowly victorious in the run-off with 50.1% of the vote against Fujimori's 49.9%. Castillo's surprise victory (he was a virtual unknown in Peruvian politics until his participation in a 2017 teachers' strike) was seen as a rebuke to the country's free-market policies pursued by successive governments, despite Peru's record as one of Latin America's top economic performers in the twenty-first century.

Chile had been hit by massive protests in 2019, culminating in Piñera's agreement to hold a national plebiscite on whether to rewrite the country's constitution, which dates from the Pinochet dictatorship. Originally scheduled for April 2020, the plebiscite was postponed until 25 October 2020 due to the pandemic, with voters overwhelmingly approving a Constitutional Convention with directly elected members. The election to this on 15–16 May 2021 resulted in a major victory by (mostly left-leaning and anti-establishment) independent candidates, with centre-right candidates from the ruling coalition winning barely one-fifth of the votes. The country's centre-left establishment candidates also fared poorly, coming in fourth. Given that the Constitutional Convention's rules state that a two-thirds majority will be needed to approve changes, the centre-right is essentially incapable of vetoing any radical proposals from the Convention's independents. As with Peru's election, the constitutional election in Chile was widely seen as a rejection of the country's free-market economic model, particularly by younger voters.

Colombia weathered the pandemic storm relatively well compared to many of its neighbours. But on 28 April 2021, massive protests erupted over a proposed tax reform by Duque's government that would have increased income taxes and VAT on basic goods (by up to 2% of GDP in additional revenue) in order to finance some of the pandemic emergency income-support measures on a permanent basis. The tax reform was widely seen as regressive. The protests quickly intensified as a result of excessive force by police and security forces, including numerous accusations of human-rights violations (around 60 deaths and more than 100 disappearances, according to several non-governmental organisations). The latter also contributed to the protests continuing even after Duque withdrew the tax reform on 2 May. Protests continued into June and resulted in the intervention of a delegation from the Inter-American Commission on Human Rights. Duque's popularity, which had been generally high throughout 2020, dropped dramatically, with potential consequences for elections scheduled for May 2022.

Aside from COVID-19-related protests, numerous scandals contributed to the declining popularity of the Bolsonaro government in Brazil. The most notable was the resignation of the three heads of the armed forces (army, navy and air force) on 30 March 2021 in response to a Bolsonaro cabinet reshuffle that resulted in the removal of the minister of defence, Gen. Fernando Azevedo e Silva. The mass resignation was widely interpreted as a demonstration of the independence of the armed forces and a rebuke to Bolsonaro's increasing militarisation of his government. A further cabinet scandal occurred on 23 June with the resignation of the environmental minister, Ricardo Salles, following allegations that he had obstructed a probe into illegal logging. Bolsonaro's poor environmental record also put him at odds with the US administration of Joe Biden, with many Bolsonaro critics urging the US president to put more pressure on enforcing environmental standards, particularly for the Amazon. The US and Brazil are currently undergoing closed-door negotiations for a potential Amazon-conservation deal.

In Venezuela, President Nicolás Maduro consolidated his rule following failed attempts by the opposition, led by Juan Guaidó, to dislodge him from power. This coincided with a decline in active US support for Guaidó in the final year of the Trump presidency. Guaidó's faltering position was made worse by the legislative elections on 6 December 2020, which the opposition mostly boycotted because of complaints over irregularities. The ruling coalition (led by the United Socialist Party of Venezuela–PSUV) won a comfortable victory, reclaiming the National Assembly following a humiliating 2015 loss. Although the election was widely condemned internationally, it prompted the European Union to cease recognising Guaidó as the legitimate president from 6 January, although the US and most members of the Lima Group (composed of most Latin American countries plus Canada working to achieve a diplomatic solution to Venezuela's political crisis) continued to do so. Early statements from the Biden administration suggested that the US would continue to put political and economic pressure on the Maduro regime.

Any prospect of his removal would likely require a much wider domestic political mobilisation against him. But the failure of protests in 2019–20 suggested even this is no guarantee of success.

Maduro's consolidation following a period of instability was broadly mirrored by another Venezuelan ally, Nicaragua, where Daniel Ortega entrenched himself further in power following a major political crisis and violent protests in 2018–19. The government undertook numerous arrests of opposition leaders, which will call into question the fairness of elections scheduled for November 2021. In neighbouring El Salvador, democracy was also eroded by the strongman tactics of President Nayib Bukele, whose heavy-handed public-security strategy and intimidation of opponents were widely condemned, yet have nevertheless made him extremely popular. His party, New Ideas, won the February 2021 legislative elections by a landslide, securing a two-thirds majority along with its allies. This power enabled Bukele to dismiss the constitutional judges of the Supreme Court as well as the attorney general on 3 May 2021, a move some labelled a 'self-coup'. Despite being gripped by COVID-19, Costa Rica and Guatemala experienced protests in October and November 2020 respectively, in the former case over a controversial IMF support programme and in the latter due to proposed budget cuts on healthcare and the judiciary.

Among the major Latin American countries, Mexico was by far the most stable, with López Obrador enjoying high levels of popularity despite pandemic mishandling and an economy that had already stagnated in 2019 well before COVID-19 hit. The country also suffered from continuous drug-cartel-related violence that left annual homicides during 2020 at 35,484, only slightly lower than in 2019. Criticism of the pandemic response gradually dissipated in 2021 once the second wave receded and the vaccination campaign picked up steam in February, leaving the ruling Morena party in a strong position ahead of the June midterm elections. The election results were a mixed success for Morena, which lost its coveted supermajority in Congress (necessary to pass constitutional reforms) but won sweeping victories in state elections, consolidating itself as a national political force outside its traditional left-wing bastion in the capital. Despite the congressional losses denting its near-total political hegemony, Morena will remain dominant in Mexican politics.

In Bolivia, the left-wing Movement Toward Socialism (MAS) party returned to power following the dramatic resignation of Evo Morales in 2019 over a contested election result, which many supporters described as a *coup d'état*. New elections were held on 18 October 2020 in which Luis Arce (a former finance minister who was the architect of Morales's economic policies) won a comfortable victory. Numerous members of the government in power following Morales's resignation are currently under investigation for sedition, including the interim president Jeanine Áñez.

Not a US priority

The Biden administration's initial policies suggested that, while some of its predecessor's more hawkish actions and rhetoric would not be repeated, the overall US stance towards Latin America would involve more continuity than change. There were, for example, few signs that Biden would roll back sanctions imposed against Venezuela or return to the Obama-era rapprochement with Cuba, despite promising to do so. The administration's tough stance against Nicaragua, and labelling of Ortega a 'dictator', also signalled continued tensions with the region's less-democratic left-wing regimes. By and large, however, Latin America did not appear to be a US foreign-policy priority and as a result may suffer from a degree of neglect made worse by the significant deterioration of US soft power in the region that resulted from Trump's hostility, particularly towards Mexico and Central America as well as Hispanics in the US.

US neglect would leave the door open to Chinese influence in the region. Excluding Mexico, China is now Latin America's largest trading partner and has committed major direct investment (Latin America accounts for over one-fifth of China's stock of foreign direct investment abroad) and financial investment (China lends more to the region than the World Bank, Inter-American Development Bank and Development Bank of South America combined). The pandemic has further helped expand China's soft power in the region through vaccine diplomacy.

A second pink tide?

The leftist resurgence in recent years has drawn comparisons with the so-called 'Pink Tide', when left-wing governments swept into office in the late 1990s and early 2000s. The left's victories in otherwise staunchly centre-right countries like Mexico and Peru is evidence of new inroads, while a further Lula victory in Brazil would leave an even larger share of Latin America's population under left-wing rule than at the height of the previous Pink Tide.

As such, the history of previous leftist governments may offer some hints at what is in store for the region over the remainder of the decade. While countries like Bolivia and Brazil were successful (at least initially) in combining pro-poor with pro-growth policies, many failed to address long-standing governance and rule-of-law issues that would come back to haunt them. Weak commitment to democracy and highly person-alistic styles of leadership enabled many of the Pink Tide's leaders to extend their mandates, often through constitutional change, with more extreme cases like Venezuela and Nicaragua eventually becoming out-right authoritarian. Bolivia's return to MAS rule under Arce, however, may offer a template for continuity of policies without the movement's leader (Morales, in the case of Bolivia). On the other hand, Ecuador's post-Rafael Correa debacle, in which Correa's successor, Moreno, made an abrupt (and rather disastrous) economic-policy shift to the right, may incentivise successful left-wing leaders to keep holding the reins of power for as long as possible.

Latin America's unique combination of inequalities, which are defined not just by income but also by geography and race, suggest that the task of achieving long-term political stability and economic growth is a daunting one. The inability to ride on a wave of booming commod-ity prices suggests that policies to improve domestic productivity and higher-value-added production will be more conducive to growth. However, such policies will require much more extensive structural reforms in areas such as education and labour markets, as well as fiscal reforms to raise taxes and thus revenue for infrastructure and social development. Many of these reforms may face stiff opposition from the public or elites, and will prove politically challenging. Chronic failures in fighting corruption and criminality will also weigh on public attitudes. Ultimately, the region's success in building more robust middle classes may prove to be the most important driver of change, as they become more demanding than their predecessors and more critical of traditional economic agendas and political establishments.

The Crisis of Mass Emigration from Venezuela
How severe and what can be done?

Major global refugee crises are almost always preceded by large-scale conflict. The Second World War, the partition of India, Bangladesh's War of Independence, the Soviet–Afghan war and, more recently, the Syrian civil war all sparked massive emigration. Estimates of displacement range from five million, in the case of the Soviet–Afghan war, to tens of millions as a result of the Second World War.

Venezuela now features on this list of the world's largest migratory outflows. According to the United Nations High Commissioner for Refugees (UNHCR), as of April 2021 there were 5.4m Venezuelan migrants and refugees abroad.[1] Other studies estimate the true figure could be up to 6m. Yet although this exodus represents a large share of Venezuela's population, which stood at around 30m in 2015, it has occurred in the absence of major civil conflict. There have been bouts of social unrest under the presidencies of Hugo Chávez, who was in office from 1999 until his death from cancer in 2013, as well as his anointed successor, President Nicolás Maduro, who has been in power since then. But while the country has grappled with deep-seated political and economic crises, it has not been at war, either internally or with external actors.

Why is this happening and how has the situation evolved?
The current situation began as an outward flow of economic migrants leaving the country voluntarily, but over time has developed into a full-blown refugee crisis. Some upper- and middle-class Venezuelans began to leave in relatively small numbers after Chávez's first election victory in December 1998 on pledges to redistribute income. Departures picked up in 2002, following a failed coup attempt and the purge of the state oil

---

1 Defining the mass displacement of Venezuelans is difficult. This essay refers to both migrants and refugees interchangeably, but acknowledges that the term 'migrant' is more of a catch-all category that includes 'economic migrants' – mainly referring to people who left in the early 2000s (primarily to North America and Spain). As time went on, the migratory flow shifted; the term 'refugee' became increasingly appropriate, referring to people who have fled on foot or by public transport, with no assets.

company, Petróleos de Venezuela (PDVSA), which sparked the emigration of many engineers in particular. Nationalisations of key economic sectors in 2007 also fuelled an increase in outward migration that same year. A study conducted by the Central University of Venezuela found that nearly 1.5m Venezuelans left the country between 1999 and 2014, of whom 90% had undergraduate degrees and 40% had either master's degrees or PhDs. Many of these people already had family overseas, including in Colombia, Mexico, Panama and the United States, where they also settled.

The scale of the crisis has escalated. While 1.5m Venezuelans left the country in 1999–2014, around another 4m did so in the six years that followed. Deteriorating political and economic conditions explained the acceleration. While Chávez had become less tolerant of criticism during his latter years in office, there was a marked shift towards a more outright form of autocratic government once Maduro took office. Elections had not been conducted in a particularly free and fair manner under Chávez, but under Maduro the scope for any sort of opposition was even further eroded. Constitutional amendments inflated the power of the executive, which facilitated crackdowns on the media, the total politicisation of the judiciary and the arrest of senior members of the opposition. The near-complete destruction of the system of checks and balances on the president persuaded many people that there was little prospect of genuine political change via electoral means. Even when the opposition managed to win a majority in parliamentary elections in 2015, Maduro created a new legislative body (reserved for representatives of his own party, the United Socialist Party of Venezuela–PSUV) that rendered the official National Assembly null and void. People who sided with the opposition feared losing their jobs, particularly in the public sector. When people took to the streets in frustration, as they did in large numbers during April–July 2017, the security forces' response was heavy handed, with over 160 people reported to have died during the protests. Many Venezuelans left the country as a result of the increasingly repressive political environment.

Venezuelan refugee and migrant flows to Latin America and the Caribbean

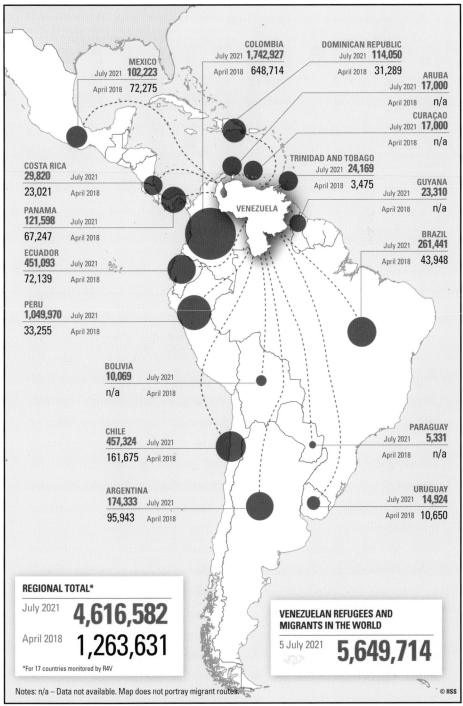

COLOMBIA
July 2021 **1,742,927**
April 2018 **648,714**

DOMINICAN REPUBLIC
July 2021 **114,050**
April 2018 **31,289**

ARUBA
July 2021 **17,000**
April 2018 n/a

CURAÇAO
July 2021 **17,000**
April 2018 n/a

MEXICO
July 2021 **102,223**
April 2018 **72,275**

COSTA RICA
29,820 July 2021
23,021 April 2018

TRINIDAD AND TOBAGO
July 2021 **24,169**
April 2018 **3,475**

GUYANA
July 2021 **23,310**
April 2018 n/a

PANAMA
121,598 July 2021
67,247 April 2018

VENEZUELA

ECUADOR
451,093 July 2021
72,139 April 2018

BRAZIL
July 2021 **261,441**
April 2018 **43,948**

PERU
1,049,970 July 2021
33,255 April 2018

BOLIVIA
10,069 July 2021
n/a April 2018

CHILE
457,324 July 2021
161,675 April 2018

PARAGUAY
July 2021 **5,331**
April 2018 n/a

ARGENTINA
174,333 July 2021
95,943 April 2018

URUGUAY
July 2021 **14,924**
April 2018 **10,650**

REGIONAL TOTAL*
July 2021 **4,616,582**
April 2018 **1,263,631**
*For 17 countries monitored by R4V

VENEZUELAN REFUGEES AND MIGRANTS IN THE WORLD
5 July 2021 **5,649,714**

Notes: n/a – Data not available. Map does not portray migrant routes.
© IISS

Source: R4V (Regional Interagency Coordination Platform for Refugees and Migrants of Venezuela, jointly led by UNHCR and IOM). R4V Venezuelan population registered by the R4V. Reporting dates and frequency vary from country to country

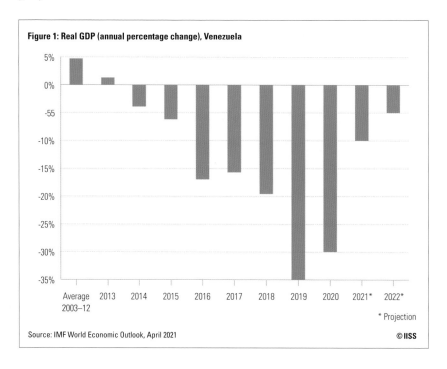

Figure 1: Real GDP (annual percentage change), Venezuela

Source: IMF World Economic Outlook, April 2021

Economic factors have also driven Venezuelans to flee the country. Economic performance had been volatile in the late 2000s and early 2010s, fluctuating in line with oil prices. A series of distortionary policies that had been introduced under Chávez, including capital controls and money-printing to cover fiscal excesses, had not been particularly troublesome when oil prices were high. However, when these began to fall abruptly in 2015, the economy went into freefall. Oil accounts for virtually all the country's export earnings, as well as a significant share of budget revenue. The nationalisations that had occurred under Chávez meant that there was very little inward investment, leaving the authorities with a large financing gap. China initially lent large sums of money to help close this gap but became reluctant to extend further finance due to Venezuela's increasingly patchy repayment record.

In order to address shortages of foreign exchange, the government tightened capital controls. It became increasingly difficult and time-consuming for individuals and businesses to access US dollars for overseas travel, import purchases and profit remittances. The ramping up of money-printing in the context of a fixed exchange rate led to a massive black market for foreign exchange. Abundant domestic liquidity quickly lifted inflation, which went from double to triple digits in 2015, before reaching quadruple digits in 2017, at which point hyperinflation took hold. Unable to defend the bolivar peg, the authorities devalued several times, even knocking five zeroes from the local currency in 2018.

The hyperinflation–devaluation spiral has decimated savings, pensions and bolivar-denominated wages. A growing number of transactions are conducted in US dollars, creating a major divide between people who have access to foreign currency (mainly courtesy of overseas relatives) and those who do not. The government has regularly hiked minimum wages, but nowhere near fast enough to keep pace with price increases, including for staple items such as food and medicines. These items are almost entirely imported and are prone to both chronic shortages and soaring prices. A Venezuelan think tank, CENDA, which tracks food prices, calculated that as of May 2021, it cost the equivalent of 92 minimum-wage salaries to feed a family. In October 2020, a joint report from the UN World Food Programme and Food and Agriculture Organization found that over 9m Venezuelans were facing acute food insecurity, with a further 17m people on the cusp of acute food insecurity.

This humanitarian crisis has been a major factor driving people from Venezuela. It has also affected the type of people who are leaving, how they are travelling and their destinations. Whereas initial migrants were mostly skilled workers who ended up in Europe or the US, virtually all those who leave now are refugees travelling either on public transport or on foot, often from their homes in Venezuela. This generates huge issues within the region, placing massive social and financial pressures on countries that have recorded large numbers of Venezuelan arrivals.

Colombia is the main destination for Venezuelan refugees. Most of the 1.7m who moved there have arrived since 2015. In absolute terms, Bogotá remains the main destination, but the border town of Cúcuta has also borne the brunt of arrivals, with social-service provision becoming increasingly strained given the town's much smaller population and thus naturally fewer resources. Those who arrive in poor health or with no money tend to remain in border areas. Although Brazil is not particularly an end destination for a large number of Venezuelan refugees, with only around 260,000 in the country as of May 2021, some border areas have become saturated, particularly in Roraima State. This has prompted the authorities to launch a relocation scheme to move Venezuelan migrants to other, less overburdened, areas of the country.

Other countries that have received large numbers of Venezuelans include Peru, with over 1m, and Ecuador and Chile, both with 400,000–500,000. The Caribbean often receives less attention, as the numbers of Venezuelan arrivals are much lower. But as a share of the local population their impact on these islands is huge. With many migrants travelling by boat, the islands geographically closest to the Venezuelan coast (Aruba, Curaçao, and Trinidad and Tobago) have received the most arrivals. The Dominican Republic has also received large numbers (it is further away, but accessible via air, meaning that most Venezuelan refugees arrived during earlier migratory waves). Local-government estimates indicate that there are around 17,000 Venezuelans in Aruba and the same again in Curaçao in addition to over 24,000 in Trinidad and Tobago. This represents 16% of the population in Aruba, 11% in Curaçao and 9% in Trinidad and Tobago.

Impact of the pandemic on the migration crisis

The COVID-19 pandemic has had a clear impact on the refugee crisis and will continue to shape it, at least in the near term. Conditions became more difficult, both for Venezuelans leaving the country and for the countries receiving them. Initial reports that the pandemic impelled Venezuelans to return home on the basis that they could not find work abroad were short-lived and the outward flow of refugees quickly resumed. However, Brazil and Colombia shut their official land-border crossings when the pandemic arrived. These currently remain largely shut, which means that virtually all Venezuelans who flee the country do so illegally, leaving them vulnerable to extortion and abuse during the journey. People leaving their homes with money and personal belongings often end up crossing the border with nothing. COVID-19-related closures of sanitary facilities have made the journey increasingly perilous. Fieldwork conducted along key routes by the Human Rights Center at the Andrés Bello Catholic University has shown that fear of catching the virus has made residents less willing to help those travelling.

The pandemic has also affected how host countries deal with the continued rise in Venezuelan refugees. It is difficult to make any kind of accurate assessment about the prevalence of COVID-19 in Venezuela, given minimal testing facilities and a heavily censored media, which hampers reporting of conditions within hospitals. However, there is a widespread consensus that infection levels are high, reflecting poor sanitary conditions and dilapidated healthcare provision. Host countries have voiced concerns that arrivals would bring the virus with them, setting up quarantine centres to protect against this (which, somewhat ironically, appear to have been vectors for spreading the virus because of cramped living conditions).

This has also affected public opinion in host countries, including Brazil, Colombia, Ecuador, Peru and the Caribbean. There was already a significant degree of scepticism from some locals, who feared that large numbers of refugees would increase crime rates, intensify competition for already-scarce jobs and place pressure on social-services provision. The pandemic has only increased this, with growing reports of xenophobic attacks against Venezuelans. As Venezuela's neighbours begin to roll out COVID-19 vaccination programmes, governments face the thorny issue of how (and when) to vaccinate refugees, particularly as the programme has yet to commence in any meaningful way in Venezuela.

Part of the difficulty in dealing with the exodus of Venezuelan refugees is that some of them are arriving without papers. For several years it has been notoriously difficult to get a passport, or other official documentation such as birth and marriage certificates, issued in Venezuela. The main reason is a critical shortage of paper and ink in the country. Reports indicate that large bribes are required to acquire these documents. But given the increasingly precarious financial position of many people planning to leave the country, some refugees are leaving with no papers. Some end up trading their documents with traffickers and many Venezuelans who have left in recent years now have expired passports, which are impossible to renew from abroad.

Why is this important and how will the situation evolve?

There is no near-term solution to the current crisis. In order to persuade Venezuelans to return home in large numbers, there would have to be a fundamental improvement in underlying political and economic conditions in Venezuela, probably involving a change in government. This appears unlikely. There had been signs in 2019 that the hitherto fragmented opposition might finally dislodge the Maduro regime, helped by growing international support for the opposition leader Juan Guaidó. But this has not yet occurred and Guaidó has become more marginalised over the past year. With most of the opposition boycotting the December 2020 parliamentary election, Maduro has an even more comprehensive grip on power. While power struggles within the ruling regime continue, there is little chance of an imminent government collapse.

Neither is there any prospect of better economic conditions. There has been some speculation that the recent rise in oil prices might help the economy recover from a severe, multi-year recession. However, this appears unlikely, as the drop in oil-production volumes is currently offsetting the increase in prices, implying little near-term respite for the beleaguered economy. Job creation remains scarce, hyperinflation is rising further and the local currency is becoming increasingly worthless.

This means that the outward flow of Venezuelan refugees will continue. The issue of how host countries deal with the large and growing numbers of Venezuelans will therefore become increasingly urgent over the next 12 months. Some countries are attempting to put up barriers in order to dissuade refugees from trying to enter, keeping land borders closed and stepping up efforts to deport illegal immigrants. The government in Chile launched the Colchane Plan in February 2021, which has increased the military's presence in northern Chile (where many migrants enter the country illegally) and authorised the expulsion of migrants. Ecuador and Peru have also introduced more restrictive measures, offering Venezuelans the opportunity to remain in the country if they have a 'humanitarian' visa, but also making a passport and supporting documentation a prerequisite, which has effectively barred access for most people. Amnesty International has criticised efforts by

Trinidad and Tobago to criminalise Venezuelans by claiming that they present a potential health risk and stepping up efforts to identify and deport immigrants.

In other countries, by contrast, there have been some notable efforts to grant legal status to Venezuelan immigrants. In February 2021, Colombian President Iván Duque unveiled a new programme – the Temporary Protected Status for Venezuelan Migrants – that aims to regularise Venezuelan refugees, allowing them to work in the country and access public services for a ten-year period. This was followed in March by the announcement that the US will provide temporary protected status to Venezuelans in the country for 18 months, although the large numbers of Venezuelans with pending asylum cases in US courts who had been deported to Mexico earlier in the year do not appear to qualify. While there are fewer Venezuelans in Costa Rica, in November 2020 the Costa Rican government unveiled a special 'complementary' asylum category that applies to Venezuelans (as well as Cubans and Nicaraguans).

The position of the international community will be important in determining how host countries respond to the refugee crisis. The Colombian government's decision was at least partly driven by the hope that a more supportive stance towards migrants would help it access the international funding that it needs to deal with the crisis. Countries hosting large numbers of Venezuelan arrivals have so far only secured a fraction of the funds they need to provide basic services to refugees. Central government budgets are under growing strain as a result of the COVID-19 pandemic, which cut revenue and raised spending virtually everywhere in 2020, prompting gaping fiscal deficits.

International organisations are accelerating efforts to encourage other countries to pursue regularisation plans. Organisations such as the UNHCR, the UN International Organization for Migration, the Organization of American States and Human Rights Watch are coordinating a campaign to increase awareness within the region that Venezuelans are not economic migrants leaving out of choice, but refugees forced to flee the country by a humanitarian emergency that is putting their lives at risk. International organisations will increase pressure on governments to recognise that this is a long-term situation that requires a long-term policy response.

There will also be greater efforts to increase awareness of the positive impact that Venezuelan migrants can bring to host economies. Although people are fleeing in very difficult conditions and with few personal belongings, they bring skills. Over 40% of Venezuelans in Ecuador have some form of technical qualification; over 50% in other countries have university degrees. This could provide benefits to local economies if harnessed effectively. International organisations and governments will also increase efforts to access donor finance to deal with the crisis. This will include measures designed to leverage private-sector support.

Huge challenges lie ahead. With the Venezuelan regime appearing firmly entrenched and the economy remaining in a critical state, there is little prospect that the outflow of migrants will cease. As Venezuelans will account for a growing share of the population in host countries, governments will come under greater pressure to respond. Encouraged by Colombia's policy, other countries are likely to introduce new programmes to regularise the status of Venezuelan refugees, particularly if external funding is more readily available. Implementation will be critical. Authorities will need to think flexibly about how to deal with issues such as lack of official documentation, and coordinate with the private sector to facilitate access to other services not provided by the state (including financial services and utilities). In conclusion, little can be done to prevent continued mass emigration from Venezuela, but actions can be taken to alleviate its impact on the region, as well as on refugees themselves.

Given the importance of human capital for economic productivity, this exodus will affect Venezuela too, deepening the economic crisis and reinforcing existing problems in many sectors, notably healthcare. The longer-term impact may be even more significant. Any successor administration to the Maduro regime would face enormous challenges in rebuilding the country. Venezuela would need skilled workers across the spectrum of economic sectors to implement a rescue plan. But many Venezuelans would already be settled abroad and unlikely to return. The current exodus will therefore have a major impact on Venezuela's longer-term prospects.

Alberto Fernández's Challenges in a Pandemic World
Can Argentina put populism and defaults behind it?

In December 2019, Alberto Fernández, leader of Frente de Todos (Front for All) – a coalition of Partido Justicialista (PJ – known as the Peronist party), Cristina Fernández de Kirchner's left-wing faction and Frente Renovador (Renewal Front) – took office as president of Argentina. He had defeated Mauricio Macri, leader of Juntos por el Cambio (Together for Change), a coalition of right-wing and centrist parties, in elections two months earlier with 48% of the vote.

Fernández's victory was mainly the result of his moderate political viewpoint, which attracted an electorate (middle-income urban households in particular) that was disappointed with the Macri administration but rejected the return of Kirchner, who had been president from 2007 until 2015. At the start of his four-year term, Fernández enjoyed considerable political capital: the ruling Frente de Todos had a majority in the Senate and a near-majority in the Chamber of Deputies (the lower house). However, this political capital has gradually eroded. After a difficult year dealing with the challenges of the COVID-19 pandemic, and facing midterm elections in November 2021, his administration may find it harder to govern.

Fernández's initial challenges

Fernández faced three major challenges at the start of his presidency. Firstly, this was the first time in a Peronist government that the main political leader (in this case, Kirchner) did not also lead the country. She had stood down as presidential candidate in May 2019 and chosen Fernández to run in order to improve Frente de Todos's electoral chances. However, clashes between Fernández and Kirchner were expected to emerge, and there were doubts as to whether Fernández could maintain his moderate policies.

Secondly, the economy had suffered a decade of stagnation, high inflation and high poverty rates. Public debt had reached unsustainable levels, and the government was forced to renegotiate it with private creditors and the IMF following the Macri government's default on private debt in August 2019. Thirdly, Fernández expected to become a regional leader in Latin America by using his moderate political style to achieve more balanced relations with the United States government, while also strengthening economic ties with China and Russia. However, the outbreak of COVID-19 in March 2020 disrupted these plans. He now faces even greater challenges after the first year of the pandemic.

Against the background of the difficult economic and social circumstances he inherited on taking office, Fernández's main priority was to restore economic growth and reduce inflation and poverty. He did not announce a comprehensive economic programme, only key priorities that were consistent with the goals of most Peronist governments: recovery of domestic consumption (through a rise of real salaries) and of production (mainly through import substitution); promotion of certain industries (such as energy, oil and mining, and information technology); and expansion of social-welfare programmes. He also aimed to promote a broad social agreement to achieve short-term macroeconomic stability. But during his first months in office, it was clear that, while he would keep some of the policies associated with Peronist governments, he would also seek to achieve fiscal equilibrium in the medium term and pursue negotiations with debt creditors, in contrast to the policies of the Kirchner administration. However, the pandemic forced a shift in priorities and a postponement of Fernández's initial goals. The overriding policy issue was now to tackle the health and economic crisis.

The lockdown and global slump hit the economy hard. In 2020, real GDP decreased by 9.9%, mainly driven by a 13.1% contraction of private consumption. Inflation climbed to 36.1%, while real wages contracted by 3% (falling for the third consecutive year) and poverty rose to 42% of the urban population. The primary deficit climbed from 1% of GDP in 2019 to 6.5% in 2020. Though nearly all countries were hit by the pandemic, the decline in social and economic conditions was largely interpreted in Argentina as a consequence of Fernández's mismanagement.

Political opponents, and parts of the electorate, criticised Fernández for his lack of an economic programme, for interventionist policies (such as exchange controls and export bans), for the long lockdown (which lasted eight months in the Metropolitan Area of Buenos Aires during 2020) and for the delayed COVID-19 vaccination programme. By the end of June 2021, Argentina's vaccination programme compared unfavourably to those of other Latin American countries: just 36.5% of the population had received at least one dose, compared to 65.3% in Uruguay and 66.3% in Chile. Kirchner's supporters, by contrast, criticised the fiscal-adjustment measures implemented by Minister of Economy Martín Guzmán (despite the crisis, in the first quarter of 2021 the fiscal deficit was the lowest for six years), and the government's less interventionist approach: though Fernández has implemented export bans and price controls, these were either temporary or more limited than those of the Kirchner administration.

When the country was hit by a second wave of COVID-19 in April 2021, the tensions between Fernández's faction (with Guzmán as its main figure) and Kirchner's supporters escalated. Fearing defeat in the November 2021 midterm elections due to a sharp decline in the government's popularity (from a peak of 67% in April 2020 to 26% in May 2021), Kirchner's faction began to press Fernández to adopt more interventionist policies and fiscal expansionary measures to reverse the decline in real incomes. Fernández partly yielded to this pressure, and in the early months of 2021 Kirchner's faction gained power within the government, weakening Guzmán's position. This internal crisis reflects the difficulties that Fernández faces as head of a diverse coalition that includes a strong political figure like Kirchner in a leading role.

A successful debt restructuring

The major economic success during Fernández's first year in office was the public-debt swap, the third debt restructuring of the last 30 years. Public debt had climbed to US$323.1 billion (89.4% of GDP) in 2019. The debt-restructuring proposal involved US$66.5bn that had been issued under foreign law and whose service was burdensome in 2020–25. In August 2020, Guzmán reached a deal with bondholders. Debt relief was achieved through the reduction of interest rates and the lengthening of the maturity profile, especially for interest payments.

By May 2021, the government still had two debt renegotiations ahead. One was with the IMF, with which it had to renegotiate a loan of US$57.1bn, of which around US$44bn was disbursed in 2018–19, in the framework of the Stand-By Arrangement that Macri had signed with the IMF in 2018. The other was a renegotiation with the Paris Club of a debt worth US$2.4bn (for a loan that had been restructured in 2014). In June, Guzmán announced that the government had achieved a 'time bridge' until March 2022 with the Paris Club: it will pay just US$430 million before that date to avert default and will seek a debt-restructuring deal in the meantime. The government aims to sign an Extended Fund Facility with the IMF for ten years, with a grace period of four years and an economic programme that includes gradual convergence to fiscal balance, given that a drastic reduction from the current high imbalance would imply significant contractionary measures (such as major cuts in public expenditure or tax hikes) that would undermine consumption and investment, damaging the expected post-pandemic recovery. The deal would be signed in the last quarter of 2021, after the midterm elections.

The need for fiscal reform

Debt restructuring, and a new IMF deal, should help to ease financial constraints in the medium term. But in the absence of a comprehensive economic programme that includes structural reforms and enjoys the support of the main political coalitions, the relief will be temporary and the country will face recurrent financial crises, as it has over the past four decades. Indeed, Argentina's fiscal problems have worsened. During periods of economic expansion, government revenues and expenditure both grow. During recessions, revenues decrease but important budget items such as social expenditure and wages are rigid and do not fall at the same rate, boosting governments' financing needs that are subsequently covered with new debt or monetary expansion. In the last three decades, primary government expenditure rose from 19% of GDP to 34%, driven by transfers to the private sector (which include social transfers and subsidies to energy and transport companies), social security and wages. Pension expenditure rose in the last decade as former workers who had not made the minimum contributions to receive a pension were included in the system. Social transfers also showed a strong expansion due to the implementation of universal social-protection programmes. Subsidies to energy and transport companies aimed to prevent tariff hikes and so improve real incomes.

On the revenue side, the ratio of tax (including federal and provincial taxes) to national income grew from 24.7% in 2004 to 30.6% in 2020. Tax pressure in Argentina is among the highest in Latin America: according to an indicator of Equivalent Fiscal Pressure prepared by the Organisation for Economic Co-operation and Development (OECD), in 2018 this index reached 31% in Argentina, placing it in the top five Latin American countries and above the regional average (25%). Though tax pressure is lower than that of some developed countries, high rates of tax evasion mean that the tax burden on those in the formal economy is comparatively higher. The informal economy is estimated to be worth up to one-third of GDP.

A sustainable fiscal programme should include tax reform that simplifies the system and reduces the burden of taxes on production and consumption. A pension reform will be more challenging, as it will have to take into account the high rate of informal labour. The prospect of reducing social transfers will depend on sustained and stable economic growth, and on the implementation of policies (including education, healthcare and basic infrastructure) that reduce structural poverty.

Currency crises are linked to fiscal imbalances. Monetary financing of the budget deficit has led to decades of high inflation that eroded confidence in the Argentine peso and hindered the development of domestic capital markets. The government's financial needs must therefore be covered by foreign debt. When a negative external shock or a domestic confidence crisis drives capital outflow, the country faces a new financial crisis. Given that budget imbalances are at the root of Argentina's debt crises, there is no guarantee that crises will not recur without deep fiscal reforms.

China and Russia expand their influence

Fernández has taken a pragmatic approach to foreign policy, distinct both from that of the Kirchner administrations – which maintained a distant relationship with the US while strengthening ties with China and Russia – and from that of the Macri government, which sought to enhance ties with the US. Fernández has aimed to become a regional leader and a reliable interlocutor for Latin America with the main global players.

However, the COVID-19 pandemic forced the president to postpone his regional aspirations to focus on the domestic crisis, while the wider foreign-policy agenda was mainly overrun by health issues. Like the rest of Latin America, Argentina was left behind in the vaccine race and turned to China and Russia for help. Fernández took advantage of good relations between Kirchner and Russian President Vladimir Putin to guarantee the country's access to Russia's Sputnik V vaccine. Argentina was the first country in Latin America to start using it (in December 2020) and will also be one of the first to produce it in the region. The government also signed an agreement with China to buy the Sinopharm vaccine. By the end of June 2021, Sputnik V and Sinopharm accounted for 61.7% of the 25m vaccine doses that Argentina had received.

Since the beginning of the century, successive Argentine administrations have sought to deepen ties with China and Russia. Even the Macri government, which was aligned with the White House, signed agreements with them. Given the growing role of China as a destination for Argentina's agro-industry products, exporters and farmers, who play a key role in the country's politics, support the strengthening of commercial relations with the Asian giant. Russia is also an important outlet for agricultural products such as meat and fruits.

China's importance as a partner for Argentina has grown steadily in the last two decades. China's share of Argentine exports grew from 3% in 2000 to 10% in 2020 – becoming Argentina's second-largest trade partner after Brazil, and the biggest for primary products, representing 15.5% of the total – and is also a significant foreign investor in strategic industries such as oil and natural gas, mining, renewable energy and transport. Its role as a source of finance has also increased in the last decade: in 2009, the Central Bank of Argentina signed a currency-swap agreement, since renewed, with the People's Bank of China, which was key to strengthening the stock of international reserves during the financial crisis of 2018–19. In February 2021, the Argentine government announced that it was working with China on a medium-term investment plan worth US$30bn for infrastructure, energy and transport projects. In January, China's President Xi Jinping had told Fernández that he was willing to build a closer relationship with Argentina. The government has already shown interest in joining China's Belt and Road Initiative.

Ties with Russia enjoyed a boost during Kirchner's presidency and have continued to strengthen since then. In 2018, president Macri signed cooperation agreements in areas such as agro-industry, transport, energy, science and aerospace. In 2019, Argentina's National Commission for Space Activities (CONAE) and Russia's State Corporation for Space Activities (Roscosmos) signed a cooperation agreement on peaceful space exploration. The Argentine government has also shown interest in strengthening military cooperation with Russia, seeking to modernise the Argentine armed forces' equipment (which had become obsolete in previous decades due to disinvestment) and revive the domestic military industry, which had played a significant regional role in the past century. Given that Argentina has historically been an ally of Western powers, the Argentine armed forces have expressed concerns about this development – although they also welcome the possibility of updating their equipment.

Given his centrist position, Fernández will seek to ensure that stronger ties with China and Russia do not interfere with bilateral relations with the US. In April 2021, two key US officials – Commander of the US Southern Command Craig Faller and Senior Director for the Western Hemisphere of the National Security Council Juan Sebastián González – visited Argentina. This was interpreted as an attempt by the Biden administration to strengthen ties with Fernández's government and so offset the increasing role of China and Russia in the region. US support will be key to Argentina achieving a favourable agreement with the IMF.

The US government has expressed its concern about the growing presence of China and Russia in key strategic industries. In 2012, China signed a cooperation agreement with CONAE, which included the construction of a space station in Neuquén province. The station's goals are space observation and exploration, as well as satellite tracking and control, although the US government has raised concerns about possible military purposes. President Donald Trump's veto in 2018 of Chinese and Russian projects to construct nuclear power stations in Argentina led to their cancellation, reflecting the influence that the US still has on domestic politics, especially by virtue of its weight in international financial institutions and credit markets.

Future challenges

The post-pandemic political scene will be shaped mainly by the results of the November 2021 midterm elections. Although Frente de Todos has a core of supporters that represents around one-third of the electorate, the ruling coalition will probably lose the centrist portion of the electorate that was key to its 2019 victory. The result in Buenos Aires province – Argentina's largest electoral district, and Kirchner's stronghold – will be key. A poor performance by her allies would undermine her influence, paving the way for a more significant role for the centrist faction of Frente de Todos, which is led by Fernández and supported by provincial governors. If the moderates gained power, there could be more progress in the economic agenda, including the discussion of pending economic reforms (such as the tax, pensions and labour reforms), which would help to attract foreign investment and strengthen the post-pandemic recovery. By contrast, if Frente de Todos's defeat affected all factions, the chance of a more complex, disrupted scenario for the final years of Fernández's term would increase, as the defeat could be interpreted as a consequence of the fiscal-adjustment policies implemented in the first half of his term. In this case, the risk of more interventionist and expansionary measures would rise, which would eventually lead to a new financial crisis.

The midterm elections will also be key to the future of Juntos por el Cambio. There are currently two main factions: one led by Macri and former security minister Patricia Bullrich, which is more right-wing and confrontational, and the other, led by Buenos Aires city mayor Horacio Rodríguez Larreta, which is more open to dialogue with other parties and social actors. If victorious, Larreta's faction would be more likely to reach agreement with Frente de Todos on long-term policies. In past decades, fierce confrontation between the two main parties undermined the progress of the economic-development agenda. Given the difficult scenario that Fernández will face in 2022–23, the chance of victory for Juntos por el Cambio in the 2023 general election looks significant.

The expected IMF agreement will be key to shaping the post-pandemic recovery. A gradual convergence to fiscal balance will help to sustain the economic rebound and gather wider political support. In the medium term, the commitments on fiscal and monetary policies will help Argentina not only to achieve macroeconomic stabilisation but to restore investors' confidence, enabling the country to return to global capital markets and therefore improve social conditions. But the pandemic will leave a difficult legacy. Prospects of a significant economic rebound in 2021 looked dimmer following the second wave of COVID-19 and consequent lockdown. In 2020, the poverty rate climbed to 42% of the urban population (it was 57.7% for children under 15 years old). People with labour problems (comprising the unemployed and those who are employed but searching for a new job) climbed to 29.4%, while informal workers accounted for 32.7% of total employment. Thousands of companies closed as a result of the pandemic. In such an adverse social and economic context, post-pandemic reconstruction, with few fiscal tools available due to budget constraints, will be Fernández's main challenge in the next two years.

Given the high levels of poverty and unemployment, social unrest and new labour conflicts such as strikes, protests and road blockades are expected in the next two years. However, most unions and social organisations identify themselves as Peronists – and thus supporters of the Fernández government – which will help to keep social tensions under control. Unions have widely been considered as the main obstacle to the modernisation of old-fashioned Argentine labour laws, but they can help contain social discontent and are a key interlocutor with the government in negotiating labour conditions. The main threat to stability will come from spontaneous protests and labour conflicts in industries where some leftist parties have a more important role in unions.

One of the main challenges for Argentina in the medium term is to restore the role of traditional political institutions as channels of society's demands. Political leaders have lost credibility, the judiciary has a poor reputation, and the three branches of power frequently lack the consensus needed to implement effective policies. The government's bureaucracy is often ineffective in implementing and monitoring public policies, and in recent decades it has become a source of employment for members of the ruling political party. Successive governments have announced that they would reform the bureaucracy and strengthen governmental institutions, but little has been done in practice.

Finally, the November elections will pose a challenge to governability, as the ruling coalition has little chance of repeating its strong 2019 performance. If third parties increase their representation in parliament, the ruling coalition will have to make more concessions to allies and opponents to get its bills passed. And if more radical factions strengthen within the two main political coalitions, there will be less room for dialogue and negotiations, making Argentina harder to govern.

Militarisation in Mexico
Many risks and few rewards?

Mexican exceptionalism

Mexico is unique among major Latin American countries in the absence of the military from its politics throughout most of the twentieth century. The Mexican Revolution of 1910–20 resulted in a military elite of revolutionary generals taking political control of the country. However, there was an impetus towards institutionalising this leadership, a process that lasted well into the 1920s and culminated in the creation of the National Revolutionary Party (PNR) in 1929, later renamed the Institutional Revolutionary Party (PRI). The consolidation of the PNR/PRI effectively set up a one-party regime that would last until 2000. The presidency of Manuel Ávila Camacho (1940–46) was the last to involve a former revolutionary general.

The end of the Ávila Camacho presidency finalised the transition from military to civilian rule, although it should be noted that he, along with his predecessors, governed as civilians. Symbolically, Ávila Camacho disbanded the military wing of the ruling party in his first month in office and prohibited active service members from participating in political activity. During the remainder of the Cold War, the one-party system presided over by the PRI provided Mexico with unprecedented political stability in comparison to many of its Latin American counterparts, and uninterrupted, peaceful transitions of power after every six-year term, even though elections were far from free or fair. During this period there were no military rebellions or attempted *coups d'état*, although the military was involved in numerous repressive activities, notably a massacre of student protesters in Mexico City on 2 October 1968 as well as anti-insurrectionist operations against left-wing guerrillas during the 1960s and 1970s, mostly in the rural south. These activities have been described as Mexico's own 'dirty war', involving widespread human-rights abuses including torture, kidnapping and killings by security forces.

The transition to multi-party democracy in 2000 did not fundamentally alter the relationship between the military and the political class, although the heads of Mexico's two main defence institutions, the

Secretariat of Defense (SEDENA) – which includes the army and air force – as well as the Secretariat of the Navy (SEMAR), continue to be led by active-duty military officers rather than civilians. However, the scale of military involvement in domestic affairs rose dramatically after December 2006 when the recently inaugurated president, Felipe Calderón (2006–12), declared a 'war on drugs' against the country's large drug-trafficking organisations (DTOs). This involved military participation in public-security operations normally assigned to police forces and set the stage for the more dramatic expansion of its role in public life after 2018.

López Obrador's about-turn

Andrés Manuel López Obrador, a populist leftist who had unsuccessfully run for president in 2006 and 2012, finally won a landslide victory in 2018 when his party (the National Regeneration Movement, or Morena), along with a few minor allies, also gained an unprecedented supermajority in both chambers (the Chamber of Deputies and the Chamber of Senators) of Mexico's Congress as well as a majority of state legislatures, the two condi-tions needed to pass constitutional reforms unimpeded.

López Obrador ran on a platform that was highly critical of his two predecessors' strategy of direct military engagement with the DTOs, pre-ferring instead to address the socio-economic causes of criminality such as poverty, unemployment and underemployment, mainly among the country's youth. This strategy was often described as 'hugs not bullets'. However, his preference for a continuation of a militarised strategy was evident in his defence of a controversial Internal Security Law passed in December 2017 by the administration of Enrique Peña Nieto, which laid the groundwork for continued military involvement in public-security duties. The law was eventually struck down by the Supreme Court follow-ing numerous injunctions over its unconstitutionality, notably because it would allow the armed forces to operate without presidential authorisation, on a permanent basis and under military rather than civilian command.

López Obrador's security agenda was initially outlined in his National Peace and Security Plan 2018–2024 on 14 November 2018, less than a month before his inauguration. The plan was notable for its tacit admission that the government had failed to defeat the DTOs and that there were no prospects of doing so in the foreseeable future. Much of the plan focused on addressing the institutional and socio-economic factors contributing to violence, but its most far-reaching proposal was the creation of the National Guard, a gendarmerie-style organisation that would enable the armed forces to avoid withdrawing from their internal-security duties. This would not be the first attempt at the creation of a gendarmerie: a similar institution created by the Peña Nieto administration was broadly seen as a failure, being considerably reduced from its intended size of 40,000–50,000 members to a mere 5,000 and organised as a division of the Federal Police rather than an independent institution.

The National Guard and its controversies

López Obrador inherited a largely unfavourable security situation when he took office on 1 December 2018. A decline in the homicide rate from a historic high in 2011 reversed in 2015 and reached a new record high of 36,661 in 2019, his first full year in office. The uptick in homicides has been attributed to numerous factors, including the success by the Peña Nieto administration in killing or capturing numerous DTO leaders. Out of a list of 122 high-profile targets, his government claimed to have arrested 96 and killed 14 during shoot-outs with security forces, including key leaders of the Juárez Cartel, Knights Templar, Sinaloa Cartel and Los Zetas. This resulted in the fragmentation of many of these organisations, which subsequently fought against each other for territorial control. Another factor was the rise of the Jalisco New Generation Cartel (CJNG), which rivalled the Sinaloa Cartel in size and power by 2019. The increased profitability of synthetic drugs such as methamphetamines, and more recently fentanyl, has also helped sustain a steady stream of financial resources, coupled with DTOs branching out into new criminal activities such as fuel theft.

Against this background of increasing violence, legislation for the creation of the National Guard was passed on 28 February 2019 and the new force was officially inaugurated on 30 June 2019. The National Guard began life with 70,000 members, composed entirely of former members of SEDENA and SEMAR as well as the Federal Police, which was to be absorbed almost entirely into the new institution (it was formally disbanded on 31 December 2019). The creation of the National Guard was marred by considerable controversy, particularly over its operational structure. According to the constitutional reform that led to its creation, all public-security institutions in Mexico, including the National Guard, are to be 'of civilian character' (Article 21). In theory, this suggested that operational control of the National Guard was to be undertaken by the Secretariat of Security and Citizen Protection (SSPC), itself a creation of the López Obrador administration (an older Secretariat of Public Security had been dissolved in 2013). In practice, the civilian character of the National Guard was virtually non-existent. Shortly after the passage of the reform, Brigadier-General Luis Rodríguez Burcio was appointed head of the National Guard, further reinforcing the institution's de facto military rather than civilian nature. A temporary coordination structure between SEDENA, SEMAR and the Federal Police was also established while elements of these three institutions were gradually incorporated into the National Guard.

The National Guard's military character was further reinforced on 6 October 2020 when the SSPC's notional control of the new institution was formally transferred to SEDENA. Although the constitution allows the selection of a military head, critics have warned that handing over operational control of the National Guard to SEDENA appears to violate the explicitly civilian character of the institution as described in Article 21.

A further problem is the overlapping of National Guard and military objectives. By law, the National Guard is tasked with 43 duties, including policing, investigation, immigration control, customs control and assisting victims of crime. However, the military performs many of these same duties in its expanded role of combatting DTOs, which further blurs the line between the two institutions. Finally, the military character of the National Guard is also evidenced by the fact that its members are subject to military rather than civilian justice, which encourages impunity. According to the National Human Rights Commission (CNDH), the National Guard received 522 complaints of human-rights violations during 2020–21, 172 of these in 2021 (as of April) – more than any other public-security institution or branch of the military.

Under military administration

If the National Guard was meant to relieve the armed forces from public-security duties, the exact opposite has occurred. A decree passed in May 2020 formalised the armed forces' continued role in public security until 2024 (when López Obrador's term is set to end) in a complementary manner to the National Guard. This decree was also highly criticised for its reversal of López Obrador's campaign promises of sending the military back to the barracks and for numerous key omissions, notably the absence of any subordination to civilian commands (as per Article 21 of the constitution), as well as the lack of external oversight and regulation of the military's public-security operations and the lack of any protocols on the use of force. The planned deployment of military forces on public-security duties on a permanent, nationwide basis also violated the supposed extraordinary (i.e., temporary and/or geographically limited) nature of this decree. Budgetary-oversight measures have not been established, essentially ensuring that military operations are not subject to transparency. In contrast to the Supreme Court's swift overturning of Peña Nieto's Internal Security Law, there has been no judicial attempt to address the numerous potential unconstitutional aspects of this decree, despite its far greater scope.

Aside from public security, the armed forces have also been tasked with operating the country's customs and ports. Of all the new duties awarded to the military under the López Obrador administration, this has widely been seen as the least controversial one, given the massive levels of corruption in Mexico's ports and border crossings largely because of DTO influence. They are major points of drugs and arms trafficking but, despite numerous efforts to modernise their administration by previous governments, little progress has been achieved. Military administration of ports is also not new, having been undertaken on a limited basis in the past: in 2013, for example, the navy took over the port of Lázaro Cárdenas, which was under the de facto control of the

Knights Templar. The handover of administrative duties to SEDENA (land borders) and SEMAR (ports) was announced on 17 July 2020 and made effective on 6 May 2021.

The military in economic life

Perhaps the most radical change in the military's role during the López Obrador administration has been its undertaking of numerous civilian infrastructure projects. This is entirely unprecedented in recent Mexican history and indeed, highly uncommon in most Latin American democracies, where it is limited to military infrastructure. The flagship project is the Felipe Ángeles International Airport, which is being constructed in the former Santa Lucía Air Force Base, north of Mexico City. This new airport is set to replace the cancelled Mexico City Texcoco Airport, which was begun by the Peña Nieto administration but abruptly cancelled by López Obrador shortly after his election victory. The cancellation was widely controversial given that around one-third of the Texcoco airport had already been built, that the cost of building a new airport on a different site represented a huge cost overrun, and that SEDENA had no experience in building a civilian project of this magnitude and complexity. In addition to its construction, SEDENA was later tasked with the airport's administration through the creation of a state-owned enterprise led by an army general, and an organisational structure composed of 26 officers from the army and air force as well as board representation by various military institutions. Revenues from the airport's operation will also be retained by SEDENA rather than going into the public coffers.

The armed forces added two more infrastructure projects to their portfolio in 2021, the first being Tren Maya, a tourist train in the Yucatán Peninsula that is one of López Obrador's flagship infrastructure projects. By December 2020, López Obrador had already announced that SEDENA would contribute to the administration of the Tren Maya as well as build three of the seven segments of the railway. However, a full handover to SEDENA was announced on 16 March 2021 and was justified on grounds that the train would cross areas close to the southern border, which for immigration-control purposes is deemed a strategic area (many migrants use the train system to travel north towards the US border). Additionally, it was argued that this would prevent its potential privatisation by future governments. As with the airport, revenues from the administration of the Tren Maya would be administered entirely by SEDENA, with the profits being used to finance pensions for military personnel.

The government also announced on 16 March that SEMAR would co-administer another major railway project, the Interoceanic Train, which will connect the Gulf of Mexico and the Pacific Ocean as an alternative to the Panama Canal. Unlike the Tren Maya, SEMAR's role in the railway's administration will be shared with four state governments that border the area. Aside from the two railway projects, it was also announced that the armed forces would operate two existing airports in the southern region, Chetumal International Airport and Palenque International Airport, as well as the Tulum airport currently under construction, bringing the total number of airports under SEDENA control to four.

In addition to the airports and railway projects, SEDENA has been involved in other smaller infrastructure projects, notably the construction of hundreds of branches of the Banco de Bienestar (a state-owned institution tasked with administering welfare benefits to the public). More recently, it was announced that it would also construct a public hospital in Mexico City.

An involvement in politics?

Despite the expansion of the role of the Mexican military in public life, it remains unclear whether it will encroach into politics – the one area where it has been shut out since the demilitarisation of government in the decades after the revolution. In this respect, prospects are much less worrying: López Obrador's coddling of the military has had the purpose of cementing its loyalty to government authority. This may have been partly to reassure the military that a left-wing administration would not reduce its influence. The military's absence from Mexican politics for nearly a century also offers few frames of reference for the kind of romanticisation of military regimes attempted by some right-wing Latin American populists – notably Brazil's Jair Bolsonaro, himself a former military officer. Indeed, Mexico is notable among its Latin American peers for its lack of far-right parties (even minority parties), making such a scenario even more unlikely – though centre-right parties could conceivably lurch further to the right to challenge Morena's left-wing populism.

The most likely worst-case scenario is that the military contributes to solidifying Morena's political dominance through an ever-increasing presence in public life, rather than by taking an active role in politics. Such a role would find fertile ground in favourable Mexican attitudes towards the military. A December 2020 survey of confidence in institutions showed the armed forces to be the most highly rated institution, with the National Guard tied for second place with universities. The region-wide Latinobarómetro surveys also show Mexicans as having above-average support for their armed forces in comparison with other Latin American countries. More worrying, however, is that Mexicans' support for democracy is low. Only 38% of Mexicans agreed that democracy is preferable to other forms of government, the fifth lowest in the region, while a similar share showed no preference for a democratic regime over an authoritarian one, the fourth highest.

Overall, the risk of further military encroachment in public life in Mexico is real. But there are some practical safeguards against this, notably Morena's loss of a supermajority in Congress in the elections on 6 June 2021, which will prevent Congress from undertaking constitutional reforms without opposition approval. The outsized role of the military is not without some benefits, notably the potential to root out some of the endemic corruption in public-infrastructure procurement and certain administrative areas like customs and ports, where the influence of DTOs was considerable (and which the armed forces are much better equipped to combat than civilian administrators, who are more prone to bribery and intimidation). Despite these benefits, the balance of Mexico's militarisation drive appears to be weighted towards mission creep into areas of policy that are better served by civilian institutions.

Index